Sounds of Other Shores

Andrew J. Eisenberg

SOUNDS OF OTHER SHORES

The Musical Poetics of Identity
on Kenya's Swahili Coast

Wesleyan University Press   Middletown, Connecticut

Wesleyan University Press
Middletown CT 06459
www.wesleyan.edu/wespress
Text and photographs unless otherwise noted
© 2024 Andrew J. Eisenberg
All rights reserved
Manufactured in the United States of America
Designed by Mindy Basinger Hill
Typeset in Minion Pro

The publisher gratefully acknowledges the support
of the General Fund of the American Musicological Society,
supported in part by the National Endowment for the Humanities
and the Andrew W. Mellon Foundation.

Library of Congress Cataloging-in-Publication Data

Names: Eisenberg, Andrew J., 1977– author.

Title: Sounds of other shores : the musical poetics of identity on Kenya's Swahili coast / Andrew J. Eisenberg. Other titles: Music/culture.

Description: Middletown : Wesleyan University Press, 2024. | Series: Music/culture | Includes bibliographical references and index. | Summary: "A cultural history of Swahili taarab, a form of sung poetry that emerged as East Africa's first mass-mediated popular music in the 1930s, using performance analyses to explore how transoceanic appropriation situated twentieth-century Mombasan taarab as a space of creative subject formation" — Provided by publisher.

Identifiers: LCCN 2023049027 (print) | LCCN 2023049028 (ebook) | ISBN 9780819501059 (cloth) | ISBN 9780819501066 (trade paperback) | ISBN 9780819501073 (ebook)

Subjects: LCSH: Taarab (Music)—Kenya—Indian Coast—History. | Swahili-speaking peoples—Kenya—Indian Coast—Music—History and criticism. | Popular music—Kenya—Indian Coast—History and criticism.

Classification: LCC ML3503.K46 E47 2024 (print) | LCC ML3503.K46 (ebook) | DDC 781.630967623—dc23/eng/20231024

LC record available at https://lccn.loc.gov/2023049027

LC ebook record available at https://lccn.loc.gov/2023049028

5 4 3 2 1

FOR KABETE

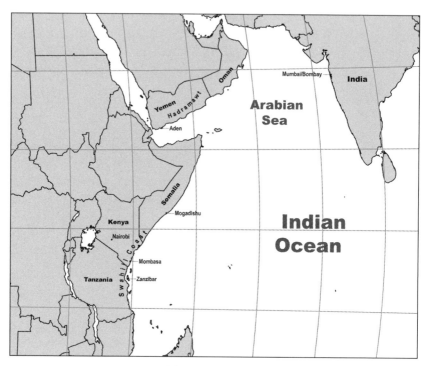

FIGURE 0.1 A map of the western Indian Ocean, showing cities and regions discussed in the book.

CONTENTS

PREFACE Hints of Elsewhere ix

Acknowledgments xiii

Companion Website xvii

A Note on Language xix

INTRODUCTION Sound, Sense, and Subjectivity in Mombasa 1

ONE A Feeling for the Boundaries: Early Recorded Taarab 24

TWO The Lullaby of Taarab: Radio and Reflexivity in the 1950s 47

THREE The Mouths of Professors and Clowns: Indian Taarab 66

FOUR "Mombasa, Mother of the World": Hadrami Ṭarab 91

FIVE The Musical Philosopher: Zein l'Abdin's Arab Taarab 112

SIX Sea Change: The Twenty-First Century 136

SEVEN Reorienting Appropriation: Swahili Hip Hop 152

EPILOGUE For a Humanistic Musical Anthropology of the Indian Ocean 174

Notes 183

Bibliography 205

Index 237

PREFACE
Hints of Elsewhere

In April 1987, eminent Kenyan writer Ngũgĩ wa Thiong'o found himself at a private gathering for the Muslim Eid al-Fitr holiday in Dar es Salaam, Tanzania (Ngũgĩ wa Thiong'o 1993, 177–94). The host and some of the guests were Muslims from the Swahili coast, and so the evening was alive with stories and laughter in the elegant, "flawless" Swahili that is the domain of the coast's Swahili-speaking Muslims (177). Though a non-Muslim from central Kenya, Ngũgĩ had grown up in close proximity to Muslims with ties to the coast. The evening was thus a nostalgic one for him, made even more so by the fact that it was his first trip back to East Africa since fleeing Kenya for his own safety five years earlier. He "savored the smell of the food; the music of the voices; the colors of the clothes; the anecdotes and the stories; the warmth of the laughter of the evening"; and the sounds of the coastal Swahili popular music known as *taarab* (177–78). All these sensations brought Ngũgĩ back not only to his childhood but also to his longstanding "dreams of one East Africa," by reminding him how the coast "had connected East Africa to the world" (181). Triggering this reflection most directly, perhaps, was the taarab music that wafted through the gathering carrying "hints of Arabia, India, Africa and even Cuba blended into one" (177).

What Ngũgĩ perceived as "hints" of different peoples and places in the sounds of Swahili taarab, ethnomusicologists and historians have described as "reflections" of "culture contact" (Topp Fargion 2002, 203) and "cosmopolitan mixture" (Fair 2001, 171; inter alia Kiel 2016; Topp Fargion 2014; Graebner 1991b). For scholars of taarab, as for Ngũgĩ, the music's hybridized sounds make audible social, cultural, and political formations that may not fit within the normative frameworks of the nation-state and area studies. This way of listening to taarab is emblematic of what Isabel Hofmeyr (2012) calls "the Indian Ocean as method." The Indian Ocean, writes Hofmeyr, is a "complicating sea" that enables writers and scholars "to think beyond the tired pieties of older ideologies" (590). Mapping its metaphorical currents is therefore a mode of critical imagining, one that ethnomusicologists Julia Byl and Jim Sykes have recently suggested as a way of moving the field of ethnomusicology beyond its stultifying "methodological nationalism" (Byl and Sykes 2020, 413; Sykes and Byl 2023a).

Swahili taarab, with its "hints of Arabia, India, Africa," is a music of the "complicating sea." But it is also a music that complicates the idea of the complicating sea, because its "hints" of other shores are, in many cases, hints in the more active sense of the word—not just characteristics to be discerned, but *intimations*, ambiguous but nonetheless *intentional* statements.

Since at least the early 1930s, when taarab first emerged as a commercially recorded popular music, the genre has served as a vehicle for *self-conscious appropriations* of Indian and Arab sounds—borrowings that signal their borrowed status by employing various degrees of irony, playfulness, and/or nostalgia. As artistic gestures, these appropriations do not so much reflect as *reflect on* sociohistorical processes. They are, in the lexicon of early twentieth-century Russian philosopher Mikhail Bakhtin (1981), "intentional artistic hybrids" that comment on the world by setting up "collisions" between different expressive idioms (360).[1] If the "Indian Ocean as method" is about attending to flows of culture in order to reimagine borders and identities, then the sounds of Swahili taarab are not only objects for this method, but also, in many cases, applications of it.

Sounds of Other Shores is about creative uses of Indian and Arab sounds in taarab as ways of reflecting on and making sense of the complexities and contradictions of identity on the Swahili coast. I describe an appropriation-centered musical poetics of identity developed in the Kenyan port city of Mombasa over the course of the twentieth century, and explore how it served for musicians and audiences as a means of assessing and sometimes reimagining their status as "paradoxical" subjects situated on a "double periphery" (Kresse 2009) between Africa and the Indian Ocean world. Working at the intersection of interpretive anthropology and musicology, I theorize with rather than just about these musicians and audiences, seeking to learn from their sonorous explorations of Kenyan Swahili subjectivity.

Like any ethnographic study of expressive culture, *Sounds of Other Shores* is an exploration of the human experience that resists reduction to a single finding or argument. But it is also a work that grows out of, contributes to, and intervenes in scholarly conversations. In the first place, *Sounds of Other Shores* reframes long-standing questions about Swahili identity in Kenya, while speaking as well to larger theoretical questions about identity and belonging in the Indian Ocean world, by offering a textured account of how Swahili-speaking Muslims of the Kenyan coast worked to make sense of Swahiliness during the twentieth century. Additionally, for the burgeoning subfield of "Indian Ocean ethnomusicology," it offers a model for a subject-centered exploration of cultural flow and exchange that avoids the intellectual cul-de-sac of cataloguing musical features and "retentions." All of these interventions—to the extent they are successful, of which the reader may be the judge—begin with an attentive ear to *musical poetics*, by which I mean a creative, communicative, and in a broad sense *rhetorical* engagement with style in musical composition and performance.

Much of the empirical data in this book comes from ethnographic fieldwork carried out in Mombasa during the first decade of the twenty-first century. During my time as a resident researcher in Mombasa, I not only socialized, conversed, and musicked with interlocutors; I also collaborated with a few of them to digitize hundreds of historical sound recordings that were stored in private collections around the city. These digitized sound recordings, now deposited as a special collection in the NYU Abu Dhabi Library, comprise the empirical backbone of the book.[2] Examples are referenced throughout the chapters that follow, indicated in the text with numbered reference tags, for instance (AUDIO EX. 1). All of these may be heard on the companion website to *Sounds of Other Shores*, www.soundsofothershores.com, or can be accessed through the publisher's website. I encourage readers to listen to the examples while making their way through the book, even if this means occasionally interrupting the flow of reading. Part of the joy of writing this book lay in sometimes losing myself in the musical performances I was writing about, many of which I listened to over and over again to discern certain details. I invite the reader to do the same.

Acknowledgments

This book is the product of many years of engaging with stories, sounds, ideas, and people. I am grateful to the men and women of the Kenyan coast who shared their time, words, and music with me, especially Jamal Hafidh Jahadhmy, Mohammed Mchulla, Omari Swaleh al-Abdi, Mbaraka Ali Haji, and the late Zein l'Abdin Ahmed Alamoody. Other denizens of the Kenyan coast who were equally generous with their assistance were Amin "Elchie" Virani, Athman Lali Omar, Stanslous Kiraga, Mohammed Abdalla "Bom Bom," Joseph Mwarandu, Salim Nasher, Swaleh Tamimi, and the late Andrew "Madebe" Burchell. *Nitoe shukrani zangu za dhati kwenu.*

Among the many scholars I have to thank, first mention goes to those I have been fortunate enough to call my mentors. My thinking about music as expressive culture has been profoundly shaped by two scholars who first introduced me to the anthropology of music over two decades ago, Steve Feld and Aaron Fox. Over the past ten years, Georgina Born has also served as a mentor and inspiration, whose influence suffuses my scholarship. And Jonathan Shannon helped me to get this book project on track in his role as my faculty mentor at New York University Abu Dhabi (NYUAD).

The seed of this book was a doctoral dissertation project at Columbia University, the output of which includes some material that is included in the book. I was immensely fortunate to have not only Steve Feld and Aaron Fox, but also Brian Larkin, as core advisors for this project. Chris Washburne and Ana Maria Ochoa provided invaluable feedback, as well, as members of my dissertation committee; and Tim Taylor and Val Daniel shaped my thinking on the project along the way. My dissertation research was also enriched by conversations with fellow students in the ethnomusicology program at Columbia University, especially Farzi Hemmasi, Elizabeth Keenan, Morgan Luker, Mandy Minks, Dave

Novak, Tim Mangin, Marceline Saibou, Matt Sakakeeny, Ryan Skinner, Maria Sonevytsky, and Anna Stirr; and my fellow Social Science Research Council (SSRC) cohort member Brett Pyper.

During my fieldwork in Mombasa between 2004 and 2006, Ann Biersteker, James Brennan, Werner Graebner, Prita Meier, Athman Lali Omar, Jeremy Prestholdt, and Clarissa Vierke all served as excellent sounding boards. James Brennan and Werner Graebner also provided assistance in the form of research materials. In addition to collaborating with me in the collection of materials related to Sauti ya Mvita, James hosted me in London as I pored through the School of Oriental and African Studies (SOAS) library. Werner, for his part, has provided me with a range of sonic and visual materials over the years, including five archival images included in the pages that follow.

My research required specialized linguistic and musical training. Prior to and during my primary fieldwork in Mombasa, I studied Swahili in the US and Tanzania with Peter Mtesigwa, Abdul Nanji, Alwiya Omar, and Peter Githinji; Arabic with Baha Saad and Iman Meiki; and Arab music performance with Tareq Abboushi and Zafir Tawil. In 2015, I attended Simon Shaheen's annual Arabic Music Retreat, where I learned a great deal in a short time from the distinguished faculty members and committed students.

A number of other musicians and scholars advised on musical works and traditions discussed in this book. Aditi Deo lent her highly trained ears and extensive knowledge of Hindi film song to my analysis of Indian taarab; Ghazi al-Mulaifi introduced me to Kuwaiti musicians and music experts, and generally served as a fount of knowledge about Khaliji music; Mahsin Basalama tracked down information relating to Zanzibari taarab; Jean Lambert, Nizar Ghanem, Mohamed Jarhoom, and Gabriel Lavin provided insights into Yemeni music traditions; Jonathan Shannon and Ginny Danielson did the same for the Egyptian and Levantine urban music traditions; and Naseem al Atrash, Yousif Yaseen, Jonathan Shannon, and Kaustuv Ganguli all assisted at various points in my efforts to transcribe and analyze taarab melodies.

NYU Abu Dhabi has provided a supportive and intellectually stimulating environment in which to work on this book. I thank my generous and inspiring colleagues in the NYUAD Division of Arts and Humanities—and those in the Department of Music at NYU in New York, as well, especially Martin Daughtry and David Samuels. I am especially grateful to my colleagues in the Music and Sound Cultures (MaSC) research group that I helped to establish at NYUAD with my colleague Carlos Guedes. MaSC has not only provided a pathway to properly archive the sound materials that I collected in the course of my research, but to work through ideas related to them as well. I thank our intrepid leader Carlos Guedes, who has been a great help (and great fun) over the years, as well as our other core members, Robert Rowe and Beth Russell. I would also like to thank everyone else who has been instrumental in establishing the Andrew Eisenberg Collection of East African Commercial Sound Recordings: NYUAD head archivist Brad Bauer, former NYUAD head librarian Ginny Danielson, digital content specialist Rebecca Pittam, and student assistants Emma Chiu and Enid Mollel. I also thank Brad Bauer and Ginny Danielson for making available the lithograph that adorns the cover of this book (especially Ginny, who had the idea to use it in the first place).

Many scholars provided feedback on material in this book over the years. In addition to my dissertation committee, those who supplied the most significant input were Abdilatif Abdalla, Kelly Askew, Irene Brunotti, Julia Byl, Annmarie Drury, Rachel Dwyer, Laura Fair, Nathalie Koenings, Kai Kresse, Michael Lambek, George Murer, Annachiara Raia, Jim Sykes, Duncan Tarrant, Farouk Topan, Julia Verne, Markus Verne, and Clarissa Vierke. I thank these scholars as well as the institutions that provided venues for me to present my work, including Bayreuth University, Columbia University, the NYU Abu Dhabi Institute, and the University of Pennsylvania. A fellowship with the Bayreuth University Academy of Advanced African Studies afforded me an invaluable opportunity to present and workshop material as I completed my book manuscript. I am grateful to Clarissa Vierke for serving as my point of contact and collaborator during my (virtual) residency.

The bulk of my field research was facilitated by dissertation research grants from the Fulbright-Hays Program and the Social Science Research Council. I also received smaller research grants over the years from Columbia University, Stony Brook University, and NYU Abu Dhabi. Some field research for chapter 7 overlapped with field research carried out as part of Georgina Born's "Music, Digitisation, Mediation" project, which was funded by the European Research Council's Advanced Grants scheme (ERC project number 249598). The National Museums of Kenya helped to arrange my research clearance in Kenya and saw to some of my other logistical needs. I am grateful for the generous support of these institutions.

Three chapters of this book have been published elsewhere in different versions. An alternate version of chapter 1 appears in Jim Sykes and Julia Byl's 2023 volume *Sounding the Indian Ocean: Musical Circulations in the Afro-Asiatic*

Seascape (University of California Press). An earlier version of chapter 3, entitled "The Swahili Art of Indian Taarab: A Poetics of Vocality and Ethnicity on the Kenyan Coast," appears in the journal *Comparative Studies of South Asia, Africa, and the Middle East* as a part of the special section "The Indian Ocean as Aesthetic Space," edited by Julia Verne and Markus Verne (2017, volume 37, issue 2). An earlier version of chapter 7, entitled "Hip Hop and Cultural Citizenship on Kenya's 'Swahili Coast,'" appears the journal *Africa* (2012, volume 82, issue 4). I thank the University of California Press, Duke University Press, and Cambridge University Press for permitting me to include these materials.

Finally, I wish to express my appreciation for the love and support I have received from my parents, Bob and Ilene Eisenberg; my sister, Eliza Millman, and her family; and my wife, Beatrice Nguthu, and our two children/lockdown buddies, Libby and Oscar. I dedicate this book to my wife Beatrice—Kabete—who has been along for the ride since my days hanging out at Zein's *maskani*. I could not have written it without her. *Asante. Nakupenda.*

Companion Website

Audio recordings for examples cited throughout this book may be found at www.soundsofothershores.com, under the Audio Examples tab.

All of the audio examples in the book, along with many other related audio examples, can also be accessed via the *Andrew Eisenberg Collection of East African Commercial Sound Recordings* AD.MC.035. Access instructions are located at https://findingaids.library.nyu.edu/nyuad/ad_mc_035/.

A Note on Language

An English speaker unfamiliar with the Swahili language should have little difficulty approximating its sounds. Swahili has five vowel sounds, all of which are consistently represented in the standard orthography: *a* is always pronounced as in the English *father*; *e* is always pronounced as in the English *bed*; *i* is equivalent to the English *ee*, as in *wheel*; and *o* is equivalent to the English *oo*, as in *moon*. Consonants are almost always pronounced as in English, with the notable exception of a few special consonant pairs: *ng'* is pronounced as in *sing*; *dh* is pronounced as in *them*; *kh* and *gh* are both pronounced as in the Scottish *loch*, with the former pair being unvoiced and the latter voiced. The stress in a Swahili word is almost always placed in the penultimate syllable.

Because Standard Swahili Roman orthography is relatively phonetic, I use it for broad phonetic transcriptions of Swahili verbal performances as well as regular transcriptions of Swahili words. For Arabic transliteration, I employ the Library of Congress system of Romanization. I use this system for broad phonetic transcription, as well, in chapter 4. With apologies to readers trained in linguistics, I generally avoid the International Phonetic Alphabet in order to make the linguistic analyses in the book accessible to a broad readership.

I have chosen to limit the use of diacritics in Arabic names, because using them would mean either inserting them into Swahili names that are commonly represented in Roman script without any diacritics (including in scholarly works and album liner notes cited in this book) or categorizing every person in the book with an Arabic-derived name as either "Swahili" or "Arab" (a challenging and problematic task). Where possible, I spell names of subjects according to their own preferences. Otherwise, I use whatever spelling I have found to be most common for the individual subject or their name on the Swahili coast.

For the sake of consistency and to facilitate dialogue with scholarship on Arab music, I use Arabic rather than Swahili for Arab musical instruments (*'ūd* rather than *udi*, *rīq* rather than *rika*, etc.) and music-theoretical terms (*Maqām Bayātī* rather than *Makam Bayati*, etc.).

Sounds of Other Shores

INTRODUCTION

Sound, Sense, and Subjectivity in Mombasa

This is a study of musical composition, performance, and listening as embodied practices of reflexive inquiry and critique on Kenya's Swahili coast. My core argument is that Swahili-speaking Muslims in twentieth-century Mombasa engaged creatively with Arab and Indian sounds in taarab and related music genres as a means of reflecting on and mediating the complexities and contradictions of being "Swahili" in colonial and postcolonial Kenya. Using a combination of oral history, interpretive ethnography, and close analyses of musical performances, I trace this tradition of reflexive cultural critique from its first soundings in the early recorded taarab of the 1930s to its decline at the turn of the twenty-first century. The result is a genealogy of music as a space of ethnic subject formation in an African-Indian Ocean nexus.

ORIENTING TAARAB IN MOMBASA

Taarab (also *tarabu*) is typically referred to as "sung poetry," because it centers on highly structured, richly metaphorical poetry. It might be better described as *musicked* poetry, however, since it always involves instrumental accompaniment, and performers and audiences place a high value on how the poetry is performed *as music*. The genre emerged around the turn of the twentieth century as a form of refined entertainment, or "amusement" (*pumbao*), for elite men and women of Zanzibar and the Kenyan coast, intended to be enjoyed while seated in quiet contemplation (Nabhany 2003, 1).[1] The word *taarab* serves as a reminder of these origins for people of the Swahili coast, whether they take it to be derived from the Arabic *ṭarab*, meaning an ecstatic state evoked by music (Racy 2003, 6), or the Arabic/Swahili *ustaarabu*, meaning "civilized Arabness" (the former etymology is almost certainly correct, but the latter is more popular).[2]

Taarab took different stylistic paths in different regions of the Swahili coast. But each of its "regional varieties" (Askew 2002, 115) incorporates a "cosmopolitan mix of Indian Oceana" in its sounds (Fair 2001, 171).[3] Such musical cosmopolitanism implies histories of *appropriation* in the broadest sense. Thus, Zanzibari writer Muhammed Seif Khatib (1992) describes taarab as an art form of the Arab world that has become "part of the local culture" (*sehemu ya utamaduni wa huko*) through active processes of "taking" (*kuichukua*) and "using" (*kuitumia*) (7). I use *appropriation* in this book in a somewhat more restricted sense, however, to mean a self-conscious, performative act that is interpretive and communicative—a *poetic* act that speaks to and about the world.[4] The paradigmatic form of appropriation in this sense is *parody*, defined by Linda Hutcheon (2000, 6) as "imitation characterized by ironic inversion." But parody stands alongside other forms of artistic "stylization," including those that employ *nostalgia* rather than irony to generate a "dialogic contrast" (Bakhtin 1981, 364).

It is in the Kenyan port city of Mombasa where practices of (self-conscious, performative) appropriation in taarab have been most pronounced. Taarab performed and recorded in Mombasa during the twentieth century was known for its dramatic, even flamboyant adoptions of Indian and Arab styles. The most popular variant of Mombasan taarab during the twentieth century was "Indian taarab" (*taarab ya kihindi*), which sets Swahili poetry to Hindi film song melodies performed in a distinctly Indian manner. It flourished alongside and in dialogue with other variants of taarab incorporating Arab elements, most notably the "Arab taarab" (*taarab ya kiarabu*) of the 1970s and 1980s that draws from urban music genres of the Arabian Peninsula as well as Egypt.

While "Indian" and "Arab" were not the only stylistic directions in Mombasan taarab during the twentieth century, their dominance was so conspicuous as to inspire the late eminent historian and Mombasa native Ali A. Mazrui (1996, 160) to describe a two-fold "'Orientalization' of Mombasa music," whereby "Swahili songs became strongly influenced by Arab music (especially Egyptian), on one side, and Indian music on the other."[5] Mazrui took a negative view of this trend, going so far as to label it "plagiarism." But a close listen to Mombasan taarab reveals something far more creative and "intentional" (Bakhtin) at play. John Storm Roberts, author of the classic text on African and Afrodiasporic popular musics, *Black Music of Two Worlds* (1998), described Mombasan taarab of the 1960s and 1970s as taking "a bit from here, a little from there" in a way that refuses to "obey anybody's rules" (Roberts 1973, 22). Rather than mindless mimicry, Roberts heard in the hybridized sounds of Mombasan taarab evidence of experimentation and invention.

What accounts for the preponderance of appropriation in twentieth-century Mombasan taarab? To the extent that scholars have addressed this question, they have done so by suggesting that the phenomenon reflects something about Mombasa's social landscape. Werner Graebner (1991b, 188) puts this argument forward most directly, when he suggests that the iconic Mombasan subgenre of Indian taarab may be explained as a result of a greater prevalence of Indian-owned cinemas and record distributors in Mombasa as compared with other Swahili port cities, and the fact that the Kenyan government after independence was more amenable to allowing foreign films to be screened than were the governments of Tanzania and Zanzibar. More recent writings on the history of Hindi films on the Swahili coast cast doubt on the notion that their cultural impact was more profound in Mombasa than in Zanzibar (Bertz 2011, 2015; Burgess 2002; Fair 2004, 2009; Reinwald 2006).[6] But in any case, this explanation misses the point of what needs to be explained. The fact that Mombasan taarab musicians during the twentieth century "Orientalized" their music more overtly than taarab musicians in other port cities does not mean that they were more influenced by Indian and Arab musics.[7] It means that they chose to engage with these influences in a particular way. The question to be asked, then, is, *What was so pleasurable and meaningful for Mombasan musicians and audiences about this way of engaging with sounds of other shores?* I propose that the answer has to do with the particular complexities and contradictions of being "Swahili" in Mombasa, an ancient Swahili town encompassed by Kenya's major port city.

From the beginning of the British colonial era in East Africa in the 1890s, Swahili-speaking Muslims of the East African coast have occupied ambiguous or contradictory positions within dominant systems of ethnic classification. As an African population partly comprised of Arabs and Indian Ocean diasporants, they confounded the British colonial administration's efforts to categorize every colonial subject as either "native" or "nonnative" (a basic *modus operandi* of British colonial rule that was given added impetus on Zanzibar and the Kenyan coast by the fact that most "nonnatives" were formally citizens of the Sultanate of Zanzibar). In Kenya, where Christians are in the majority and "tribe" has been the prime mover of politics since the independence struggle, Swahili-speaking

Muslims' efforts to achieve or maintain "nonnative" status under colonial rule came to haunt them after independence, marking them as people who were "neither completely African nor, by extension, Kenyan" (Prestholdt 2011, 6). This is especially true of Mombasa, where the "paradoxes" (Parkin 1994; Mazrui 2000) of being "Swahili" have always been part of the fabric of everyday experience.

THE EXPERIENCE OF PARADOX

To speak of paradox in relation to Swahili-speaking Muslims of the East African coast is to invoke the debate that exercised Swahili studies during the 1970s over how to define "the Swahili" (Arens 1975; Eastman 1971; Salim 1985; Shariff 1973; Swartz 1979). Most contributions to this debate accomplished little more than a rehashing of colonial-era attempts to "characterize the inhabitants of [East Africa's] coastal towns according to [Western] racial categories" (Glassman 2011, 300; Mazrui and Shariff 1994). But as anthropologist David Parkin (1994) suggests, we can "sympathize with those who raised the question" (1), because East Africa's Swahili-speaking coastal Muslims—particularly those residing on the coast of Kenya—do, indeed, "[bask] in a parade of paradoxes" (ibid.). It is just that these paradoxes—what I will call the *paradoxes of Swahili subjectivity*—are not conceptual problems to be worked out by applying theoretical models. They are historically constituted *experiences* of social and political in-betweenness, ambiguity, and disjuncture.

Sounds of Other Shores listens to the paradoxes of Swahili subjectivity on the Kenyan coast as "structures of feeling," in Raymond Williams's sense of "meanings and values" that are "actively lived and felt" in everyday life and often re-presented in artistic expression (Williams 1977, 132; 2020, 56). Sherry B. Ortner (2005) argues that investigating structures of feeling helps to us to get inside "how people (try to) act on the world even as they are acted upon" (34). By taking an ethnographic ear to paradoxes of Swahili subjectivity in Mombasa during the twentieth century, I aim to reveal something of how Swahili-speaking Muslims of the Kenyan coast actively engaged with their changing conditions of social identification and belonging from the late-colonial era to the dawn of the new millennium. Given that this time period saw the consolidation of Swahili identity on the Kenyan coast (Eastman 1994b), this book represents a study of Kenyan Swahili ethnogenesis, albeit one with a particular focus on music as a way into matters of subject formation.[8]

David Parkin opened the door to a study of paradox as an historical experience on the Kenyan coast in his work on "being and selfhood" among "Swahili Mijikenda" (Parkin 1985, 1989). The Mijikenda are nine closely related ethnolinguistic communities that claim parts of the rural hinterlands of the Kenyan coast as their ancestral homelands, and have historically maintained social and economic ties with urban Swahili-speaking Muslims, typically as subaltern clients.[9] The peoples Parkin calls "Swahili Mijikenda" (or "intermediary Swahili") are Muslim Mijikenda who "[aspire] to Swahili Islamic values and life style" (Parkin 1989) and thereby navigate a space "betwixt and between different criteria of evaluation in modern coastal Kenya" (163). More recently, Kai Kresse (2009, 2012b) situated the experience of paradox at the center of his ethnographic inquiry into Swahili Islam on the Kenyan coast, probing how Swahili-speaking Muslims in Mombasa navigate their position on the "double-periphery" between the Christian-dominated Kenyan state and the global Muslim *umma* (community of believers). *Sounds of Other Shores* builds on these works to offer a musical perspective on Swahili cultural identity and ethnogenesis on the Kenyan coast.

The term *paradox* is imprecise, of course, being a shorthand for conceptual tensions that may be grounded in perceived antinomies. Parkin's use of the word *parade*, however, though clearly chosen for the sake of alliteration, is quite apt. *Parade* suggests a "continuous multiplicity" that can only be divided into discrete elements by "[placing] ourselves along the transition" and "making cross cuts therein in thought" (Bergson 1911, 302; Deleuze 1988, 38–39). This is precisely how paradoxes of Swahili subjectivity have been experienced on the Kenyan coast. Even "the most basic" of these paradoxes—the perception of Swahili people as neither "Arab" nor "African" but somehow both (Topan 2006, 55)—is not unitary but multiplicitous, implicating race, ethnicity, space, culture, and citizenship. And this is but one paradox in the parade.

Making the requisite "cross cuts in thought," we can identify three overarching paradoxes of Swahili subjectivity that have been part of daily life for Swahili-speaking Muslims of the Kenyan coast since the colonial era: a social and political *in-betweenness* related to their existence on the "double-periphery" (Kresse) between Africa and the Indian Ocean world; an *ambiguity* of identity related to the complexity of social categorization in coastal Swahili society and the contested nature of the Swahili ethnonym; and a *disjuncture* of social belonging related to the co-presence of two mutually contradictory *regimes of ethnicity*. I shall review these in turn.

In-Betweenness

For centuries, port cities of the Swahili coast and their inhabitants have been "situated between different kinds of cultures, ethnic groups, economic systems and religious and political forms of authority and control" (Kresse 2012b, 86). Since the advent of the state in East Africa, this experience of in-betweenness has also been one political *dissociation*, as the state in East Africa, as elsewhere within and beyond the African continent, has been in large part a project of transforming fluid "cultural identities" into fixed "political identities" (Mamdani 2001, 21–24).[10]

A sense of in-betweenness and dissociation has been especially acute for Swahili-speaking Muslims in Mombasa since the early twentieth century, for reasons having to do with the very contours of the city. On a map, Mombasa Island appears almost totally engulfed by the mainland, to which it is today connected by a bridge, causeways, and a ferry system. The Old Town is situated on the eastern portion of the island, on the edge of a protected harbor, over which countless battles had been fought between local communities and conquerors from Portugal and Oman between the beginning of the sixteenth century and the *Pax Britannica*. Until the turn of the twentieth century, the Old Town was the whole of urban Mombasa. By linking the Mombasa area to the African interior by rail, the British colonial administration initiated the emergence of a "New Mombasa" with a new mix of inhabitants that included large numbers of migrants from up-country, situated just outside the bounds of (what then became) the Old Town. By the end of the twentieth century, Old Town's tight assemblage of "Swahili"- and "Indian"-style buildings abutted a sprawling metropolis populated by nearly one million Kenyans of various geographical, ethnic, and religious backgrounds. And since the demographics of the Old Town remained relatively stable through this transformation, this division of urban space has served to reflect and maintain a sharp "cultural dissociation" between the city's long-standing population of urban Muslims and those who came to the city from other parts of Kenya (Hoyle 2001, 184).[11]

Many Mombasans during the colonial era experienced their dissociation from the state as a privilege. During the 1950s, Mombasa's Swahili-speaking Muslim elite enjoyed a "cultural, educational, and economic revival" at the very same time that the British colonial government was restricting rights and privileges of up-country Kenyans in response to the anticolonial Mau Mau uprising, detaining and torturing many (Salim 1973, 214). But this changed after independence, as the coast was flooded with "men who were hand-picked by President Kenyatta to ensure the incorporation and integration of the coast (remote, exotic, and largely Muslim if viewed from Nairobi, and certainly a former KADU [opposition party] stronghold) into the mainstream of Kenya's economic and social life" (Yahya 1998). In this context, Kenya's coastal Muslims found themselves situated as "second-class citizens," often prevented from securing civil service jobs and national identity documents, and facing harassment at the hands of police (Goldsmith 2011, 18; Mazrui and Shariff 1994, 44; Prestholdt 2011, 7). In response, many came to embrace the mantra, "*Pwani si Kenya*" (the Coast is not Kenya), formally introduced as a slogan by the coastal separatist party the Mombasa Republican Council in 1999 (Goldsmith 2011; Walibora 2021).

The second-class status of coastal Muslims in postcolonial Kenya has been exacerbated by the symbolic positioning of the coast as a foil "in opposition to which non-coastal Christian Kenya may construct an identity" (Porter 1995, 147). As an ideological construct, the postcolonial Kenyan nation was built on independence leader Jomo Kenyatta's conception of the national community as a "United Nations in miniature" (Kenyatta 1968, 247; cf. Lonsdale 2004) whose constitutive communities are conceived along African "tribal" lines. The coast and its people came to be coded as the *margin* of this miniature United Nations, where the nation dissolves into its constitutive outside. *Our Nation, Kenya* (Wegulo and Ondieki 1987), a primary-school textbook used during the 1980s and 1990s, presents the coast's ancient urban heritage as an anomaly that can only be explained by the influence of Arabs and Portuguese, who are described using the loaded (and in the case of Arabs, misleading) term "foreign" (31–33). The fact that this depiction of coastal Swahili society was first promulgated by British and German Orientalists during the colonial period and has been heavily critiqued since the 1960s seems not to have bothered the authors or approvers of this text.[12]

To the extent that the coast has found a place in Kenya's postcolonial national imaginary, it is as something of an internal Orient. This is due to the Swahili coast becoming a popular destination for European tourists, a situation that John Middleton, mincing no words, calls the region's "final and perhaps the most degrading exploitation" (1992, 53). The particularly "degrading" aspect of tourism for coastal Muslims is the "corrupting influence" of "tourists and their hangers-on," who "bring new commercial and sexual mores" (ibid.). But a more subtle form of exploitation stems from the "Orientalizing strategy" (Kasfir 2004, 340) of Kenya's coastal beach resorts. As with all images and narratives associated with the tourism industry in Kenya, the touristic Orientalization of the Swahili coast has been "part of the local discourse in the country" (Ntarangwi 2003, 5), shaping how Kenyans understand themselves.

Ambiguity

The late anthropologist John Middleton (1992, 198) wrote of a "thread of ambiguity of identity" running "throughout Swahili culture." By this he meant that ethnic and racial categories in coastal Swahili society have always been to some extent nebulous. This "thread of ambiguity" has been thickened, coiled, and knotted since the late nineteenth century, by constant wrangling over the Swahili ethnonym.

The word *Swahili* comes from the Arabic *Sawāḥil*, meaning "borderlands" or "coastlands." In the maritime context, *Sawāḥil* often denotes a "coastal region with entrepôts for goods from its hinterlands" (see Collins 1990, 64n9). Arab sailors used the term to refer to segments of the East African littoral at least as early as the thirteenth century CE (Horton and Middleton 2000, 16; Collins 1990, 64). Presumably, the idea of a "Swahili" person (*Mswahili*; plural *Waswahili*) is as old as the first mentions of the *Sawāḥil* by Arab geographers. But until the nineteenth century, *Mswahili/Waswahili* likely "existed only as an epithet of reference, used mainly by foreign visitors," while denizens of the Swahili coast "identified primarily with their clan or village or with the ruler of the city-state to which they owed political allegiance" (Glassman 2011, 25).

In the 1890s, a group of Swahili-speaking Muslim writers led by Mtoro bin Mwinyi Bakari described "the Swahili" (*Waswahili*) as a "people of the coast" whose "[customs] are virtually the same" from Lamu, on the northern coast of present-day Kenya, to Lindi, on the southern coast of present-day Tanzania (Bakari 1981, 1). This definition resonates with how the term is often used today within the international field of Swahili studies as well as by intellectuals on the Swahili coast. But it has not been a straight line between Mtoro's writings and contemporary discourses. Even while Mtoro and his colleagues were putting pen to paper, the notion of what it meant to be "Swahili" was being radically transformed by the Omani ruling class and other elite Arabs, who had begun using the word as a shorthand for any coastal African who was unable to claim Arab descent (Allen 1981, 223). The British colonial administration amplified the conceptual split between *Arab* and *Swahili*, and the negative valence of the latter, by reserving *Swahili* as "a catch-all designation for what was considered to be the mass of disreputable and detribalized or alien African population"

(Arens 1975, 433; Willis 1993, 110–11). By the late 1950s, Dutch anthropologist A. H. J. Prins (1967) found *Swahili* to have a distinctly negative connotation on the Swahili coast: "locally in Zanzibar, Lamu, or elsewhere, hardly anybody likes to be called a Swahili himself, though people of higher social strata in any given community readily refer to their inferiors as Swahili" (11).

Prins's characterization of the Swahili ethnonym in the late 1950s is perhaps a bit reductive, as there were some denizens of the Swahili coast at the time who certainly did embrace the "Swahili" label, including large numbers of rural subalterns who sought to elevate their status by insinuating themselves into urban networks, thereby "becoming Swahili" (Cooper 1980, 159; Fair 2001, 36; Glassman 2011, 55). But in any case, the situation had changed by the time Prins's work was published in 1967, especially in Kenya. The integration of the Kenyan coast into an independent African nation-state that equated citizenship with membership in an African "tribe" made the idea of a Swahili "ethnic group" far more relevant (Eastman 1994b). In 1968, historian F. J. Berg reported that Mombasa's Swahili-speaking patrician elites, who had traditionally identified as members of specific "tribes" (*mataifa* or *miji*) and "clans" (*mbari* or *milango*), were beginning to embrace "a more generalized idea of 'Swahiliness,' contrasted with other elements in the modern city" (Berg 1968, 38).

By the end of the twentieth century, it seemed equally possible to describe the existence of a Swahili ethnic group in Kenya either as a long-standing "myth" that had become a "reality," or a long-standing "reality" that had long been denied as "myth." The former position was voiced by the late cultural anthropologist Carol Eastman, in the same volume in which Parkin called for a focus on paradox as a defining feature of the Swahili experience (Eastman 1994b). Synthesizing ideas from a panel on Swahili ethnicity held at the meetings of the *American Anthropological Association* in 1991, Eastman argues that while a distinctive "pattern of culture" recognized as "Swahili" has existed for centuries, especially on the northern Kenyan coast, it only became an essential determinant of social belonging for Swahili-speaking Muslims of the Kenyan coast in the postcolonial era. The latter position was voiced in the same year by two scholars who identify as ethnically Swahili: Kenyan sociolinguist Alamin M. Mazrui, and Zanzibari artist and literary theorist Ibrahim Noor Shariff, in their influential book, *The Swahili: Idiom and Identity of an African People* (1994). Taking a critical lens to discourses of Swahili identity in Swahili studies (including earlier work by Eastman), Mazrui and Shariff "attempt to demonstrate that [the] seeming muddle as to the definition of a Swahili is not intrinsic to Swahili identity; it is, rather, a problem that is fused into the tinted glasses of Eurocentricity, through which the Swahili have been viewed over the years" (4).

Disjuncture

Mazrui and Shariff's critique of discourses of Swahili identity attempts to shift the focus from the supposed ambiguity of Swahili identity, which they suggest exists primarily in the minds of foreign scholars, to the *disjuncture* between what I will call Kenya's *modern regime of ethnicity* and the *traditional Swahili regime of ethnicity*. I use the phrase *modern regime of ethnicity* in roughly the same way that Jonathan Glassman (2000, 397) uses *exclusionary national categorical order*: it is "an intellectual paradigm in which humanity is assumed to be divided into mutually exclusive national groups—or (to be more precise), into mutually exclusive ethnicities or ethnic groupings, each of which ought 'naturally' to control its own polity." I prefer the Foucauldian idea of a *regime*, however, in order to keep in view how this "intellectual paradigm" extends beyond the confines of formal academic and political discourses. To borrow from Stuart Hall's (not unrelated) discussion of the race concept, a regime of ethnicity is a "regime of truth" (Foucault 2000) that "makes a certain kind of sense of the world, constructs an order of intelligibility, organizes human practices within its categories, and thus comes to acquire real effects" across disparate areas of social practice (Hall 2017, 81).[13]

A modern regime of ethnicity is "modern" in the sense that it is part of a broader, global trend since the nineteenth century toward an emphasis on "attributional identity" (Ingold 2018, 47–48) in relation to "autonomized" (Fardon 1987) ethnic categories. In African countries like Kenya that experienced colonial indirect rule, a modern regime of identity was cemented by the "discursive repertoires" (Lynch 2017, 96) of colonial administrations that embraced the assumption that "every African belonged to a tribe, just as every European belonged to a nation" (Iliffe 1979, 323).[14] These same discursive repertoires then set the terms for postcolonial nation building and struggles over citizenship. This is especially true of Kenya, where the triumph of the "politics of recognition" over the "politics of redistribution" (Branch 2011, 16-19; drawing on Fraser 1995) situated ethnicity as a means for elites "to make political and economic demands on the state" (Ogot 2012, 11).

Like all Kenyans, Swahili-speaking Muslims of the Kenyan coast have had to navigate the modern regime of ethnicity since the advent of colonial rule. At the same time, they have also had to navigate a traditional regime of ethnicity that works in a fundamentally different way. Under the traditional Swahili regime of ethnicity, social belonging is tied to processes of situating oneself within, or in relation to, the social landscape of the Swahili town (*mji*, plural *miji*). These towns, which include Mombasa's Old Town, have dotted the East African littoral for over a thousand years. The ones that are still inhabited today have been continuously inhabited for centuries and remain socially as well as architecturally "Swahili." They range from "closely built-up places with mostly stone-built houses set in narrow streets and as clearly urban as anywhere in the world, to what appear more as large villages with mud and palm-leaf dwellings dispersed among overhanging coconut palms" (Horton and Middleton 2000, 11). Until the mid-twentieth century, all were interconnected as part of "a single mercantile system of considerable complexity," forming a "social landscape" that extended beyond their physical boundaries to incorporate other locales and other peoples (ibid.). Within each, social belonging was inseparable from ideas about power and privilege with respect to physical space. In other words, ethnicity was a matter of urban "citizenship" (Meier 2016, 30).

The Space of Swahili Ethnicity

In order to approach how the disjuncture of the modern and traditional Swahili regimes of ethnicity has been experienced and negotiated since the colonial era, it is necessary to delve into the historical foundations of the traditional Swahili regime of ethnicity. This task begins with a look at the social dynamics of the Swahili town prior to the abolition of slavery in the first decade of the twentieth century.

In terms of social and political form, the preabolition Swahili town had much in common with the ancient Greek *polis*, generating "a complex array of categories within citizens and between citizens and strangers and outsiders" (Isin 2002, 78). The primary citizens were the *waungwana* (sing. *mwungwana*), typically translated as "patricians," among whom where groups considered to be the "owners" (*wenyeji*) of the town. Most patricians claimed distant Arabian or Persian ("Shirazi") ancestry, though it was only the sharifs (descendants of the Prophet Muhammad) among them who could trace their lineages back across the Indian Ocean.[15] Reflecting Mombasa's long history as a site of political struggles and warfare (the original name for the city, Mvita, literally means "place of war"), the town's patricians comprise twelve communities, called the "Twelve Tribes"

FIGURE I.1 A man walks down a narrow street in the Forodhani area of Mombasa Old Town in 2006. Photo by Salim Nasher. Used with permission.

(*Thenashara Taifa*). This category was further divided into two "confederations"—the Three Tribes of the Kilindini (*Thelatha Taifa*) and the Nine Tribes of the Mvita (*Tisa Taifa*)—and further still into many dozens of clans (*mbari*).[16] The confederations divided the town into two competing moieties (*mitaa*)—a common feature of Swahili towns, which had "the structural function of making unity through opposition" (Horton and Middleton 2000, 130; cf. Ranger 1975, 18–19; Middleton 1992; Prins 1967, 1971; el-Zein 1974).

The wealth of Swahili patricians came from commerce. Until well into the twentieth century, these coastal subjects "provided the center of far-reaching mercantile relations with both Africa and Asia," thereby managing to prosper without ever becoming "landed aristocrats" (Horton and Middleton 2000, 18). Ultimately, however, it was slave ownership that secured their social status. Owning slaves made patricians "freeborn peoples" (another possible translation of *waungwana*), thereby solidifying their claim as owners of the town. It also enabled them to devote much of their time to religious worship and leisure activities. In a word, it made them "civilized." As Thomas Spear writes, "To be [*mwungwana*] was to be 'civilized' in the town mode—respected, creditworthy, dressed in the Swahili manner, well-spoken in Swahili and adept at Swahili verse, and learned in Islamic knowledge" (1984, 294–95). Along with *uungwana* ("patricianness"), this civilized way of being was referred to as *ustaarabu* (literally, "Arabness"), a concept introduced in the nineteenth century by the Omani ruling class.

The other citizens of the nineteenth-century Swahili town included elite Omani Arabs and Hadrami sharifs. Together with the patricians, these communities constituted what Mombasan Islamic scholar and social critic Sheikh al-Amin bin Ali Mazrui refers to in his writings during the 1930s as the "coastal peoples" (*wapwani*) (Kresse 2017). The paradigmatic *non*citizens, meanwhile, were the enslaved residents. For the most part, citizens treated enslaved peoples as "personal dependents, rather than chattel." But they also viewed them as "outsiders, whose chief defining quality was their origin as people who had been wrenched from their natal communities" in the rural hinterlands (Glassman 1995, 81; cf. Cooper 1977). Those hinterlands and their inhabitants—described by the patricians and other higher-status townspeople as *washenzi*, or "barbarians"—served as a constitutive Other, dividing coastal Swahili society "in true structuralist fashion between [the] town—representing order, civilization (*uungwana*), and predictability—and the world outside it—representing chaos, barbarity (*ushenzi*) and the fear-inspiring unknown" (Pouwels 1987, 30). Thus, in political theorist Engin Isin's (2002) terms, the participation of enslaved peoples in town life transformed a dialectical "logic of exclusion" into a "logic of alterity" animating social relations within the space of the town.

British colonial rule introduced new "struggles for Swahili citizenship" (Glassman 1995; Fabian 2019) in Swahili towns, as the process of "becoming Swahili" came to serve as a way for coastal subalterns to "step outside the colonial framework of control" (Willis 1993, 107). After the abolition of slavery, new contexts emerged for subalterns to join urban Swahili society from below. The most important of these during the colonial era was the competitive dance society, which could immediately situate newcomers within a moiety (Fabian 2019, 152–62; Kresse 2007, 53; Mirza and Strobel 1989; Ranger 1975; Strobel 1979; Willis 1993, 104). Another, which has remained relevant into the present, is domestic labor, which maintains the category of *utumwa* (serfdom, slavery) as "a membrane through which outsiders might be integrated in society" (Kresse 2007, 54), and a mediating category that enables those within the Swahili context to distinguish "between what is *uungwana*, 'civilized, high class, cultured' and what is *ushenzi*, 'barbaric, low class, foreign'" (Eastman 1994a, 102; see also Kresse 2007, 52–55; Hillewaert 2016).

The abolition of slavery in 1907 undermined the power of Swahili patricians along the entire coast. Mombasa's patricians were then dealt an additional blow in 1926, when the completion of new deep-water berths at Kilindini Harbor effectively moved all major shipping away from the Old Town (Middleton 2000, 112; Janmohamed 1978, 161). But patrician status has remained salient to this day in Mombasa and elsewhere on the Swahili coast. Rather than melting away with patricians' wealth, patricianness (*uungwana*) became a "residual" institution, remaining "active in the cultural process" (Williams 1977, 122). Set in opposition to the idea of barbarism (*ushenzi*), and in relation to the mediating category of serfdom/slavery (*utumwa*), it has continued to serve as the basis of a logic of alterity underpinning notions of identity and belonging in the Swahili town (Kresse 2007, 51–55). This is what I am calling the traditional Swahili regime of ethnicity.

One way in which the traditional Swahili regime of ethnicity has remained salient is in the fundamental spatiality of ethnic identification in the coastal Swahili context. To this day, coastal Swahili speakers most often approach ideas about what it means to be "Swahili" through the spatial notion of *uswahili*. *Uswahili* may be glossed as "Swahiliness" or "Swahili culture." However, it always carries a spatial connotation. When used with a locative suffix (*-ni*), it takes on an explicitly spatial meaning, expressing an idea akin to "Swahili-land." But even without this suffix, the spatial dimension is always present (cf. Shariff 1973, 68). In other words, *uswahili* is not just a quality or an essence, not just a *-ness*, but a *domain*. In discourses of ethnic identification, coastal Swahili speakers make use of this conflation of identity and space to express an "ethnic schema" (Brubaker et al. 2004) that I call *Swahili-space*.

The Swahili-space schema posits Swahili ethnicity as a territory that individuals and communities dwell within or move into or out of. This harmonizes with lived experience on the Swahili coast, where being or becoming "Swahili" has always implied existing within or entering into the cultural and moral context of the Swahili town (Kresse 2007, 36–69). In this way, the Swahili-space schema captures not only the poetics of Swahili ethnicity but also its dynamics, serving as a vernacular sociological model. Like any vernacular sociological model, it is often deployed normatively, as when Kenyan Swahili poet Mahmoud Mau implores, "Let us remain in Swahili-space [*uswahilini*], and not allow ourselves to be snatched from it!" (*Tubaki uswahilini, Natusiweni mateka*).[17] But it can also provide a relatively value-neutral way of objectifying the structured porosity of Swahili ethnicity, especially when discussing processes of "becoming Swahili" (Glassman 1995; Willis 1993), in which subalterns elevate themselves socially by moving into closer physical and social proximity to the patrician "owners" of Swahili towns. Unlike notions of cultural conversion, exemplified in the verb *kustaarabika* ("to become civilized in the manner of an Arab" [Sacleux 1939, 815]), the idea of moving into Swahili-space doesn't necessarily assume the inferiority of non-Muslim Africans. Thus, in describing Mijikenda-born taarab singer Maulidi Juma Iha, one proud, non-Muslim Mijikenda community leader told me, "he has entered very far into Swahili-space" (*ameingia uswahilini sana*).

MAKING SENSE IN SOUND

The most profound impacts of being "paradoxical" for Swahili-speaking Muslims in Mombasa have been those that amount to denials of full citizenship (or "non-native" status during the colonial era). But the quotidian *experience* of paradox for these subjects has always been one of navigating concrete and abstract *spaces* of identity, including a coastal "double periphery" and an urban neighborhood (Old Town) that is at once an arena of Swahili-space and a constituent part of Kenya's major port city. This has lent a special weight to practices of sounding and listening in the everyday lives of Mombasa's Swahili-speaking Muslims, as such practices are powerful modalities for developing "senses of place" (Feld

1996). In my earlier research on the Islamic soundscape in Mombasa Old Town, I develop Steven Feld's (ibid.) notion of an "acoustemology of place" to outline how sounding and listening practices serve as ways of experiencing and negotiating the disjuncture between coastal-Muslim and Kenyan political subjectivities.[18] *Sounds of Other Shores* expands on this work, by exploring secular music in Mombasa during the twentieth century as a site in which Swahili-speaking Muslims engaged *creatively* and *reflexively* with senses of place and identity.

An essential starting point for my investigation of music as a creative and reflexive engagement with place and identity is the recognition that music serves as a medium of *sensemaking*, by which I mean an active and dialogic process of generating meanings by making patterns, gestures, images, and qualities available to the senses (one's own senses as well as the senses of others). I draw here on the double meaning of *sense* as both a "vital communication with the world" (Merleau-Ponty 1962, 48) and a particular dimension of *meaning*, a rhetorical move I borrow from British philosopher Victoria Lady Welby and the American pragmatists John Dewey and Charles Sanders Peirce.[19] For Welby, Dewey, and Peirce, ruminating on "sense in all its senses" (Welby 1903, 48) was a way of getting at the role of the *aesthetic*, in the Aristotelean sense of "sensorial experience" and "sensuous knowledge" (Meyer and Verrips 2008, 21), in meaning. Their insights have been developed in more recent years by Eugene Gendlin, in his writings of "felt meaning" (1997), and Mark Johnson, in his investigations into "embodied cognition" (1997, 2007, 2013).

The idea of sensemaking, as I develop it here, begins from Johnson's (2007) dictum that "meaning is not just a matter of concepts and propositions, but also reaches down into the images, sensorimotor schemas, feelings, qualities, and emotions that constitute our meaningful encounter with our world" (xi). *Sense* is the domain of experience in which "images, sensorimotor schemas, feelings, qualities, and emotions" first take shape. Phenomenologically, it is *immediate* and *direct*. But this is only because it is mediated by *habit*, the domain of socially acquired "ways of using and incorporating the environment" (Dewey 1922, 15). The dialogic interrelation of sense and habit provide an aesthetic substrate for social relations, an "embodied sensitivity" (Ostrow 1990, 10) that facilitates intersubjectivity. Practices of sensemaking are creative engagements with this substrate that objectify and enable reflection upon notions of self and other.

Music is a particularly rich medium of sensemaking. It has often been observed that musical expression and experience are richly *sensual*, intimately connected to both bodily activity and spatial experience (Fisher and Lochhead

2002; Lidov 1987; Cox 2016; Johnson 1997; Zuckerkandl 1956; Di Bona 2017). But musical expression also involves the *reenactment* and *manipulation* of sense. As the late anthropologist Roy Wagner (2001, 163) put it in one of his audacious works on meaning, music is "a surrogate autonomy of sense" through which human beings explore and experiment with ways of being-in-the-world.

Practices of sensemaking in music may involve a greater or lesser focus on "interpretive moves" (Feld 1994b) that introduce articulated meanings, depending on how the music is framed in the encounter. Sensemaking in taarab tends to involve a fairly robust focus on interpretive moves, because of the historical emphasis in the genre on contemplative listening. Even though taarab has been commonly performed as a dance music since the mid-twentieth century, the music is still largely conceptualized as a contemplative art. Traditionally, taarab is understood in opposition to *ngoma*, a concept of music broadly shared by speakers of Bantu languages throughout equatorial and southern Africa that centers on the drum (also *ngoma* in Swahili) and the activities it enables. Whereas *ngoma* connotes a social event or ritual involving dance, music, and song, in which the separation of performers and audience is absent (Askew 2003, 612; Campbell and Eastman 1984, 467; Franken 1994, 99), *taarab* connotes an event with a separation between performers and audience, and an atmosphere of focused, contemplative listening.[20] Thus, the late Zanzibari taarab musician, educator, and arts administrator Seif Salim Saleh (1988) defines taarab as an exceptional form of *ngoma* that centers on "songs and instruments" rather than "dancing," and in which listeners remain "totally silent as they turn their ears to the sounds of the instruments and the voice as well as the words delivered by the taarab singer" (*taarab huwa kimya kabisa wasikilizaji wakiwa wametega masikio yao katika milio ya vinanda na sauti na maneno aimbayo mutribu muimbaji*) (9).

THE MUSICAL POETICS OF IDENTITY

Acts of appropriation orient musical sensemaking toward questions of being and selfhood, inaugurating a *musical poetics of identity*, a sonorous practice of questioning and commenting on relations of self and other. This poetics necessarily takes place at the level of *style*, which is to say within the patterning of sonic gestures that lends a felt coherence to a musical composition or performance. Style in music, according to Leonard B. Meyer's influential formulation, is a matter of "learned habits" that are "internalized" by musicians and listeners, and experienced "as a complex of felt probabilities" (Meyer 2010, 116).[21] These "internalized habits," as ways of *in-habiting* the world, tend to be perceived as unmediated, authentic expressions of identity (Turino 1999, 241; Gaunt 2006, 37–55). This is why, as decades of ethnomusicological research has shown, music provides a powerful means of self-understanding as well as "knowledge of other peoples, places, times and things, and ourselves in relation to them" (Stokes 1994, 3).

In broad terms, mimetic appropriation in music turns style into a medium for a poetics of identity by slotting a metaphoric gesture of *sounding as other* in place of a metonymic gesture of *sounding as self*. This is accomplished in part through the production of a mood such as irony or nostalgia that introduces an "awareness of difference, of a second reality" (Friedrich 1991, 32). Such moods, which are produced both within and outside of the text/performance, raise the suggestion that what is expressed is not identical to what is meant, thereby eliciting "interpretive moves" (Feld 1994b) oriented toward active decoding.

There is a direct connection between the musico-poetic process I am describing here and what Roman Jakobson (1960) calls the "poetic function" in language, the essence of which is an insertion of a paradigmatic resemblance (metaphor) in place of a syntagmatic connection (metonymy)—as, for example, when a rhyme is used to connect two ideas in a poem (372; see also Ricoeur 2004, 223).[22] In music as well as language, the poetic act of inserting metaphor in the place of metonymy draws attention to the formal characteristics of an utterance, "promoting the palpability of [its] signs" (Jakobson 1960, 356). This, in turn, places the utterance within "a special interpretive frame" that promotes reflexivity (Bauman and Briggs 1990). As Bauman and Briggs write, the poetic act "objectifies [the utterance], lifts it to a degree from its interactional setting and opens it to scrutiny by an audience" (73).

An investigation of musical poetics is also a musical poetics, in a slightly different sense. As a scholarly methodology, *poetics* is about parsing the internal workings of a text (in the broad sense of "any coherent complex of signs" [Bakhtin 1986, 103]), in order to lay the groundwork for the *hermeneutic* task of specifying situated meanings. Its focus is "the rules and conventions that enable the text to have the meanings and effects it does for [audiences]," the formal elements and relations that create the "conditions of possibility of such meanings" (Culler 2020).[23] The musical poetics I develop in the chapters that follow draws heavily from the *literary* poetics of twentieth-century Russian philosopher Mikhail Bakhtin. While Bakhtin never explored music in depth, he embraced expansive definitions of "language" and "text" that may be said to include music (Bakhtin 1986, 103–31), and made frequent use of vocalic concepts (*voice*, *double-voicedness*, etc.) that provide a bridge to thinking about musical expression. Importantly, the vocalic concepts in Bakhtin's work are not purely metaphorical. For Bakhtin, "*voices* allude to the ideological position *embodied* in the world" (Petrilli and Ponzio 2005, 406).

Bakhtin's extended essay "Discourse in the Novel" (1981, 259–422) lays out an approach to style in literary prose that provides a powerful model for an approach to musical style. Described by Bakhtin as a "sociological stylistics" (ibid., 284), this approach posits style as a space in which an author explores the texture of the social world by engaging creatively with the "dialogism" (the intersubjective and relational character) of language. In adapting Bakhtin's sociological stylistics to music, I attend to the special forms of dialogism not considered in Bakhtin's work—namely, those related to how musical expressions reverberate and resonate within and between human subjects and physical spaces. Most importantly, I attend to the heightened potential for "multivocality" in the performance of song, which involves the literal embodiment (and possible "misembodiment" [Brayton 2011]) of an actual voice or voices, typically set in a (literal and figurative) polyphonic relationship with other voices and/or musical sounds (Samuels 2004, 20; Meizel 2020).

From Bakhtin, I also garner insights into the role of ethnography in poetics. In his ruminations on "the problem of the text," Bakhtin stresses the need to constantly shift focus between text and context in analysis, and to recognize the inherent difficulty of demarcating the line between them (Bakhtin 1986, 103–31). This is, of course, the very essence of an ethnographic approach to expressive culture. Notably, he points to vocal timbre, something to which I attend to closely in this book, as an element of a performance that cannot be said to reside completely within or outside a text (ibid., 105–6).

MIMESIS AND THE SWAHILI WORLD

In moving from sensemaking to poetics, via appropriation, I have skipped over a concept that potentially provides a different way into transoceanic musical appropriation: *mimesis*. *Sounds of Other Shores* enters into a dialogue with a growing literature on mimesis in the "Swahili world" (the East African littoral plus the Comoro Islands and Swahiliphone northern Madagascar).[24] *Mimesis* refers to "reduplicative action" that is "both interpretive and assimilative" (Walker 2010, 33) and carried out with a "communicative purpose" (Donald 2005, 286). A propensity for mimesis has long been recognized to be part of what it means to be human.[25] But scholarly accounts of mimesis in the Swahili world often suggest or explicitly state that mimesis plays a special role in the region, serving as a "general social praxis" (Walker 2005, 192; 2010; Prestholdt 2008; Ivanov 2014, 2017) and/or a cultural logic evident in such domains as material culture and architecture (Ivanov 2017; Meier 2016; Prestholdt 2008), poetry and music (Vierke 2011, 423; 2017), and spirit possession (Larsen 2008).[26] Some scholars have argued that cultures of the Swahili world are especially mimetic as a result of the region's history as a mercantile contact zone in which urban dwellers must constantly engage with influential outsiders. This position has been put forward most convincingly by anthropologist Iain Walker and historian Jeremy Prestholdt in separate works on the Comoros. Walker (2005) characterizes mimesis on the Comorian island of Ngazidja as a mechanism for social inclusion, stability, and change; and Prestholdt (2008, 13-33), writing about nineteenth-century social life on the Comorian island of Mutsamudu, identifies a mimetic practice of "similitude" by which local actors shaped the "perceptions and policies" of hegemonic outsiders (18). Their works recall A. H. J. Prins's (1965, 263–75) earlier speculations about a cultural "ethos" of "adaptivity" on the Swahili coast that enables (Muslim) foreigners to quickly become locals, and locals to "easily and often adapt themselves" to new circumstances and even identities (268–69). They resonate, as well, with Edward Simpson and Kai Kresse's (2008) more recent argument about a distinctive "Indian-Ocean cosmopolitanism" centered on the cultivation and maintenance of forms of knowledge and dispositions necessary for thriving within "an ever-changing community of strangers" (Simpson and Kresse 2008, 3, 26; see also Kresse 2012a).

    The evidence of a mimetic "ethos" (Prins 1965) in the Swahili world is difficult to ignore, even accounting for the propensity of Western scholarship to generate "topological stereotypes" (Appadurai 1992, 44). But if, indeed, mimesis is a special feature of culture in the Swahili world, it is not always so "functional," in the classical anthropological sense of the word, as Walker and Prestholdt suggest. Drawing on Michael Taussig's (1993) reassessment of anthropological theories of mimesis, Swahilist philologist Clarissa Vierke (2017) describes mimesis in Swahili poetry as a "specifically aesthetic act" that seeks to "connect sensuously with what has been copied and hence evoke some of the original's force" (327, 333). Like Vierke, I approach mimesis on the Swahili coast as an aesthetic act. But whereas Vierke proposes bracketing questions of meaning in this act, I am specifically concerned in this book with its poetic valences, which is to say, in Aristotle's terms, how it moves from *mimesis* to *poiesis*, from sensuous engagement with "the actual" to creative exploration of possibility (Martin 2020; Aristotle 1902).

A GENEALOGY OF APPROPRIATION

The chapters in this book comprise a series of chronologically ordered case studies, each centering on a particular era or form of popular music in Mombasa. While most concern taarab, two chapters explore other, related music genres that are part of the story of transoceanic musical appropriation in Mombasa. Despite its historical sweep and overriding focus on taarab, *Sounds of Other Shores* is not a history of Mombasan taarab. It is, rather, a history—or, more properly, a *genealogy*—of a cultural practice (transoceanic musical appropriation) that happened to emerge mostly within the space of Mombasan taarab. Among other things, this means that I place a greater emphasis on certain musicians over others who might receive greater attention in a proper historical account of Mombasan taarab.

My use of the term *genealogy* follows from Arjun Appadurai's discussion in *Modernity at Large* (1996) of history and genealogy as distinct yet complementary approaches to examining the diachronic dimensions of social and cultural formations. Whereas history for Appadurai is concerned with linking events and phenomena "to increasingly larger universes of interaction," genealogy homes in on "cultural dispositions and styles that might be embedded both in local institutions and in the history of the local habitus" (74).[27] In the chapters that follow, I sometimes situate local musical practices within "increasingly larger universes of interaction." But the primary narrative of the book is a genealogical one, centered on aesthetic forms and practices, and processes of subject formation that are bound up with relatively local communities and publics.

I begin my genealogy of transoceanic musical appropriation in Mombasa with two originary moments when the social, technological, and aesthetic conditions for the phenomenon took shape. The first, explored in chapter 1, is commonly thought of as an originary moment for Swahili taarab, in general: the interwar years. The massive success of the first commercial recordings by the legendary Siti binti Saad and her Zanzibar-based collective, released between 1928 and 1930, transformed taarab into a modern, mass-mediated popular music. Developing an analytical approach to musical style inspired by Bakhtin's "sociological stylistics" (Bakhtin 1981, 300), I reveal how the early recorded works of the binti Saad collective situated the sounds of taarab as an important medium for critical reflection on ethnic boundaries, a matter of rising concern at the time for Swahili-speaking coastal Muslims.

Chapter 2 turns to the 1950s, a decade in which taarab in Mombasa thrived, thanks in part to the existence of a dynamic sonic mediascape centered on the locally operated radio station Sauti ya Mvita (Voice of Mombasa). I argue in this chapter that the broadcasts of Sauti ya Mvita nurtured a reflexive approach to musical style in Mombasan taarab by presenting Swahili-speaking Muslims in Mombasa with a powerful sonic portrait of what it meant to be culturally "Swahili" at a time when they, like all colonial subjects, were caught up in the politics of "ethnic territoriality" (Lynch 2011).

Chapters 3, 4, and 5 are case studies of transoceanic musical appropriation in Mombasa during the second half of the twentieth century. Chapter 3 concerns Indian taarab, arguably the most popular form of taarab on the Kenyan coast during the latter half of the twentieth century. Taking an ethnographic ear to the dialogics of (multi)vocality in Indian taarab performance, I argue that this subgenre's paradoxical presentations of Indian sounds as Swahili expressions positioned it as a vehicle for public reflection on Swahili ethnicity. I pay special attention to the more comedic Indian taarab singers, who, I argue, engaged in a musical poetics of identity centered on the act of amplifying and recasting the Indianness that resonates in Swahili-space.

Chapter 4 moves out of the genre space of taarab to explore the literal and figurative resonances of Hadrami Arab music in Mombasa. The central focus is the genre of Hadrami Arab popular song known in Mombasa as *ṭarab*, which has been performed on the Kenyan coast since the early twentieth century. While Hadramis of the Swahili coast can rightfully claim Hadrami *ṭarab* as their own, I suggest that their engagements with it nonetheless constitute a reflexive mode of *appropriation* similar to—and, indeed, connected to—transoceanic appropriation in Mombasan taarab. The heart of the chapter is an ethnography of *ṭarab*-centered Hadrami men's wedding celebrations. Drawing on anthropological theories of ritual and performance, I describe these events as cultural performances in which participants reflect upon the experience of existing on the diasporic edge of Swahili-space.

Chapter 5 takes a close look and listen to the life and work of the late Kenyan-Swahili singer and *ʿūd* virtuoso Zein l'Abdin, who was known for a distinctive brand of "Arab taarab" that blends elements of Egyptian, southern Arabian, and coastal African musics. During the 1970s, Zein developed his Arab taarab repertoire in collaboration with renowned Swahili poet Ahmed Sheikh Nabhany (a fellow transplant from the northern coastal island of Lamu). I describe the musical settings that Zein composed in collaboration with Nabhany as a musical strand of what Kresse (2007) characterizes as Nabhany's program of conserving Swahili culture. I argue that Zein expanded Nabhany's program of conservation, by presenting, in and through musical form, a theoretical model of Swahili culture that manages to addresses the paradox of "authentic hybridity" (Ballinger 2003, 245–65).

Chapters 6 and 7 bring the genealogy of transoceanic musical appropriation in Mombasa into the twenty-first century. Chapter 6 outlines how and why Mombasa's tradition of transoceanic musical appropriation has evaporated, focusing on the disparate roles of Islamic reformism and heritagization in eroding the conditions that had allowed an appropriation-centered musical poetics of identity to thrive. Chapter 7 then examines the revival of transoceanic musical appropriation in Mombasa, in a new, outward-facing form, in the realm of hip hop-oriented youth music. I explore what this phenomenon reveals not only about the possibilities of transoceanic appropriation as an outward-facing project, but also about the broader conditions of "cultural citizenship" (Ong 1996, 737) for Swahili-speaking Muslims of the Kenyan coast in the twenty-first century.

I close with brief reflections on the burgeoning field of "Indian Ocean ethnomusicology," and a call for a humanistic musical anthropology of the Indian Ocean that attends to creative practices of sensemaking.

ONE

A Feeling for the Boundaries
Early Recorded Taarab

A shout of "*Sahani Odeon!*" (Odeon record!) rings out as Mbaruk Talsam strikes the first tones on his *ʻūd* (Arab lute). A violin and *rīq* (Arab tambourine) enter a moment later, and a buoyant melody takes shape over a lightly syncopated beat. Seventeen seconds later it reaches an end, leaving only the soft decay of Mbaruk's final note.

After a moment, Mbaruk gets things started again, this time with his voice as well as his *ʻūd*. Now the tempo is slower, and the rhythmic structure more complex. Time stretches, lopes, as Mbaruk intones Swahili words in his gristled tenor:

U muongo! Basahera, u muongo! (Liar! Basahera, you liar!)
Tena Basahera, u muongo! (Basahera, still a liar!)

The song then moves on to a string of words transported on a winding melody. Unlike the words that came before, these seem to hide their meanings beneath a thicket of metaphor:

Kuna kijiti kimoja kikasitawisha jengo? (Can a single stick hold up a building?)
Huna pau huna nziba huna ng'ongo (You have no pole, filling, or thatching)
Nenda ukakate miti nije nikuonye jengo (Go and cut a tree and I'll show you
    a building)

Now the *U muongo* refrain returns, this time with additional voices, including the unmistakable, soaring voice of the region's first true popular music icon, Siti binti Saad.

Thus proceeds the first minute of Mbaruk Effendi Talsam's "Basahera Umuongo" (AUDIO EX. 1), recorded in 1930 in a makeshift recording studio in Mombasa for the German record label Odeon.[1] This is one of the earliest commercial recordings of Swahili taarab. The very first taarab records had only recently been released on the HMV label—the fruits of recording sessions undertaken at the Gramophone Company's recording facility in Bombay in 1928 and 1929. Consumers in towns and cities across the Swahili coast had snapped up tens of thousands of those records (not to mention gramophone players to play them), prompting a veritable scramble for Swahili taarab that saw Odeon, France-based Pathé Records, and US-based Columbia Records all get into the business of recording and distributing the music during the course of 1930 (see Graebner 1989b, 2004b; Fair 1998; 2001, 1–2).[2] As one of the trailblazing musicians featured on the first taarab releases, Mbaruk was in high demand. Born around 1892 into a wealthy Arab family in Mombasa, he was one of the finest musicians of his generation on the Swahili coast. After losing his vision to smallpox around age ten, he dedicated his life to poetry and music, becoming a virtuoso in both fields. Around 1920, he moved to Zanzibar to chase success in what had become the most dynamic music scene of the Swahili coast. There he became a member of a musical collective led by the now-legendary female taarab singer, poet, and composer Siti binti Saad. Siti can be heard singing with the chorus in "Basahera," while another key member of the collective, Buda Swedi, can be heard on violin.[3]

As Michael Denning describes in his *Noise Uprising* (2015), early recorded Swahili taarab was among the many "vernacular phonograph musics" that arose in colonial port cities during the early electrical recording era (roughly 1925–1930). All of these musics, Denning asserts, cultivated new social imaginaries that were at once modern and indigenous, thereby presenting an early challenge to the colonial order. What Denning doesn't point out is that taarab was special, if not unique, among these musics, for how it fostered critical reflection on the new social imaginary it was helping to create. Before any of its sounds were ever etched in shellac, taarab was already a genre that engendered discussions of social norms and values. Audiences derived pleasure from uncovering social commentaries buried in the verbal texts, which employ a mode of allegorical indirection known as *mafumbo* (from the transitive verb *fumba*, meaning "close" or "wrap up"). (The stanza of "Basahera" above exemplifies the *mafumbo* style of poetic composition, though, as I will discuss, it happens to be borrowed from another genre of Swahili poetry.)[4] In her account of the reception of the binti Saad collective's music in working-class Zanzibar during the interwar years, historian Laura Fair (2001, 169–225) describes how conversations about the meanings of taarab song texts that began during or directly after performance events would reticulate through the community to "spur public debate of the religious, social, and cultural principles that contributed to the constitution of community" (183–84). While she focuses mostly on song texts whose underlying meanings reside near the surface or circulated along with the songs in the form of rumors, "Basahera" can help us to imagine how this process might have unfolded in relation to songs for which this was not the case. The somewhat ambiguous surface allegory in the first stanza clearly invites interpretations relating to themes of sincerity and responsibility, which would naturally flow into discussions of social roles and expectations.

The transition to a "phonograph music" amplified the public-making potential of taarab, by enabling listeners to imagine themselves as part of a larger community of addressees without eliminating traditional practices of social interpretation. "In these early days of Swahili records," writes one firsthand witness to life in Zanzibar in the 1930s,

> the coffee shops and eating houses were flooded with members of the public listening to the songs of Siti binti Saad. Members of the public who played them inside their houses were astonished to hear encores from listeners outside their houses. The people were proud and pleased with this new invention in their national language. (Suleiman 1969, 86–87)

As is clear in this writer's use of the phrases "members of the public" and "national language," while listening to recorded taarab on the Swahili coast in the 1930s was often akin to attending a live performance, it was also an engagement with a public text, and therefore a way of relating to the multitude of strangers who comprise the larger, imagined communities to which every modern urbanite belongs. The addition of this "stranger-relationality" (Warner 2002, 75) necessarily amplified the reflexivity of listeners' metadiscourses, by situating them as "practices of circulation" (Novak 2008) that brought disparate groups of listeners on the Swahili coast into the same broad conversation. In this way, the recorded output of the binti Saad collective constituted what might be called *a medium of social reflexivity*, a form of public culture that encouraged and enabled critical evaluation of aspects of social life.

Siti binti Saad and her collaborators were not the only Swahili taarab musicians to get swept up in the global "musical revolution" of the electrical recording era (Denning 2015). By 1930, a number of groups from the Kenyan coast had also recorded, or were just about to record, for HMV and other international labels.[5] But Siti and company are the only taarab musicians from this era who are still widely remembered anywhere on the Swahili coast, including in Mombasa.[6] Laura Fair provides a partial explanation for this, by showing us how the lyrics of their songs resonated with the subaltern denizens of Zanzibar (Fair 1998, 2001). Notwithstanding Mbaruk's elite background, the collective was situated, literally and figuratively, among the working-class people of Zanzibar, in the area of Ng'ambo (literally, "The Other Side"). Fair's oral-historical research reveals how the collective's songs "gave poetic form to the often trenchant critiques of economic and political power that circulated in . . . Ng'ambo during the period between the two world wars" (Fair 2001, 169). This chapter offers a different, complementary perspective on the matter, by exploring how the *sounds* of the binti Saad collective's early recordings resonated with residents of cities and towns across the entire Swahili coast. Taking a critical ear to musical form in the collective's early recorded works, I argue that the *sounds* of these works were meaningful (in multiple sense of the word) for audiences on the Swahili coast during the interwar years for how they enabled critical reflection on matters of cultural identity and difference in coastal Swahili society.

Though rarely emphasized in Swahili- or European-language writings on the life and art of Siti binti Saad, Siti and her collaborators developed a sophisticated approach to musical style that made the sounds of their songs every bit as layered and socially dialogic as their widely celebrated and studied lyrics. This approach, I contend, situated taarab as a powerful medium for critical reflection on cultural identity and difference, thereby setting the stage for the cultural phenomenon of transoceanic appropriation in Mombasan taarab. Subsequent chapters will trace the genealogical connections between the early recorded works of the binti Saad collective and later forms of taarab in Mombasa. My focus in this chapter is the social resonances of these works on the Swahili coast in their historical moment. Developing an approach inspired by Bakhtin's "sociological stylistics" (Bakhtin 1981, 300), I investigate how the collective worked with the sounds of other shores in their early recordings, with an ear toward the "internal politics" of their stylistic appropriations.

THE HYBRIDIZED SOUNDWORLDS OF THE
BINTI SAAD COLLECTIVE

While poetry is always the centerpiece of taarab, the members of the binti Saad collective were admired for their musical artistry as well as their verbal prowess. Siti, for her part, was renowned for the "quality of her voice, her range of tones, resonance, nasality, and intonation[, which] is said to have moved her listeners to another plane of existence" (Fair 2001, 181); and her male collaborators were all considered to be the finest singers and instrumentalists in the region (cf. Matola et al. 1966). They were also, as we will see, highly skilled and innovative *composers*, who developed a novel approach to stylistic hybridization.

We can hear the binti Saad collective's novel approach to stylistic hybridization in Mbaruk's "Basahera." Two basic aspects of the performance may be described as generically "Arab": the orchestration, which is typical of urban ensembles throughout the Arab world in the early twentieth century; and the use of *Maqām*, the Arab system of melodic modes, as the structural basis of the melodic material (the song is mostly set in *Maqām Bayātī*, save for a brief modulation that I will describe shortly).[7] Atop this broad Arab foundation, Mbaruk and his collaborators construct a more heterogeneous musical edifice. The instrumental prelude is a *dūlāb*, an Egyptian musical form commonly featured at the time on Arab music records produced in Cairo.[8] But the style of the song proper is not Egyptian at all. Its more complex rhythmic foundation—a compound meter involving a 3:2 polyrhythm—is typical of coastal East African music, but also of musics of the Arabian Peninsula. Meanwhile, Mbaruk's vocal performance reflects the music culture of the Swahili coast, in ways both obvious and subtle. Most obvious, of course, is his use of the Swahili language. But his vocal delivery, which is syllabic and devoid of the ornamentation that one would expect of Egyptian or Gulf Arab song, is also distinctly Swahili. At a deeper level, the peculiar melody of the first stanza is a direct reference to *ngoma* (traditional social dances) of the northern Kenyan coast, which is the original context of the "Basahera" poem. Mbaruk, who had spent years studying with master poet-musicians in the northern coastal port of Lamu, executes this reference with exquisite finesse. His melody's convoluted motion beautifully mimics how *ngoma* singing across the Swahili coast tends to abandon form in favor of delivering an entire stanza in a single breath (Abdalla 1974), while a brief modulation to a new melodic mode (*maqām*) with a "half-flat" tonic elicits a strong flavor of the northern coast.[9] A half-flat tonic grants a melody a special quality, described by Palestinian Arab musicians Johnny Farraj and Sami Abu Shumays as an "unusual feeling of tonicization and resolution" (Farraj and Shumays 2019, 388), which has been an iconic feature of traditional Swahili music of the northern Kenyan coast since at least the early twentieth century (Eisenberg In prep.).

"Basahera" offers a good example of the stylistic approach taken by the binti Saad collective in their early recorded works. Each of these works features its own *hybridized soundworld* incorporating some combination of elements drawn from *ngoma* traditions, Egyptian Arab music, Arab musics from the Arabian Peninsula, or Indian musics. To be sure, there are some stylistic threads that weave through most of the works. These include an Arab-style heterophonic texture, in which all instruments and voices perform the same melody in unison but with distinct variations and ornamentations; the use of melodic modes (frequently, but not always, Arab *maqām*s); an Egyptian-style introductory prelude (*dūlāb*) as an introductory gesture; and, most importantly, Siti binti Saad's reedy yet powerful voice. Beyond these threads, however, what characterizes the style of the binti Saad collective's early recorded works is the absence of a characteristic style.

The perspective I am outlining here on the relationship between style and identity in the early recorded works of the binti Saad collective challenges the notion that the collective developed "a truly typical Indian Ocean style" (Topp Fargion 2014, 55–56). The stylistic approach that the binti Saad collective developed in their early recordings was not simply an organic result of the Indian Ocean context in which they were working. It was, rather, an *intentional and reflexive aesthetic project*. My choice of terms here draws from Bakhtin's (1981) distinction between "organic" and "intentional" processes of linguistic hybridization, which has been extended by postcolonial theorists to discussions of hybridization in culture and identity (Werbner 1997; Young 2005, 18–21). "Organic hybridization," as Pnina Werber (1997) puts it, is the largely "unreflective" process through which all cultures, "despite the illusion of boundedness . . . evolve historically" (4), whereas "intentional hybridization" is an artistic act oriented toward reflecting upon—objectifying, playing with, ironizing—this process. Both organic and intentional modes of hybridization involve "borrowings, mimetic appropriations, exchanges and inventions" (ibid.), but in the latter case they are reflexive "artistic interventions" (5) that seek to generate a "collision between differing points of views on the world" (Bakhtin 1981, 360). The hybridized soundworlds of the binti Saad collective were just these sorts of interventions, crafted to resonate with a listening public for whom questions of cultural boundaries—that is to say, of *ethnicity*—had become especially important.

The era in which the binti Saad collective developed their unique stylistic approach and first presented it to a phonographic public was one of changing ideas about ethnic categories and boundaries on the Swahili coast. In the wake of the first world war, the British colonial administration in East Africa worked to assert greater control over the population and colonial economy through new laws and policies relating to labor and taxation. Their efforts, grounded at every turn in the idea that every colonized subject belonged either to an African "tribe" or a non-African "racial" community, sparked a range of controversies and disputes over ethnic categories and boundaries among colonized subjects. In the Zanzibar archipelago, new labor policies created an influx of migrants from the mainland that reshaped ethnic categories. Incoming migrants began to identify as "Swahili" in order to escape the social stigma and other deficits of their "tribal" origins, prompting the islands' indigenous communities to reject this label in favor of narrower "ethnic categories associated specifically with the isles" (Fair 2001, 36; Glassman 2011, 55). Meanwhile, in Mombasa, the administration's efforts to clarify the distinction between "natives" and "nonnatives" for purposes of taxation sparked discord and even incidents of violence between elite Arabs and Swahili patricians. Both communities actively lobbied for "nonnative" status to escape new taxes on "natives" as well as the perceived indignity of being lumped in with "native" Africans. The administration's decision to grant this coveted status only to those classified as "Coast Arabs" created a cleavage at the heart of urban Swahili society on the Kenyan coast (Kindy 1972, 27–45; Salim 1976).

TOWARD A SOCIOLOGICAL STYLISTICS

Understanding how the hybridized soundworlds of the binti Saad collective were received in the interwar years presents a challenge. While musicians and commentators handed down stories about intended and received meanings of some poems from the binti Saad collective, they did not do the same for any of the musical settings through which these poems were conveyed.[10] This surely has much to do with the fact that Swahili poetry has always been viewed on the Swahili coast as a vessel of cultural knowledge worthy of preservation. But it is also possible that listeners did not talk about the sounds of the music using the sort of (meta)language that would lend itself to transmission through formal writing, as speech about music is often highly associational and metaphorical (Feld 1994b, 92–93).

Garnering insights about the early works of the binti Saad collective from actual, living subjects might seem to be a straightforward task, given that some of these works are still performed today on the Swahili coast. But in truth, the musical sensibilities of the early commercial recording era are mostly alien to contemporary taarab musicians and audiences. Even the Swahili musicians who perform works by the binti Saad collective today are often puzzled by what they hear in the collective's earliest recordings.[11] This may seem especially remarkable in light of the fact that there now exists a music school on Zanzibar oriented toward teaching the taarab as it was established by the binti Saad collective. The Dhow Countries Music Academy (DCMA), founded in 2001, offers formal instruction in Swahili taarab performance.[12] Students there are taught to perform songs by the binti Saad collective, and a photo of Siti hangs in a place of honor in the main performance space. But while these students and their instructors are rightly seen as heirs to the tradition of Siti binti Saad, they received this tradition from later generations who transformed it in significant ways. Notably, the late singer and drummer Bi Kidude, who was largely responsible for reviving interest in the repertoire of binti Saad in the late twentieth century, brought her own aesthetic sensibility to the music, "modernizing" it and infusing it with a dose of *unyago*, a rural women's *ngoma* danced for weddings and initiation rites (Graebner 2005a; Saleh et al. 2008). In many cases, she completely recomposed the settings of the binti Saad collective songs she performed, thereby transforming those songs in the popular consciousness as well.[13]

One musician from whom I was able to garner valuable information and perspectives for this chapter was Kenyan taarab musician Zein l'Abdin (1939–2016), whose career and work will be explored in chapter 5. For Zein, as for the DCMA faculty, any discussion of the history, aesthetics, or formal characteristics of taarab necessarily began with a consideration of the work of "*akina Siti*" ("Siti and company"). But Zein's focus was always on the music *as it was recorded*. He had a collection of recordings by the binti Saad collective on cassette, courtesy of his nephew Jamal Hafidh Jahadhmy, an avid music collector.[14]

Zein convinced me that stylistic hybridization in the works of the binti Saad collective needs to be understood as intentional and reflexive. He took seriously every aesthetic choice the collective made in their recorded performances, and spoke with reverence about their compositional abilities. In one of our conversations, he admonished me for asking a clumsily worded question that seemed to downplay the collective's creativity. Earlier in the conversation, he had used the Swahili verb *kuiba* (to steal) to refer to an act of musical appropriation. Unable to come up with a better verb in the moment, I seized upon it to ask about the binti Saad collective's penchant for borrowing Egyptian melodies (something they did in at least a few instances [cf. Kiel 2012]). Zein bristled at my insinuation that the binti Saad collective ever perpetrated any kind of musical "theft." "All the old songs are [the musicians'] own, *original* creations!" (*Nyimbo zote za zamani ni wenyewe, ni* original *zao!*), he proclaimed, accentuating the English word *original* to make sure I got the message.

Zein's emphasis on the artistic integrity of the binti Saad musical compositions provided a methodological opening for me. It suggested that the collective's hybridized soundworlds should be treated as, in Bakhtin's terms, "artistic hybrids" that are "stylized through and through, thoroughly premeditated, achieved, distanced" (Bakhtin 1981, 366). In musical terms, this meant approaching these soundworlds as tapestries of musical structures, some of which function as "musemes," or musical signs (Tagg 2013).

To the extent that they function "musematically" (semiotically), mimetic appropriations of style in the hybridized soundworlds of the binti Saad collective are necessarily "intermusical" (Monson 1994), alluding to other musics and their associated social contexts. Such intermusicality is clearly at play in how Mbaruk incorporates the style of northern coastal *ngoma* into the melody of the first verse of "Basahera." In the context of the song, the momentary sonic gestalt of a winding melody and a half-flat tonic is explicitly *citational*; it is a reference, an allusion, rather than just an organic component of the composition. An even more conspicuous example of an intermusical allusion to another style can be heard in Siti binti Saad's 1930 recording of her song "Wewe Paka" (You Cat), which Janet Topp Fargion presents as a representative example of the early sound of the binti Saad collective (Topp Fargion 2014, 54–55; 2007, 6–7).[15] As Topp Fargion notes, "Wewe Paka" brings together African, Arab, and Indian stylistic elements. The vocal performance is broadly "African," but the orchestration and use of an introductory *dūlāb* situate the performance as a whole "recognizably in an Arabic idiom" (Topp Fargion 2014, 54). Meanwhile, the melody is loosely based on an Indian melodic mode (*rāg*), and glides along on a pulse from "a small bell" that evokes the sound of "the Indian *tāl*, small cymbals used to maintain meter in the performance of dance and songs" (54). Topp Fargion characterizes this remarkable stylistic mélange as a "[symbol] of Zanzibari society" (Topp Fargion 2007, 6), and suggests that it shows how "[t]*aarab* music was emerging as a truly typical Indian Ocean style" (Topp Fargion 2014, 55–56). While there is truth to this assessment, by failing to account for the play of intermusicality, it misses something essential about Siti and her collaborators' engagement with

Indian style in this instance. As a sonic gestalt composed for one particular song, the combination of a *tāl* bell and *rāg* tonality clearly announces itself as an appropriation, asking to be heard as an evocation of India/Indianness.

I use the phrases *announces itself* and *asking to be heard* not to impute agency to musical expressions, but rather to refer to the "reflexive diagramming" that is the essence of *citationality* (Nakassis 2013). "Citations," writes linguistic anthropologist Constantine V. Nakassis, "do their work by pointing to the ways in which they are not what they reanimate" (ibid., 70). The references to *ngoma* in "Basahera" and Indian music in "Wewe Paka" are both citational in this sense, because they are bounded and *intergeneric* (drawn from another genre). The intergeneric aspect is key here—not only to the citationality of the stylistic appropriations but also to their potential meanings. In Philip Tagg's terms, these borrowings are "genre synecdoches," mimetic appropriations of style that connote other "paramusical" contexts—other places, times, culture, "other sorts of people" (Tagg 2013, 525).

A discussion of intermusicality naturally moves from poetics to hermeneutics, from how the music works to what it *means*. In this case, the move is still a bit premature. Before we can approach the question of how this music may have been received by denizens of the Swahili coast in its contemporary moment, it is necessary to delve deeper into the formal aspects of its *genre*, that is to say, its "orienting frameworks, interpretive procedures, and sets of expectations" (Hanks 1987, 670). This will require taking a step back, to examine the context in which the binti Saad collective first developed their stylistic approach.

TAARAB FROM THE OTHER SIDE

The particular form of taarab that the binti Saad collective launched into public circulation at the end of the 1920s was, as Fair (2001, 171) puts it, a "revolutionized version" of what had been a distinctly elite form. It was "unofficial" (Barber 1987; Bakhtin 1984b), unmoored from, and to some extent opposed to, the tastes and expectations of the elite members of coastal Swahili society for whom the sounds of taarab "celebrate[d] and reaffirm[ed] the power and exclusivity of Zanzibar's Omani ruling class" (Fair 2001, 171).

When the collective began their work together after the end of the first world war, taarab was a genre performed by and for elite Arabs and Swahili patricians of Zanzibar and the Kenyan coastal town of Lamu. The Zanzibari variety of this elite taarab was sung mostly in Arabic and firmly grounded in Egyptian aesthet-

FIGURE 1.1 Siti Binti Saad and her collective in Bombay, 1929. From left to right: Maalim Shaaban, Subeit bin Ambar, Siti Binti Saad, and Buda Swedi.

ics and performance practices. It emerged, in a sense, out of the sultan's court, developed by elite men's social clubs as a public version of the Egyptian-style Arab music that had been performed at court since the reign of Sultan Seyyid Barghash (1870–1888) (ibid., 171–73; Graebner 2004a; Khatib 1992; Topp Fargion 2014, 37–92). The Lamu variety of elite taarab also had roots in the nineteenth century, but was otherwise quite different. It was a genre of sung Swahili poetry traditionally accompanied by a locally constructed lute called the *kibangala* (a version of the southern Arabian *gambus*) (Graebner 2014; Nabhany 2003). Like Zanzibari taarab, it was historically associated with elite Arabs, but in this case Swahiliphone "old Arabs" rather than Omani suzerains. It also differed markedly from Zanzibari elite taarab with respect to its gender dynamics. The late Lamuan poet Ahmed Sheikh Nabhany (2003) stressed the essential contributions of women like poet and musician Bi Salima Zeina, who performed for elite Swahili and Arab women around the turn of the twentieth century. Musicians and audiences on the Swahili coast in the first decades of the twentieth century recognized the two elite forms of taarab as distinct yet interconnected, and actively worked to bring them together. Swahili songs from Lamu made up a large portion of the Swahili repertoire of Zanzibar's elite taarab orchestras in the earliest years (Graebner 2004a, 183–84; Topp Fargion 2014, 43–50); and at least one important Lamuan musician, Mohamed Kijuma, actively experimented with importing the Egyptian sounds of Zanzibari taarab into Lamu taarab (Abou Egl 1983, 403).[16]

To be sure, elite taarab laid the foundation for the work of the binti Saad collective. Zanzibar's men's orchestras opened up the field of taarab on the island, by bringing the music out of the sultan's court and introducing some repertoire in Swahili (Fair 2001, 172). Meanwhile, Lamu taarab directly influenced the stylistic approach of the collective via Mbaruk, who had spent years on Lamu studying with master poet-musicians Mohamed Kijuma and Bwana Zena before arriving on Zanzibar (Jahadhmy, in Matola et al. 1966, 65–66). But in important respects, the binti Saad collective operated outside the world of elite taarab. In the first place, the members were all strangers to elite Zanzibari society, albeit to different extents and for different reasons. Mbaruk was one of two members who would have had relatively little trouble navigating elite Zanzibari society, including the world of elite taarab. The other was the renowned poet, singer, and percussionist Maalim Shaaban Umbaye, who, as his title "Maalim" (teacher) suggests, was a teacher of Islamic studies. Both Mbaruk and Shaaban had come from relative wealth, and received formal education and musical training at local Qur'anic schools. Despite their elite credentials and upbringings, however, these men were still outsiders to elite Zanzibari society, because they were "immigrants from the mainland" (Fair 2001, 176). Mbaruk was a true newcomer (*mgeni*), having come from the Kenyan coast as a fully formed adult complete with Mombasan-accented Swahili.[17] But Shaaban also held this status to some degree, having been born in Malawi. The other members of the collective were all strangers to elite Zanzibari society because of their humble origins. Siti's case was singular in this regard. As a descendant of enslaved peoples, she began life about as far from elite Zanzibari society as it was possible to get, but slowly closed this gap over the course of her lifetime. Much like the Egyptian singer and national icon Umm Kulthum, with whom she is often compared, Siti's fame, talent, and upstanding comportment in public life enabled her to transcend the perceived infirmity of her birth in the eyes of her audience.[18] One sign of this was her Arabic honorific, "Siti," which is said to have been bestowed upon her by an elite Arab admirer. The name replaced her given name, Mtumwa (literally, "servant"), which was then "reserved for socially marginal, unfree members of coastal society" (Fair 2001, 316). Another was the fact that she was ultimately invited to sing at the sultan's palace.[19]

Even more than the social positioning of individual members, the physical positioning of the binti Saad collective outside of Zanzibar's patrician Stone Town, in the working-class area of Ng'ambo ("The Other Side"), placed them and their music outside of elite Zanzibari society. As a fixture of Ng'ambo, the collective was part of a vibrant, working-class cultural scene that included music groups associated with a range of African and Hadrami Arab social clubs. Such groups had been Zanzibar's main source of public entertainment until the advent of public taarab (Topp Fargion 2014, 46–47). During the 1920s and 1930s, the collective composed and rehearsed at Siti's home in Ng'ambo, in dialogue with area residents as well as Zanzibaris of higher social status. Siti famously hosted regular musical gatherings that gave guests opportunities to provide feedback, including specific ideas for songs (Fair 2001, 182–85; Mgana 1991, 40–41; Topp Fargion 2014, 52).

A COMEDY OF SOUND

To begin to understand how the working-class context of Ng'ambo shaped the stylistic approach of the binti Saad collective, let us return again to "Basahera." The second half of the performance (side two of the record) begins not with a *dūlāb* or improvisation, or even by launching into a new verse, but with talking—playacting, to be precise. Two male characters, one played by Mbaruk, engage in a brief argument that would seem almost Dadaist if it didn't relate directly to the *fumbo* (enigmatic metaphor) in the first line of the first stanza. Mbaruk's character begins by calling the other a liar and demanding to know, "When have you ever seen me trying to use a single stick to build a house?" (*Umepataje kuniona mimi nimechukua jiti moja kuja kujengea nyumba?*). The second character responds, "You always do it!" (*Daima unafanya hayo!*). The argument gets more heated from there, until it begins to get buried beneath the sounds of Mbaruk plucking at his *'ūd* strings. The skit eventually ends with the two characters gruffly parting ways as the musical performance starts up again.

This moment in "Basahera" reflects an essential aspect of the approach to taarab that the binti Saad collective developed in the decades leading up to their first recordings: an emphasis on the interplay of song and theatrical expression. Theatrical forms, including miming (*natiki*), dramatic plays (*michezo ya kuigiza*), and comedic skits (*vichekesho*), were central to the collective's live performances (Fair 2001, 224; Topp Fargion 2014, 53–54), and became an important part of their phonographic performances as well.[20] During their spate of recording sessions in 1930, the collective devoted at least one full 78-speed record (six minutes) to a theatrical performance that is billed as a "story" (*hadithi*) but might just as easily be called stand-up comedy. In it, Maalim Shaaban relates a humorous tale about a woman, her servant, and an annoying rooster, as another male member of the collective (likely Mbaruk) and Siti respond with questions and pointed jibes. All the while, a mixed-gender "audience" supplies peals of laughter (AUDIO EX. 2).[21] Along with this and any other similarly nonmusical sound performances the collective may have recorded in the interwar period, the binti Saad collective also incorporated playacting of various sorts into their *musical* recordings. Despite being compelled by the media technologies of the era to limit each recorded performance to three minutes (or six, with a break in the middle), many of their recorded musical performances include a brief comedic skit like the one in "Basahera." And of those that do not, a good portion feature other sorts of extramusical vocalizations—shouts, comments, laughs, etc.—that offer a taste of playacting. Sometimes these vocalizations are attempts by Siti to lend her imprimatur to the recordings of her colleagues, as when she "thanks" them for their performances with a dramatic "*Asante!*" followed by their name. Even in those cases, however, the effect is that of a live performance that is centered on music but not limited to musical utterances.

The binti Saad collective's emphasis on playacting and comedy had to do, in part, with the theatrical and comedic abilities of its members, especially Siti and Mbaruk. Siti developed considerable theatrical skills while hawking pottery on the streets of Zanzibar before taking up a career as a musician (Fair 2001, 179; Robert 1967, 5). Mbaruk, meanwhile, was by all accounts a born comedian (Jahadhmy, in Matola et al. 1966, 62; Suleiman 1969, 88).[22] By the time he joined the collective he was nearly as renowned for his comedy as for his musicianship. His lively performances for British and African troops in Mombasa during the latter half of World War I famously included humorous parodies of European folk songs and military marches (Jahadhmy, in ibid., 67; Ward 2011, 78). These earned him the affectionate nickname "Meja Mbaruk," which he proudly retained for the rest of his life. Mbaruk's mentors on Lamu likely encouraged and nurtured his theatrical abilities, as they had both been flamboyant performers in their younger days. Among other things, they had both been key figures in *beni ngoma*, a form of competitive group performance that drew from European military parades and featured music, movement, and costumes (Abou Egl 1983, 69–81; Ranger 1975, 18–25).[23]

But the fact that the members of the binti Saad collective happened to be skilled at playacting and comedy does not, in itself, explain why they incorporated these elements into their performances. For that, we need to think in terms of "orienting frameworks, interpretive procedures, and sets of expectations"—that is, of *genre* (Hanks 1987, 670). Toward that end, I suggest that it may be useful to consider the binti Saad collective as purveyors of *comedy*, by which I mean a mode of performance that generates a "self-reflexive theatricality" through a special emphasis on the mimetic process (Dolar 2017, 588). "Comedy," writes philosopher Mladen Dolar, "is mimesis in action." Rather than simply representing reality, it "redoubles its own presentation; it mimics itself; it creates its own mimesis, not simply the mimesis of preexisting models in reality" (ibid.). Comedy in this sense is not just about laughter—though laughter is essential. More fundamentally, it is about a particular orientation or attitude toward representation, one centered on the idea of generating copies *as copies*, copies that (in the manner of a citation) are "reflexive about that very fact" (Nakassis 2013, 57).

The appropriateness of the comedy label for the work of the binti Saad collective comes into sharp focus when we consider how and why the musicians inserted campy miming into a performance of "Kijiti," a chilling song that recounts the story of a murder and a miscarriage of justice. Laura Fair, who retrieved this memory from her Zanzibari interlocutors, is surely correct that the sight of the musicians mimicking "lawyers hoisting up their trousers around protruding bellies" would have functioned as a kind of comic relief, "[allowing] audience members to temporarily forget their cares and to rejuvenate the courage they needed to carry on" (Fair 2001, 224–25). But this explanation doesn't account for how such whimsy could have made artistic sense to the musicians and their audience in the performance of a song that "had the power to bring tears to people's eyes" (ibid.). Understanding the performance as a comedy, in which all representations, from the horrifying to the absurd, maintain a general "self-reflexive theatricality" helps make sense of this apparent incongruity.

Rather than a classificatory box, we can think of comedy as an interpretive frame, one that is similar to irony in its emphasis on the idea that "what is said is not what is meant" (Friedrich 1991, 31). Placing musical expression in such a frame provokes a particular mode of reception or species of "interpretive move" (Feld 1994b) oriented around the search for "what is meant." In other words, it inaugurates a way of approaching musical sound akin to how taarab listeners in the early twentieth century were expected to approach verbal texts. The *mafumbo* style of early twentieth-century taarab compelled listeners to search for meanings deep "inside" (*ndani*) of the words. While *mafumbo* is most often understood as a way of using language, one can think of it more broadly as a culturally specific way of exploiting the "power of ambiguity" to invite active interpretation (Vierke 2012). This expanded sense of the term suggests the possibility of a musical form of *mafumbo* that leverages the inherent ambiguity in any musical utterance to provoke a critical engagement.

A FEELING FOR THE BOUNDARIES

A comedic frame in musical expression impels a listener to hear mimetic appropriations of style as representations, *images*, even when they are realized as fully formed, authentic expressions of what has been appropriated. This is the essence of what Bakhtin terms "stylization." In his essay "Discourse in the Novel," Bakhtin defines stylization as a mimetic appropriation of stylistic elements oriented toward creating "an artistic representation of another's linguistic style, an artistic image of another's language" (ibid, 362).[24] By *language* here, as elsewhere in his writings, Bakhtin means a system of communication that is "stratified not only into dialects in the strict sense of the word . . . [but also] into languages that are socio-ideological: languages belonging to professions, to genres, languages peculiar to particular generations, etc." (ibid., 271–72). An "image of another's language," then, is an image of another's situation in, and situated perspective on, the social world. Stylization achieves this image by setting up a productive tension, a "dialogic contrast," between "two individualized linguistic consciousnesses" (ibid., 362–64). As such, it "delineates the boundaries of languages, creates a feeling for these boundaries, compels one to sense physically the plastic forms of different languages" (364).

Not every mimetic appropriation of an alien style constitutes *stylization*. One can simply *imitate* a style or, at another extreme, *caricature* it in a fashion that fails to "give it its due . . . as possessing its own internal logic" (ibid., 364).[25] Though they sit at opposite ends of a spectrum, imitation and caricature are similar in how they assume full control over the appropriated style. This is precisely what stylization does *not* do. Instead, stylization allows the appropriated style to "[reveal] its own world" (ibid.), thereby maintaining an "internal dialogism."

For the most part, the binti Saad collective's appropriations of foreign styles are too faithful to their sources to be heard as caricatures. On the other hand, some of their appropriations of foreign styles would certainly have been heard by listeners of the time as simple imitations. This is especially true of their Egyptian gestures—the use of an introductory *dūlāb*, for example—given the normative status of Egyptian style in Zanzibari taarab. But the presence of a comedic mood would have situated most of the binti Saad collective's appropriations of foreign styles within the realm of stylization for their listeners. A comedic mood lends a parodic element to appropriation, infusing what might otherwise be heard as a simple imitation with a "dialogic tension."

Thinking of the binti Saad collective's mimetic appropriations of style as acts of stylization opens up a perspective on how they resonated with the listening public of the Swahili coast during the interwar years, one that differs slightly from those offered by Laura Fair and Janet Topp Fargion. Based in part on Topp Fargion's work, Fair argues that the collective's hybridized soundworlds provided "a musical space that widened the boundaries of belonging" (Fair 2001, 174).[26] There is surely a large grain of truth in this, especially for the Zanzibari context. But when we approach these soundworlds as arenas of stylization, it becomes clear that they did more than simply *reflect* the diversity of the Swahili coast for listeners. They also *reflected on* it, exploring its dynamics, tensions, and contradictions. With this in mind, I suggest that for coastal Swahili audiences in the interwar period, these soundworlds ultimately did more to *objectify cultural boundaries* than to widen the boundaries of belonging. By *objectify* here I mean, specifically, *to make available for scrutiny by granting sensuous form and presence*. To borrow a turn of phrase from Bakhtin, what the binti Saad collective's hybridized soundworlds offered listeners was *a feeling for* the boundaries of culture, a kind of tactile awareness of them that enabled and encouraged reflection.

The mimetic appropriations that comprise the hybridized soundworlds of the binti Saad collective constitute a mode of musical stylization that enabled listeners on the Swahili coast in the interwar years to feel the boundaries of and between different music cultures of the Swahili coast, and thereby to consider questions of cultural identity. "Basahera," for example, would have offered listeners of the time a feeling for the boundaries of Swahili music culture within the broader context of commercially recorded musics in global circulation, and of coastal Kenyan music culture within the broader context of Swahili music culture. In other words, notions of Swahili cultural identity and coastal Kenyan cultural identity would have emerged for listeners in (or *as*) sensations of, feelings for, their boundaries. Admittedly the metaphor of *boundary* starts to reveal its limitations here, as it is only the boundaries of these identities that become sensible, not anything *within* them. But Bakhtin's notion of cultural boundary is precisely non-Euclidean in this way. He insists, "the realm of culture has no internal territory: it is entirely distributed along the boundaries, boundaries pass everywhere, through its every aspect" (quoted in Morson and Emerson 1990, 51).

"YA DANA DANA"

I want to bring this discussion back to the ground by considering another recorded performance by Mbaruk from the same Odeon sessions in Mombasa.

This one, titled "Ya Dana Dana," offers one of the most remarkable examples of musical stylization in the binti Saad *oeuvre*, because the performance is explicitly framed as a critical exploration of cultural boundaries.

Like "Basahera," "Ya Dana Dana" (AUDIO EX. 3) extends over two sides of a 78-speed record; however, I have only been able to locate a copy of the first side.[27] The performance opens with Mbaruk and Siti speaking over one another to announce the name of the record label. Siti seems to be having fun with the task. The mellifluous "*Sahani Odeoni*," Swahili for "Odeon record," rolls quickly off her tongue in a playful judder. Next, we hear Mbaruk and another man engaged in a brief conversation. Speaking in fast, slightly garbled Arabic, one of them calls to the other and coaxes him to "come see the *dāna dāna*!" All of this—the announcement of the record label and the introductory skit—lasts just eleven seconds.

The musical performance begins with a simple melody played on *'ūd*, violin (or possibly *kamanjā*, a traditional Arab fiddle), and *nāy* (end-blown reed flute), backed by a steady pulse played on the jingles of a *rīq*. The melodic instruments all play the same line together in a heterophonic texture, each presenting the melody in its own idiomatic fashion. But Mbaruk's *'ūd* is audibly in the lead role, supplying a quick upbeat before the other instruments join in and pushing the pulse forward with forceful articulations. The melody employs only a few pitches, rhythmically patterned in a danceable triple meter. It is set in *Maqām 'Irāq*, and emphasizes the mode's distinctive "half-flat" tonic.

After the initial instrumental exposition, the melody repeats, this time with voices taking the lead and the instruments lightly doubling the melody while interjecting short connecting phrases. The melody is now revealed in full, with the addition of a slightly varied consequent phrase. The first vocalist we hear is Mbaruk, who performs the antecedent phrase alone. Two or three vocalists then follow with the consequent phrase. They sound distant, but Siti's clarion voice is clearly audible among them. The words they sing are not words at all, but various combinations of three vocables: "*yā*," "*dān*," and "*dāna*."

The meaning of "come see the *dāna dāna*" now becomes clear with the introduction of the vocables. This "*dān*" singing, which is found in genres of music and sung poetry throughout the Arabian Peninsula, is perhaps most strongly associated with the music culture of Hadrami Arabs, an ethnic community from the Hadramawt region of southern Yemen that has spread throughout the Gulf and western Indian Ocean regions, including the Swahili coast (Braune 1997, 192–94; Urkevich 2014, 270–71; Hassan 1998). Beginning in the late nineteenth century, the Swahili coast has been home to a thriving Hadrami diasporic community, established and sustained by immigrant men (and some women) who traveled to East Africa in search of economic opportunities (see chapter 4).

The *dān* vocables in "Ya Dana Dana" are not an isolated reference to Hadrami culture. Rather, the performance as a whole is generically Hadrami. In form and execution, it fits the mold of *dān ṭarab*, a Hadrami genre of accompanied popular song. Unlike other forms of Hadrami sung poetry that incorporate *dān* singing, *dān ṭarab* is entertainment music "sung for the pure enjoyment of poetry and song" (Hassan 1998, 4). Toward the end of the performance, Siti adds jubilant shouts to give a sense of the festive atmosphere of an authentic *dān ṭarab* event.

Around forty seconds into the performance, Mbaruk introduces the song's refrain—two lines of Swahili poetry, set in a typical taarab meter, with the first repeated to fit the form of the melody:

> *Kanga mbili za mkasi, zimenikata maini* (Those *kanga*s with scissors on them have cut me deeply)
> *Kanga mbili za mkasi, zimenikata maini* (Those *kanga*s with scissors on them have cut me deeply)
> *Mwambie bwana afunge mlango, leo asitokaini* (Tell him to close the door, he should not go out today)

As with many taarab refrains, this one includes esoteric references and possibly borrowed material. I am not fully confident in my translation of the first line. A *kanga* is a colorful printed cloth that typically includes a short poetic saying or message on it. Since the early twentieth century, women on the Swahili coast have commonly used *kanga*s to send veiled insults and challenges to rivals. The line "*kanga mbili za mkasi*," which literally translates as "the two *kanga*s of scissors," is ambiguous. For this translation, I have taken my cue from Abdilatif Abdalla, who believes the scissors may refer to a specific, notoriously insulting line of *kanga*s that bore the image of scissors.[28] But it is also possible to understand the line as referencing the fact that kangas are usually sold as a single piece of cloth containing a matching pair that must be separated by the consumer (with scissors). This is how one younger Zanzibari taarab musician who performs the song explained the line to me. In either case, Mbaruk seems to be playing with the vivid imagery in the common Swahili idiom "*kukata maini*," which is a way of saying "to hurt (someone's) feelings" but literally means "to cut the liver."

The introduction of Swahili taarab poetry, redolent with *mafumbo*, transforms the performance into a cultural hybrid, a combination of Hadrami *dān ṭarab* and Swahili taarab (a kind of *dān* taarab). This hybrid is fleshed out even further as the performance continues. After the Swahili refrain there is another *dān* refrain, and then an instrumental refrain punctuated by Siti's exhortations (in Swahili). The Swahili refrain then returns again, followed again by another *dān* refrain. After a minute and a half of this vacillation, Mbaruk sings the only full stanza of Swahili poetry in the three-minute side. As he does, Siti and a male backing musician echo key phrases in heightened speaking voices, mimicking the sort of "ecstatic feedback" that one finds in traditional settings of Arab music performance (Racy 1991; Shannon 2003, 75). The lines he sings are as follows:

> *Pesa zangu mbili, hanunue kibiriti* (Two months' salary doesn't even buy matchsticks)
> *Ni vinani tu makanda, tenda chukua kaniki* (It's just empty grain sacks, go grab a laborer's shirt)
> *Usiku kucha silali asili, kwa kuhesabu boriti* (I don't sleep at night, just count the ceiling beams)

Unlike the refrain, the stanza connects thematically to the style of the performance, albeit obliquely, by expressing the point of view of a manual laborer, a common profession for Hadrami men in East Africa during the interwar years.[29] While grounded in reality, the conceptual linkage that is achieved at this point in the performance between the (musical) image of Hadrami culture and the (poetic) image of struggling laborer was to some extent politically charged. The fact that most Hadramis who arrived in East Africa in the late nineteenth and early twentieth centuries were mostly peasants who had come to escape abject poverty back home positioned them as a kind of untouchable class in the highly stratified coastal Swahili society. Tellingly, Hadramis on the Swahili coast have never been referred to as "Arabs," a distinction traditionally reserved for communities of higher social status. During the interwar years, they were typically referred to as "*Shihiri*," a reference to Al-Shihr, the Arabian port from which the new arrivals among them had started their journey to East Africa (Le Guennec-Coppens 1989, 186; Salim 1976, 78). While this label has fallen out of use today, it remains uncommon to hear a Hadrami described as "Arab" on the Swahili coast, even as many of them have achieved success as entrepreneurs and business owners (chapter 4).

While we cannot know exactly how audiences on the Swahili coast in 1930s received Mbaruk's Hadrami-Swahili musical hybrid, it seems clear that it would *not* have been heard as a simple mockery (or *rhetorical parody*, in Bakhtin's terms). The Hadrami style is performed too beautifully for that. Upon hearing the recording for the first time, Yemeni musician and music researcher Nizar Ghanem opined that the performance bears a distinct "Hadrami taste."[30] It did not sound to him like an inauthentic imitation, much less a "gross and superficial destruction" (Bakhtin 1981, 364); it simply sounded "Hadrami." Nevertheless, the performance would certainly have been heard as *parodic*. The introductory skit establishes a playfulness and general sense of irony, which is then amplified by the introduction of Swahili poetry. Given that Hadramis on the Swahili coast, as elsewhere in the Indian Ocean world, have historically "dropped their own language for the local one" within a generation (Le Guennec-Coppens 1989, 190), the idea of Hadrami music sung in Swahili is not all that strange. But Mbaruk's highly sophisticated Swahili poetry, with its complex *mafumbo*, is a strange fit with a performance that so vividly reflects the culture of recent Hadrami immigrants.

The ironized hybridization of Hadraminess and Swahiliness in "Ya Dana Dana" does not offer a direct statement or commentary. What it offers, rather, is *a feeling for the boundaries* of Hadrami culture in coastal Swahili society. This would have been compelling for audiences of the time on the Swahili coast, I suggest, because it would have enabled them to reflect upon one of the more paradoxical facets of social belonging in this society: the status of Hadramis as both insiders and outsiders. While Hadramis spoke Swahili and participated in the same religious and cultural practices as most other Swahili-speaking Muslims, their subaltern status kept them apart from other Swahili-speaking Muslims, encouraging a degree of insularity (see chapter 4). Their residence patterns reflected this situation quite vividly: in Mbaruk's home town of Mombasa, for example, Hadramis who were fortunate enough to live outside of the migrant laborer housing settled in Bondeni, right on the edge of the Old Town, the traditional neighborhood of elite Arabs and Swahili patricians (Le Guennec-Coppens 1997, 168n41).

Another paradoxical aspect of the Hadrami position in Swahili society is that there often is no boundary between Swahili and Hadrami *cultures*, since many "Swahili" religious and cultural practices actually have Hadrami origins (Pouwels 1987, 32–54). Intentionally or not, Mbaruk subtly references this situation in the structure of his melody, which is built on the same relatively rare melodic mode (*Maqām ʿIrāq*) that he also uses in "Basahera" to capture the sound of the northern Kenyan coast. This is a rather subtle reference, to be sure, but it seems likely that Mbaruk and his listeners would have sensed it at some level, if only as an added bit of tension in the "dialogic contrast" of the Hadrami-Swahili soundworld.

MOMBASAN RESONANCES

I have offered an account of how the sounds of the early recorded works of the binti Saad collective resonated on the Swahili coast during the interwar years. These sounds are often cast as "Zanzibari" today, as Siti binti Saad has become something of a national icon for the semiautonomous Republic of Zanzibar.[31] The overriding focus on the context of Zanzibar in scholarly accounts of the collective has amplified this particular hearing. But these sounds circulated well beyond Zanzibar, making their ways into public and private spaces, and the minds and bodies of the people who inhabited them, in towns and cities along the entire Swahili coast. This was particularly true of Mombasa, which was not only on its way to becoming the largest port city on the Kenyan coast, but also happened to be home to one of the binti Saad collective's key members.

FIGURE 1.2 Mbaruk Talsam in his later years. Werner Graebner collection, used with permission.

Early Recorded Taarab **45**

Mbaruk was not simply Mombasa-born. He was a true *Mvita* (Mombasan). Mombasa was where he was raised, where he learned to make his way in the world (first as a sighted boy, then as a blind man), where he found his initial fame, and where he spent his final years. And Mombasans—especially Mombasan *musicians*—revered him. The first time Zein l'Abdin mentioned Mbaruk to me in conversation, he added pointedly, "he was Basheikh," and jutted his chin in the direction of the nearby Basheikh Mosque, where Mbaruk was laid to rest in 1959.[32] This was a specific way of paying homage to Mbaruk, which emphasized his respectability. Though Mbaruk was raised as a member of the wealthy Talsam family of Basheikh Arabs, his legitimacy as a Basheikh was open to question because he had been born to one of his father's enslaved concubines (Jahadhmy, in Matola et al. 1966, 61). Mbaruk ultimately earned the respect and admiration of the Basheikh and the rest of Mombasa's Swahili-speaking Muslim elites through his achievements as a poet and musician. Some well-heeled members of the Basheikh clan demonstrated this respect by supporting him in retirement, enabling him to spend is final years playing his ʿūd on the veranda of a comfortable home in Mombasa Old Town (Jahadhmy, in ibid., 69–70).[33]

By maintaining a focus on songs recorded by Mbaruk in his home town of Mombasa in this chapter, I have sought to keep in view the fact that the story of the binti Saad collective is not simply a Zanzibari one. This is because, against the prevailing winds of scholarly and popular opinion, I want to suggest that the aesthetic approach of the collective's early recorded was carried forward most powerfully in the taarab of *Mombasa*.

TWO

The Lullaby of Taarab

Radio and Reflexivity in the 1950s

THE SEA OF MOMBASAN TAARAB

Mbaruk Talsam lived long enough to witness his home town become the site of a dynamic sea of taarab (to use a common Swahili metaphor) with multiple aesthetic currents. The decade leading up to his death in 1959 was an important one for the formation of this sea. Mombasa during the 1950s provided an almost ideal environment for taarab to flourish. Largely untouched by the Mau Mau uprising that convulsed the Kenya Colony, the city enjoyed a stability and prosperity that allowed large celebrations for weddings and other occasions to become commonplace. Such events provided constant work for taarab ensembles large and small. At the same time, the sounds of taarab reverberated daily in private homes and public squares in Mombasa, thanks to the simultaneous emergence of a regional recording industry and local radio broadcasting.

East Africa's first independent record company, East African Sound Studios, Ltd. (later renamed East African Records, Ltd.), began releasing music on its Jambo label in 1948 (see Harrev 1989). Though based in Nairobi, much of their output was taarab from Mombasa. Meanwhile, multinationals operating under the umbrella of EMI began marketing Swahili taarab again in East Africa, pressing rereleases and previously unreleased materials, along with new recordings. Many of the new releases were recorded locally in Mombasa, by Indian-owned shops that were also the main distributors of records in the region (Graebner 2004b, 12). One of these shops, Assanand & Sons, Ltd., established the Mzuri label, which served as an essential vehicle for Mombasan taarab from the mid-1950s to the mid-1970s (ibid., 14–17). Throughout the 1950s, taarab recordings were amplified, literally and figuratively, by the Mombasa-based radio station Sauti ya Mvita (Voice of Mombasa), which situated them (along with their own recordings and live broadcasts of the music) within a sonic mediascape oriented toward coastal Muslims.

My interlocutors in Mombasa who were old enough the recall the 1950s remembered it as an era of large taarab orchestras. This trend, which also extended to other urban centers of the Swahili coast (ibid., 12), was part of a broader, regional trend toward large dance bands featuring Western brass and woodwind instruments introduced to the region through the conduits of colonial government and military bands. Taarab orchestras differed from "colonial dance bands," however, by virtue of incorporating instruments and influences from mid-century Egyptian popular song and Hindi film music in addition to jazz and Latin American popular musics (Tracey 2006).

Small taarab ensembles in Mombasa also took on new configurations during the 1950s. While some remained centered on traditional Arab instruments, others adopted Indian instruments, including the hand-pumped harmonium and tabla drums. Many also incorporated the *tashkota* (or *tuntunia*), a two-stringed keyed zither of Japanese origin (see examples in chapter 5, Figure 5.2 and chapter 6, Figure 6.1).[1] First imported by Indian traders as a novelty item, the *tashkota* became a professional instrument in Mombasa during the 1950s thanks to singer and multi-instrumentalist Yaseen Mohamed Tofeli (1922–1985), who worked as a talent scout, producer, and studio musician for Assanand & Sons. Yaseen achieved a remarkable virtuosity on the instrument and modified it to add electrical amplification (Gesthuizen 2019).

THE CROSSCURRENT OF REFLEXIVITY

Along with developing a new timbral diversity, Mombasan taarab in the 1950s also branched out in different stylistic directions. The decade saw the advent of what Ali A. Mazrui, a resident of Mombasa at the time, later described as the two-fold "'Orientalization' of Mombasa music" (1996, 160). At the same time, it saw various efforts at creating a "Swahili" style of taarab in relation to the "Orientalized" ones. All these currents gained strength in succeeding decades, leading to the emergence of subgenres of "Indian taarab" (chapter 3) and "Arab taarab" (chapter 5) as well as a popular "Swahili" style of taarab grounded in women's *ngoma* rhythms (Graebner 2004c, 2020).

The new stylistic currents of Mombasan taarab developed in tandem with what I will call a *crosscurrent of reflexivity*, meaning an audible emphasis on style as a space of (re)presenting and mediating cultural identity. This crosscurrent first took shape during the interwar years, in the work of the binti Saad collective, and then flowed into Mombasan taarab during the 1950s. My aim in this chapter is to outline the historical conditions that enabled the latter influx, focusing on the role of Sauti ya Mvita. Throughout the 1950s, Sauti ya Mvita threaded Mombasan taarab and Arab popular music recorded in Cairo (and to a lesser extent, Aden) into a sonic mediascape also consisting of Islamic recitations and sermons, news, topical discussions, recited poetry, and traditional songs in Arabic and Kimvita (Mombasan Swahili). This mediascape reached listeners along the entire coast, and even as far afield as southern Arabia. But it was created by and for Arabs and Swahili patricians of Mombasa, for whom it represented "the fount and focus of a coastal Muslim cultural revival" (Salim 1970, 216). Examining the content of Sauti ya Mvita's broadcasts in the context of the era, I argue that the station enhanced the crosscurrent of reflexivity in Mombasan taarab by putting into circulation a particular portrait of Swahili cultural identity to which local taarab musicians were, in a sense, compelled to respond.

BROADCASTING TERRITORIALITY[2]

Technically, Sauti ya Mvita was a propaganda outlet of the British colonial administration. Established in the wake of a dockworkers' strike in 1947, it was shored up in the mid-1950s to counter anticolonial Arabic and Swahili broadcasts from Cairo. But the station operated largely under local community control until 1959, at which point directorship was transferred to Nairobi. During its era of local control, Sauti ya Mvita was effectively a project of and for elite Arabs and Swahili patricians of Mombasa. The station's advisory council was mostly comprised of elite Arab men, who had stepped in to support the station early on when it was underresourced (Brennan 2015, 21–22); and prominent Swahili patrician Hyder Kindy played an important role in content development as the assistant provincial information officer for the Coast (Kindy 1972, 163–75). The largely volunteer production staff and on-air talent were mostly Arabs and Swahili patricians, as well.

Sauti ya Mvita's content catered almost exclusively to Arab and Swahili patrician listeners. According to the colonial Legislative Council documents, "During 1957, the population nominally served by Sauti ya Mvita included 21,000 Arabs, 13,000 Swahili, 390,000 Coastal Africans, and some 45,000 'up-country' Africans; yet Ki-Mvita took up 24.5 hours per week, Arabic took up 12.5 hours per week, and 'up-country Swahili' took only 7 hours per week" (Brennan 2015, 28). Unsurprisingly, non-Muslim coastal residents voiced displeasure at this situation. Letters of complaint appeared in the *Mombasa Times* newspaper. One writer went as far as to decry the Arabic and Islamic programming as failing to cater to "the real Coast people," by which she or he meant the Mijikenda and other coastal African "tribes."[3]

It is difficult to overstate the resonance of Sauti ya Mvita among Arabs and Swahili patricians in Mombasa during the 1950s. A 1954 survey found that more than half of "Arab-Swahili" households in Mombasa owned a radio receiver—"nearly twice as many as the next-largest 'tribe' (Kikuyu/Embu/Meru) in town and three times that of 'Coastal' Africans [i.e., Mijikenda]" (ibid., 25; cf. Wilson 1958). Given that radio listening also took place at formal and informal listening stations in public spaces, it is reasonable to assume that a sizable majority of Swahili-speaking Muslims in Mombasa were listening to radio on a regular basis by the mid-1950s. Sauti ya Mvita was by far the most popular station for this community—its only real competition being Radio Cairo, whose anticolonial broadcasts were a major reason for the British colonial administration's support for Sauti ya Mvita (Brennan 2015, 22).

During the interwar years, it would have been difficult to imagine Arabs and Swahili patricians in Mombasa successfully sharing control of a media outlet. The colonial administration's efforts to limit the number of coastal Muslims who could claim "non-native" status had pitted the communities against each other.[4] But the advent of Sauti ya Mvita coincided with the rise of a new ethnic sensibility centered on the idea of an "Arab-Swahili" community. In part, this new sensibility was a result of Swahili patricians having finally attained something of a *de facto* "nonnative" status, gaining "privileges once limited to Arabs, such as the right to enroll in Arab schools and vote for Arab Legco [Legislative Council] seats" (Prestholdt 2014, 256). But an even more important uniting factor for Arabs and Swahili patricians in the 1950s was the specter of decolonization. Trepidation about a future in which traditional elites of the coast might be at the mercy of upcountry Africans served to align the communities against an Other defined along religious and racial lines: Christian "Africans" (with "African" understood as a racial category to which neither Arabs nor Swahili patricians belonged). This alignment remained fundamentally intact even as rising anti-Arab rhetoric among African nationalists in the mid-1950s prompted a renewed "closing of ranks" (Salim 1970, 218) among the Swahili-speaking Muslim communities, with Swahili and Bajuni communities reactivating old ethnic organizations and "some Swahili political thinkers . . . [deciding to emphasize] their distinction from Arabs" (Prestholdt 2014, 256n26).

The understanding of "Arab-Swahili" identity that prevailed in 1950s Mombasa was grounded in the traditional regime of Swahili ethnicity that I outlined in the introduction. But its more immediate source was the politics of "ethnic territoriality" (Lynch 2011) that was then taking hold across the entire region as colonial subjects worked within the confines of local, ethnically defined organizations to imagine, agitate for, and negotiate the terms of a postcolonial future (Prestholdt 2014, 259; Ogot 1995). The most overt expression of Arab-Swahili ethnic territoriality was the *Mwambao* ("coastline") movement for coastal autonomy, which lasted from around 1953 until the Kenyan coast was formally joined to mainland Kenya on the eve of independence in 1963 (Brennan 2008). Though supported by various communities at various moments, *Mwambao* was spearheaded by Arabs and Swahili patricians in Mombasa, who crafted a narrative of coastal sovereignty based on the legal fiction of the Sultan of Zanzibar's ownership of the Kenyan coast (Salim 1970; Brennan 2008).

Sauti ya Mvita was more than just an expression of Arab-Swahili ethnic territoriality. It was also an engine of it. The station directly promoted an image of the Kenyan coast as part of the Sultanate of Zanzibar, bookending daily broadcasts with its national anthem and occasionally airing speeches by the sultan (Brennan 2008, 843–44). More significantly, it instantiated ethnic territoriality as a *felt understanding*, by engendering what historian James R. Brennan (2015), borrowing a concept from Birgit Meyer (2009), describes as an "aesthetic formation" that made Arab-Swahili identity sensible.

Brennan stresses the roles of language and religion in Sauti ya Mvita's aesthetic formation. He notes that the directors of the Sauti ya Mvita rejected the use of Standard Swahili and embraced, instead, the Kimvita dialect of Mombasa's native Swahili speakers (Brennan 2015, 29); and, in dialogue with my work on the Islamic soundscape in contemporary Mombasa (Eisenberg 2013), he describes how "Sauti ya Mvita . . . amplified the particular rhythms of Mombasa's pious soundscape," thereby "[sharpening] listeners' mental geographies of a Muslim coast standing athwart a vast non-Muslim interior where political power lay" (2015, 25).

An aspect of Sauti ya Mvita's aesthetic formation that receives somewhat less attention in Brennan's analysis, but which is essential for my argument here, is what Kenyan Swahili historian Ahmed Idha Salim describes as the station's efforts to "revive, in sound . . . the Arab-Swahili culture of the whole coast" (Salim 1973, 217). Sauti ya Mvita undertook this project of cultural "revival" by curating and presenting traditions of orally performed verbal art associated with the urban elite of the Swahili coast.

SOUNDING CULTURE

The traditions of urban Swahili oral performance promulgated by Sauti ya Mvita included poetry recitation, storytelling, and patrician *ngoma* songs. One might say it included taarab, as well. But I will argue below that taarab had a special place in Sauti ya Mvita's broadcasts, which situated it both within and outside of the domain of urban Swahili oral performance.

Poetry recitation, an art form that has always enjoyed broad popularity among Swahili-speaking coastal Muslims (see Kresse 2011; Raia 2020), lay at the heart of Sauti ya Mvita's soundscape of urban Swahili oral performance. The station frequently aired recitations of poems by renowned local poets, performed by professional reciters who set each poem "to a pattern of melody based on one of the Arabian modal scales and characterized by stereotyped turns of mood and pitch" (Harries 1966, xiii). Notably, the revered poet Ahmad Nassir Juma Bhalo, discussed further in chapter 3, "came to regional prominence through Sauti ya Mvita broadcasts, while in Mombasa the broadcast of his poetry became an integral part of local Ramadan observance" (Brennan 2015, 28). As Lyndon Harries notes, "many of the poems" in Ahmad Nassir's internationally published translated collection *Poems from Kenya* "were written especially for performance at the Mombasa radio station and so reached a much wider audience than the traditional poet ever thought possible" (Harries 1966, xiii).

Storytelling was a rare addition to Sauti ya Mvita's broadcasts, unless one includes the storytelling that was interwoven into discussion programs. In that case, it was anything but rare. Popular presenter Maalim Said frequently interpolated storytelling into the religious and moral advice that was the main theme of his program. He was known for presenting "enticing pictures of the paradise awaiting his listeners after their life on earth, with rich references to *miraaj*, the Prophet Muhammad's Night Journey," all delivered in what his fellow broad-

FIGURE 2.1 A group of Swahili men dressed in finery perform the traditional men's *ngoma* called *chama* at the Swahili Culture Festival in Mombasa in October 2004: a scene that recalls the *diriji* and *twari la ndia* performances of decades before. Photo by author.

caster Faraj Dumila would later describe as a "beautiful voice, a natural voice" (Brennan 2015, 27).

Ngoma performances were the least common form of urban Swahili oral performance presented on Sauti ya Mvita, but in some ways the most important. When *ngoma*s were aired by the station, the project of cultural revival was out front. The only surviving recordings of Sauti ya Mvita broadcasts that I know of are a small collection of programs from the early 1950s in which Hyder Kindy presents performances of *diriji* by the Afro-Asian Social Club.[5] *Diriji* was one of two men's *ngoma*s that served during the early twentieth century as a form of competition between the two "confederations" of the Twelve Tribes (the other being *twari la ndia*, which I will consider in chapter 5). According to Marc Swartz (1996), these were "highly formal and prestigious men's dance performances requiring long hours of rehearsal, meticulously disciplined movement, and the careful maintenance of the highest-quality clothing" (242). Both involved sung poetry, often religious in nature, which was set to accompaniment of slow and deliberate rhythms provided by an ensemble of frame drums (*matwari*). By the time of Kindy's broadcasts, *diriji* and *twari la ndia* were already on the wane in Mombasa. Kindy therefore frames the performances as an effort to "remember" (*kumbuka*) and "value" (*thamini*) a disappearing tradition. He closes one of the broadcasts by saying that the aim of airing such materials is to "remind ourselves of our grandeur" (*tujikumbushe fahari zetu*).

Sauti ya Mvita's soundscape of urban Swahili oral performance profoundly influenced intellectuals and artists on the Kenyan coast, including those who would go on to shape postcolonial discourses of Swahili identity. A notable example is Mombasan writer and educator Shihabuddin Chiraghdin (1934–1976), who became a prominent voice in the postcolonial, "nationalist phase" of Swahili studies, articulating "one of the most compelling and ardent propositions for the existence of the Swahili" as a distinctive ethnic group (Waliaula 2013, 13).[6] Chiraghdin had a close relationship with Sauti ya Mvita, which began with him helping to organize the *diriji* performances presented on air by Hyder Kindy in the early 1950s. He was a young man at the time of these broadcasts, just heading off to (or perhaps on a visit back from) university. Between 1952 and 1955, he studied at Makerere University in Uganda, then "the intellectual capital of East and Central Africa" (Ngũgĩ 1993, 182), but regularly traveled home to Mombasa to visit family and teach at local schools. During his visits home, he interviewed family members and collected literary materials for essays and articles about Swahili language and culture, some of which he published in the student-run journal that he edited (L. Chiraghdin 2018, 48–50). The broadcasts of Sauti ya Mvita, including those of his mentor Hyder Kindy, were surely a constant companion for him as he carried out this research. After completing his degree at Makerere, Chiraghdin returned home and rekindled his efforts to revive Swahili traditions in partnership with Sauti ya Mvita (ibid., 81).

During my fieldwork, taarab musician Zein l'Abdin and the men he hosted most evenings in his sitting room (see chapter 5) often reflected nostalgically on the impact of Sauti ya Mvita's soundscape of urban Swahili oral performance. This discourse became especially animated at the end of 2004, in the wake of the inaugural broadcasts of Radio Rahma, the first radio station oriented toward Kenya's coastal Muslims to emerge since the demise of Sauti ya Mvita.[7] Radio Rahma's programming in the early days was an eclectic mix of call-in shows on topics ranging from issues of morality to how to go about getting a visa to enter Yemen, along with recordings of Qur'anic recitation from the Arab world, Islamic devotional music from Indonesia, and Swahili- and English-language sermons from local and foreign sources. Zein and his circle were quick to express disappointment with this content, which they felt paled in comparison to what Sauti ya Mvita had provided. Specifically, they lamented Radio Rahma's lack of attention to the sounds of Swahili expressive culture.[8] The broadcasts served for them as a painful reminder of what they had lost.

"If you want to know why things have deteriorated here," Zein l'Abdin's nephew Jamal Hafidh told me, "you can start with the demise of Sauti ya Mvita." Sometime later, I heard this same sentiment from former Sauti ya Mvita presenter, translator, and presenter Abdalla Mbwana, who worked at the station from 1958 until it was phased out.[9] "The death of Sauti ya Mvita contributed greatly to the stagnation of culture," he opined, calling Mombasa "a case study in the rise and fall of a culture." The bitterness in these statements comes not only from a sense of loss, but also from a righteous indignation about the active role of the Kenyan government in facilitating this loss. Sauti ya Mvita did not simply fade away for lack of an engaged audience. It was consciously phased out as part of a broader strategy of "Africanizing" the Kenyan media (Brennan 2015, 31). Compounding both the injury and the insult of this policy decision, the station's tapes were transported to Nairobi when the station was closed, where they were then either discarded or (according to rumor) squirreled away in private collections.

AN ACOUSTEMOLOGY OF URBANITY

Sauti ya Mvita's soundscape of urban Swahili oral performance provided a relatively narrow portrait of Swahili expressive culture, centered on the voices of elite men in an elite Swahili town (Mombasa). For a brief time in 1957, this portrait broadened to include a greater diversity of locales and voices. As part of an effort by the Department of Information to expand the reach of Sauti ya Mvita beyond Mombasa, Hyder Kindy traveled to northern coastal towns to engage with the local communities as well as "to record local musicians, poets, and other artists." In Malindi, Mambrui, Kipini, and Lamu he "recorded individuals, bands, reciters of poetry, orchestras, witchcraft dancers and even witchcraft love-cure dancing" (Kindy 1972, 173). Using these materials, he launched a special program aimed at introducing "coast folklore and music [with] the appropriate cultural and historical background" (174). According to Kindy, the program was well liked, especially outside of Mombasa. However, it was cancelled abruptly after about a year. Kindy describes this cancellation merely as an unfortunate "administrative decision" (173). But one can infer from his account that the men who had the greatest say in the direction of Sauti ya

Mvita were uninterested in, if not opposed to, changing the station's approach to urban Swahili oral performance.

The narrowness of Sauti ya Mvita's soundscape of urban Swahili oral performance would not have sounded random to the station's primary audience. While it may not have reflected the breadth of Swahili expressive culture, it reflected very well the dominant understanding of "vocalic space" (space as produced by the soundings of socially situated voices [Connor 2000]) in the Swahili town, where it is the "pronouncing" men who are meant to be audible in public (Hirsch 1998). As such, it amplified a particular acoustemology of Swahili cultural identity—a way of knowing, in and through sound, what it meant to be culturally "Swahili"—that was bound up with traditional Swahili concept of "urbanity" (*utamaduni*).

In contemporary Standard Swahili, the word *utamaduni* is generally taken to mean "culture" in the anthropological sense. On the Swahili coast, however, it has historically meant something closer to its Arabic etymon, *tamaddun*, which comes from the same root as *madīna*, meaning "town" or "city." It connotes a "refinement" and "purity" traditionally associated with the patrician "owners" (*wenyeji*) of the town (Horton and Middleton 2000, 115). Sauti ya Mvita's soundscape of urban Swahili oral performance rearticulated the traditional values of *utamaduni* within a modern project of cultural revival. This move bore a profound emotional resonance for members of the Arab-Swahili community living an era of ethnic territoriality, such that some would come to experience the loss of the soundscape as nothing less than the "fall of a culture."

THE RESPONSIBILITY OF TAARAB

What did Sauti ya Mvita's promotion of an acoustemology of *utamaduni* as part of a project of cultural revival mean for Mombasan taarab? I argue that the impact was indirect yet profound. While, as sung poetry, taarab can be understood as a form of urban Swahili oral performance, as a cosmopolitan popular music that often featured women's voices it resonated at a slightly different frequency (metaphorically speaking) than Sauti ya Mvita's soundscape of urban Swahili oral performance. There was thus a subtle tension between the sounds of taarab on Sauti ya Mvita's airwaves and the project of cultural revival that listeners understood (and *felt*) to be the station's core mission. Taarab musicians in Mombasa necessarily incorporated this tension into their "responsive understanding" (Bakhtin 1981, 280–81), their active sensitivity to the potential impacts of and responses to their creative work, and in this way nurtured the crosscurrent of reflexivity. This phenomenon is most obvious in the ways in which Mombasan taarab musicians during the 1950s experimented with ways of sounding "Swahili."

ORCHESTRATING SWAHILINESS

The orchestral taarab of the 1950s was self-consciously cosmopolitan in style. In most cases, orchestras adopted a style that "owed much to the influences of Egyptian film orchestras in the *firqah* style" (Graebner 2004b, 12). Such was the case with Jauharah Orchestra Musical Club. But the leaders of this group nonetheless incorporated into their work an abiding concern with the idea of sounding "Swahili."

Like many of the large taarab orchestras on the Swahili coast during the 1950s, Jauharah was organized as a men's social club.[10] The members first came together as a soccer team, playing under the name Chelsea. But they soon discovered music to be an even greater shared interest among them. Hugh Tracey, who recorded Jauharah for the Trek and Gallotone labels in 1952, described the group in his fieldnotes as "an enthusiastic amateur band of Swahili young men on the East Coast of Africa [whose members] reflect that class of the community which has adhered to the largely Arab culture from the Persian Gulf" (Tracey 2006). They held their first public performance on a Saturday night in April 1951, at Tononoka Social Hall, north of the Old Town, for a large audience that included VIPs like Sheikh-Sir Mbarak al-Hinawy, who had just retired from his post as the liwali (governor) of the Coast.[11] The group must have been a sight to behold—thirty-six musicians playing a wide range of Arab and Western instruments (*'ūd*, violin, accordion, mandolin, saxophone, guitar, clarinet, and more), and dressed in fine evening jackets and fez hats. They modelled their look as well as their music on archetypes from Hollywood jazz films and Egyptian films (Daniels 1996, 422). Their sound, immortalized in the recordings they made with Tracey, was rough around the edges, albeit lively and compelling. Zein l'Abdin, who performed with the group when he was starting out in the mid-to-late 1950s, recalled that few of Jauharah's members had had much training or experience in music. With the exception of a couple of older men in the violin section, Zein was the only skilled instrumentalist.[12] Nevertheless, the orchestra had a reputation for professionalism, which they earned by taking themselves seriously and rehearsing for long hours.

Jauharah's commitment to an Egyptian style was strong in the early years,

FIGURE 2.2 Members of Jauharah Orchestra pose outside their clubhouse during a recording session with Hugh Tracey in 1952. Photo by Hugh Tracey or assistant. Copyright the International Library of African Music. Used with permission.

such that many of their songs used popular Egyptian melodies. But Zein l'Abdin and other taarab musicians and aficionados I spoke with in Mombasa described their most famous song of the 1950s, "Kasha Langu" (My Strongbox), as an iconic example of a "Swahili" composition. "Kasha Langu" first became widely known thanks to continuous airplay on Sauti ya Mvita, presumably the station's own recording of a performance by Jauharah (Shariff 1988, 81). It remained popular on the Swahili coast for decades, and then received even wider recognition in the late 1980s and 1990s, after Kenyan Afropop band Mombasa Roots recorded a cover version and made it a staple of their performances. It has been performed by many different taarab singers and groups in Mombasa over the years, but is most strongly associated with Jauharah singer Athman Abdalla Kajungu, known as "Athmani Kasha," who first popularized it in the 1950s and recorded multiple versions over the years (AUDIO EX. 4) is a version from the 1970s).[13]

The popularity of "Kasha Langu" has much to do with its highly allegorical verbal text, composed by Hadrami-Swahili poet and musician Abdel-Rahim

Said Mohammed Basalim (1920–1978)—a beautifully constructed variation on a traditional Swahili theme of a man's despair over his betrothed's lost virginity (Shariff 1983, 17). But as P. J. L. Frankl and Yahya Ali Omar note, audiences have always been strongly drawn to the song's melody, as well. This melody, Frankl and Omar write, is "neither Arabic nor Indian but Swahili—a truly local product" (Frankl et al. 1998, 18). In the same article, Janet Topp Fargion suggests that the Swahiliness of the "Kasha Langu" melody has to do with its compound meter. She mentions "the use of a 6/8 triplet lilt" (24). This is an apposite description, though 12/8 may be the more suitable time signature. In fact, the melody of "Kasha Langu" lines up almost perfectly with a common variant of the 12-beat "standard timeline pattern" that links the rhythms of traditional Swahili *ngoma* to those of other African and African-diasporic musical traditions (see chapter 5; Eisenberg In prep.).

It may seem fair to characterize "Kasha Langu" as an exception to the rule of Jauharah's stylistic Arabness during the 1950s. But founding Jauharah member Mbarak Rashid insisted to me in 2005 that the group's stylistic approach had always been "Swahili," particularly with respect to melody (*lahani*).[14] In providing examples of Jauharah's "Swahili" approach to melody, he did not mention "Kasha Langu," but rather three of the songs that the group recorded with Hugh Tracey in 1952: "Mimi" (a name), "Maashuki" (My Love), and "Damu Imenikauka" (My Blood has Dried Up).

On the surface, the claim that these songs are "Swahili" in style is puzzling. Not only are none of them set in a compound meter like "Kasha Langu," but all are clearly Latin American in style. The musical setting for "Mimi" (AUDIO EX. 5) is actually taken from a tango-style song of the same name made famous by Syrian-Egyptian icon Farid al-Atrash.[15] The other two songs appear to be Jauharah's own compositions; however, they are similarly grounded in Egyptian versions of Latin American styles. "Damu Imenikauka" (AUDIO EX. 6) is also an Egyptian-style tango in terms of its rhythmic foundation, melodic form, and arrangement; and "Maashuki" is an Egyptian-style rumba. In short, all three of the musical compositions that Mbarak Rashid pointed to as exemplars of Jauharah's "Swahili" approach to melody are Swahili stylizations of Egyptian stylizations of Latin American styles. Even so, Mbarak Rashid had a relatively clear idea of what made the melodies to these songs "Swahili."

A "Swahili" melody, Mbarak Rashid explained during our interview, follows the natural prosody of a Swahili text: "How you pronounce the words is how the song will be sung" (*Yale matamshi yako, nyimbo itakavyoiimbwa*). As he spoke, another founding member of Jauharah, Abdalla Jemadari, interjected that particular *maqām*s are also integral to a "Swahili" approach to composition. Specifically, he named *Sīkāh* and *Hijāz*, though he made it clear that more could be added to the list.

The vocal melodies of "Mimi," "Maashuki," and "Damu Imenikauka" do, indeed, feature a natural-sounding fit with their Swahili texts. The settings are predominantly syllabic and rarely go against the normal accentuation of the words, producing an almost conversational effect. With respect to *maqām*, both "Mimi" and "Damu Imenikauka" are set in *Maqām Nahāwand* (similar in pitch structure to the Western minor scale), while "Maashuki" is in a variant of *Maqām 'Ajam* (similar in pitch structure to the Western major scale).[16] The use of *Nahāwand* in two of the songs lends support to Jemadari's assertion that certain *maqām*s are more "Swahili" than others, as this is also the *maqām* of "Kasha Langu." Interestingly, the way in which *Nahāwand* is used in "Mimi," emphasizing the third scale degree, is reminiscent of "Kasha Langu," suggesting a formal basis for hearing the melody of "Mimi" as "Swahili," despite it having been composed by an Egyptian.

According to Jauharah's criteria, then, "Mimi," "Maashuki," and "Damu Imenikauka" are, indeed, "Swahili." Even so, to actually hear these melodies as Swahili in the context of their performances requires that one embrace a particular epistemic (or acoustemic) commitment: namely, that Swahili and Arab cultural expressions can be distinct without being mutually exclusive. This commitment stands in tension with the understanding of colonial administrators and many foreign scholars during the 1950s that Swahili culture must either be "Arab" or "African" (Topan 2006). The colonial epistemology of Swahili culture is evident in the notes of the British scholar and entrepreneur who immortalized Jauharah's performances of "Mimi," "Maashuki," and "Damu Imenikauka." In reference to "Mimi," Hugh Tracey wrote, "There appears to be a tendency to distort the Swahili language when singing in the Arab style, just as there is when African words are set to an English tune" (quoted in A. Tracey 2006). It is difficult to know what if any detail of Mbarak Rashid's vocal performance inspired this note. Whatever the case, it seems clear that Tracey was primed to hear an antinomy of "African" and "Arab" elements in Jauharah's music. In contrast, Jauharah heard a dialogue of distinct "Swahili" and "Arab" elements in their music. This conception of Swahiliness as a distinctive feature that is not necessarily mutually exclusive with Arabness grows organically out of an epistemology/acoustemology of *utamaduni*.

Whereas Jauharah's project of developing a "Swahili" approach to melody was clearly nurtured by Sauti ya Mvita's sonic enactments of *utamaduni*, other approaches to sounding "Swahili" in 1950s Mombasan taarab engaged in a dialogic counterpoint with them. I present two examples here, each of which left a lasting impression on Mombasan taarab.

"ARABIAN CONGA"

Barriers to women's participation in the nascent East African recording industry resulted in a relative dearth of women's voices in Mombasan taarab recorded in the 1950s (Graebner 2004b, 12). Siti Ganduri was one of the few women who managed to find a place for herself in the recording industry of the time, presumably because she was already a respected elder of taarab. Ganduri had begun her career during the interwar years (hence, her use of the honorific "Siti," adopted by many female taarab singers in the wake of Siti binti Saad's rise to stardom). After the second world war, she enjoyed a comeback with her somewhat awkwardly named ensemble Siti Ganduri and Party of Ras Maalim Revue. During the early 1950s, she recorded in Nairobi for both local and international labels. Among her biggest late-career hits were two songs in a style that she labelled "Arabian *conga*." The first, titled "Arabian Conga," was released in 1950 on the Columbia label;[17] the second, "Kitabu Nimekifungua" (I Have Opened the Book) (AUDIO EX. 7), was released on the Jambo label in 1952.[18]

Siti Ganduri's Arabian *conga* style manages to be at once self-consciously "African" and wholly cosmopolitan. On the surface, it seems to be an adaptation (stylization) of *ngoma*, with a high-energy rhythmic feel, ululations, and some lyrics that suggest a festive occasion (particularly in "Arabian Conga," which is overall "a song of welcoming" [Ward 2011, 67]). But it does not draw from any specific *ngoma*. The most *ngoma*-like aspect—the syncopated rhythm performed on resonant hand drums along with struck idiophones (sticks or claves) and shakers (possibly a raft shaker)—is quite clearly adapted from the Afro-Cuban *conga* style popularized worldwide by the likes of Chano Pozo and Desi Arnaz in the 1940s (Moore 1998, 77–80). It is an allusion that speaks to influences of the Western music industry and Hollywood.

In both examples of Siti Ganduri's Arabian *conga* style, the vocal melody is nearly the same, revealing a specific approach to melody as a key to Ganduri's conception of her invented idiom. The melodies descend to the tonic on every phrase, locking into the *conga* rhythm along the way. This descending gesture strongly evokes traditional Mijikenda melodies, which always follow the descending melodic contour of Mijikenda speech patterns. A Mijikenda-tinged melody, colored with ululations, would have signaled the "bush," or *nyika* (a word literally synonymous with "Mijikenda" at the time), for urban(e) taarab listeners during the 1950s; just as a *conga* rhythm signaled the "African jungle" for audiences around the world who had been exposed to its uses in Hollywood movies as a trope of savagery (Garcia 2017, 156). Thus, Ganduri's Arabian *conga* style playfully juxtaposes local and global icons of musical Africanness to imagine an emphatically "African" style of taarab. It is difficult to imagine a portrayal of Swahili cultural identity further removed from the traditional conception of *utamaduni*. And yet, Ganduri's Arabian *conga* songs are taarab through and through. As if to compel her listeners to dwell on the tension between this manifestation of "Swahili" music culture and notions of utamaduni, Ganduri flamboyantly posits the idea that the songs are as much "Arabian" as "African": the phrase "Arabian *conga*" is presented on the record label as well in verbal introductions for both songs.

"ROCK THE BABY"

The most famous and influential dialogic response to Sauti ya Mvita's acoustemological intervention came from a singer whose legendary status stands at odds with the relative paucity of his output: Ali Mkali (1935–2005). Born Ali Salim Hanzwani, Ali Mkali earned the nickname Mkali, "the Fierce One," playing soccer in his youth. He began singing in the early 1950s, inspired by his love of Hindi musical films. After brief stints with Morning Star Orchestra and Jauharah, he started his own smaller group, which he named Mvita Orchestra. While Mkali generally composed his own melodies, his sound was broadly aligned with Indian taarab. His vocal delivery evoked Hindi film playback singers, and his ensemble included the typical "Indian taarab" instruments of harmonium, tashkota, and tablas (chapter 3).

Ali Mkali's "Bembeya Mtoto" (Pamper the Child/Rock the Baby) (AUDIO EX. 8), which premiered on Sauti ya Mvita around 1956, was one of the biggest Mombasan taarab hits of the 1950s—perhaps second only to "Kasha Langu."[19] There would seem to be a few factors that contributed to the deep and lasting popularity of this song. One is the structure of the main melody, which includes an unusual and affecting modulation in the refrain. The melody is set entirely in *Maqām Kurd* (equivalent in pitch structure to the Western Phrygian scale and Indian *raag Bhairavi*); however, it tonicizes the third scale degree in the refrain, momentarily lifting and brightening the mode. While the melody is probably based on a traditional Swahili melody (or melodies), the modulation would seem to have been Mkali's own innovation.[20] Another factor in the success of the song is the "poeticity" (Jakobson 1987) of the song's titular phrase. *Bembeya* means "cajole" or "pamper" in Kimvita and Kiunguja (the Mombasan and Zanzibari dialects of Swahili, respectively).[21] But it exists in other Swahili dialects and related coastal languages as a variant of the Kimvita/Kiunguja *pembea*, which means (to) "swing" or "rock" (as in a baby).[22] The phrase *bembeya mtoto* thus combines two images of childrearing in a compact statement. That audiences appreciated this word play is evident in how the phrase quickly made it onto *kanga*s (colorful wraps worn by women on the Swahili coast, which often feature proverbs or other short sayings) (Beck 2000, 112).

A third factor in the success of "Bembeya Mtoto"—and the one that most concerns us here—is its creative engagement with a traditional genre of women's lullaby singing that I will call the *howa* lullaby. The *howa* lullaby centers on the use of a particular vocable, *howa*, which African communities on the Swahili coast and beyond sing to soothe an infant.[23] Though functional, the *howa* lullaby is also a literary genre that serves as a vehicle for poetry combining traditional and newly composed stanzas (Senkoro 2005).

"Bembeya Mtoto" doesn't actually use the *howa* vocable, but it incorporates other content from traditional *howa* lullabies, most notably the iconic line, "*Ukila waniliza, wanikumbusha ukiwa*" (When you cry you make me cry; you remind me of my loneliness) (cf. ibid., 2). At some point, Mkali also composed another *howa* lullaby song, entitled "Howa Howa" (AUDIO EX. 9), which does feature the *howa* vocable, along with a melody similar to that of "Bembeya Mtoto."[24] Renditions of both songs are included on the first cassette that Ali Mkali recorded with Mbwana Radio Service in the 1980s.

Ali Mkali's *howa* lullaby songs are intertextual in more than one respect. They draw not only on the traditional *howa* lullaby genre, but also on the first iterations of the *howa* lullaby taarab song in the early recordings of the binti Saad collective. The binti Saad collective recorded two stylized *howa* lullabies around 1930, one by Siti binti Saad and another by Maalim Shaaban.[25] Siti's "Mbembeleze Mtoto" (Comfort the Child) (AUDIO EX. 10), whose title is essentially the more standard version of the phrase "*bembeya mtoto*," was still widely remembered among my older interlocutors in Mombasa in the twenty-first century. Taarab audiences in the 1950s would surely have heard Ali Mkali's "Bembeya Mtoto" as an allusion to this earlier *howa* lullaby song.

In their portrayals of childrearing and the hardships of women in society, the binti Saad collective's stylized *howa* lullabies are of a piece with their general emphasis on themes of domestic relations and the struggles of women and the downtrodden in colonial Zanzibar (Fair 2001, 211). But the songs reflect on these themes in a particular way, which involves a play on Swahili norms of vocalic space.

The sounds of the *howa* lullaby belong to the domestic space, understood on the Swahili coast as a domain restricted to women and the family, a space of "privacy" in the Arabo-Islamic sense of "sanctity-reserve-respect" (El Guindi 1999, 77–96). The ideal-typical Swahili patrician house contains an area called the *ndani* (literally, "inside") that is reserved specifically for women and the family and understood as a space of "sanctity-reserve-respect." The *ndani* is situated in the uppermost part of the house, furthest from the outside porch (*baraza*), which is understood as a domain of men (Allen 1979; Donley 1982; Donley-Reid 1990; Ghaidan 1975). The *baraza* extends outward to public streets and squares, which are even more strongly associated with men. In this way, lived space in the Swahili town bears an "intimacy gradient" (Ghaidan 1975, 75) that (re)produces a set of dispositions and sensibilities based upon the analogy *female : male :: private : public*.[26]

The *howa* lullaby trope in mass-mediated taarab plays with the norms of vocalic space in the Swahili town. In the context of a local mediascape it constitutes a gesture of *disclosing* the *ndani*, of sounding the *ndani* out into public space and circulation. This gesture is amplified, perhaps, when the singer is a man, as a taarab singer's voice is always "situated and gendered" (Ntarangwi 2001, 24). Ali Mkali's *howa* lullaby songs play up the tension between the masculine voice and the feminine setting, by using veiled language (*mafumbo*) to maintain a surface connection to the lullaby genre while engaging in gendered discourse. "Bembeya Mtoto," for instance, is generally taken to reflect a man lamenting the difficulty he finds in satisfying his wife's emotional, economic, or sexual needs (Beck 2000, 112). Mkali heightens this tension further by employing an *ngoma* rhythm—*chakacha*—that is associated with Swahili girls initiation rites.

The poignancy of Ali Mkali's particular dialogic response to Sauti ya Mvita's acoustemological intervention is evident in how the *howa* lullaby trope was picked up by other Mombasan taarab musicians in later years. The first Mombasan to record another *howa* lullaby in the wake of the success of Ali Mkali's "Bembeya Mtoto" was Yaseen. During the 1950s and 1960s, Yaseen recorded a number of singles with his wife Mwanasaada Said Kondo, who went by the professional name Mimi. Their "Nimepata Mwana," written to commemorate the birth of their son in 1962, includes creative allusions to the *howa* lullaby (AUDIO EX. 11).[27] The musical setting is broadly Indian, with a verse melody that may be borrowed from a Hindi film song. But the refrain echoes Maalim Shaaban's "Howa Howa Mwanangu," using the same words and a similar melodic shape. Interestingly, the performance works to erase any suggestion of a lullaby. It is blazingly fast, and includes virtuosic soloing on tashkota and Clavioline (an early analog synthesizer that Yaseen also used for his Western pop-oriented recordings [see Gesthuizen 2019]). Though it may seem an odd choice for a lullaby, the agitated mood of the performance works nicely with the song's lyrics, which express a man's anxiety about supporting his new child.

Juma Bhalo, whose name became synonymous with Indian taarab (see chapter 3), also recorded a *howa* lullaby song during the 1960s (AUDIO EX. 12).[28] The verbal text, possibly composed by the eminent Swahili poet (and Bhalo's cousin) Ahmad Nassir, is brilliantly crafted to conjure a woman's experience while still being sung by a man, using formal devices of prayer to navigate the gulf between normative male and female ways of speaking to and about a child. The words are set to a lyrical melody in a slow triple meter, making the song one of Bhalo's very few non-"Indian" performances.

Later in the 1970s, Zuhura Swaleh (1947–) brought the *howa* lullaby back into the hands (or voice) of a woman. Hearkening back to Siti's "Mbembeleze Mtoto," Zuhura's "Silie Mwanangu" (Don't Cry My Child) (AUDIO EX. 13) poignantly reflects on the position and experience of women on the Swahili coast. The words portray "the life of single parenthood which has driven this woman not into desperation, but to a cry of self-confidence which was unheard of before in this male-dominated society" (Senkoro 1995, 132; see also Ntarangwi 2003, 241–42). Like Ali Mkali, she sets the song to a *chakacha* rhythm.

In addition to a gendered critique of the acoustemology of *utamaduni*, the *howa* trope in taarab can be heard as a (meta)reflection on reflexivity in taarab. The gesture poses the idea that the sounds of taarab disclose aspects of Swahili culture that may not always be audible in public space but are nonetheless essential to what it means to be culturally "Swahili." In light of this, it is not surprising that the two men who took up the *howa* trope after Ali Mkali were both Indian taarab stars. As we will see in the next chapter, style in Indian taarab has historically been a site of a musico-poetic engagement with senses of place and identity.

THREE

The Mouths of Professors and Clowns
Indian Taarab

March 4, 2005. There was a momentary fracas around the VCD deck, as a few of the regulars of Zein l'Abdin's nightly men's gathering argued over how best to finesse the temperamental machine. The task complete, Bombom was the first one back on his floor cushion, a stick of khat in his teeth and his feet resting on an old PA speaker with the words "Zein Musical Party" emblazoned in stencil font on its front mesh.

I shifted forward on my own cushion to grab the abandoned VCD case.

"*Teesri Manzil*," Salim said as I studied the VCD case. He was seated next to me, nursing a fagot of khat and a small coffee cup in front of his crossed legs. I stared at him nonplussed, with an expression he probably recognized as linguistic processing. "*Teesri Manzil*," he repeated, tapping the VCD case. "It is the title of the movie. It means 'Third Floor.'"[1]

"So you speak Hindi?" I asked in mocking reverence.

"*Kushinda Kiswahili!*" (Even better than Swahili!), Salim answered with a laugh.

At this, Bombom, usually the one making the jokes, interjected without a hint of sarcasm. "You know, we used to watch these films *every day*." His didactic tone signaled that I should take note. "*Nasikia yote!*" (I understand everything!).

The film turned out to be a classic from the late 1960s, when most of

> the men in the room would have been in their teens or twenties. Bombom, Kibasha, and Salim sang along to every song. By the middle of the film, I was singing along, too—as best I could. Occasionally, the men substituted some Hindi words with similar-sounding words in Swahili. It was a game of sorts, to see who could find the most clever substitutions. Everyone had a particularly good time with the song "Aaja Aaja" (Come), which accompanies a nightclub scene in which the entire dancefloor breaks into "the Shake" (an Anglo-American fad dance from the 1960s). The song's refrain begins with a sputtering "*A-a-a-aja a-a-a-aja*," and then moves on to a melodious release: "*Aaja aajaaaaa!*" Bombom was the first to tackle the Hindi phrase "*aaja aaja!*" turning it into "*hajaja*" (he hasn't arrived yet). No one was going to top that: a perfect phonological fit that played on a false cognate. Salim was undaunted, however. He added a variation on Bombom's theme, replacing "*hajaja*" with "*yuaja*" (he's coming). Now the newly invented Swahili refrain took on a dramatic tension. It was a song waiting to be written.

This moment from my fieldwork offers a sense of the creative engagements with Hindi films and their soundtracks that gave birth to what is probably Mombasa's most distinctive form of Swahili taarab, the subgenre known as "Indian taarab" (*taarab ya kihindi*). The practice of setting new words to popular Hindi film melodies—what we might call "Bollywood *contrafacta*"—is common in Africa and other parts of the Global South (Booth 1993; Chernoff 1979, 129–30; Lambert 1993, 181; Larkin 2004; Manuel 1993, 131–52; Marcus 1994; Waterman 1990, 2). Hindi film music invites this sort of play, by virtue of its propensity for intertextuality and cultural borrowing. It is a promiscuous art, open to reinterpretation (Novak 2010, 50). But Indian taarab stands out among all the documented examples of Bollywood *contrafacta*. At its heart is a paradox: despite its highly cultivated "Indian" sound, it has come to stand as an icon of a *non*-Indian identity—Swahili.[2]

No one has embodied the tension between the sonic Indianness and symbolic Swahiliness of Indian taarab more than the famed singer Juma Bhalo (1942–2014). At Bhalo's funeral in Mombasa in April 2014, Ahmed Yasin of the National Museums of Kenya lauded his role in preserving Swahili dialects, while Stambuli Abdillahi Nasser, a politically active intellectual from Bhalo's clan, celebrated his renown in Swahili towns and villages across the East African coast (Mwakio 2014).[3] It was not the first time Bhalo had been eulogized in this way. Similar pronouncements about his importance to Swahili culture, language, and community had been proffered in private conversations in Mombasa as well as on local talk radio after Bhalo had declined to perform at the 2005 Swahili Culture Festival in Lamu, and again in 2007, after he had announced his retirement. The eulogies at Bhalo's funeral were merely the most poignant airing of a discourse that had already been well established. In light of this, it is remarkable that Bhalo not only borrowed melodies from Hindi film soundtracks for nearly *all* of his songs, but also cultivated a distinctly Indian style, both in his vocal delivery and in the sound of his ensemble. Bhalo's poetry may have been "Swahili," but his music was "Indian."

In this chapter, I argue that Indian taarab's paradoxical presentation of Indian sounds as "Swahili" expressions was part of what attracted performers and audiences to the genre during the twentieth century. Indian taarab came into its own in the 1960s, just as a "generalized idea of 'Swahiliness'" was taking hold within discourses of ethnic identification among Swahili patricians and elite Arabs in Mombasa (Berg 1968, 38), and continued to flourish through the latter half of the century as the idea of Swahili ethnicity took root. I contend that the disjuncture of identity at the heart of Indian taarab offered Mombasans who saw themselves as "Swahili" a way of taking pleasure in the recognition and exploration of the paradoxical character of this ethnic subject position.

A POETICS OF VOCALITY

Indian taarab is a singer's art. As an instrumentalization of the bodily faculty that is most involved "in the production of social and cultural being," the singing voice serves as a powerful technology of public reflexivity (Feld et al. 2004, 334). A human listener, endowed with his or her own body, voice, and innate orientation toward mimesis, confronts an other's singing voice as a reflection and refraction of the self (Meizel 2011). This inherent reflexivity in the reception of the singing voice can never be wholly subjective, given the fundamentally social lives of the voice and the self. Nina Eidsheim illustrates this point in her discussion of the reception of jazz vocalist Jimmy Scott. By flouting normative gender expectations, Eidsheim argues, Scott's voice "holds up a mirror to the audience" (Eidsheim 2008, 235). Indian taarab singing similarly holds up a mirror, albeit at a different angle, reflecting and refracting Swahiliness for listeners who understand themselves to be "Swahili."

Indian taarab singing becomes most deeply reflexive in the hands (or mouths) of those singers I will describe as the genre's "clowns." By using this term I mean to connect this type of Indian taarab singer to the possibly universal figure of the harlequin or trickster, whose role in ritual or art is to upend and invert norms and expectations (Turner 2012). Indian taarab clowns upend the ethnic categories of coastal Swahili society by drawing attention to and playing with the paradox of an Indian voice emanating from a Swahili mouth. This move constitutes a *poetics of Swahili identity*, a performative exploration of the "network of interrelated tropes" (Fox 2004, 29) through which social actors on the Kenyan coast have historically understood what it means to be "Swahili." Drawing on the locally salient ethnic schema of "Swahili-space" (*uswahili*), I describe this poetics below as a matter of *making audible the Indianness that already resonates in Swahili bodies and places*.

My focus on articulations of ethnically marked voices and bodies in musical practice places my analysis in this chapter within the interdisciplinary research area that Steven Feld, Aaron Fox, Thomas Porcello, and David Samuels term "vocal anthropology" (Feld et al. 2004, 340). Following other works in this area that explore the intersections of vocality and identity, I home in on the multidimensional materiality of the voice as sound "produced through bodily actions" (Weidman 2015, 235). Specifically, I attend to the dialogic cultivation and choreography of the Indian voice in Indian taarab, in order to get at its social meanings.[4]

THE ORIGINS OF INDIAN TAARAB

While Indian taarab still exists to this day, its heyday had passed even by the time of my fieldwork in the first decade of the twenty-first century. The only relatively young Indian taarab bandleader working in Mombasa at the time of my research was Lamu-born Mohamed Yusuf "Tenge," who began his career in the mid-1980s as a protege of Juma Bhalo. Tenge was struggling to get by during my time in Mombasa, despite being one of Mbwana Radio Service's best-selling artists. Unable to establish himself there permanently, he frequently went home to Lamu for long periods. At one point, shortly before I arrived in 2004, he had been gone from Mombasa for so long that he was rumored to have died. The local affiliate of KBC radio (Kenya's national radio network) even aired a tribute program.

There are two reasons for the decline of Indian taarab at the end of the twentieth century. First, the declining local economy and rising popularity of television and video drove all but one of the town's Indian-owned cinemas out of business. Hindi musical films were still quite popular in Mombasa during my fieldwork. But there were no longer any *current* hit movies, soundtracks, or songs that everyone in town could be expected to have seen/heard. Second, and perhaps more significantly, the rise of religious opposition to live music in Mombasa Old Town severely reduced performance opportunities (see chapter 6). The Swahili women's wedding celebration (*kupamba*), Indian taarab's primary live context for decades (see Fuglesang 1994, 111), nearly disappeared in Mombasa Old Town. *Kupamba*s and larger, mixed-gender wedding celebrations featuring taarab music still go on today in Mombasa, but mostly on the outskirts of town and in more rural areas, where bands working in the more danceable "modern taarab" idiom pose stiff competition.

To reconstruct the history of Indian taarab, I have relied upon the memories of consultants with first- and secondhand knowledge of past figures and events. In the course of hanging out nearly every evening for more than a year at Zein l'Abdin's home in Mombasa Old Town, I conducted informal and formal interviews with middle-aged and older musicians and aficionados of Indian taarab. I sometimes listened with them to recorded performances of Indian taarab to elicit free-flowing talk about the music. Zein was particularly helpful, as he had been a performer of Indian taarab in the 1960s before developing his "Arab" style (chapter 5). But it was his nephew, Jamal Hafidh Jahadhmy, who served as my key interlocutor and collaborator. Jamal is not himself a musician, but he recorded and promoted Indian taarab groups during the 1980s, and he has long been an avid collector of Swahili cultural artifacts. He supplied some of the recordings I worked with and assisted me in collecting and analyzing others. I supplemented my work with Jamal Hafidh and other members of Zein l'Abdin's circle with conversations and interviews with other taarab experts, including noted Swahili poets and local Indian musicians who had worked closely with Indian taarab musicians during their careers.[5]

As I explained in chapter 1, commercially recorded taarab incorporated Indian elements from the very earliest days. A close examination of the earliest commercially recorded taarab reveals influences from Urdu genres such as *qawwali* (Muslim devotional music) and early recorded *ghazal* (light classical song).[6] While it has been suggested that Siti binti Saad's appropriations of Indian style resulted from her experiences in Bombay, it is also the case that Indian records "were available almost to the exclusion of any other type of music on the Swahili coast" at the time (Topp Fargion 2007, 7). Another possible source of Indian influence in early recorded taarab was the urban popular musics performed by local Hadrami musicians and Hadrami musicians visiting from southern Arabia. Hadrami popular song (*ṭarab*) has incorporated Indian influences and, indeed, Bollywood *contrafacta* since the interwar years (Lambert 1993, 181; chapter 4). While I have not found any direct link between Bollywood *contrafacta* in Hadrami *ṭarab* and the development of Indian taarab, some degree of influence may be assumed.[7]

Indian taarab emerged as early as the late 1930s. At least two singers, Chuba Shee and Jumbe Ali, recorded recognizable Indian taarab for His Master's Voice between 1938 and 1946.[8] But the ground for Indian taarab became more fertile after the Second World War, as denizens of the Kenyan coast fell in love with Hindi musical films. From the 1950s to the mid-1990s, going to see a Hindi musical film at a local Indian-owned cinema was among the most popular leisure activities for Swahili-speaking Muslims in Mombasa. By the time I arrived in Mombasa to begin my fieldwork in 2004, most of Mombasa's Indian-owned cinemas had gone out of business. But the culture of cinema going and its importance to the local sea of taarab was still a recent memory. The late British music producer Andrew Burchell, who had been living in Mombasa since the 1990s, recalled how he once found himself sitting next to Indian taarab singers Maulidi Juma and Tenge at a Bollywood move in the mid-1990s. He was struck by how the musicians were "taking notes" and whispering to each other about how they had the perfect idea for this or that song.[9]

It is tempting to assume that Indian taarab borrowed from the popularity of Hindi musical films in Mombasa, just as it borrowed from the content of these films. But it may also be the case that an already established proclivity for Indian music helped attract Swahili-speaking Muslims to Hindi musical films. There are, of course, reasons why Swahili-speaking Muslims took to Hindi musical films that have little to do with music: as Brian Larkin argues in relation to Hausa audiences in northern Nigeria, Swahili-speaking Muslim audiences in the postwar period were surely attracted to Hindi musical films for their "images of a parallel modernity to the West, one intimately concerned with the changing basis of social life, but rooted in conservative cultural values" (Larkin 1997, 410). And as historians Ned Bertz and Laura Fair discuss in relation to Zanzibar, the films were also attractive for how they enabled African audiences to imagine new global alliances and social futures on the eve of decolonization.[10] But given the importance of music to the affective power of Hindi musical films, it is clear that a familiarity with and fondness for Indian sounds played a role in the reception

FIGURE 3.1 A "Young India" record in its original packaging. Photo by author.

of these films among Swahili-speaking Muslims of the Kenyan coast—which, in turn, means that Indian taarab is not an ancillary offshoot of the Swahili love affair with Bollywood, but a key component of it.

That the popularity of Indian taarab continued to grow during the 1950s is suggested by the success of an odd minigenre of Swahili-language Bollywood *contrafacta* produced in India, by Indians. This was the effort of the Young India record company in Bombay, an early "'indigenous' effort at record production" that focused mainly on "amateur and upcoming artists."[11] Presumably spurred by the presence of Swahili-speaking Indian singers who had recently relocated from East Africa, Young India produced a few dozen such songs during the latter part of its years of operation (ending in 1955). These recordings feature verbal texts that appear to be mostly direct translations of the original film songs, all sung in distinct Indian accents over lush orchestral accompaniments.[12] Whether or not these recordings were considered to be taarab at the time, they nevertheless left a lasting impact on some Swahili musicians and listeners, as we shall see.

During the 1960s, when small taarab ensembles were beginning to replace the large orchestras of the colonial-era social clubs in Mombasa, Indian taarab came to dominate Kenyan coastal taarab. As a music performed by small groups led by individual stars, Indian taarab thrived in this new environment. Juma Bhalo and other Indian taarab stars became popular along the entire stretch of the Swahili coast, from Dar es Salaam to Mogadishu. But the Kenyan coast was where the genre really took hold, becoming the primary form of live entertainment for Swahili women's wedding celebrations and a staple of local record production and radio broadcasts.

MAKING TAARAB INDIAN

Three musical instruments imported to East Africa by Indians during the twentieth century helped spur the development of Indian taarab: the hand-pumped harmonium (largely supplanted by the synthesizer since the 1980s), the paired tabla drums, and the tashkota. The harmonium and tabla drums are typical South Asian instruments, widely used across the Indian subcontinent. The tashkota, as noted earlier, is a keyed zither of Japanese origin, originally imported as a novelty item and established as a professional instrument by Yaseen Mohamed Tofeli. While it has been used by Swahili taarab musicians in a variety of contexts, its timbral similarity to Indian chordophones used in Hindi film music made it an especially good fit for Indian taarab.

As with Hindi film music, the most important instrument in Indian taarab is the human voice. Unusually for Swahili taarab, Indian taarab is predominantly associated with male singers. While female taarab singers sang songs based on Hindi film songs during the twentieth century, they rarely, if ever, came to be known as Indian taarab singers in the generic sense. The most famous Kenyan female taarab singers of the late twentieth century, Zuhura Swaleh and Malika (1940–, *née* Asha Abdo Suleiman), each performed and recorded some Bollywood *contrafacta* during their careers. Both achieved their greatest renown, however, for songs set in the style of the Swahili women's dance known as *chakacha*. Malika's "Vidonge," based on traditional *chakacha* song, was not only her most popular song, it was arguably "the most popular taarab song to appear in the early 1990s" (Graebner 2004c, 251). More to the point, neither Zuhura nor Malika ever truly adopted the vocal style of a Bollywood playback singer. One can perhaps hear in their voices shades of the constricted vocal timbre developed by Lata Mangeshkar and Asha Bhosle. But female taarab singers have cultivated a similar timbre since at least the days of Siti binti Saad, who predates Mangeshkar and Bhosle. Mastery of the Mangeshkar/Bhosle vocal style was never a primary concern for either of them. When asked about their influences, Zuhura mentioned the American country singer Jim Reeves, while Malika mentioned male taarab singer Ali Mkali.[13] Sitara Bute, whose career was cut short by her untimely death in 2001, seems to my ear to have been the female taarab singer with the most abiding interested in developing a Mangeshkar/Bhosle style. Her reputation, however, was more that of a modern taarab singer (Ntarangwi 2001).

The gender disparity in Indian taarab singing seems to have stemmed in part from local understandings of Hindi film song as having a special power to stoke romantic passion. The use of Indian taarab as a vehicle for romantic fantasy in Swahili women's celebratory gatherings created a steady demand for suave male singers like Juma Bhalo during the years when the genre was obligatory at any such event. A sense of how this situation was understood locally can be garnered from a one-man comedy performance recorded by Assanand & Sons during the 1950s or 1960s. In it, a talented vocal acrobat named Lamu Omari acts out a scene in which a Swahili man catches his new Mijikenda *boi* (male domestic servant) serenading his wife with a Hindi film song performed in an uncannily authentic tone and accent (AUDIO EX. 14).[14] A number of norms and expectations are at play in this scene, including the notion that the cultivation of an "Indian" voice is an inherently Swahili practice. But most of all, the joke is on the passion of Swahili women for Hindi film song and the anxiety it provoked in Swahili men. One might expect that this anxiety would have stoked opposition to male Indian taarab singing, if not the genre as a whole among Swahili men. To be sure, Swahili women's attraction to male Indian taarab singing proved controversial in coastal Muslim society—Juma Bhalo was on more than one occasion accused of wooing married women—but the situation was accepted, or at least tolerated, by Swahili men for decades, until the rising influence of Islamic reform began to curtail *all* live music in Swahili neighborhoods toward the turn of the twenty-first century (see chapter 6).

Another possible explanation for Indian taarab's gender disparity lies in the similarity between Indian taarab singing and other traditionally masculine Swahili activities like speaking Arabic or Omani-style men's dancing (Eastman 1984). All of these activities involve intensive mimetic engagement with other Indian Ocean cultures. Given that female taarab singers have always, by definition, defied normative gender roles, one might expect that they could also inhabit the masculine role of culture broker. But the mimetic engagement in Indian taarab happens through a cultivation of the voice, and a taarab "singer's voice is . . . not neutral but situated and gendered" (Ntarangwi 2001, 24).

An Indian taarab singer takes pains to cultivate an "Indian" voice in his performances. In at least one important respect—the preparation of the verbal text—this may entail a collaborative process. Swahili poets working in the realm of Indian taarab work just as hard to marry their poems to Hindi film songs. At the semantic level, this means paying close attention to the thematic content of the source songs. While a set of Indian taarab lyrics is hardly ever a direct translation of a Hindi film song, they often reference the imagery and narratives of the source film, especially when that film was popular at the time they were composed. For instance, Yaseen Mohamed Tofeli's "Sina Nyumba" (I Have No Home), recorded in the 1950s by Assanand & Sons, references the theme of the film song upon which it is based, the global hit "Awaara Hoon" (I Am a Vagabond) from the 1951 Raj Kapoor classic *Awaara* (Vagabond).[15]

Indian taarab poets take even more exacting care at the level of prosody. The late Swahili poet and acknowledged cultural expert Ahmed Sheikh Nabhany (see chapter 5) told me that a skilled Indian taarab poet aims to set Swahili words to a Hindi film melody so perfectly as to momentarily fool an Indian listener into believing they are hearing their own language.[16] To accomplish this, he or she attends closely to the structure of the song's melody—Indian taarab is, in fact, the only form of taarab in which verbal texts are always composed to fit an existing melody[17]—as well as to the phonetics of the original Hindustani words. At least one poet, Ahmad Nassir (discussed below), was known to study the original Hindustani song texts in detail as part of his process of composing Indian taarab poetry, demonstrating the multilingualism that has traditionally been held up as an essential aspect of Swahili *umalenga*, "poetic genius" (Chiraghdin 1971, 18).[18]

Not surprisingly, Indian taarab poets take advantage of any Hindustani-Swahili cognates that might be present in the source song. Such cognates occur as a result of the presence of Arabic lexemes in both languages.[19] Since Arabic-derived words have mostly entered Hindi film music via the Urdu poetry tradition, they typically relate to key romantic and philosophical themes (Ganti 2004, 22–23). In some Indian taarab songs, cognates are used to forge a thematic connection to the original film song. Such is the case in Yaseen's "Sina Nyumba" (AUDIO EX. 15). The poet (presumably Yaseen himself) inserts the Arabic/Swahili/Urdu word *duniya* (world)—a word loaded with philosophical connotations for Muslims (Ho 2006, 229)—at the same climactic point at which this word occurs in the original song. Yaseen's performance amplifies the connection, by employing the exact melismatic ornamentations that occur in the original performance. Given the phenomenal popularity of the source film, *Awaara*, the effect for a listener on the Swahili coast in the mid-twentieth century must have been synesthetic.

He or she would have pictured the vagabond (Raj Kapoor) standing in a humble, dusty village—not unlike what much of Mombasa looked like at the time—lifting two naked children to his chest as he sings.

Of course, achieving an "Indian" voice takes more than just getting the right words to sing. An Indian taarab singer trains his vocal apparatus for the task. This is not a formalized process—there have never been any "schools" or formal apprenticeship programs for Indian taarab—but it certainly takes concentrated effort. I insist on the term *cultivation* to describe the work of the Indian taarab singer, in order to keep in view that he does not simply adopt an Indian voice for the purpose of a song or album. In most cases, an Indian taarab singer's Indian voice is the *only* singing voice that he ever presents to the public. While it is the product of "a highly sophisticated and evolved choreography," it must come off as completely natural (Eidsheim 2008, 268). To accomplish this, Indian taarab singers engage in an embodied learning process, what Pierre Bourdieu (1980) calls "practical mimesis." Bourdieu sums up this idea with the axiom, "What is 'learned by body' is not something that one has, like knowledge that can be brandished, but something that one is" (73).

A well-cultivated "Indian" voice in Indian taarab blurs the boundaries between Swahili and Indian languages and styles. For the Indian taarab clown, as I have already intimated, this blurring is about subverting given ideas about vocality and identity. But not all Indian taarab singers are clowns. For many Indian taarab singers, including the most successful one—Juma Bhalo—the blurring of languages and styles is, rather, about eliminating any sense of parody in order to enable listeners to lose themselves in the performance. While I am most concerned in this chapter with the activities of Indian taarab clowns, a closer look at Juma Bhalo is in order, as his case teaches us a great deal about the cultivation of the voice that lies at the heart of the form.

THE PROFESSOR

Juma Bhalo—"Professor Bhalo," as he was often called—is the quintessential example of a type of Indian taarab singer I call the "professor." His vocal performance was expressive, yet controlled—even understated. Seated at his keyboard in his buttoned-up suit, moving slightly as he sang, he exuded a debonair detachment that reflected the seriousness with which he took his craft.

Like Siti binti Saad and many other Swahili taarab singers, Bhalo first realized his vocal talent studying *tajwīd*, the science of Qur'anic recitation.[20] He began singing professionally in the late 1950s in Tanga, Tanganyika, at first accompanying himself on the mandolin. Around 1966, he moved to Mombasa, where he replaced his mandolin with a hand-pumped harmonium and began to establish himself as a wedding performer and recording artist.[21] His made his first recordings in the mid-1960s with Assanand & Sons, all released on 7-inch singles (45s) on Assanand's Mzuri label (some also carrying the Philips label, evidently released in partnership with the multinational Grammophon-Philips). By the late 1960s, however, he was releasing longer recordings, including live performances, on magnetic reel and, later, compact cassette, through Mbwana Radio Service. In the 1980s, after years of disputes with Mbwana over royalty payments, he set up his own studio and cassette kiosk just across the street.

In the traditional fashion of Swahili poets and musicians, Bhalo fostered his fame through competition. His first nemesis was another Indian taarab professor, Swaleh al-Abdi.[22] Swaleh might have surpassed Bhalo if he hadn't died relatively young in the 1970s. Two Indian musicians I spoke with who had performed with Swaleh praised his flawless Hindi and Urdu pronunciation, which they attributed to his being an Arabic speaker. After Swaleh's death, Bhalo began a long and bitter rivalry with another Indian taarab singer, Maulidi Juma Iha (1941–). Maulidi is a unique figure in Mombasan taarab. Born in a village outside of Malindi town, he is of Giriama (Mijikenda) descent. He started his first taarab group in the Malindi area as a teenager, before giving it up to go back to fishing. He then restarted his music career in Mombasa in 1971, briefly collaborating with Zein l'Abdin (see chapter 5) before starting his own group, Maulidi and Party, in partnership with Lamu-born keyboardist and tashkota player Mohamed Adio Shigoo (also known as Mohamed Mbwana). Though the majority of his work falls within the realm of Indian taarab, he has also ventured outside of the form—like Yaseen Mohamed Tofeli, but in a different way. Most strikingly, he has incorporated a few Giriama songs (songs that are Giriama in every way save for the taarab instrumentation) into his repertoire.

The bitterness of the rivalry between Bhalo and Maulidi stemmed from the fact that Maulidi and Party effectively replaced Bhalo at Mbwana Radio Service, becoming the company's new star group and recording studio mainstay. By all accounts, Bhalo felt personally betrayed by this, as he had to some extent taken Maulidi under his wing before that. Exacerbating the rivalry further was the social divide between the two men, Bhalo being a member of an elite clan within urban Swahili society and Maulidi being of rural Mijikenda descent (Ntarangwi 2001, 59). The different backgrounds of the two men amplified the sense of factionalism between their supporters, and made it difficult to find a third party who could effectively mediate between them.

The rivalry first took musical shape in the mid-1970s. As Mwenda Ntarangwi describes,

> Live performances at weddings became arenas for metaphorical compositions that centered on each other's *aibu* [shame]. The metaphors were initially mild, but clear enough to both artists and their fans to discern the intended meanings. They soon established a pattern whereby each would compose a song to attack or challenge the other. (Ntarangwi 2000, 60)

In terms of musical style, many of the challenge songs from the two singers were not Indian but rather *chakacha*, drawing rhetorical force from the manifestation of a Swahili *ngoma* traditionally associated with challenge songs.

After Bhalo set up his own kiosk across from Mbwana, the rivalry effectively spilled out onto the streets of Old Town. For a while, recordings of salacious insult songs were continually broadcast from each of the competing kiosks, blanketing Pigott Place, one of the central public squares of Old Town. The most unseemly aspects of these songs (suggestions of sexual perversion and the like) were veiled with cagey metaphors (*mafumbo*). But the situation was nonetheless beyond the pale for upstanding town residents. Eventually, the chief of Old Town intervened in the name of public decency.

Most people who dealt professionally with Bhalo were keen to call him "professor." One man who was exempted from this protocol was Bhalo's older cousin, the renowned poet Ahmad Nassir Juma Bhalo (1936–2019), who was himself often accorded the title of "professor," albeit the Persian/Urdu/Arabic version, *ustadh*.[23] Ahmad Nassir is responsible for much of the poetry that Bhalo sang throughout his career. As such, he reserved the right to refer to Bhalo as the "mouth" (*mdomo*) and himself as the "brain" (*ubongo*). Interlocutors familiar with Bhalo's process in the 1980s and 1990s reported that "mouth" and "brain" used to complete each "volume" (sixty- or ninety-minute cassette) only after a painstaking process that involved choosing the proper material, setting each song with the appropriate poetry, and making various decisions regarding the performances. They were known to place Indian friends in advisory roles during this process. One such friend, deceased by the time of my research, was nicknamed Dugu (literally "Big Brother"). He helped out by transliterating and translating Hindi film songs, aiding both the "mouth" with problems of declamation and the "brain" with problems of content rendering.[24]

FIGURE 3.2 Maulidi Musical Party perform at a wedding in Mombasa in the early 1980s. Maulidi Juma Iha stands at the far right. Jumaa Bakari Chera on bass (background left), Ali Tihu Suleiman on *rīq*, Mohamed Abdallah Mfaume on accordion (background), Bakari Aziz Omar on bongos, Ali Abdurahman Ali on tabla, and Mohamed Adio Shigoo on organ. Werner Graebner collection, used with permission.

FIGURE 3.3 Ahmad Nassir Juma Bhalo (left) and Mohamed Khamis Juma Bhalo (right), ca. 2005. Used with permission of Anwar Bhalo.

Bhalo's meticulous process reveals Indian taarab as more than a simple appropriation of popular melodies or an attempt at "harnessing the glamour and transnational prestige associated with Indian films," as Larkin suggests in the case of Hausa *bandiri* music (2004, 105). As much a discipline as an art, Indian taarab requires training and labor in addition to raw talent. An Indian taarab song is a true "artistic hybrid" in Mikhail Bakhtin's terms—"stylized through and through, thoroughly premeditated, achieved, distanced" (Bakhtin 1981, 366). But when it is done well it doesn't seem this way at all. It seems much more natural, because the "stylization" is not something that happens in the words, melodies, rhythms, or timbres, but in the body. In other words, stylization in Indian taarab literalizes Bakhtin's metaphorical notion "that the stylizer constructs his utterance so that the voice of the other will be heard to sound within his own" (Morson and Emerson 1990, 151). This takes us from Bakhtin's notion of stylization to that of Judith Butler (1999). The cultivation of an Indian voice is, in Butler's words, a "stylization of the body," a practice of self-making akin to what every person does in moving through the world as a social being (179).

THE CLOWN

An Indian taarab singer's stylization of the body is always intensive, but not always quite as *serious* as Bhalo took it to be. Unlike the professor, the Indian taarab clown approaches the stylization of the body as a form of play. By placing his performance within a "play frame," he keeps the parodic nature of Indian taarab in focus (Turner 1986, 107). He revels in the strangeness of the genre's "misembodied voice" (Brayton 2011), transforming his performance into a work of "cultural translation" in Homi Bhabha's sense of a staging of cultural difference (Bhabha 1994, 325).

If Indian taarab professors channel the spirit of Mohammed Rafi, the Hindi-film playback singer who took his work so seriously that another singer once had to be brought in to perform "the nonmusical utterance 'yahoo'" in a song, the clowns channel Kishore Kumar, the playback singer whose skill for comedy made his considerable virtuosity easy to overlook (Ranade 2006, 382–83). Indian taarab clowning seems to have begun in the earliest days of the genre: the surviving recordings of Chuba Shee and Jumbe Ali suggest that both were clowns. But the earliest clown that my Mombasan interlocutors recalled was a half-Indian, half-Swahili Zanzibari entertainer who went by the name Musa Maruf ("Famous Musa").

Musa Maruf frequented Mombasa from the 1940s until he took up permanent residence there after the 1964 revolution in Zanzibar. As a member of the Nizari Ismaili Muslim community, his relocation was a matter of self-preservation: seen as allies of the sultan, Ismailis were targeted along with Arabs in the violent ouster of the Omani ruling class (Nagar 1996, 67). But he was more than welcome in Mombasa, having already achieved a degree of celebrity there. Older Mombasans remember hearing Maruf's distinctive voice, not only as it emanated from 78-speed records and Sauti ya Mvita radio broadcasts, but also as it resounded in the physical spaces of Mombasa's Old Town and market area. Just like Siti binti Saad in her pre-celebrity days, Maruf was a hawker, earning a living from his ability to transmit his voice through public streets and squares (Shaaban bin Robert 1967, 5). His primary hawking work was in promoting *lesos*, colorfully patterned wraps with Swahili sayings. When he wasn't performing his distinctive hawker's cry, "*Badilisha! Badilisha!*" (Exchange! Exchange!), he enthralled passersby in the *leso* district of Biashara Street with everything from puppet shows to elaborate comedic performances in drag.

While his street performances would have been enough to make him famous, Maruf was also one of the most talented East African musicians of his generation—an expert harmonium player with a piercing tenor capable of performing powerful *qawwali*-style melismas. He began his career recording for the Nairobi-based Jambo label in the late 1940s. His songs set Swahili poems to otherwise authentic-sounding Indian melodies (some of which may have been his own compositions), all sung in a distinct Indian accent.[25]

Maruf's music is marked by layers of multivocality and intertextuality. His Jambo recording "Mpenzi Wangu Kanitoka" (And Then My Love Left Me), based on the song "Jaba Dil Hi Toot Gaya" (When the Heart Is Broken) (AUDIO EX. 16) from the 1946 film *Shahjehan* (dir. Abdul Rashid Kardar) provides a rich example.[26] In a nasal tenor reminiscent of Bollywood playback singer K. L. Saigel's performance of the source song, Maruf sings, "*Moyo wangu 'mevunjika*," literally "my heart is broken." This image comes directly from the source song,[27] but it also recalls the Swahili expression *-vunjika moyo*, which is generally translated as "(to) be discouraged." In other words, the song's lyricist, who I assume to be Maruf himself, is engaging in a bit of esoteric wordplay that could only be picked up by someone who speaks both Hindi and English. It is possible that the intended audience for this wordplay was Indian Zanzibaris, who have historically been known to adopt Swahili as a mother tongue whether or not they sought to become "Swahili" in any other respect (Padgaonkar 2002). But the wordplay could also be taken as a clever attempt to translate the concept of lost love into a Swahili context, just as Hindi films at the time were translating ideas of romantic love for young Swahili viewers interested in ideas of self-determination (Fair 2009). Maruf's accent, which turns *wangu* into *wangul*, brings the playfulness to the surface in a way that an Indian taarab professor like Juma Bhalo would try to avoid. It is impossible to forget that this is Swahili poetry inflected with Hindi, all wrapped up in an Indian voice emanating from an Indian-Swahili mouth.

The next Indian taarab clown to emerge bore many similarities to Musa Maruf. Junaidi Al Noor, popularly known as Mzee Mombasa ("Old Man Mombasa"), was a Swahili musician and performer who achieved national fame in Kenya. As a young man he endured backbreaking and dangerous labor on Indian Ocean ships in order to avail himself of opportunities to perform music and comedy in South Asia as well as East Africa. Having garnered experience in South Asian musical forms in Lahore, he marketed himself as an Indian musician for Indians and others back in East Africa, "taking [the music] to faraway places that it could not have reached by itself" (Anonymous 2000, 182). No doubt his performances were appreciated by discerning Indians in far-off places like Bukoba, on Lake Victoria. But there was also a farcical aspect to his Indian persona, evidenced by the fact that he coupled musical performances with comedic plays in which he always portrayed an Indian man with a "spot" on his forehead (ibid.).

By the time Mzee Mombasa began playing accordion with Zein l'Abdin's taarab group in 1971, he had already wrapped up his acting career in favor of more lucrative opportunities in deep-sea fishing. Whether it was the opportunity to perform again or the desire to live a life without the threat of sharks (he was treated for stress after one close call), he began working with Zein full time, going with him as far as Rwanda and Burundi to perform for weddings. This was around the time that Zein began to move away from borrowing Indian melodies, preferring Arab melodies and his own compositions based on Arab *maqāms* (melodic modes), a move no doubt influenced by the steady influx of Hadrami Arab business owners willing to lay out money for wedding bands to suit both Arab and Swahili tastes. Thus, Mzee Mombasa, who had molded himself into a bridge between the coasts of South Asia and East Africa, was now stretching himself toward southern Arabia.

From the end of his time with Zein l'Abdin until the mid-1990s, Mzee Mombasa worked as a nationally recognized actor in Kenya, first on radio and then later on television. By 1995, however, his failing health forced him to retire. Shortly before his death in 2002, he experienced his last bit of public acknowledgment through the rather odd channel of an Australian cultural studies journal, where his oral history is recorded (Anonymous 2000).[28]

On stage, behind the microphone, in the public square—and, it would appear, in the more private quarters of their imaginations—Musa Maruf and Mzee Mombasa each played with the relationship between Swahiliness and Indianness. This play was entertaining for Swahili-speaking Muslim audiences, but also thought provoking. But this should not be surprising, as a clown often exceeds his ostensible role as mere entertainer, becoming a kind of cultural critic working through an embodied methodology, "a rogue who dons the mask of a fool in order to motivate distortions and shufflings of languages and labels" (Bakhtin 1981, 404–5).

THE RESONANCE OF INDIANNESS

The work of the Indian taarab clown accrues particular meanings for Swahili-speaking Muslim listeners on the Kenyan coast because of the enigmatic status of Indian identity in coastal Swahili society. While members of coastal Swahili society have at their disposal a range of historically constituted ideas about what it means for a person to be at once "Swahili" and "Arab," the same cannot be said for what it means to be at once "Swahili" and "Indian." To be sure, there is no shortage of opinions on the matter on the Kenyan coast. But one cannot identify any that are close to universally shared. The late anthropologist John Middleton, relying (perhaps a bit uncritically) on input from Swahili patricians, stated categorically, "Indians are never counted as 'Swahili'" (Middleton 1992, 13). To the extent that this represents a dominant opinion among self-described "Swahili" on the Kenyan coast—and I'm not sure that it does—it sits in an uneasy relationship with the general understanding that many "Swahili" individuals and clans have Indian ancestry. The same interlocutors who informed Middleton that "Indians are never counted as Swahili" surely knew of the Bhalo clan, which has given coastal society some of its most famous "Swahili" men, including Juma Bhalo and Ahmad Nassir. As part of the larger Badala community of the Kenyan coast, members of the Bhalo clan trace their roots to Gujarat (Salvadori 1989, 194). They are "Swahili," but also, as one of my interlocutors in Mombasa put it, "in some way part Indian." By drawing attention to the strangeness of an Indian voice emanating from a Swahili mouth, Indian taarab clowns bring to the surface the enigma of Indian identity in coastal Swahili society.

The inherent reflexivity of Indian taarab clowns' performances was amplified

Indian Taarab

during Indian taarab's heyday by the genre's literal and figurative resonance within the *casbah*-like Swahili neighborhoods of the Kenyan coast. Indian identity holds the same enigmatic status in these concrete spaces as it does in the abstract space of Swahili ethnicity. In the Swahili stone towns of Mombasa, Malindi, and Lamu one cannot escape the Indian decor, fashion, and cuisine that have been integral to Swahili material culture ever since the coast's Arab suzerains turned them into signs of aristocratic taste in the late nineteenth century (Allen 1981, 222; Prestholdt 2008, 78–85). And yet, the places themselves are never referred to as "Indian." They are "Swahili" or "Arab" places that just happen to be infused with Indian sights, smells, and sounds.

As I adumbrated in the introduction, Swahili speakers on the Kenyan coast often employ the spatial schema of "Swahili-space" (*uswahili*) to make sense of ethnic identification in coastal Swahili society. To employ a sonic metaphor, we can say that while Arabness *reverberates* in Swahili-space, revealing its various contours and edges, Indianness *resonates*, existing as a palpable yet ungrounded presence, a "sounding after an unlocatable origin" (Radano 2003, 11). "As resonance is received," writes Ronald Radano in relation to Black music in the United States, "moreover, so is it repeatedly recast, rearticulated, and heard within the social" (11). Taking inspiration from Radano's work, I suggest that Indian taarab clowns engaged in a musical poetics of Swahili identity by recasting and rearticulating the resonance of Indianness in Swahili-space. The following section examines this poetics in greater detail, by focusing on one particularly skillful and adventurous Indian taarab clown.

A HARLEQUIN POETICS

One of the most talented Indian taarab clowns was a little-known singer named Mohammed Hassan, who went by the stage name Bonzo (presumably referring to Ronald Reagan's simian co-star in the 1951 film *Bedtime for Bonzo*). I want to focus on one of Bonzo's most remarkable performances: a song titled "Sisi Isilamu" (We Muslims) (AUDIO EX. 17), recorded by my interlocutor Jamal Hafidh in 1985.[29] What makes this performance so valuable for the present discussion is the deliberateness with which it plays with and upon the genre of Indian taarab itself.

"Sisi Isilamu" uses not one, but two Hindi film songs as source material. Its buoyant refrain is based on "Door Koi Gaye" (Someone Sings in the Distance), from the 1952 film *Baiju Bawra* (dir. Vijay Bhatt). This happens to have been

FIGURE 3.4 Mohammed Hassan "Bonzo" records a comedic song before a small audience in Mombasa, ca. 1985. Photo by Jamal Hafidh Jahadhmy. Used with permission.

one of the Hindi film songs that were set with Swahili lyrics by Indian singers working with the Young India record company in the mid-twentieth century. Bonzo references this history near the end of his performance, by breaking into the refrain of the Young India version: "*Sauti yako nzuri kama santuri / Napenda nikusikie mara kwa mara*" (Your voice is as beautiful as a gramophone / I want to hear you all the time) (AUDIO EX. 18).[30] The second melody of Indian origin is a lively ditty in the Indian mode of *Bilawal* (corresponding to the Western major scale), which is used for the verses. An intervallic relationship of a fourth between the tonics of the two sections gives the song as a whole the semblance of a simple song composed in the Western tonal system.

Like the refrain, the musical material for the verse was retrieved secondhand. In this case the source was a Musa Maruf recording.[31] Thus, while it may have been perceived only by Bonzo, his band, and others close to them, "Sisi Isilamu" clearly references the role of Indians in the development of Indian taarab. Bonzo pays a peculiar homage to this history by taking on the persona of a flamboyant Indian vocalist who sings in the pidginized Swahili of an East African Indian who does not live among native Swahili speakers.[32] Adding another layer of absurdity, we quickly discern that Bonzo's fictitious persona, who sings with gusto about being Muslim, is actually Hindu (*Banyani*), when he interjects a spontaneous "*Hare Krishna*" after the first line of the first verse.

Bonzo besets his Hindu alter ego—at some point he introduces himself as "Baburao Gabbar Singh Guru," a reference to a character in the 1975 Hindi film *Sholay* (dir. Ramesh Sippy), but I will simply call him "Bonzo Banyani"—with an impossible task. Unlike "Sauti Yako Nzuri" or any of the other songs recorded by the Young India singers, "Sisi Isilamu" cannot reasonably be sung by a Banyani. In the first place, the song text is written from the point of view of a Muslim. Beyond that, the text features a multitude of words with Swahili phonemes that pose the most difficulty for Indians, many of which would be uncommon for any Hindu to encounter in the first place since they have to do with foods eaten during the Muslim holy month of Ramadan. Despite all this, Bonzo Banyani tackles the song with gusto, seemingly unaware that he is rendering it virtually incomprehensible. The first line of the refrain, "*Sisi Waislamu tunafunga Ramadhani*" (We Muslims fast on Ramadan), comes out as "*Sisi Isilamu funga marajani*"; the second line, "*Futari ndizi kojozi na samaki mkizi*" (Breakfast of soft bananas and cuttlefish), as "*Futari jiji kojoji na samaki makiji*." Later on, Bonzo Banyani encounters his most difficult challenge when he breaks into an old Swahili children's song about a Segeju man who refuses to have his cows mix with other cows.[33] The song is completely nonsensical in the given context, but it contains the phrase "my cows," and therefore offers a perfect opportunity to underscore the two most glaring errors that Indians typically make in speaking Swahili: the velar nasal *ng'* [ŋ] in *ng'ombe*, the Swahili word for cow, becomes a simple *ng*, and the possessive modifier *wangu* becomes *zangu* (a construction that suggests the cows to be inanimate objects).

Unlike most taarab poems, "Sisi Isilamu" has little coherence on the written page. This is because the point of the song is not the text but *the text in the mouth of the singer*. Its meaning lies in what Roland Barthes terms the "diction of the language," "that apex (or depth) of production where the melody really works at the language—not at what it says, but the voluptuousness of its sounds-signifiers, its letters—where melody explores how the language works and identifies with that work" (Barthes 1977, 182).

TABLE 3.1 A broad phonetic transcription of Mohammed Hassan's vocal performance in "Sisi Isilamu," with Standard Swahili and English translations

	AS PERFORMED ("BANYANI" CHARACTER)	STANDARD SWAHILI	ENGLISH
REFRAIN	Sisi Isilamu funga marajani	Sisi Waislamu tunafunga Ramadhani	We Muslims fast on Ramadan
	Futari jiji kojoji na samaki makiji	Futari ndizi kojozi na samaki mkizi	Breakfast of soft bananas and cuttlefish
1	Wahindi wa zamani najitendekeze sana	Wahindi wa zamani wakijitendekeza sana	Indians of the past were very proud
	Kama wewe piga ngumi wao baki tajama	Kama wewe ungalipiga ngumi wao wangalibaki na kutazama	If you hit them they would just stand and stare
	Lakini Wahindi wa lewo (... Hare Krishna)	Lakini Wahindi wa leo	But the Indians today
	Kama wewe piga ngumi	Kama wewe ungepiga ngumi	If you punch them
	Wao [inaudible] tajama bali pigaji pijana	Wao hawatatazama bali wakijipigania [?]	They will fight back
2	Segeju iko gombe nami niko gombe zangu	Msegeju ana ng'ombe nami nina ng'ombe wangu	The Segeju has his cows and I have mine
	Mwambia tutanganya naye nanikataliye	Nilimwambia tuungane naye alinikatilia	I told him we should let them mingle but he refused
	Bye bye, *mein aawjo* [Hindi/Gujarati], leo naenda zangu		Bye bye, mein [Hindi, "I am leaving"] aawjo [Gujarati, "goodbye"], I'm leaving today
3	Jina langu Baburao Gabber Singi Guru		My name is Baburao Gabbar Singh Guru
	Shali, hapana sahau figili, Mosijiti Nuru (kama nakula nateuka)	Shali, usisahau figili, Msikiti Nuru (kama nakula nateuka)	Shali, don't forget [to bring] the radishes [to] Nuru Mosque (if I eat them I burp)
	Na Daku wali wa pilau (tangawiji ndani, manga manga), na machuuzi ya nguru	Na Daku wali wa pilau (tangawizi ndani, manga manga), na machuuzi ya nguru	And Daku [Ramadan midnight meal] of pilau (loaded with ginger and black pepper), and fish sauce

TABLE 3.1 *Continued*

	AS PERFORMED ("BANYANI" CHARACTER)	STANDARD SWAHILI	ENGLISH
4	Wewe [...] wachukua uji	Wewe [...] uchukue uji	You [...] take the porridge
	Gomvi, hapana leta, kwisha shiba uji	Gomvi, usilete, nimeshiba na uji	Gomvi, don't bring it, I'm already full of porridge
	Kuja hapa teja karata; karata na turufu mavi ya buji[?]	Njoo hapa, cheza karata; karata ya turufu ni mavi ya mbuzi[?]	Come and play cards; the trump card is goat[?] shit
CODA	Sauti zako nduri kama santuri	Sauti yako nzuri kama santuri	Your voice is as beautiful as a gramophone
	Napenda nizisikize mara kwa mara	Napenda nikusikie mara kwa mara	I want to listen to you all the time

In the "diction" of "Sisi Isilamu," Bonzo's ludicrous presentation of a Swahili (Mohammed Hassan) parodying a Hindu Indian (Bonzo Banyani) parodying a Muslim (the supposed composer of "Sisi Isilamu") parodying a Bollywood playback singer (the performer of the original Hindi film song) takes on a critical edge as a play on mimesis. Take the case of the letter *w* in Bonzo Banyani's declamation. Each *w* is pronounced in true Indian style as a labiodental approximant [ʋ]—that is, somewhere between a *w* and a *v*. I considered representing these sounds with the letter *v* instead of *w* in my transcription but quickly realized that this would be misleading. It would imply that Bonzo performs a vulgar parody of this phoneme. In fact, Bonzo performs the labiodental approximant perfectly, because it also exists in northern-coast Swahili dialects. He doesn't need to *imitate* this sound, just *accentuate* it, something that even Indian taarab professors do. A listener is forced to wonder whether the sounds are truly parodic. Are they "Banyani" or just "Swahili"?

Bonzo Banyani is certainly an unflattering caricature.[34] But "Sisi Isilamu" is not only—or even primarily—about East African Indians; the joke, really, is on Indian taarab and the (Swahili) people who perform and enjoy it. By masterfully layering parody on top of parody (on top of parody on top of parody . . .), Mohammed Hassan upends the genre of Indian taarab, compelling listeners to consider the nature and role of parody in this iconically Swahili art of sounding Indian.

THE INTIMACY OF INDIAN TAARAB

I have suggested that we may hear the playful performances of Indian taarab clowns as reflexive explorations of Swahili ethnicity. By placing an Indian voice at the center of Swahili-space, where Indianness already resounds, Indian taarab clowns enable and entice Swahili listeners to reflect upon their status as subjects situated in closer cultural, historical, and geographical proximity to India than other non-Indian citizens of the Kenyan nation-state. As such, Indian taarab performances may be described as articulations of "cultural intimacy," in Michael Herzfeld's (2016) sense of the "rueful self-recognition" that often lies at the heart of group identity formation in the modern world.

In line with Herzfeld's model of cultural intimacy, Indian taarab clowns foster a sense of shared sociality by trafficking in notions of cultural identity that "are considered a source of external embarrassment" (ibid., 7). This was a particularly poignant move during the 1960s and 1970s, when being Indian in Kenya came to mean being quintessentially non-African. Stereotypes of the Indian as insular, a carpetbagger, and an exploiter were part and parcel of the discourses of nation building in Kenya after independence. During the 1970s, one sociologist reported, "anti-Asian ideology is the bread and butter of many a local politician," and "the implementation of the Ugandan option [Idi Amin's expulsion of Indians] is a political possibility at any time in Kenya" (Ferudi 1974, 358).

It may seem strange that non-Indian Kenyans would embrace an imagined proximity to India and Indianness at such a precarious time for Indians in Kenya. But, of course, this proximity is more than just imagined. Part of the reflexivity of Indian taarab derives from how it reveals and explores the very real proximity and *familiarity* (a different sort of "intimacy") between Swahili and Indian peoples on the Kenyan coast. The significance of this familiarity for Swahili subjectivity on the Kenyan coast was driven home for me as I listened to Omari Swaleh al-Abdi, son of the late Indian taarab singer Swaleh al-Abdi, speak on the phone with an Indian musician with whom his father used to perform. Omari was hoping to borrow a harmonium for a recording session. To break the ice, he playfully introduced himself as the "*chokra*" of Swaleh al-Abdi. *Chokra*, a Gujarati word for "boy" and Hindi word for a "servant boy," entered the Swahili lexicon at least as early as the late nineteenth century, presumably as a result of Indians employing African boys as servants and employees (Sacleux 1939, 146). More recently, it has entered into up-country Kenyan slang as a term for a homeless child who roams the city streets committing petty crimes (Mbaabu and Nzuga 2003, 4). No self-respecting up-country Kenyan would ever refer to himself as a *chokra*. But from the mouth of a Swahili man in Mombasa (not to mention the son of an Indian taarab singer) the word finds a different resonance. Like the musical performances of his father and other Indian taarab singers, Omari's telephone performance revealed an intimate relationship with Indians and Indianness, recalling a shared Indian-Swahili experience on the periphery of the Kenyan nation.

FOUR

"Mombasa, Mother of the World"

Hadrami *Ṭarab*

September 24, 2004. Omari directed the driver of our taxi through a dark maze of narrow streets, until we reached the mouth of an alley softly thrumming with distant sounds of live music pumped through PA speakers. Stepping out of the car, I could make out the sounds of a man singing in Arabic, his tone forceful yet constricted, with subtle melodic dips at the ends of his phrases. I also heard an *'ūd* punctuating the melody and rolling along tremulously between each phrase, along with the faint jingling of a *rīq*.

I followed Omari through the darkness, into another, larger alley illuminated at the far end by floodlights aimed at a trestle with red-and-white theatrical curtains. Omari, now silhouetted in front of me, led us toward the spectacle. Before long we reached the edge of a throng of men and boys seated on straw mats. Placing our footwear in our hands, we began to make our way through like hunters through a thicket.

Eventually, we came upon an open space where men in sarongs danced with quick strides, skips, and elaborate turns. At the risk of losing Omari, I paused to take in the sight. It was something new to me. Until that point, I had only seen Muslim men on the Swahili coast dance in the context of traditional Swahili *ngoma*s, which involve highly controlled, regal or martial movements. The music was louder now, and more distinct; I could hear a polyrhythmic pattern being played on a pair of drums. The music also seemed to have greater presence. It took me a moment to realize that this was because it was coming at me from multiple directions. In addition to the speakers that were facing outward from the curtains, there were two more behind me aimed back toward them. Meanwhile, the concrete buildings lining the alleyway acted as additional sound sources, by efficiently reflecting the sounds that reached them.

Beyond the clearing, the straw mats gave way to an expanse of Persian rugs that extended onto a stage situated beneath the trestle. The musicians were seated cross-legged on the stage, soda bottles, small bundles of khat, and crumpled Kenyan shilling notes littered around them. They were still midsong when we reached them, so greetings would have to wait. The lead musician, a young man I would eventually come to know as Salim Bagmesh, was singing and playing ʿūd. He was flanked by two percussionists—one playing a rīq, the other a pair of synthetic-skin bongos propped vertically on his leg. As the rhythm rolled along, Salim and his percussionists traded short vocal phrases in a lively refrain. Omari took his place next to the bongo player, adjusted a waiting dumbek drum on his leg, and began striking low, resonant tones.

After another choral refrain, Salim let his ʿūd take over the melody. At this point, a group of men seated in a circle up against the stage began clapping in multiple, interlocking parts. At their last downbeat, Omari let out a joyful "*Aywah!*" ("Yes!" in Arabic).

The end of the song brought no cessation of sound. As Salim and Omari deliberated in Swahili about which song to perform next, the men in front of the stage yelled to each other, and over each other, with smiles on their faces. I could make out both Arabic and Swahili speech in the cacophony. One or two of the men echoed bits of the melody of song that had just ended, keeping the music alive in the night air as the musicians prepared to start up again.

During my fieldwork, I accompanied percussionist Omari Swaleh al-Abdi to a handful of musical events in Mombasa hosted by men of the local Hadrami Arab community. Most of the events were men's wedding celebrations, festive gatherings held to honor a newly married man and usher him off to consummate his marriage. Since the mid-twentieth century, these occasions have been among the most conspicuous public displays of Hadrami presence on the Kenyan coast—second only to the annual festival of *Maulidi* (the birthday of the Prophet Muhammad) on Lamu Island, which is organized annually by Hadrami religious elites. They have played an essential role in the maintenance of Hadrami identity in Mombasa, a project that seems to have grown in importance for Mombasan Hadramis as their community has become further removed from the immigrant experience. Technically speaking, the music performed at the events, typically referred to by the performers as *ṭarab* (the Arabic etymon of *taarab*), is a case of cultural *transmission* rather than *appropriation*. But it is nonetheless an essential part of the story of transoceanic musical appropriation Mombasa. During the latter half of the twentieth century, it provided a segment of Mombasa's Swahili-speaking Muslim community with a sonorous medium of collective self-reflection—just as Indian taarab and "Arab taarab" (discussed in this chapter and in chapter 5) did for other segments of the community. Moreover, as we will see, it directly influenced Arab taarab.

Though my aim is to situate Hadrami *ṭarab* in Mombasa within a genealogy of musical practices in the twentieth century, this chapter draws heavily on data from participant observation carried out in the early twenty-first century. I take it as given that the Hadrami community, Hadrami *ṭarab,* and the Hadrami men's wedding celebration in Mombasa have all changed over the years. Indeed, I reflect on the nature of those changes throughout the chapter. My intent in using a classical ethnographic approach is to enable a productive engagement with the anthropological literature on ritual and "cultural performances," particularly the writings of Victor Turner and others who have developed and refined his insights into the dynamics of "public reflexivity" (MacAloon 1984; St John 2008a; Turner 2012, 1969, 1974, 1979, 1982, 1984). Working in a Turnerian mode, I explore how the musical atmosphere of the Hadrami men's wedding celebration enables Hadrami subjects to represent and critically examine their existence on what we can call the diasporic edge of "Swahili-space."

HADRAMIS IN SWAHILI-SPACE

Hadrami Arabs comprise an "old diaspora" of the Indian Ocean region (Ho 2006; Manger 2010).[1] They began settling on the Swahili coast as early as the eleventh century CE, and arrived in especially large numbers between 1890 and 1950, enabled and encouraged by the "material and political conditions" of the *Pax Britannica* (Le Guennec-Coppens 1997, 158; Bang 2019). Because the vast majority of the immigrants were men who went on to marry local women, Hadramis on the Swahili coast have typically adopted Swahili as a first language within a generation and otherwise taken on local, "Swahili" cultural norms (Walker 2008, 49). But they have rarely been accepted as ethnically "Swahili." In part, this is because Hadramis on the Swahili coast, "especially in Mombasa," have placed a high value on "maintaining a distinct Hadrami identity" (Salim 1983, 121), even establishing a tradition of "[sending] the sons back to Hadramawt as children to learn the ways of their homeland" (Walker 2008, 49). But it is also because elite Swahili and Arabs have traditionally viewed most of them as social inferiors who exist on the outer edge of Swahili-space.

One part of the Hadrami community has always resided at the *center* of Swahili-space: Hadrami sharifs (Swahili *masharifu*, sing. *sharifu*), religious elites who are understood to be descended from the Prophet Muhammad, have been among the landed gentry of Swahili stone towns since at least the seventeenth century (Bang 2019; el-Zein 1974; Martin 1974; Pouwels 1987; Hoffman 2012).[2] While their religious and political authority in coastal Swahili society has diminished over the past century with the rise of "Islamic reformist ideologies that denounce traditional veneration of the Prophet and his descendants as heresy" (Hoffman 2012, 194; Bakari 1995b; Le Guennec-Coppens 1989, 189; 1997, 172), sharifs have nonetheless retained their position in Swahili towns and Swahili-space. Indeed, this position has been solidified with the emergence of a modern notion of Swahili ethnicity in Kenya in the postcolonial era, as it is impossible to imagine a distinct "Swahili" culture without recognizing the sharif contributions to it (Trimingham 1964, 22; Le Guennec-Coppens 1989, 191). In addition to establishing the Shāfiʿī school of Sunni Islam as the dominant form of Islam in the region, sharifs introduced sufi practices that are broadly accepted as iconic expressions of coastal Swahili culture (notwithstanding occasional arguments to the contrary by Islamic reformists [Kresse 2003, 303]) and the *buibui* veil that has been adopted as the traditional form of sartorial purdah among Swahili women (Allen 1981, 299). Sharifs were also among the key figures in the development of Swahili poetry as a "scriptural" form (Vierke 2016, 227; Martin 1974, 383; Allen 1977, 15).

But sharifs have not been the only Hadramis to immigrate to the Swahili coast. As historian Randall Pouwels (1987) writes, Hadramis who arrived on the Swahili coast "in greatest numbers and who had the greatest effect on coastal society and economy" during the influx of Hadramis in the late nineteenth and early twentieth centuries "were the peasants (*ḍaʿīf* and *maskīn*), artisans, and merchants" (112). Newly arrived Hadrami peasants were "despised [by elites] for their lowly occupations, such as water carriers" (ibid., 112; Salim 1983, 141). The artisans and merchants enjoyed somewhat greater respect, but were similarly excluded from elite Swahili society (Pouwels 1987, 113; el-Zein 1974, 92–93). Only the unmarried women among these groups (which is to say, daughters, since unmarried adult women would not have been among the initial arrivals) could hope to elevate themselves through marriage, due to the strong predilection for hypergamy among Swahili patricians and elite Arabs.[3] Broadly speaking, then, Hadrami immigrants to the cities of the Swahili coast during the late nineteenth and early twentieth centuries found themselves divided into two categories: sharifs who could claim membership in elite Swahili society, and economic migrants who were "assigned low status within the Swahili social hierarchy" (Beckerleg 2009, 293). The latter were situated outside or on the edge of Swahili-space, just as they were situated in a more literal sense outside or on the edge of Swahili stone towns, in places like the *majengo* settlements that were set up to house poor laborers in Mombasa, or Bondeni, a residential neighborhood on the northwest border of Mombasa Old Town (el-Zein 1974, 15; Fuglesang 1994, 68; Sheriff 1987, 149; Le Guennec-Coppens 1997, 168; Salim 1983, 93; Strobel 1975, 37).

To be sure, there were some non-sharif Hadrami immigrants who managed to insinuate themselves into elite Swahili society as elite "Arabs." This would have been easiest to achieve for non-sharif Hadramis of high social standing, namely, other religious elites (*masheikh*) or "tribespeople" (*makabila*, from the Arabic *qabā'il*).[4] But the divide between the sharifs and the rest of the Hadrami community was well defined in urban spaces of the Swahili coast, to the point of being ethnically marked: whereas the sharifs were referred to as "Arabs" (*Waarabu*), other Hadramis were called "*Washihiri*" (sing. *Mshihiri*), meaning people from the southern Yemeni port of Shihr (Le Guennec-Coppens 1989, 186; Salim 1976, 78).[5] The *Shihiri* ethnonym fell out of use by the late twentieth century. But many coastal Swahili speakers have continued to mark the distinction between sharifs and other Hadramis in their speech, by reserving the "Arab" moniker only for the former group and referring to the latter only as "Hadrami" (*Wahadhrami*). During my fieldwork in Mombasa in the first decade of the twenty-first century, all of my Arab, Swahili, and Hadrami interlocutors observed this rule, only referring to Hadramis as "Arabs" in specific contexts.

The demise of the *Shihiri* epithet is testament to the economic success of Hadramis on the Swahili coast. By the mid-twentieth century, Hadramis had largely moved out of manual labor professions and into trade and retail, and some had achieved great success in business and even national politics (Le Guennec-

Coppens 1989, 189; 1997). Hadramis on the Swahili coast have succeeded, as so many immigrant communities throughout history have, by developing strong intracommunal networks of mutual investment, aid, and support. As part of this strategy, they have worked to maintain their ethnic coherence, which has meant working to remain on the *diasporic edge of Swahili-space*. Since at least the late 1960s on the Kenyan coast, the men's wedding celebration has been among the most important forms that this work has taken.

HADRAMI ṬARAB

As is common among Muslim communities of the Swahili coast and throughout the Muslim world, wedding traditions of Hadramis on the Kenyan coast involve separate celebrations for men and women. Following the custom in Hadramawt (Elsner 2002), both men's and women's celebrations among Kenyan coastal Hadramis involve music making. The Hadrami men's wedding celebration on the Kenyan coast is a joyous and raucous affair centered on the performance and enjoyment of Hadrami *ṭarab* music.

The genre that my musician-interlocutors in Mombasa referred to as "Hadrami *ṭarab*" is more precisely described as a Hadrami strand of a near century-old tradition of Yemeni popular song centered on a genre of vernacular Arabic poetry known as *ḥumaynī*.[6] Though Yemen and the Arabian Peninsula have been the primary loci of this music, the Swahili coast has also played a significant role in its development, as we will see. On both sides of the Indian Ocean, Hadrami *ṭarab* has always been a men's music, performed almost exclusively by men, and almost exclusively for men's events. Traditionally, it is performed by a small ensemble led by a singer who accompanies himself on *'ūd*, though larger ensembles are now common in southern Arabia. In terms of form, it is characterized by melodies constructed with short phrases set in a single mode, call-and-response refrains, and upbeat rhythms orchestrated with interlocking, polyrhythmic drum patterns.

Hadrami *ṭarab* first took shape during the interwar years as a "tradition of urban music" involving lute (first gambus, then *'ūd*) and violin, whose aesthetics lay "at the crossroads of many influences, from India, Africa and the Gulf" (Lambert 2002, 656). The major figure in the development of the tradition was Muhammad Juma Khan (1903–1963), aptly described by Gabriel Lavin (2017) as a "troubadour of the Indian Ocean." The son of a Punjabi military officer employed by Hadramawt's Qu'aiti Sultanate, Khan spent his formative years performing in government ensembles, one of which was an "Indian" ensemble that performed "a mix of Western European and Indian music" (ibid.). By the late 1930s, he had picked up the *ʿūd* as his primary instrument and developed a repertoire of Arabic songs. He set some of these songs in a style that combined traditional Hadrami melodic structures and rhythms (including some rhythms of East African derivation) with elements of Egyptian Arab music; and others in an "Indian style" (*lawn hindī*) akin to (Swahili) Indian taarab. By the mid-1940s, his music was in circulation throughout the Arabian Peninsula and beyond, thanks to the emergence of a dynamic recording industry in the British-controlled Yemeni port of Aden.

When Muhammad Juma Khan cut his first recordings in Aden in 1939, he solidified his distinctive brand of urban popular song as a Hadrami strand of Aden's local output, which had until then been largely dominated by urban popular song of Sanaa and Aden.[7] As musicians and record companies in Aden worked to diversify their output in response to the expansion of radio and the phonograph beyond the metropoles, this Hadrami strand evolved in tandem and dialogue with other strands of popular song from other regions of Yemen, including not only Sanaa and Aden but also Lahij and Yafi.[8] Cross-pollination of these regional "colors" of Yemeni popular song began early on, and intensified during the latter half of the twentieth century, as the poets deemphasized dialectical differences in favor of developing a unitary, "metropolitan" variety of *ḥumaynī* (Liebhaber 2011, 257; cf. Wagner 2009, 243–76).[9] Hadrami *ṭarab* is thus a decidedly cosmopolitan form, incorporating elements associated with other regions of Yemen as well as the Indian Ocean world.

The history of Hadrami *ṭarab* on the Kenyan coast stretches back to the earliest years of the genre's existence. During the first half of the twentieth century, Hadrami musicians frequently performed in coastal cities for their own events as well as for events of Swahili and Arab elites (Topp Fargion 2014, 46–47; Curtin 1984, 144). The historical record offers few details about the musics Hadramis performed on the Swahili coast prior to World War I. Certainly, much of it would have fallen into the broad category of *ngoma*, which is to say traditional dances associated with southern Arabia and/or the Swahili coast, accompanied by drumming, singing, and sometimes *zumari* (a double-reed aerophone with conical bore, similar to the Egyptian *mizmār*). But the fact that Hadramis were among the founders of the first Swahili taarab ensembles in Zanzibar (Topp Fargion 2014, 43–45) suggests that at least some of them were also performing *ḥumaynī* songs with lute and/or violin accompaniment.

By the interwar years, Hadrami *ṭarab* had found a foothold on the Swahili coast, as evidenced by Mbaruk Talsam's parodic stylization of *dān ṭarab* (see chapter 1) and the fact that Muhammad Juma Khan traveled to Mombasa to perform in the late 1930s (Lavin 2017, 16). During the 1950s, Hadrami *ṭarab* reverberated as part of the local mediascape, thanks to a regular program on Sauti ya Mvita by the station's senior Arabic producer Mahfood Bawazir (Boninger 1956). Presumably, most of the music featured on this program came out of Aden's recording industry, but some may have been locally sourced.

By the mid-1960s, Hadrami men's wedding celebrations had become a regular occurrence in Mombasa and other cities and towns of the Kenyan coast, providing a career path for local Hadrami musicians who might otherwise have confined their musical activities to evening khat chews with small groups of men. The presence of a robust local recording industry in Mombasa between the 1950s and the 1970s promoted a sense of professionalism among the Hadrami musicians who lived in and around the city, fostering the rise of a Hadrami *ṭarab* scene that remained strong into the 1980s. A fair number of Hadrami musicians who worked in Mombasa during these decades ended up relocating (or returning) to southern Arabia after cutting their teeth on the Kenyan coast. In something of a late echo of this trend, Salim Bagmesh's uncle, Awadh Bagmesh, moved to Saudi Arabia shortly before my time in Mombasa, leaving his ensemble in Salim's hands.

By the time of my fieldwork, it had been several decades since any Hadrami *ṭarab* had been recorded in Mombasa. Taking advantage of my presence and willingness to help, Salim Bagmesh's group produced an album of classic Hadrami *ṭarab* songs during my stay. The album was something of a novelty, however, mostly given away for free as a way to market the group. I engineered, mixed, and mastered it in my apartment in Old Town, using a jury-rigged setup involving a small mixing board, the preamp of my Marantz field recorder, and an Apple Powerbook running an early version of Garageband. The other recordings of local Hadrami *ṭarab* that I found during my fieldwork were all from the 1950s and 1960s.

With the assistance of Jamal Hafidh Jahadhmy, nephew to Zein l'Abdin and an avid music collector, I collected copies of around a dozen Hadrami *ṭarab* songs produced and sold in Kenya during the 1950s and the 1960s. Table 4.1 provides information for the five that I retrieved directly from the original 78s.[10] In addition to the performers' names, the song titles, and the record label information, I provide brief notes on style dictated by Dr. Muhammad Ahmed Jarhoom, an expert on Yemeni culture with whom I consulted in 2009.

TABLE 4.1 Five Hadrami *ṭarab* songs recorded in Mombasa, 1950s–1960s

	PERFORMER	SONG	RECORD INFORMATION	NOTES ON STYLE BY MUHAMMAD AHMED JARHOOM
1	Ahmad Mahfouz Bin Brek	"Bā Nuṭlub al-Mūla" (We will Beseech God)	Mzuri AM 572 sides A and B, listed on the record label as "Banatlub El-Mola" by Bin Brek	Hadrami song performed with a modified Lahiji rhythm
2	Ahmad Mahfouz Bin Brek	"Bā Sāmir al-Zayn" (I will enjoy the evening with the beautiful one)	Mzuri AM 499 sides A and B, listed as "Basamir Azzein" by A. M. Bin Brek	Hadrami style, close to the personal style of Muhammad Juma Khan
3	Yaseen Abdallah Fara	"Māl al-Gamīl Mā Luh" (What Happened to the Beautiful One?)	Mzuri AM 358 sides A and B, listed as "Mal El Gamil" by Yaseen Fara	Adeni style, close to the personal style of Ba Swayd
4	Saleh Abdulla El Antari	"Yā Munyatī" (O' Desired One)	HMV MA 241 OAF 382, listed as "Wanahibak Ya Salaam" by Saleh Abdulla El Antari	A famous song from Lahij, composed (music and words) by Prince Ahmad Fadl al-Qumindan
5	Saleh Abdulla El Antari	"Akhafu Akhaf In Dārat" (The Passage of the Days Worries Me)	HMV MA 241 OAF 383, listed as "Akhafu Akhaf Indarat" by Saleh Abdulla El Antari	Hadrami Indian style (lawn hindī); close to the personal style of Muhammad Juma Khan.

1. AUDIO EX. 19
2. AUDIO EX. 20
3. AUDIO EX. 21
4. AUDIO EX. 22
5. AUDIO EX. 23

Two stories about Hadrami *ṭarab* in the Indian Ocean world are embedded in this small sampling of songs. One is about music and mobility across the Ocean, and is told by the record containing songs 4 and 5. Unlike the other records, which were all released on the Mzuri label, this one was released on an international label (HMV) and possibly recorded in Nairobi rather than Mombasa. The artist, Saleh Abdallah El Antari (1905–1965), is one of the most famous Yemeni musicians of the twentieth century. He was neither Hadrami nor a resident of the Swahili coast, but he performed in a variety of regional styles and traveled extensively in East Africa (Lambert and Al-Akouri 2019, 67; Lambert and Mokrani 2013, 244–45). Evidently recorded during one of El Antari's East African trips, this record seems to have been intended to appeal to local Hadrami audiences. One side features an Indian-style song, whose melody was appropriated from a Hindi film song; the other a famous Lahiji song performed in an unusual, Hadrami style, with an Indian-inflected rhythm.[11] El Antari's use of Indian rhythms for both sides hints at the fact that one or more of his accompanying percussionists may have been local Indians. Even if that isn't the case, the story of this record stands as a remarkable example of the layered complexity of "the Indian Ocean as a cultural milieu" (Bose 2006, 11): a musician from northern Yemen performs in an Indian style in order to appeal to an audience from southern Yemen residing in East Africa.

The other story embedded in Table 4.1 is about the intensive dialogue between Hadrami *ṭarab* and Swahili taarab on the Kenyan coast during the last quarter of the twentieth century. It is told by the inclusion of two songs by Ahmad Mahfouz Bin Brek, one of which, "Bā Nuṭlub al-Mūla," is a paean to the Hadrami diaspora in East Africa that praises the city of Seiyun in Hadramawt and some of the places in East Africa where Hadramis have settled, from the coast of Somalia to the Rift Valley. Though he was born in Hadramawt and retired there in the early 1980s, Bin Brek's musical career on the Kenyan coast took him deep into Swahili-space. Along with his work in Hadrami *ṭarab*, he led a Swahili taarab trio in Malindi (north of Mombasa) and recorded a number of his own Swahili taarab songs for the Mzuri label in the 1960s (Graebner 2005b, 22).

Bin Brek was not the only musician involved in *ṭarab*-taarab genre crossing between the 1960s and 1980s. He was joined in this endeavor by two other *ʿūd*ist-singers, Omar Badbes and Zein l'Abdin. For decades, these three men competed with each other for work at both Hadrami men's wedding celebrations and Swahili "men's taarab" wedding occasions. The latter tradition, which we shall come to in the next chapter, is in some respects similar to the Hadrami men's wedding celebration, but more subdued and centered on the Swahili taarab subgenre of "Arab taarab." A somewhat rarer type of event for which the three men also found themselves in competition was the Hadrami-Swahili wedding, a women's or mixed-gendered celebration featuring a mix of *ṭarab* and taarab.

Zein l'Abdin is a special case among Mombasa's *ṭarab*-taarab genre crossers. Unlike Bin Brek and Badbes, he was not actually a member of the Hadrami community. He traced his lineage to a clan of Hadrami sheikhs, but his paternal ancestors had arrived on the Swahili coast prior to the Omani era, making him an "old Arab," which is to say a member of the Arab-Swahili community at the center of Swahili-space. His limited facility with the Arabic language meant that he could not compose any of his own *ṭarab* songs. Nor could he sing *ṭarab* songs as convincingly as Bin Brek or Badbes. He partially made up for these deficiencies, however, with his musical skills, including his unparalleled virtuosity on *ʿūd*. These skills earned him respect within Hadrami community, and at least one opportunity that he treasured as a crowning achievement of his career: when legendary Hadrami singer Abu Bakr Salim Balfagih (1939–2017) visited Kenya in 1986, Zein was tapped to perform with him at a concert in Mombasa sponsored by a patron from the local Hadrami community.

Zein was perhaps the only non-Hadrami musician to ever find any degree of success as Hadrami *ṭarab ʿūd*ist or singer on the Kenyan coast. But a number of non-Hadrami percussionists have performed in Hadrami *ṭarab* ensembles in Mombasa over the years. One of them was my consultant Omari Swaleh al-Abdi, who provided my entree into the world of Hadrami music culture in Mombasa. Omari, who remains active in both Hadrami *ṭarab* and Swahili taarab to this day, was one the most experienced performers of Hadrami *ṭarab* during my fieldwork. His paternal grandfather had been a native Arabic speaker, giving him about as much exposure to spoken Arabic as any Kenyan Hadrami of his generation. But he was nonetheless an outsider to the Hadrami community, something I was reminded of every time he spoke to me about "their" (i.e., the Hadramis') culture and traditions.

The participation of non-Hadrami percussionists in Hadrami *ṭarab* on the Kenyan coast has been facilitated by the similarity between the traditional rhythms of southern Yemen and those of the Swahili coast, itself a consequence of the long history of cultural exchange across the Indian Ocean. What is probably the most popular southern Yemeni rhythm today, *sharh*, has an underlying structure identical to that of traditional Swahili rhythms used in women's dances like *kumbwaya* and *chakacha* (see chapter 5, Table 5.3). That structure, described by Charles Capwell as "an ambiguous compound duple that confuses duple and triple rhythms in a constant hemiola" (Capwell 1995, 85), is often characterized by musicians in southern Yemen as being of "African" origin.[12] Indeed, it is also known in Yemen as *"sawāhilī,"* meaning "coastal" but surely also referencing exchange across the Indian Ocean.

THE HADRAMI MEN'S WEDDING CELEBRATION

A typical Hadrami men's wedding celebration on the Kenyan coast lasts late into the night and ends with the groom being sent off to consummate his marriage.

Relatively subdued at the start, it slowly builds in intensity and climaxes at the very end, offering a template for what is meant to happen afterward in the privacy of the marital bedroom. Though it may seem chaotic for those in the thick of it, the celebration's climax is highly structured. It is at this point that the event takes the form of a classic life-crisis ritual, proceeding as "a patterned process in time, the units of which are symbolic objects and serialized items of symbolic behavior" (Turner 1967, 45). Two collective symbolic acts are involved in this moment, each of which refers metonymically to the bridegroom's passage into a new stage of life. One of these acts, referred to as the *kupamba* (Swahili for "decoration"), sees the bridegroom's male peers slather jasmine-infused henna paste over his head and torso. When Omari first explained this tradition to me, he clarified that "*kupamba*" is an ironic reference to the *kupamba* rite of women's wedding celebrations on the Swahili coast, in which a bride's hands and feet are decorated with delicate designs using the same henna paste (Le Guennec-Coppens 1980; Thompson 2011, 435). In stark contrast to the women's *kupamba*, the Hadrami men's *kupamba* is something of a violent hazing. In order to keep the bridegroom from getting injured in the melee, the trays of henna paste are delivered by a procession of married women led by an imposing "auntie" capable of keeping him safe.

The intrusion of the women's procession into the space-time of the men's wedding celebration, and their eventual departure with the appropriately "decorated" bridegroom, constitutes the other collective symbolic act of the climax of the event. Whether the bride is Hadrami or Swahili, this procession typically involves the performance of *vugo*, a women's *ngoma* historically associated with the Swahili patricians but also performed by elite Arabs and Hadramis. When the women's procession arrived during the first Hadrami men's wedding I attended, Omari put his hand to his ear to signal me to listen. Through the din of the *ṭarab* music and revelry, I heard the clap of sticks striking buffalo horns, and a chorus of women's voices singing in unison with a powerful, nasal tone. These were the unmistakable sounds of *vugo*, which centers on the performance of sung poetry over a 12-beat rhythmic cycle of which the women play the first and third beats on their buffalo horns (see chapter 5). The women, all clad in black *buibui*s, paused in an adjoining alley before bringing the henna forward, allowing the sounds of their horn strikes, singing, and ululations to seep into the men's event.

Vugo processions, once commonly performed by Swahili and Arab women for weddings and other occasions, have become increasingly rare in Mombasa since the late twentieth century.[13] But even today, when a Hadrami groom's family goes through the trouble of putting on a proper men's wedding celebration, it is likely that the women will perform *vugo*, even if it means hiring specialists to help. Though it has historically been practiced by Swahili-speaking Muslims of various ethnicities and classes, *vugo* has always been most strongly associated with Swahili patricians (Hinawy 1964; Topan 1995). When they intrude upon the Hadrami men's wedding celebration, the sounds of vugo index the Swahili-space into which the groom's future progeny are, in a sense, already placed.

The Celebratory Space-time

I describe the Hadrami men's wedding celebration as a *celebration* that incorporates a "rite of passage" (Van Gennep 1960; Turner 1969), rather than the other way around, in order to keep in view the experience of all participants, not just the groom and those closest to him. From this perspective, the event comes into view as a "rite of intensification" (Chapple and Coon 1942; Burnett 1969), a ritual centered on the collective rather than the individual, which often serves in modern societies to bolster values, traditions, and images of identity that are under threat (Peña 1980). By cordoning off space and time with physical objects, sounds, and spatial practices, participants in the Kenyan Hadrami men's wedding celebration establish a resonant "time out of time" (Falassi 1987) and "space beyond space" (Beidelman 1997, 88) for "unashamed" displays of "emblems of culture" and the "plenitude" of community (Abrahams 1982, 161). This celebratory space-time privileges the collective over the individual and flattens the stratifications that exist in everyday life. It temporarily restructures—or, better, *unstructures*—social relations. Participants take up particular roles (clappers, dancers, etc.), but these roles bear no homologous relationship to social roles outside of the celebratory space-time. And when the cartons of soda bottles are passed around, no participant, not even the ethnographer, is left out. In a word, the event elicits *communitas*, a "mode of relationship" wherein individuals confront one another stripped of their everyday roles and positions (Turner 1969, 1982; E. Turner 2012).

Music—the beating heart of the Hadrami men's wedding celebration—plays a key role in activating the event's celebratory space-time and its concomitant atmosphere of communitas. "Music," as Edith Turner writes, "can be pure communitas" (Turner 2012, xi). As a "manifestation of time eventuating" (Zuckerkandl 1956, 233), musical performance, understood in the broadest sense to include dancing and other forms of musicking-in-the-moment, enacts a "vivid and continuous present" that enables shared subjective experience (Kapferer 1986, 198–99). This ecstatic quality of musical experience has been a key theme of post–World War II

Western music scholarship. In the 1950s, phenomenologists Alfred Schutz (1951) and Victor Zuckerkandl (1973) called attention to how music "draws us into time" (Zuckerkandl 1973, 253) to effect a "mutual tuning-in relationship, [an] experience of the 'we'" (Schutz 1951, 92); while Charles Seeger (1951) proposed the elaboration of a concept of "music space-time" as the key to developing a "systematic" branch of musicology. Later, ethnomusicologists integrated these perspectives as part of a turn toward music's role in "social entrainment" (Clayton et al. 2005, 18–19). Working in a Durkheimian mode, John Blacking (1983) emphasized music's propensity to engender a "bodily resonance" that amplifies "fellow feeling"; and Charles Keil and Steven Feld (1994) worked to place music's capacity for placing subjects "in the groove" at the center of an anthropology of music that could address issues of social identification and power in radically different contexts.

As Ali Jihad Racy notes, musicians and music theorists in the Arab world have long recognized the ecstatic quality of musical experience in their use of the word *ṭarab*, which denotes a psychological or emotional state brought on by listening properly to music performed in a beautiful way (Racy 2003, 194). Often glossed as "ecstasy" or "enchantment," *ṭarab* involves an out-of-timeness that "may result both from the experience of being lifted from normal temporality . . . and from being brought back into it" by the music and its occasion (Shannon 2003, 88). In many parts of the Arab world, forms of music that are oriented toward eliciting this experience are referred to generically as "*ṭarab*." Appropriately, this is how the musicians who perform at Hadrami men's wedding celebrations on the Kenyan coast refer to the Yemeni popular song they perform. In Yemen and the Arabian Gulf, the same music might be referred to as "song" (*ghīnā'*), but *ṭarab* is also used as a genre title in some contexts (e.g., *dān ṭarab*, discussed in chapter 1), and the musicians are often referred to as *muṭribs*, or purveyors of *ṭarab* (Miller 2007, 223).[14] The use of the word *ṭarab* among Hadramis on the Kenyan coast surely has something to do with the existence of a Swahili music genre by the same name (i.e., taarab). But it also reflects the particular characteristics of the music as it is experienced by participants in Hadrami men's wedding celebrations—its presence as enveloping sonic vibrations, its rhythmic intensity—and how these characteristics work to enact a suspended space-time.

The Reflexive Frame

Victor Turner famously argued that cultural performances are inherently reflexive. He viewed them as large-scale "social dramas" that exist in large part to

FIGURE 4.1 Scenes from Hadrami men's wedding celebrations in Mombasa, 2005. Top right: Salim Bagmesh performs with Omari Swaleh al-Abdi (background) and Ali Swaleh (foreground). Photos by author.

provide a social group with "a bordered space and a privileged time within which images and symbols of what has been sectioned off can be 'relived,' scrutinized, assessed, revalued, and, if need be, remodeled and rearranged" (Turner and Turner 1982, 34; Turner 1979, 468; 1984). This model has largely held up over decades of engagement, refinement, and critique by anthropologists, literary theorists, and others (St John 2008b, 18). But it remains an open question as to exactly how the ecstatic "flow experience" of communitas helps to establish a "reflexive frame." For Turner, the answer lies in the "subjunctive mood" of cultural performances, which is engendered most powerfully in the "liminal" facets of these events, such as the "phase of seclusion from the centers of daily action" that is common in most life-crisis rituals (Turner 1984, 21). Perhaps more relevant for the analysis of the Hadrami men's wedding celebration, however, is Bruce Kapferer's (1984) suggestion that cultural performances generate reflexivity by granting certain participants—or perhaps all participants, at certain moments—"the ability . . . to assume the role of audience, that is to be distanced from their

Hadrami Ṭarab

own actions and the actions of others" (187). This would seem to be especially true of celebratory rites of intensification, which typically enable participants to move in and out of a contingent space-time and engage with the same "emblems of culture" (Abrahams) from different vantage points. In the thick of a celebratory space-time, participants are liable to relate to cultural emblems in ways consistent with what Roy Rappaport (1999) calls "high-order meaning," a type of meaning(fulness) in which "the distance between signs, significata, and those for whom they are meaningful may be greatly reduced, if not annihilated," making it seem (or better, *feel*) "totally subjective," a matter of immediate affect, "a state of being" (73). But from outside or on the cusp of the celebratory space-time, the same participants may approach the same cultural emblems as objects of contemplation or discussion.

In the Hadrami men's wedding celebration, as in any celebration, the boundaries of the celebratory space-time are not coterminous with the boundaries of the event. There is always an outside, and thus a vantage point from which to contemplate the meanings and significance of the event and its component parts. This outside exists at once on the other side of a literal spatial boundary, where the event may still be seen and heard but at a remove, as well as within the space of the event, in moments when participants pull themselves out of the ongoing activity for conversation or individual introspection. In the celebrations I attended, there were always men and boys milling about beyond the straw mats. Though they may have been enjoying the music, they were beyond the boundary of the celebratory space-time, engaged in their own social interactions. Meanwhile, those seated on the outskirts of the event often seemed to be on the cusp of the celebration, fully absorbed in (entrained by) the music one moment and then involved in side conversations the next. Deeper within the space-time of the event, participants were more fully absorbed in the goings-on, but there were still side conversations and visible signs of inattention. Through this constant shifting between intensive participatory engagement and passive spectating, participants in the Hadrami men's wedding celebration achieve a balance of immersion and distance that enables and invites them to reflect on the emblems of Hadrami culture in the sounds and movements all around them.

SOUNDING DIASPORA

The "emblems of culture" in a Hadrami men's wedding celebration primarily reside in the *ṭarab* music. These emblems lend themselves to two distinct processes of collective reflexivity, which, borrowing from two separate anthropologists, I will label *diasporic calibration* and *cultural intimacy*. I borrow the notion of diasporic calibration from linguistic anthropologist Patrick Eisenlohr, who develops it in relation to a different part of the Indian Ocean world (Eisenlohr 2004). Grounded in Michael Silverstein's notion of "pragmatic calibration" (1993), the term refers to a process by which members of a diasporic community deploy indexical signs to construct a sense of "temporal equivalence" between a lived space and "a diasporic source conceived as a spatially removed homeland" (95). This process can be found in everyday contexts of communication (nostalgic talk, for example), but cultural performances provide the sort of intensive diasporic calibration that has the power to shape a durable diasporic consciousness, in the sense of shared feelings and ideas about existing and potential relationships between one's self, one's diasporic "homeland," and one's place of residence.

Hadramis on the Kenyan coast participate in a number of events rich in diasporic calibration. The most striking example is Lamu's Maulidi Festival, which is organized annually by a sharif clan on the island. The tradition has always incorporated the notion of temporal calibration with Hadramawt. Indeed, as el Zein (1974) writes, "When Ḥabib Saleḥ adopted the Maulidi [at the beginning of the twentieth century], he celebrated it on the same day and at the same time as it was celebrated in Ḥadramaut. In other words, he read the Maulidi in his mosque on the same day and at the same time as Ḥabib Ali ibn Mohammed al Ḥabshy read his Maulidi" (330). The Hadrami men's wedding celebration is another rich site of diasporic calibration, and the *ṭarab* music is what lends the vast majority of the indexical signs to the process.

The fact that they are listening to and performing the same music as their counterparts in southern Arabia makes every note of *ṭarab* a diasporic calibration for participants of a Hadrami men's wedding celebration on the Kenyan coast. Beyond the repertoire, the competences involved in playing, clapping with, singing along with, dancing to, and otherwise responding appropriately index a diasporic habitus linking enculturated bodies across the Indian Ocean. In terms of Peircian semiotic theory, such expressions of cultural competence are "dicent-indices," which "are among the most direct and convincing sign types because typically they are interpreted as being real, true, or natural" (Turino 1999, 229). Music and dance, as Thomas Turino argues, are particularly rich in dicent-indices, which is why they are so often utilized in the reproduction of cultural identity.[15] One of the most poignant moments I observed in a Hadrami men's wedding celebration in Mombasa involved a display of dicent-indices: a young boy around age five began dancing in the center of the clapping circle, to the clear delight and pride of his father and the other men. The boy's face showed signs of fatigue—he seemed even to be sleeping—but his body was performing Yemeni dance steps with a virtuosity that could put all other dancers at the event to shame.

Displays of cultural competence seem to have become more valuable to Hadramis on the Kenyan coast as the community has gained distance from the experience of immigration. This is evident in the fact that during my time in Mombasa, Zein l'Abdin was never hired to play a Hadrami men's wedding celebration, save for a guest appearance at the wedding celebration for Salim Bagmesh's brother. I was told by some members of the Hadrami community that as beautiful as Zein's playing was, his singing wasn't quite "Hadrami" enough. It seems that as time has moved on since the most recent influx of Hadrami immigrants, Hadramis who invest in live *ṭarab* for their sons' weddings have become more interested in an authentic "Hadrami" voice. In other words, Zein's "Swahili accent" has become less acceptable to members of the Hadrami community, as the community itself has, in a sense, taken on more of a Swahili accent.

The irony of Zein's exclusion from the Hadrami men's wedding circuit in the twenty-first century is that reflection on the "Swahili accent" of the local Hadrami community has been an essential aspect of the event since at least the late 1960s. Indeed, this reflection is consciously elicited through the performance of a special type of song specifically suited to the task. I call this type of *ṭarab* song the *ludic* ṭarab *song*. Ludic *ṭarab* songs are locally composed songs that employ Arabic-Swahili code mixture as a way of playing with and on the cosmopolitan experience of Hadramis on the Swahili coast. Their raison d'être would seem to be to elicit the "rueful self-recognition" that is the essence of what Herzfeld (2016) terms "cultural intimacy."

I encountered two ludic *ṭarab* songs during my time in Mombasa, both of which had been composed decades earlier. One was performed by Zein l'Abdin, to an exuberant response, when he briefly took the stage at Salim Bagmesh's brother's wedding celebration. It involves a dizzying mixture of phrases in Arabic, Swahili, Somali, Hindi, Italian, and English.[16] The other, entitled "Mombasa Umm al-Dunyā" (Mombasa, Mother of the World), was performed at every Hadrami wedding celebration I attended. Following a tradition established well before his time, Salim Bagmesh always used it to underscore the *kupamba*, the "decoration" of the groom that marks the climax of the event.

"Mombasa Umm al-Dunyā" is a Hadrami-style song written by Saleh Said Baisa, a musician who migrated to the Kenyan coast from the Hadrami city of

Al Mukalla and later moved to Jeddah, Saudi Arabia, where he died in 2006 at the age of eighty.[17] Salim told me that it was first performed at his own uncle's wedding in 1969, and thereafter became a standard part of the Hadrami wedding music repertoire in Mombasa. Perhaps unsurprisingly, it has also circulated throughout the Hadrami diaspora, such that one can find videos online of renditions by Hadrami singers in the Gulf and elsewhere.[18] Lyrically, the song is a play on a category of Hadrami song that my consultant Muhammad Jarhoom calls the "passion of place," a good example of which is Bin Brek's "Bā Nuṭlub al-Mūla."[19] It is ostensibly a paean to Mombasa, but its eponymous line, "*Mombasa umm al-dunyā*," carries a hint of irony. In referencing the popular Egyptian saying, "Egypt, mother of the world" (*Misr umm al-dunyā*), it playfully alludes to the backwater status of the Swahili coast when viewed from the Arab world.

On the surface, the verbal text of "Mombasa Umm al-Dunyā" tells a story about a *ṭarab* musician (*muṭarib*) who has a brief but successful encounter with a patron. As is common in Arabic sung poetry, all verbs are set in a "generic masculine" form that may be understood as feminine when attributed to the object of a male singers' amorous desire (Racy 2003, 150). Thus there is also a veiled suggestion of a sexual encounter, which adds a ribald element. The key feature of the poem, however, is not its narrative, but its intensive mixture of Arabic and Swahili. It employs the trope of reported speech to effect a complex interweaving of the two languages. The code mixture is fast and fluid, with few lines set wholly in either language. To a certain extent, this is normal for code mixture in *ḥumaynī* poetry, in which elements from regional dialects often show up as individual words or phrases (Wagner 2009, 36).[20] But the play of cognates in "Mombasa Umm al-Dunyā" adds another dimension to the blending of languages, making it difficult at times to sense the boundary between them. The transcription provided in Table 4.2 shows how this works. Arabic words are rendered in a broad phonemic system based on the US Library of Congress standard Romanization, while Swahili words are set in standard Swahili orthography and placed within triangle brackets. Cognates are set in bold to give a sense of how they are employed—and how they might be perceived by a listener familiar with both languages. The transcription is based on a recording of Zein l'Abdin performing the song in the early 1980s (AUDIO EX. 24) as well as a reference recording that I made of Salim Bagmesh's group performing the text as it is written in Zein's Arabic songbook. The version that Salim Bagmesh typically performed during my time in Mombasa was slightly different. Working

TABLE 4.2 Broad Phonemic Transcription and Translation of "Mombasa Umm al-Dunyā," by Saleh Said Baisa

REFRAIN	Wadān āʻlan dāna...	
	Mombasa umi *duniyā*, fihal *kher[a] ṭayyārī*	Mombasa, mother of the world; it has a lot of goodness in it.
1	Shufti zayn itmasha, rayaḥ *Mammba Ṭayyārī*	I saw the beautiful one walking, headed toward Mwembe Tayari.
2	Gultilo <jambo sana,> ya *ḥilwā* ū *sukkārī*	I told him, "Jambo sana, you are beautiful and sweet."
2 (alt. version)	Gultilo <jambo sana, ya *hali* wa sukari>	I told him "Jambo sana," with sugary sweetness.
3	Gultilo <wewe mzuri,> ya *ḥilwā* minībārī	I told him, "You are a beautiful person; your beauty is from God."
4	Gultilo *sāʻa* <moya,> sharafnā ilā dārī	I told him seven o'clock, please come to my home.
5	Gālī <kwako mapesa, mimi hapa> *ṭayyārī*	He asked me, "What do you charge? I'm ready now."
6	Gultilo <sina kwangu,> *rasilmālī* autārī	I told him, "I've no charge, my wealth is just my (oud) strings."
7	Gālī ahalan bil-muṭarib, wakhalīhā alā bārī	He told me, "Welcome ṭarab artist, and leave it to God."
8	Gālī <twende pamoya>, bīt <ndani ya gari>	He told me, "Let's go together to the house, [traveling together] in the car."
9	Baʻdil *farḥa* wirdaʼn, gultilo <haya, kwa heri>	After happiness there is a farewell; I told him "Goodbye."
10	Gālat <lini tarudi>, gultilo mānādārī	I asked him, "When should I return?" He told me, "I don't know."

with friend who was a new arrival from Hadramawt, he had altered the text a bit, making it his own.[21]

The code mixture here elicits cultural intimacy at multiple levels. In the first place, it reflects a pattern of Hadrami speech on the Kenyan coast—that of Hadrami immigrants, who still speak Arabic but find themselves in a Swahili linguistic environment. Accordingly, the Swahili phrases are set off as reported speech, giving the impression of a story being told in Hadrami Arabic about verbal interactions conducted largely in Swahili. But at the same time, the code mixture reflects *on* the experience of being Hadrami in a Swahili linguistic environment, by playing with the intimate relationship between the Swahili and Hadrami languages. Take, for example, the phrase "*sāʿa <moya>*" (seven o'clock) in line 4. In Swahili, *saa moya* literally means "hour one," referring to the first hour after either sunrise or sunset. It is thus a particularly Swahili way of telling the time. But the word *saa* is performed with a pharyngeal (*sāʿa*), a phoneme that doesn't exist in Swahili. The phrase is thus a Swahili phrase with an emergent Hadrami essence—or vice versa. Something similar happens with the word *ṭayyārī*, a Hadrami Arabic word borrowed from Swahili that is used in two different ways in the song. The Swahili word *tayari*, derived from Hindi, means "already." It is used in Hadrami Arabic primarily as a place name, in reference to the popular Swahili place name Mwembe Tayari (or "the mangoes are ready") (Al-Saqqaf 2006, 77). This is how the word is used in line 1. But in the refrain and line 5, it is used in a way that would only make sense to a Swahili speaker, despite being pronounced in Hadrami Arabic. This phonetic play, as we might call it, also occurs on a broader level throughout the song, thanks to the *dān* singing ("*wadān āʿlan dāna*") that repeats throughout. The confluence of *dān* singing and Arabic-Swahili code mixture in "Mombasa Umm al-Dunyā" juxtaposes signs of creolization with signs of cultural purity. Icons of Hadraminess keep returning, like echoes, throughout the song, but are constantly reframed with the sounds of Swahili.

The phonetic play in "Mombasa Umm al-Dunyā" and other ludic Hadrami *ṭarab* songs is not only a play of language, but also a play of *vocality*, similar to what we find in Indian taarab clowning. Indeed, just as in Indian taarab clowning, the point of "Mombasa Umm al-Dunyā" is not the text but *the text in the mouth of the singer*. This connection should not be surprising, however. Hadrami *ṭarab* and Indian taarab are linked not only by a shared history, but also by a shared structure of feeling, constituted by questions and concerns about the paradoxes of Swahili subjectivity on the Kenyan coast. As diasporants committed to maintaining diasporic connections and a diasporic identity, Hadramis have experienced and navigated these paradoxes in particular ways. But these ways may not be so far removed from those of other Swahili-speaking Muslims. After all, if we think about diaspora in its broadest sense as a matter of "dwelling-in-displacement" (Clifford 1994, 310), then all individuals and communities who inhabit Swahili-space have what James Clifford describes as "diasporic dimensions (moments, tactics, practices)," as well.

FIVE

The Musical Philosopher
Zein l'Abdin's Arab Taarab

April 9, 2005. It was after 11 p.m. by the time the first sounds rang out from the aging PA system. Zein plucked an open string on his *'ūd* as he adjusted the knobs on the small mixing board in front of his crossed legs. He was seated on a fiber mat at one end of the courtyard, flanked on both sides by his accompanying musicians, who were busy positioning their own instruments and microphones. Immediately to his left sat Sururu Yakuti, a wiry man around the same age as Zein (mid-sixties). Sururu would be playing an instrument of Zein's own design, which had been a key component of Zein's music for decades. It consisted of two metal dumbeks of different sizes, stacked one on top of the other so they can be played like a set of Arabian *bingiz* (bongos). No one had ever bothered to give this instrument a name, but I had taken to calling it the *maradufu* ("double"), to the amusement of Zein and his musicians. Complementing Sururu's percussion work would be Mohamed "Bombom" Abdalla on the *duf* (the local term for a large *rīq*). A third drum, a bass dumbek, lay on the end, for me to play when I wasn't attending to my video camera. To Zein's right was Saidi Mberera, who would be playing the *nāy*. Mberera, an Arabic speaker who had spent time working in Saudi Arabia, was no master of this difficult instrument, but he could supply the flowing, highly ornamented melodic lines that are so valued in traditional Arab music as a complement to the percussive sounds of *'ūd* and drums.

Around a dozen men were in the audience, all seated on fiber mats. Each had his own supply of stimulants laid out before him: a faggot of khat (locally called *miraa* or *mirungi*) and a bottle of Coke or Fanta. The caps of all the soda bottles had been perforated by a nail rather than being fully removed, so that the contents could only drip out slowly. The point was to lubricate mouths for khat chewing without filling up bladders.

The sound check was brief. The acoustics of the concrete courtyard were favorable, offering just enough reflection to allow all the musicians to hear each other and balance properly. Zein took on a thoughtful expression as he moved his attention from the mixing board to his weathered notebook of poems—his Swahili songbook. After flipping through a half dozen pages, he pressed the book down flat, leaned back, repositioned his plectrum with the nimble fingers of his right hand, and struck his first tones. The brief solo that followed was nothing fancy—especially not for Zein, who was known to dazzle audiences with his virtuosity—just some halting phrases in *Maqām Sīkāh*. It seemed more like an attempt to remember a lost melody. Mberera noodled around on his *nāy* as Zein proceeded, seemingly trying to get his own bearings.

After about a minute, Zein strummed a quick rhythmic figure and then immediately launched into the fully fleshed-out melody. Sururu, who had just finished a swig of water, put down his cup and slipped effortlessly into a *kumbwaya* pattern. Bombom then joined in, as well, expanding the frequency spectrum and texture of the percussion, as Zein nodded his head to cue Mberera to begin the melody again from the top. Men in the audience added yet another percussive element with their hands: some clapped a slow, steady pulse, while others clapped a syncopated rhythm connected to the *kumbwaya* pattern. The rest of the men in the audience remained respectfully quiet, their khat-fueled concentration directed solely at the music.

Finally, Zein began to sing, his midrange voice as robust and centered as always. The first phrase of the first line revealed the title of the song: "Aso Subira Hanali" (One Who Lacks Patience Had Nothing). I had spotted the poem before in Zein's Swahili songbook—one of his own compositions from the 1970s—but I hadn't yet heard it performed. Zein sang the first lines twice. The first go-around, he stumbled a bit, breaking up words in odd places. But he did so with a relaxed confidence and composure, nicely

> exhibiting the patience about which he was singing. He settled into the song just in time for the first refrain, which the other musicians and some in the audience sang with him.

The event described in this narrative is a Swahili men's wedding celebration, a tradition associated with elite Swahili-speaking Muslims of the Kenyan coast, especially those of Arab descent like Zein l'Abdin himself. Both the event and the music that Zein supplied for it were anachronisms by 2005. Rising religious conservatism on the Kenyan coast had slowly chipped away at both of them since the early 1990s, until, by the first decade of the twenty-first century, they had nearly disappeared (see chapter 6). This event, organized for the wedding of singer and political activist Habib Swaleh Ahdaly (1953–2022), a nephew of Zein's who mostly resided in the UK, was the only Swahili men's wedding celebration that Zein played during the year and a half that I spent in his orbit. All of his other performances were at cultural festivals or Arab-themed beach resorts, appropriate settings for music from a bygone era. But for much of his half-century-long career in Mombasa, Zein played multiple Swahili men's wedding celebrations per week.

The style that Zein performed at this event in 2005, and for which he became famous in the latter half of the twentieth century, is variously called "Arab taarab" (*taarab ya kiarabu*) or "men's taarab" (*taarab ya wanaume*).[1] Of course, most forms of taarab are to some extent "Arab," employing formal structures and aesthetic orientations of Arab music. Arab taarab is more robustly "Arab," however, in both its sonic form and its typical settings. That an Arab style of music would be popular among Arabs and others who value "civilized Arabness" (*ustaarabu*) is not surprising. Indeed, Arab taarab provides as good an example as any of the phenomenon that sociologist Paul Willis terms "socio-symbolic homology," by which a cultural form takes shape as a mode of group self-identification and celebration within a stratified social context (Willis 1978, 247–66; Trondman et al. 2011). But a closer listen to Zein's particular version of Arab taarab reveals a more complex relationship between musical style and social meaning. As I will describe, Zein worked closely with the renowned poet Ahmed Sheikh Nabhany (1927–2017) during the 1970s to create a style of taarab that explored, in and through musical form, the nature of *Swahili* culture and identity.

EDUCATION OF AN ARAB TAARAB MUSICIAN

Zein l'Abdin Ahmed Alamoody—often addressed and referred to using the honorific *Ustadh*—was born in 1939 in a village on Lamu Island. During the nineteenth and early twentieth centuries, Lamu's port town was an important center of commerce, Islamic learning, and arts. Though in decline by the time Zein was born, it was still a place rich with poetry and music. Zein's father and maternal uncle were both musicians. His father, who worked as a port clerk, was little more than an amateur, but his maternal uncle Seyyid Ali Basakuta was a renowned *'ūd* player and acknowledged expert on local musical traditions. Basakuta had grown up playing the *kibangala*, a local variant of the southern Arabian *gambus* lute, and then switched to *'ūd* around the year Zein was born. By that time, the sound of the *'ūd* had become familiar to local ears through the circulation of recordings of Egyptian music and Egyptian-influenced Zanzibari music (Graebner 2014, 313; 1991b).

During Zein's childhood, his father held regular gatherings with Basakuta and other local musicians. Occasionally, they were joined by musicians from Kuwait who worked aboard trading vessels that were plying the waters between the Kenyan coast and the Arabian Peninsula. Kuwaiti crews almost always included skilled musicians, as Kuwaitis considered music an integral part of seafaring (Mulaifi 2021). These musicians often took time while on shore to exchange knowledge with local musicians. According to Basakuta, it was visiting Kuwaiti musicians who initially introduced him to the *'ūd* (Askew 2000, 27).

Zein's childhood experiences at his father's musical gatherings instilled in him a desire to play music. After his father's death in 1951, Zein moved to Mombasa to live with an uncle. He attended school there until 1954, and then, as a result of family disagreements, returned to his mother on Lamu. By this point he had started on his path to becoming a musician, so the pull of the larger, more dynamic city of Mombasa was too great to resist. He moved back to Mombasa around 1956 to pursue music, carrying with him an old *'ūd* that had been circulating within his family. To pay the bills initially, he took up a day job as a hotel clerk.

Although he grew up surrounded by music and musicians, Zein was largely self-taught in music. There were no schools for musicians on the Swahili coast, and he never undertook any kind of formal apprenticeship—not even with his master-musician uncle, Basakuta. As German ethnomusicologist and taarab chronicler Werner Graebner writes, Zein "learned by seeing, listening to and asking other *ʿūd* players questions" (Graebner 1989a). In Mombasa, he "often went to the home of the tailor, Omar Awadh Ban, a well-known *ʿūd* player of the time (who recorded for the Jambo label in the late 1940s), and stayed whole nights playing and discussing music" (ibid.). But he also learned by studying recordings. The advent of consumer magnetic tape recorders in the 1960s enabled him to create a reference library for his studies, which included, as Graebner notes, "BBC Arabic music broadcasts [that] explained the various maqamat (modes)." Zein's most essential reference recordings were *ʿūd* improvisations by the legendary composer Riad al-Sunbati and famed "King of the *ʿūd*" Farid al-Atrash, two giants of the twentieth-century Cairo scene. From listening to and copying these masters, Zein internalized the workings of the Arab *Maqām* system as well as idiomatic phrasing and ornamentation on the *ʿūd*. He was especially enamored with Farid al-Atrash, whom he called his "teacher" (*mwalimu*). Zein even modeled himself personally on Farid, channeling the Syrian-Egyptian star's suave demeanor in performance and everyday life.

When Zein arrived in Mombasa, the local taarab scene was still dominated by large orchestras. In 1956, Zein joined Jauharah. But his time with them lasted for less than two years. After the Orchestra's leaders declined to include him in an historic performance for the Sultan of Zanzibar, he resigned. Next, Zein worked with Lamuan poet and musician Ali wa Lela, who had learned to play the *ʿūd* at Zein's father's house in the 1940s. It was at this point that Zein began finally to see himself as a professional musician: he quit his day job and finally acquired his own *ʿūd*, made by a local craftsman. When Ali wa Lela departed for a job in the Gulf around 1958, Zein was ready to chart his own course as a solo artist. By the early 1960s, he was leading his own group, Zein Musical Party, and had built a reputation as a major force in Mombasa taarab. He recorded his first singles in the early 1960s for the Arrow label, before establishing a relationship with Assanand & Sons and becoming a mainstay of the Mzuri catalog until the mid-1970s. From the mid-1970s on, he recorded cassette albums at Mbwana Radio Service, and at live performances. Unlike most other taarab musicians in Mombasa, he took care of his own distribution, duplicating and selling his own cassettes. He also made his own recordings at live performances.

During the 1960s and early 1970s, Zein experimented with his aesthetic approach, "flirting with various styles and ensemble sizes" (Graebner 2020, 10). For a while, he aligned himself with the Indian current of Mombasan taarab. Many of his songs used Hindi film-song melodies, and his ensemble sound, dominated by accordion and *tashkota*, had an Indian sheen. Sometimes on his

FIGURE 5.1 Zein Musical Party performs in Nyali, Mombasa, 1987; Sururu Yakuti on *maradufu* (double dumbek) and Omari Swaleh al-Abdi on *duf*.
Photo by Werner Graebner. Used with permission.

early recordings he even sang with a bit of added nasality, though he never fully embraced an Indian taarab vocal style. But by the mid-1970s, he had abandoned the Indian direction in favor of an "Arab" style centered on a "small group sound, featuring his *ʿūd* virtuosity and his own lyrical voice" (ibid.).

During his period of experimentation, Zein collaborated with other singers. From around 1971 to 1973, Zein Musical Party featured two talented singers who were just starting out in Mombasa at the time, Maulidi Juma Iha and Zuhura Swaleh. I introduced Maulidi in chapter 3. Zuhura, mentioned briefly in chapter 2, is a Muslim of Kikuyu descent who, as they say, "entered far into Swahili-space." She settled on the Kenyan coast as a newly married young woman in the early 1960s, and began her singing career during the same decade. In addition to singing with taarab groups, she recorded with other popular musicians in Nairobi, and even starred with Kenyan popular music luminary Fadhili William (of "Malaika" fame) in one of Kenya's first feature films, *Mrembo* (Beautiful, dir. Ragbir Singh and Kuljeet Pal, 1968).[2] In 1970, after separating from her husband, she moved to Mombasa.

Zein also performed on and off during the 1970s with Asha Abdo Suleiman "Malika." Malika hails from the Bajuni Islands off the coast of southern Somalia, and is of Bajuni and Barawa descent (two Swahili-speaking Muslim communities

Zein l'Abdin's Arab Taarab **117**

FIGURE 5.2 Zuhura Swaleh performs at a wedding in Mombasa, 1980s. Mohamed Kombo Bajees on tashkota. Photo by Werner Graebner. Used with permission.

historically reckoned as distinct ethnic groups). After Somalia gained independence from Italy in 1960, she moved to Mogadishu and became a regular singer for Radio Mogadishu. She began performing taarab in Somalia and on the Kenyan coast during the 1970s, developing a style grounded in traditional Bajuni rhythms and melodies. When war broke out in Somalia in the 1980s she settled in Mombasa on a more permanent basis, staying there as a precarious resident for a decade until being granted resettlement in the United States.

After departing from Zein Musical Party, Maulidi and Zuhura both founded their own groups. Maulidi established Maulidi Musical Party with Lamu-born keyboardist and tashkota player Mohamed Adio Shigoo, who was also playing with Zein Musical Party at the time; and Zuhura established Zuhura Swaleh and Party with tashkota player Mohamed Kombo. Both groups cultivated performance styles appropriate for women's wedding celebrations. Maulidi and Party crafted a danceable brand of Indian taarab. Zuhura Swaleh and Party developed a style centered on the women's *ngoma* called *chakacha* (Graebner 1991a), which became a driving force of the "Mombasa-Tanga small-group taarab style" that would ultimately lay the groundwork for the synthesizer-driven "modern taarab" of the 1990s (Graebner 2004c, 258; 2020; Askew 2000). When Malika settled in Mombasa, she took cues from both Maulidi and Zuhura, developing a *chakacha*-oriented approach that also picked up elements of Maulidi's high-energy Indian taarab style. Her musicians were all drawn from Maulidi and Party.

In light of the success of Maulidi and Zuhura, and later Malika, in the women's wedding circuit, Zein's turn toward Arab taarab may be seen as a way of focusing on a market that he was better positioned to dominate. But Zein generally described his Arab turn in a different way—as a matter of being true to his own identity. "For some time I too have sung with an Indian tone like the others," he told Werner Graebner in 1989. "But I realized it is of no use. I have my own culture, I live my traditions, it is awkward for a musician like me to follow foreign music. It does not sound good" (Graebner 1989a).[3] He put the matter to me in similar terms decades later, telling me in 2005 that he had turned to an Arab style because he had come to understand that human beings appreciate listening to music more when it is anchored in the performer's own culture.[4]

Zein may have developed this identity-focused narrative about his Arab turn partly in retrospect, through interactions with Western interlocutors committed to the idea of music as an expression of identity. After all, in addition to his interactions with ethnomusicologists in the 1980s and 1990s, he also recorded his first international release with British producer Ben Mandelson, who was partly responsible for coining the term "world music" in the 1980s (Cottrell 2010). But as we will see, Zein had been concerned with the relationship between his music and his identity before he ever met Mandelson.

MAPPING A REPERTOIRE

Stylistically, Zein's Arab taarab songs are all artistic hybrids, in Bakhtin's sense. But unlike in the work of the binti Saad collective, each of Zein's musical settings has a fairly clear stylistic orientation determined mostly by its rhythmic foundation. It is possible to divide Zein's Arab taarab repertoire into four geographically defined categories: *Egyptian* songs employ the duple-meter *maqsūm* rhythm; *Latin American* songs employ a rumba or samba rhythm, and often feature melodies that suggest harmonic motion; *Kuwaiti* songs employ the *ṣawt shāmī* rhythm, and incorporate other aspects of the Kuwaiti genre of popular song known as *ṣawt*; and *Swahili* songs are all set in one of a half-dozen or so traditional *ngoma* rhythms of the northern Kenyan coast. The *Swahili* category is the largest, accounting for over half of Zein's Arab taarab songs. The rest of the categories are fairly small in terms of the number of songs they contain, but each includes songs that Zein performed frequently and over many years. The Egyptian category includes some of Zein's most beloved songs, including "Moyo Wakupenda Hauna Subira" (The Loving Heart Has No Patience) (AUDIO EX. 25), which uses a famous melody composed by Riad al-Sunbati for Umm Kulthum;[5] and "La Waridi" (The Rose) (AUDIO EX. 26), which transforms a languid melody by Mbaruk Talsam into an upbeat refrain set to a *maqsūm* rhythm.[6] The smallest category is Kuwaiti, which includes only a few songs. It was a category of special importance for Zein, however, as I will discuss below.

Because most of Zein's Arab taarab songs fall within Swahili category, the rhythmic feel of *ngoma* provided a through line in his performances. The most common *ngoma* rhythms in Zein's Arab taarab songs—*chakacha, goma, kumbwaya,* and *vugo*—are all grounded in a 12-beat compound meter, and to varying degrees incorporate the 12-beat "timeline pattern" that has come to be known among African music specialists as the "standard pattern" for its prevalence in African and African diasporic musics (Agawu 2006).[7] Table 5.1 uses Time Unit Box System (TUBS) notation to show the basic drum melodies of the *chakacha, goma, kumbwaya,* and *vugo* rhythms, as they are generally performed by taarab percussionists in Mombasa—each set against the standard pattern.[8] The *duf* player generally plays the standard pattern on the cymbals, albeit with a high degree of variation. The pattern also structures the rhythms at a more fundamental level, shaping not only the percussion patterns and variations through which they are expressed, but also how melodies are composed and performed to them.

THE HADRAMI THREAD

Another category of songs that Zein performed during the 1970s was Hadrami *ṭarab*. Of course, *ṭarab* is its own genre—and one that Zein engaged with only as a performer, not a composer. But Zein did not always keep the two genres separate in his performances. He brought them together most intensively at what I have called Hadrami-Swahili wedding celebrations. Zein's cassette album *Zein Concerts 9*, recorded at one such event in the early 1980s, features his renditions of Abu Bakr Salim's "Hiya Hiya al-Sanīn" (These are the Years) and Saleh Said Baisa's "Mombasa Umm al-Dunyā," along with an array of Arab taarab songs falling into the Swahili, Egyptian, and Kuwaiti categories.[9]

In addition to sometimes bringing his Arab taarab into dialogue with Hadrami *ṭarab*, Zein also infused his Arab taarab with a general stylistic Hadraminess. As

TABLE 5.1 Basic drum melodies of the most common ngoma rhythms in Zein l'Abdin's Arab taarab, with standard pattern

Chakacha

	1	2	3	4	5	6	7	8	9	10	11	12
Timeline	X		X		X	X		X		X	X	
High 1		X			X			X			X	
Low 1	X		X	X			X			X	X	
High 2			X	X						X	X	
Low 2	X				X		X					

Goma

	1	2	3	4	5	6	7	8	9	10	11	12
Timeline	X		X		X	X		X		X	X	
High				(X)	X	X				(X)	X	X
Low	X						X					

Kumbwaya

	1	2	3	4	5	6	7	8	9	10	11	12
Timeline	X		X		X	X		X		X	X	
High		X	X		X	X						
Low	X						X					

Vugo

	1	2	3	4	5	6	7	8	9	10	11	12
Timeline	X		X		X	X		X		X	X	
Vugo horn	X		X									
High 1			X			X			X			
Low 1	X			X			X	X		X		
High 2					X	X	X	X				
Low 2	X		X									

much as he may have been inspired by Farid al-Atrash, his style of *ʿūd* accompaniment was actually more in line with Hadrami performance practice—rhythmic and percussive with occasional strummed chords. Additionally, his double dumbek invention, which was directly inspired by the Yemeni *bingiz*, gave the percussive foundations of his performances a texture and intensity reminiscent of Hadrami *ṭarab*.

In 2005, a group of Hadrami musicians from Yemen took pleasure in recognizing Zein's stylistic debt to Hadramawt. Members of Seiyun Popular Arts ensemble had traveled from Hadramawt to Zanzibar to perform at the Sauti za Busara (Voices of Wisdom) music festival, where Zein was also performing. Though they never got the chance to interact with Zein, they managed to catch his performance with the Zein Trio, a stripped-down ensemble that Zein often performed with in later years consisting only of him, Omari Swaleh al-Abdi on the *maradufu*, and Anasi Shembwana on *duf*. The Hadrami musicians noted that Zein had "the same percussive and highly rhythmic style of *ʿūd* playing as Yemeni musicians, and after he had finished, [they] danced for a few moments in front of the stage to show their appreciation" (Hughes-Smith 2005).

Remarkably, in all our interviews and conversations, Zein never mentioned Hadrami music as a source of influence for his Arab taarab. One deceptively obvious reason for this omission has to do with class politics. Because Zein's Hadrami ancestors were sheikhs who had arrived on the coast prior to the nineteenth century, he was, in local terms, an "Arab," and enjoyed an elevated social status relative to Hadramis. Given that his Arab turn was in part a project of self-fashioning, it is reasonable to see his downplaying of the Hadrami contributions to his music as a way of asserting his elevated social status. But what is more likely is that he was keen to stress the very real differences between his Arab taarab and that of his Hadrami competitors, Badbes and Bin Brek. Zein's experience with and commitment to Swahili music far outstripped those of Badbes and Bin Brek. This comes through when comparing how the musicians approached the task of setting Swahili words to "Arab" melodies. As John Storm Roberts (1973, 22) puts it, the Arab taarab performances of Bin Brek and Badbes "show a twisting of the Swahili to fit Arabic melody lines," whereas Zein's do not. This is because Zein always made sure his Arab taarab melodies fit with the natural prosody of their Swahili texts—even, as we will see, when those melodies were taken directly from Arab sources.

THE CONSERVATOR

Zein was an accomplished poet, and confident in his own ability to navigate what he describes in one of his poems as the "choppy waters" (*maji yakikombeni*) of the "sea of poetry composition" (*bahari ya tungu*). But he saw himself as a musician first, and enjoyed working with poems by men and women whose reputations for verbal artistry matched his own reputation as a musician.[10] None of the poets who supplied Zein with poems ever expected a share of the revenue Zein brought in by performing the works. Traditionally, a Swahili poet does not expect a monetary reward for composing. Rather than money—which, as Ahmad Nassir puts it in one of his poems, is "nothing but a flower" that gets left behind when you die (Harries 1966, 78–79)—the Swahili poet is motivated by a passion for the art as well as a desire to achieve respect and renown. Skilled performers—musicians as well as reciters—are the key to achieving the latter. Thus, many of "the best and most highly respected local poets" on the Swahili coast, including those with "regional and even international reputations," have supplied poetry to taarab musicians (Kresse 2007, 109).

Zein's first poet-collaborator was Khuleita Said Muhashamy (1950–2013), a woman from a prominent Mombasan Mazrui Arab clan who would go on to become one of the most renowned Swahili poets of her generation. Out of the first twenty-five poems in the Swahili songbook that Zein began keeping in the early 1970s, eight were Khuleita's—the same number as were written by Zein himself—and one was co-authored by Khuleita and Zein. Khuleita continued to write new poems for Zein into the 1980s, by which point she was better known as the main poet for Malika (Graebner 2020, 15). By the mid-1970s, however, Zein had also established a closer working relationship with poet, intellectual, and fellow Lamuan Ahmed Sheikh Nabhany. Zein spoke of both poets with equal reverence. But his working relationship with Nabhany was special, based on a shared artistic vision as well as a love of the literary and musical traditions of *Kiwandeo* (roughly, "Island of Pride," an old moniker for Lamu that Nabhany used in many of his poems [cf. Shariff 1985]) and the northern coast of Kenya more broadly.

Sheikh Nabhany received a traditional education in Swahili poetic composition and performance while growing up in Matondoni, a fishing village situated amid the mangrove forests of Lamu, where a contingent of the Nabhany clan of Omani Arabs have resided since the nineteenth century. He began his studies with his grandmother, Amina Abubakar Sheikh (ca. 1880–1975), who became his primary caregiver after his parents died when he was a child. "A lady of immense erudition" (Allen 1968, 114), Amina Abubakar was widely recognized as one of the finest poets on Lamu during Nabhany's youth. Nabhany's first lessons in Swahili poetry came through his exposure to her regular meetings with other female poets on the island (Vierke 2011, 397). Later, Nabhany undertook a more formal apprenticeship with two male *shaha*s, or "master poets," Abdalla Kadara and Faraj Bwana Mkuu, until he received his own certification as a *shaha* from

FIGURE 5.3 Sheikh Nabhany speaks at a workshop at the British Institute in Eastern Africa in Nairobi, 2009. Photo by Clarissa Vierke. Used with permission.

the latter upon successful completion of a public examination involving *ad hoc* composition (ibid., 399; Said 2012, 2).[11]

Nabhany moved to Mombasa in the 1960s while working as a civil servant in the office of the district commissioner. By this point he had married Khadija Husein, a talented poet in her own right who would remain at his side until her death in 2005. By the 1970s, he had begun to make a name for himself both regionally and internationally through the publication of his poems in local newspapers, journals, and books, and his involvement in international research projects and publications (Kresse 2007, 112; Vierke 2011, xvi–xvii). By the 1980s, he had made a career as a consultant for European scholars, and through this work "contributed strongly to shaping (if not constructing) academic views of the Swahili coast" (Vierke 2011, vxii).

Much of Nabhany's poetry is explicitly oriented toward documenting and preserving traditions of the Swahili coast. It has been suggested that this conservationist aspect of his output represents a Eurocentric perspective that Nabhany internalized through his collaborations with foreign scholars (Brown 1997). But two of Nabhany's later scholarly collaborators, Kai Kresse (2007, 125–131) and Clarissa Vierke (2011, xvi), have pushed back on this, describing it instead as a response to social change rooted in the Swahili poetic tradition. In any event, Nabhany's "program of conservation," as Kai Kresse (2007) calls it, found fertile ground among local intellectuals on the Swahili coast in the 1970s, particularly the Swahili nationalist scholars who were working to promote an image of the Swahili language as, in Shihabuddin Chiraghdin's words, "a dynamic, living language of dynamic, living people" (quoted in L. Chiraghdin 2018, 171).

Nabhany and Zein presumably met for the first time in the 1960s. But the two only began to work together intensively in the 1970s, after Zein's decisive turn toward Arab taarab. Nabhany's interest in collaborating with a musician of Zein's caliber followed naturally from his deep interest in Swahili traditions of oral performance. Though Nabhany never mastered any musical instrument and didn't have much of a singing voice, his knowledge of Swahili traditions of oral performance was vast. Evidence of this is available in archival materials that he left behind. Nabhany started making documentary recordings of Swahili poetry recitation and song in the mid-1960s, performing examples with assistance of his wife Khadija. His first recordings were commissioned by philologist J. W. T. Allen in 1965 (Allen 1968, 115).[12] Later, he made recordings for the UCLA Ethnomusicology Archive with the assistance of Kenyan ʿūd player and professor of medicine Alwi Shatry.[13]

Nabhany's work with Zein went beyond supplying Zein with his own poetry to set to music. He also supplied Zein with older poems from Lamu's golden age of the late nineteenth and early twentieth centuries, many of them handed down from his grandmother. Additionally, he collaborated with Zein in setting all these poems to music, offering input up to and including traditional melodies. Through this intensive collaboration, Nabhany effectively brought Zein into his program of conservation, as Zein also brought Nabhany into his program of Arab taarab.

MUSICAL PHILOSOPHIZING

The repertoire that Zein developed in collaboration with Nabhany in the 1970s—a couple dozen or so songs that he continued to perform for the remainder of his life—centers musically on a device that I will call *nostalgic pastiche*, meaning a form of appropriation and hybridization that signals a longing to return to a bygone time or place (specifically, in this case, turn-of-the-twentieth-century Lamu). Nostalgic pastiche promotes cultural conservation by reviving old expressions and texts and investing them with emotion. But at the same time, it serves as a mode of exploring—indeed, theorizing—culture, by establishing novel relations among expressions/texts and inviting a hermeneutic engagement.

Noting that poetry has historically been understood on the Swahili coast as an important medium of critical reflection, Kai Kresse (2007, 71) describes Nabhany's "program of conservation" as a mode of "philosophizing." Swahili music has not always been viewed in this same light. But a closer look at the contexts of the creation and reception of Zein's Arab taarab reveals that it was, indeed, understood as a mode of thought.

Zein's nephew Jamal Hafidh Jahadhmy provided the most detailed picture of how Nabhany and Zein carried out their work together during the 1970s. According to Jamal's account, Nabhany would bring poems to the regular men's social gatherings at Zein's home in Ingilani, a residential neighborhood on the edge of Old Town. Then, fueled by khat and Turkish coffee, Nabhany and Zein would discuss the intricacies of the poems, and work through how best to set them to music. During some of these sessions, Nabhany composed new poems on the spot. For the most part, Zein would take primary responsibility for composing the melody (*lahani*) for each setting, while Nabhany helped to advise on the rhythm and general stylistic approach (*mahadhi*).[14] But in some cases, Nabhany supplied Zein with traditional melodies.

Jamal explained all this to me as we sat huddled in conversation on the floor cushions of Zein's sitting room, at a gathering much like the ones at which Zein and Nabhany undertook their collaborations three decades earlier. The venue was different—in the intervening years, Zein had gotten divorced and moved from Ingilani to a flat on Ndia Kuu ("Main Street"), in the heart of the Old Town—and some of the accoutrements of media consumption had changed—there was now a television and DVD player, but no more reel-to-reel tape player—but everything else was much the same, down to the viscous Turkish coffee that Jamal and I drank as we talked. I had become a regular participant at Zein's evening conclaves soon after my arrival in Mombasa, and remained one throughout my time there. Sometimes I would show up early, before evening prayers, to have an *'ūd* lesson with Zein and then take him out to dinner at the local Swahili restaurant, Island Dishes; at other times, I would come after dark like every other attendee, greet everyone present, remove my shoes, find a cushion on the floor to sit on, and join in whatever conversation or activity was happening.

Those of us who regularly attended Zein's gatherings referred to them as Zein's *maskani*. This word, derived from Arabic, literally means "dwelling place" (TUKI

2001, 187). But Swahili speakers on the Kenyan coast mostly use it to describe a particular type of men's social gathering as well as the locality where such a gathering regularly occurs. Generally speaking, what constitutes a *maskani* is talk, from informal conversation to formal lectures and debates (Kresse 2007, 72). In this sense, it serves as a synonym for *baraza*, another Arabic-derived Swahili term referring to a time, place, and situation of homosocial conversation. In his *Philosophising in Mombasa* (ibid.), Kai Kresse describes how *maskani*s and *baraza*s are integrated into the rhythm of everyday life in Mombasa Old Town:

> Every evening, groups of younger and older men meet up, sitting on wooden benches around a coffee-seller in the street, in or next to a *hoteli* (tea-house or cafe), or on the stone benches outside a house or mosque. They meet mostly according to age groups, preferably before sunset, that is before *magharibi*-prayers, and after around eight p.m. after *isha*-prayers. This is a more or less regular daily practice of exchanging the news of the day (local, national and global), discussing and interpreting them, and reflecting upon them. It is also, of course, recreational chatting. (72)

Mombasa Old Town's "*baraza* culture," as Kresse calls it, has nurtured many local intellectuals, including some who have achieved international renown as poets and/or scholars despite having had very little formal schooling. Kresse focuses on two such men in his book, both of whom resided in the same Kibokoni section of Old Town that Zein also called home during my fieldwork. As it happens, both were renowned poets who wrote for taarab singers: Ahmad Nassir Juma Bhalo (see chapter 3) and Nabhany.

Zein's *maskani* deserves to be understood as part of the broader *baraza* culture of Mombasa Old Town. But it was not exactly like other *baraza*s that Kresse describes. Zein's regular guests marked this difference by only ever referring to it as a "*maskani*," and never a "*baraza*." While *the two words* are often used as synonyms, they carry different connotations. *Baraza*, which derives from an Arabic word for "platform" or "protrusion" (Loimeier 2007, 19), is the older and more widespread term. It is used not only on the Swahili coast, but also up-country to refer to official functions involving discourse and debate among experts. Its primary meaning—which coastal Swahili speakers generally know, but up-country East Africans may not—is a stone bench built into the front entryway of a traditional Swahili patrician house. Swahili patricians have historically used these structures as spaces for men to meet and converse. *Maskani*, meanwhile, seems to have originated as an ironic reference to socialist Tanzania's official "*maskani*s," which were huts placed in every locality to be used for party meetings (Kresse 2007, 256n6). It thus carries a connotation of informality, akin to the English "hangout," whereas *baraza* is more like "salon."

For Zein and his circle of male family and friends, a *maskani* was a meeting over coffee and khat that could involve serious conversation but more often centered on relaxation and enjoyment through media consumption and musical performance. If, as Roman Loimeier (2007) suggests, the *baraza* finds an analog in the Gulf Arab institution of the *majlīs*, then Zein's *maskani* was like the "music *dīwāniyya*" of Kuwait, a special type of men's *majlīs* oriented around music making. This analogy is apt, both because Kuwaiti music *dīwāniyya*s have come to serve as important institutions for conserving cultural traditions (Mulaifi 2021; Alsalhi 2016, 36–37; Lavin 2016), and because Kuwaiti sounds played a special role in Zein's work with Nabhany (as I will discuss below).[15]

The men who had the good fortune to be present at Zein's *maskani* when Nabhany and Zein undertook their collaborative work would certainly have heard Zein's musical poetics as thought*ful*. Those who paid close enough attention might have also heard it as *thought*, philosophy (*falsafa*). The same goes for many who encountered Zein's music outside of his *maskani*, because Zein's primary performance context at the time—the Swahili men's wedding celebration—is the epitome of a contemplative taarab context, where participants are expected to attend to, appreciate, and reflect upon the music.

Though it may involve merriment, conversation, singing, clapping, and even a bit of Yemeni-style dancing, a Swahili men's wedding celebration is a space for stimulant-fueled, active engagement with the highly metaphorical language of taarab poetry and the music by which it is delivered. The emphasis on nostalgia in Zein's aesthetic approach would have served to enhance the framing of his music as an object of contemplation. On the Swahili coast, nostalgia has long been associated with philosophical reflection. The most famous work of coastal Swahili philosophy is arguably the early nineteenth-century poem *Al Inkishafi*, which illustrates the decline of a once-great Swahili city state in order to "pose and examine the essence of life and how [one] should relate to the world and especially its deceptive material aspects" (Mberia 2015, 100; see also Kresse 2007, 71). Suffused with images of ruin, abandonment, and loss, *Inkishafi* casts a critical light on the world by evoking what sociologist Bryan Turner describes as the "paradigm of nostalgia" that lies at the heart of Abrahamic theologies, centered on "the sense of historical decline and loss, involving a departure from some golden age of 'homefulness'" (Turner 1987, 150). The core audience for

FIGURE 5.4 The musical philosopher at home. Two photographs of Zein l'Abdin taken three decades apart. Left: Zein looks through his Swahili songbook at his home in Mombasa Old Town, 2005 (photo by author). Right: Zein rehearses at his home in Ingilani, Mombasa, ca. 1970s (Werner Graebner collection, used with permission).

Zein's music during the 1970s was comprised of men who had learned to recite *Inkishafi*, among other canonical Swahili poems, as part of their intellectual and moral education. For them, Zein's musical nostalgia would have borne a distinct philosophical aura.

A MUSICAL POETICS OF SWAHILI CULTURE

The majority of Zein's work with Nabhany fell into two broad projects, each of which employed nostalgic pastiche in a particular way. One involved the creation of a set of stylized *vugo* songs that combined traditional melodies with old and new poems in Lamu's Kiamu Swahili dialect. I examine this project elsewhere in technical detail, considering it as a study of Swahili melody that Zein used in developing his compositional approach (Eisenberg In prep.). The other project, of more direct relevance to the present study, involved an exploration of Swahili music culture through practices of transoceanic appropriation. I doubt that Zein or Nabhany viewed this as a single project. I describe it as such here in order to draw out its connecting strand, which was an emphasis on *cultural ambiguity*.

The musical settings that Zein composed as part of what I am calling his and Nabhany's cultural ambiguity project all present musical expressions as in some way belonging to both the Arabian Peninsula and the Swahili coast. In each case, the nostalgic mood deepens the sense of ambiguity, by casting the act of appropriation as one of recovery or restoration.

Arabian Contrafacta

Two of the songs that I place within Zein and Nabhany's cultural ambiguity project may be described as examples of *contrafacta*. Zein's setting for the poem "Kamba Haipigwi Fundo" (The Rope is Not Tied) (AUDIO EX. 27) by Sharif Mohamed Saggaf takes the melody and associated instrumental figures from the popular Gulf Arab song "Shuwaykh min 'Arḍ Miknās" (A Little Sheikh from the Land of Meknes), which was made famous by Bahraini musician Ahmed al Jumairi during the 1980s.[16] "Shuwaykh" was an extremely popular song in the Gulf and Yemen, performed by many different singers. Zein would have expected his Hadrami audiences, in particular, to recognize the source of the appropriation.

Zein's other Arabian *contrafactum* is a setting for the early twentieth-century poem "Loho ya Kihindi" (The Indian Writing Tablet) (AUDIO EX. 28). Zein had at least two different settings for this poem in his repertoire. The one that is featured on his second international release, *The Swahili Song Book* (2000), is a recitational-style melody. More commonly, however, he used a classic Kuwaiti ṣawt melody that was first put on recording by Abdullatif al-Kuwaiti in 1928.[17] It wasn't just the ṣawt melody that Zein borrowed for this setting, but also the ṣawt form, including the coda section (*tawshīha*) and the appropriate rhythm (ṣawt shāmī, which Zein referred to simply as "Kuwaiti"; see Table 5.2). He also adopted the forceful styles of vocal delivery and 'ūd picking that mark traditional ṣawt.

Unlike a typical Indian taarab *contrafactum*, Zein's Arabian *contrafacta* do not feature lyrics specially crafted for the melodies. In both cases, the appropriated melodies were already well structured for taarab poetry, with eight-note phrases that provide excellent vehicles for the eight-syllable lines found in the most common variants of the *nyimbo* ("song") form typically used in taarab (Knappert 1977; Shariff 1988, 45–49). In his performances, Zein worked to make sensible

TABLE 5.2 Basic drum melody of "Kuwaiti" (ṣawt shāmī)

	1	2	3	4	5	6	7	8
High				X				X
Low	X					X		

the naturalness of the fit between the Arabian melodies and Swahili words. This is most audible in his recorded performance of "Loho ya Kihindi," in which he blends Swahiliness and Kuwaitiness at the level of "diction," in Roland Barthes's sense of the "apex (or... depth) of production where the melody really works at the language—not at what it says, but the voluptuousness of its sounds-signifiers, of its letters—where melody explores how the language works and identifies with that work" (Barthes 1977, 182–83).

Emulating how the poem was likely performed on Lamu in the nineteenth century, Zein sings "Loho ya Kindi" with a mixture of Kiamu pronunciation (executed as only a native speaker can) and Arabic (or Arabicized) pronunciation. Take, for example, the second stanza of the poem, which is rendered in Standard Swahili and (rather freely) translated by Jan Knappert (1979, 40) as follows:

> *Yameningia moyoni* (It has entered my heart)
> *kwa sahihi ya aini* (forsooth, oh pupil of my eye,)
> *kana wanja wa machoni* (you are like cool antimony.)

Each line of Zein's rendering is different than Knappert's Standard Swahili version, but the most significant differences are in the phrases *"sahihi ya aini"* (the truest kind) and *"wanja wa machoni"* (field of vision). Zein performs the former in an Arabic[ized] manner as ṣaḥīḥī lī-'aīnī, using emphatic and pharyngeal phonemes that don't exist in Standard Swahili; and the latter with proper Kiamu pronunciation as *wanḍa wa maṭoni*, using dental phonemes in place of the postalveolar affricates that are more common in Standard Swahili.

The Kuwaiti Sounds of Swahili Streets

"Loho ya Kihindi" is just one example of what I referred to earlier as Zein's Kuwaiti style. All the songs that fall within this category are grounded in the style of ṣawt, a genre of urban art song from Kuwait that Zein referred to simply as "Kuwaiti." Zein had a passion for ṣawt, which grew out of his early exposure to the genre at his father's *maskani*. In our interviews, he described ṣawt—or "Kuwaiti"—as a major source of inspiration for his musical career. Once, he even called it his favorite type of music. But his uses of ṣawt in his work with Sheikh Nabhany were always about more than the pleasure of performing in a beloved idiom. They were also excursions into history.

Ṣawt originated in the nineteenth century as a cosmopolitan genre performed not only in urban salons of the Arabian Peninsula but also "alongside the dominant sea music on the trading boats connecting Kuwait" to India and East Africa (Killius 2017). Zein knew this history well, having learned it from his uncle Basakuta, the "walking thesaurus of Swahili musical traditions" (Graebner 1989a) whose close engagements with Kuwaiti musicians I noted earlier. In the 1980s, Basakuta related to Werner Graebner that musicians and audiences in 1930s Lamu had realized that dances from the Arabian peninsula "[fit] incredibly well with ngoma rhythms from Lamu," and hypothesized that this likely spoke to "an earlier link between these two traditions" (ibid.). The "Kuwaiti" settings that Zein composed (or appropriated) in collaboration with Nabhany constitute explorations of Baskuta's hypothesis. All of them use poems from Lamu's golden age, which would have been the same era when Kuwaiti sailors first started bringing ṣawt to the Kenyan coast.

Zein's setting for Mohamed Kijuma's poem "Maneno Tisiya" (Nine Words) (AUDIO EX. 29), is a special case among his Kuwaiti musical settings.[18] In the first place, it features an original melody, composed in a melodic mode that Zein considered to be distinctly "Swahili." As it is used in "Maneno Tisiya," this mode is best described as *Maqām Bayātī* on A. But Zein called it *Swaba*, suggesting that it was a version of the Arab *Maqām Ṣabā* rather than *Maqām Bayātī*. In truth, nothing in the melody suggests *Maqām Ṣabā* as that mode is normally conceptualized in Arab music traditions (certainly not in Egyptian/Levantine music, which was the main source of Zein's *maqām* terminology). Exactly what Zein meant by *Swaba* in formal terms remains a mystery to me, because he also applied the label to an entirely different mode that he used in other compositions. That other version of *Swaba* is closer to *Maqām Sīkāh*, which is distinct from both *Maqām Bayātī* and *Maqām Ṣaba*.[19] What is clear is that Zein heard something essentially "Swahili" in both of his *Swaba* variants. Whether that Swahili element can be identified at the level of form is an open question. But a *maqām* is ultimately about more than just notes and how they are organized. It is possible that what Zein heard in his *Swaba* variants relates to broader aesthetic, or possibly even metaphysical, ideas.

The use of a distinctly "Swahili" melodic mode is just the start of how Zein worked to evoke cultural ambiguity in his performances of "Maneno Tisiya." As documented in the liner notes for his 1989 international release (Graebner 1989a), Zein often chose to describe the rhythm of "Maneno Tisiya" not as *ṣawt shāmī*, but as *twari la ndia* ("drum of the street"), a patrician men's *ngoma* closely related to *diriji* (see chapter 2). In other words, he used his rigorously "Swahili" setting of "Maneno Tisiya" to make a specific historical claim: that the rhythm of *twari la ndia* (or one of them, at least) was exactly the same as *ṣawt shāmī*. It is difficult to know whether Zein was correct on this point, as *twari la ndia* has not been performed for many decades. But it does seem plausible, given that the *diriji* performances aired on Sauti ya Mvita in the early 1950s feature spacious rhythms structured in 8-beat cycles—not unlike *ṣawt shāmī*. In any event, in the times and places when Zein chose to communicate this to his audience, he opened up a way of hearing Kuwaiti rhythm as an icon of Swahili urban space and urbanity (*utamaduni*).

Compounding Culture

As mentioned in chapter 4, the compound-meter rhythms of Swahili *ngoma* are structurally similar to Hadrami rhythms that are known to be of African origin. The most striking connection between the two domains is that between the Swahili *chakacha* rhythm and the Hadrami *sharh* rhythm (also called *sawāhilī*). While the basic drum melodies of these two rhythms are not exactly the same, they are played with the same polyrhythmic accents (Table 5.3). In a sense, the rhythms are culturally as well as metrically "compound"—at once Swahili and Hadrami. Two of the musical settings that Zein composed during the era of his collaboration with Nabhany play with this connection by setting melodies that are essentially Hadrami to a *chakacha* rhythm: Zein's setting for the late nineteenth-century Lamuan poem "Mnazi Wangu Siwati Kwa Mkoma" (I Won't Trade a Date Palm for a Doum Palm) (AUDIO EX. 30) features a melody similar to one composed in the 1940s by Hadrami *ṭarab* progenitor Muhammad Juma Khan; and his setting for his own "Mwiba wa Kujitoma" (A Thorn in the Flesh) (AUDIO EX. 31) features a melody similar to one composed by Said Marzuq (1911–?), "one of the best *dān* composers the [Hadramawt] valley had ever known" (Hassan 1998, 4–5).[20]

ARABNESS RESOUNDING

Given the long history of the Swahili coast as a contact zone, and the general understanding among its local denizens that their society is a "mixture" (*mchanganyiko*) (Ivanov 2017, 375), any conception of "Swahili culture" as something that can and should be "conserved" necessarily runs up against the paradox of "authentic hybridity" (Ballinger 2003, 245–65). Ken Walibora Waliaula (2013) argues that this paradox remains unresolved in much of the "nationalist" work in

TABLE 5.3 Comparison of the basic drum melodies of chakacha and sharh, showing corresponding accents

Chakacha

	1	2	3	4	5	6	7	8	9	10	11	12
High 1		X			X			X			X	
Low 1	X		X	X			X			X	X	
High 2			X	X					X	X		
Low 2	X				X		X					

Sharh

	1	2	3	4	5	6	7	8	9	10	11	12
High Bongo		X			X			X			X	
Bongo Snap			X			X			X			X
Low Bongo	X			X			X			X		
Low	X						X		X			X

Swahili studies, pointing to the inherent "contradiction" in "Mazrui and Shariff's ... insistence on the Swahili not being a hybrid product even as they gesture toward the flexibility of Swahili identity and admit that Swahili ethnic purity is fallacious and inconceivable" (13). As Kresse (2007, 212) suggests, Nabhany's program of conservation also fails to address the paradox, embracing instead an idea of a "pure and desirable 'Swahiliness' that is grounded in the past and still provides a normative standard for the present." But what Nabhany was unwilling or unable to accomplish in words, Zein accomplished—with Nabhany's help—in sound.

Zein's musical poetics of cultural ambiguity offers an image of Swahili culture as an emergent property of processes of appropriation and indigenization, like a sailing vessel that is unquestionably local though constructed in part from foreign materials. This is an answer to the paradox of authentic hybridity, one that may be best encapsulated by French anthropologist Jean-Loup Amselle's (1998) provocative coinage, "originary syncretism."

I suggested in chapter 3 that with respect to discourses of ethnic identification, conceptions of Arabness do not so much resonate on the Swahili coast as *reverberate*, making sensible the contours and boundaries of Swahili-space (*uswahili*). Zein's musical poetics of cultural ambiguity suggests that in Swahili *culture* (also commonly described in spatial terms as *uswahili*), Arabness does have some resonant qualities, even if it also reverberates. Phenomenologically speaking, there is actually an ambiguous middle ground between reverberation and resonance—a space of *becoming-resonance*, where reverberation coalesces into resonance and resonance carries traces of reverberation (Morris 2002). English does not provide a word for this phenomenon, but Swahili does. The Swahili verb *-vuma*, historically used in the maritime context to refer to the "roaring" of the sea near a shore or the "humming" of the wind on a boat's rigging (Prins 1965, 307), expresses the idea of sound in a liminal state between reverberation and resonance. We might say, then: Zein's musical poetics reveals how Arabness *vuma*s in Swahili culture, existing as a discernible element always ever on the cusp of becoming an essence.

SIX

Sea Change

The Twenty-First Century

Questions and anxieties about the paradoxes of Swahili subjectivity persist on the Kenyan coast to this day. It seems, however, that the sounds of other shores have become less relevant to Swahili-speaking Muslims in Mombasa as a means of making sense of them. The heyday of Indian taarab is past, and Arab taarab effectively "left the Earth," as the Swahili euphemism goes, along with Zein l'Abdin, after decades on the wane. More broadly, the contemplative approach to taarab that nurtured an appropriation-centered musical poetics of identity in Mombasa during the twentieth century has largely evaporated, and recent attempts to reconstitute it have taken a form that has not been conducive to transoceanic appropriation. This chapter briefly outlines and contextualizes these changes.

THE NEW ENVIRONMENT

In June 2005, I traveled with Mombasan taarab musician Mbaraka Ali Haji (1958–) to Kisauni, a peri-urban area on the outskirts of Mombasa, to meet with Indian taarab icon Maulidi Juma Iha. Maulidi wasn't at home when we arrived, so we waited for a while on the veranda of his home. Mbaraka studied me as I looked around at the dusty, sun-baked town. He knew that my experience of Mombasa up to that point had been one of narrow streets lined with multistory concrete buildings. After a minute or two, he interrupted my reverie. "This is where taarab is played these days" (*Hapa ndipo taarab inapochezwa siku hizi*), he said. "Places like this" (*Maeneo kama haya*).

Indeed, there were almost no live taarab performances in Mombasa Old Town during my fieldwork. Outside of Zein's performance discussed in chapter 5, the only other live taarab performance that I attended anywhere on Mombasa Island was a small one in Mwembe Tayari, a kilometer or so outside of Old Town. The group performing was Mbaraka's own Diamond Star, best known for their work with singer Sitara Bute in the 1990s. Specializing in dance-oriented taarab in the mold of Zuhura Swaleh and Party, Diamond Star were active in areas like Kisauni, but almost never performed "in town." This performance in Mwembe Tayari was an oddly sparse women's wedding celebration with little more than twenty attendees. The men who were present stood at a remove, keeping watch. It was only the dozen or so women and one *shoga* (a flamboyantly feminine man who is often in the company of women and presumed to be homosexual) who seemed to be enjoying themselves. As the other men stood silently, the women and their lone male friend raised their hands in the air and sang their favorite lines toward the sky. During the dance riffs, they tied *kanga*s around their hips to properly dance *kiuno*, the traditional hip-rotation dance associated with women's initiation *ngoma*s. The men keeping watch responded to the dancing by stiffening their backs and glancing around to make sure there were no uninvited spectators.

Even the sounds of *recorded* taarab were rarely audible in public spaces of Mombasa Old Town during my fieldwork. There were only two areas of the neighborhood where I regularly encountered them. One was near the border with the Central Business District, where a social hall nestled among ice cream shops and internet cafes regularly hosted loud wedding celebrations featuring a DJ playing recordings of Tanzanian "modern taarab," *bhangra* (South Asian diasporic youth music), and Egyptian/Lebanese pop. The other was a small alley off of Pigott Place, where the kiosks of Mbwana Radio Service and Bhalo Songs were situated.[1] Bhalo Songs was often silent in those days, as Juma Bhalo had recently entered into semiretirement and didn't always have someone to run the kiosk. But sometimes his songs were playing. The daytime soundscape in front of Mbwana's kiosk was more reliable, only going silent during calls to prayer. Half the time, however, the music they played was Giriama *ngoma* songs rather than Swahili taarab. Giriama music had become a major output for the company since the mid-1990s, thanks to Maulidi Juma Iha's connections to the Giriama community.[2]

The main reason for the demise of live taarab in Mombasa Old Town, Mbaraka argued, was "religious politics" (*siasa ya kidini*). Taarab musicians had always had to navigate the demands of some religiously conservative residents in Old

Town, he said. But in the past this had meant adhering to strict gender separation by placing the band behind a wall or curtain. In the 1990s, the sounds of the music had begun to be heard as taboo as well, because of a new "environment" (*mazingira*, literally "surroundings") wrought by the growing influence of Salafi-style Islamic reformism.

Transnational discourses of Islamic reform have had a presence on the Swahili coast since the early twentieth century (Bakari 1995b, 172–73; Kresse 2003, 2009, 2018; Mathews 2013). It was only in the 1990s, however, that Islamic reformism "gained a position of social dominance" in the region (Kresse 2003, 302). As elsewhere in the Muslim world, this change may be attributed to the simultaneous emergence of new communications media and political Islamism as a way for "deprived masses and disaffected intellectuals [to] reconstruct meaning in a global alternative to the exclusionary global order" (Castells 2010, 21–22; see also Chome 2019, 544).

The political situation in Kenya during the 1990s afforded coastal Muslims good reasons to see themselves as part of a global struggle against an "exclusionary order." Under intense pressure from local activists and international bodies, Kenya's autocratic president, Daniel Arap Moi, was slowly releasing his tight grip on the body politic, establishing a path toward a return to multiparty democracy and a liberalization of the media. At the same time, however, he and his ruling party, the Kenya African National Union (KANU), undertook various machinations to hold onto power, many involving the instrumentalization of violence (Mazrui 1997; Branch 2011, 183–216). Like other ethnic communities in the country, coastal Muslims saw the move toward multiparty democracy as an opportunity to address "colonial injustices [that] have been carried over into the post-independence era" (Bakari 1995a, 250). Their efforts to do so, however, situated them as targets of repressive tactics by KANU. The resulting tensions between coastal Muslims and the state came to a head in 1992, after the government refused to register the Mombasa-based Islamic Party of Kenya (IPK). Though IPK was not an Islamist party, it was nonetheless banned on the grounds of its religious basis.[3] The result was explosive:

> On May 19 and 20, 1992, Muslims went on a rampage in Mombasa, Kenya's second largest city. Some Muslim preachers were arrested publicly when addressing a Muslim audience. This led to the two-day Mombasa riots, where four Muslims were shot dead by the police. A young volatile and restless Muslim activist named Khalid Balala was delivering inflammatory speeches, made

possible by the new-found freedom of expression, on Muslim demands and the need for Muslims to take their destiny into their own hands. The riots and arrests led to the burning of the cars of two island K.A.N.U. Muslim politicians. (ibid.)

The IPK violence inaugurated a cycle of repressive tactics from the Kenyan government and further politicization of Islam among coastal Muslims, which only intensified after the bombing of the US embassy in Nairobi in 1998 brought the Kenyan coast within the purview of US counterterrorism activities (Prestholdt 2011). In this context, Islamic reformism on the Kenyan coast not only expanded its reach. It also took a "dogmatic turn" that transformed its historical emphasis on "reason, rationality and self-reliance . . . into an (irrational) absolutism" (Kresse 2003, 305).

Following the lead of Wahhabi reformists in Saudi Arabia (Otterbeck 2012), some reformist imams and activists on the Kenyan coast in the 1990s began to decry secular forms of entertainment, including music, as sinful. Some took direct aim at taarab (Ntarangwi 2003, 181). In rare cases, there were direct confrontations between Islamic leaders and taarab musicians, as in the following story recounted by Mwenda Ntarangwi:

> [O]n January 10, 1997 . . . [the late taarab singer] Sitara Bute was entertaining Muslims in Majengo-Msaji in Mombasa to usher in the holy month of Ramadan. This performance drew opposition from conservative Muslims. About twenty Muslim youths led by the local Imam, Sheikh Mohammed Idris, disrupted the performance amid shouts of *"takbir! takbir!* (God is great)." The youths, who had come from the nearby Sakina Mosque after *twareh* (special prayers before the beginning of Ramadan), had the music stopped, as the Imam grabbed the cordless microphone seeking to know why Muslims were enjoying music during the eve of the month of Ramadan. As the youth group got rowdy, threatening to lynch the participants if they did not stop, Sitara Bute abandoned the performance and ran off-stage. (Ntarangwi 2003, 180–81)

Mbaraka happened to be performing with Sitara Bute at the time of this incident. In one of our interviews, he clarified that the dispute had occurred because agents of Sakina Mosque were intent on substantiating the idea that Ramadan had already begun on the previous evening, as per the calendar drawn up by Wahhabists in Saudi Arabia.[4] In other words, it was part of a larger and longer-running struggle between reformists and "traditional" or "Sufi" Muslims over religious authority.[5] He also noted that the dispute did not end so quickly. The next Friday, instead of speaking on a more general, Ramadan-related topic, the preacher of Sakina Mosque delivered a sermon that used the dispute as a religious object lesson. A week later, presumably in response to Sitara's refusal to admit wrongdoing, the same or another preacher from the mosque spoke on the incident yet again. At some point, the leadership of Sakina Mosque took their argument to a second medium, distributing written pamphlets on the alleged sins of Sitara and her fellow musicians.

Mbaraka is a pious, practicing Muslim. When discussing the dispute between Sitara and Sakina Mosque, he drew my attention to the callous on his forehead, acquired through daily contact with a prayer mat. But he had no compunction about taking Sitara's side in this dispute. He opined that the real reason some Islamic leaders in Mombasa decry taarab is that they covet the "fame" (*umaarufu*) and "adulation" (*wasifu*) that taarab musicians are able to garner. While this may sound dismissive, Mbaraka did not take lightly the dangers posed by Islamic preachers (*khatibs*) who choose to target taarab musicians. These men, he explained, wield powerful "weapons" (*silaha*) in their disputes with taarab musicians: namely, the "pulpit" (*minbar*) and the authority to recite verses from the Qur'an. When combined with modern technologies of acoustic amplification, these "weapons" afford a preacher with what we might call "acoustemic authority." In Islamic practice, the space in which a preacher's voice resounds serves as an extension of the mosque, marking "a sacred enclosure, belonging to God and therefore to the whole community" (Gaffney 1994, 43; cf. Eisenberg 2010, 2013, 2019). While pious Muslims may disagree with a sermon and even voice these disagreements in appropriate fora of public discourse, they are prevented from rejecting the authority of the preacher's voice in the space and time in which it resounds. To do so is to commit a transgression against the entire community. This places taarab musicians at a serious disadvantage in disputes over the propriety of performing in certain spaces and times.

The episode involving Sakina Mosque and Sitara Bute reveals a great deal about the "environmental" change that prompted a decline in live music performance in Mombasa Old Town during the 1990s—but not directly. Sakina Mosque is not located within Old Town, and is in many ways unrepresentative of mosques in Old Town. Established in the 1930s, it is one of a number of "non-communal" Sunni mosques in the newer section of the city, whose founding was "stimulated by quite modern yearnings for pan-Muslim solidarity and alarm about the increasing permeation of society by secular values" (Berg and Walter 1968, 75). Since the 1990s, Mombasa's noncommunal mosques have been run by reformist imams and preachers (often foreign trained) who approach the Friday sermon as an instrument for direct engagement with social and political issues.[6] Mosques within Old Town have been less amenable to this sort of preaching, and so "blowups" (Göle 2002) of the sort that ensued between Sakina Mosque and Sitara Bute have been less common, or at least less heated, within the bounds of the neighborhood. But if anything, the reformist critique of secular music has had an even *stronger* resonance within Old Town. To understand why, we must return to Mbaraka's notion of the social "environment."

As I have discussed elsewhere (Eisenberg 2010, 2013, 2019), since the emergence of Mombasa as a modern port city in the early twentieth century, the neighborhood of Mombasa Old Town has been a place where an "Islamic communitarian privacy" (Ammann 2006, 98–110) is constantly produced and reproduced in a tension-filled relationship with the new part of the city—and by extension, the Kenyan state. The phenomenon of communitarian privacy in Islamic urban spaces is classically described in the scholarly literature as a function of architectural form: winding streets and mazes of courtyards make public space "defensible" (Abu-Lughod 1987, 170) by fostering multiple "[gradations of] private, semi-private and semi-public space" (Ammann 2006, 102). But as I have argued, it is also an acoustical, or *acoustemological*, phenomenon, because of the centrality of the sounded word in Islamic practice. Mombasa Old Town is every day awash with electrically amplified male voices delivering Islamic devotional and moral texts in Arabic and Swahili. Five times a day a polyphony of cantillated Arabic calls to prayer emanates from the rooftop loudspeakers of dozens of neighborhood mosques, its "soaring yet mournful, almost languid harmonic webs" (Hirschkind 2006, 124) somewhat harshened by the crackling of overstressed or substandard sound reproduction technologies. The constant rhythm of this key "sound-mark" (Schafer 1994) is further punctuated each week by the polyphony of Arabic and Swahili sermons that emanate from many of these same loudspeakers. Between these periodic sonic events, a random assemblage of radios and computer speakers in local shops and homes supply the neighborhood's private and semiprivate spaces with layers of qur'anic recitations, sermons in Arabic, Swahili and sometimes English, and religious songs in Swahili and Arabic—producing a continuous (e)merging of pious vocal performances that leave no space for secular sounds.

While there weren't any significant "blowups" around music making in

Mombasa Old Town during my fieldwork, smaller and more subtle (micro) controversies were frequent. Being a man with no direct family ties to the local community, I mostly learned about these controversies through second- and thirdhand accounts. For instance, a fellow researcher told me about an incident at a women's wedding celebration she attended in the neighborhood in which women from the groom's side of the family put a stop to the live music and demanded that all attendees spend the rest of the evening in prayer. I also heard from various interlocutors about a group of sharif women who had begun performing religious songs (*kaswida*, or "maulidi songs") at women's wedding celebrations. I sometimes heard their performances, which involved singing accompanied only by *twari* drums, at night on the streets of Old Town, reverberating out from private homes in the wealthier areas of the Kibokoni section. According to some sources, one of the most favored performers in the group set off a minor scandal by setting religious texts to well-known melodies from Tanzanian modern taarab hits. Discussion ensued among respected women of the town about whether this was proper, as listeners might enjoy the *music* of the performance at the expense of the poetry.[7]

TAARAB MODERN

Taarab still had a significant presence in Mombasa during the 1990s, but its epicenter had shifted away from the Old Town—and away from the contemplative orientation. Mwenda Ntarangwi's (2003) ethnographic study of Mombasan taarab poetry in the late 1990s describes performances by the likes of Zuhura Swaleh and Maulidi Juma Iha in areas such as Majengo (outside of Old Town) and Kisauni (outside of town altogether) for all-female or mixed-gender audiences who enjoyed the music in large part through dance.

By the time of my fieldwork, taarab in Mombasa had moved even further afield from Old Town and the contemplative orientation. Though Maulidi Juma was still actively performing, he was having a difficult time finding well-paying gigs. "Taarab doesn't pay anymore" (*Manufaa ya taarab hakuna tena*), he told Mbaraka and me when we sat down to talk in 2005. He went to on say that old taarab singers have all died poor or are still living in poverty, having nothing to show for their music careers save their stories about the past.[8] In early 2020, he repeated the same sentiment in an interview on Kenyan television, speaking openly about his own financial difficulties, and expressing regret about not having chosen a different career (NTV Kenya 2020).

The taarab groups that were finding work were those that were even more strongly dance oriented than Maulidi Musical Party, and located in areas even further out from the center of Mombasa. These groups generally aligned themselves with "modern taarab," a dance-oriented form of taarab that rose to prominence in Tanzania in the 1990s, nurtured by patronage from political parties during the country's transformation to a multiparty democracy (Askew 2002; Graebner 2004c).[9] While modern taarab exists "in different shades and hues" (Khamis 2005, 149), it has some defining features, including danceable rhythms drawn from *ngoma* and Latin American musics, synthesized string sounds and electric guitar, and synthesized trumpet solos that evoke *beni ngoma*. A large proportion of Tanzanian modern taarab centers on a style of poetry called *mipasho*, meaning "telling things openly and bluntly" (Khamis 2002, 200), which are oriented toward women's experiences and revolve around backbiting (*kusengenya*) (Topp Fargion 2014). Women in Swahili-speaking communities throughout East Africa incorporate *mipasho* taarab songs into everyday micropolitical struggles with other women, for example by playing them loudly in the home for others to hear (an especially effective strategy for a rivalry with a neighbor) or sending meaningful glances while tipping the singer at a live performance (Askew 2002).

Though heavily influenced by Tanzanian modern taarab, modern taarab in Mombasa actually grows out of the dance-oriented taarab that flourished in Mombasa and Tanga during the 1970s and 1980s (what some of have called "first modern" taarab [Graebner 2020]), and so bears its own characteristics. In addition to a reduced emphasis on *mipasho* poetry, Mombasan modern taarab is marked by the occasional use of melodies from Hindi film songs (though without the intensive stylization of Indian taarab). One of the most popular Kenyan modern taarab groups in Mombasa during my fieldwork—Silver Star Modern Taarab, founded by the poet Sheriff Maulana "Badmash"—had a few such Indian songs in their repertoire.[10]

The most lively and well-attended taarab performances I experienced in Mombasa were those of modern taarab groups in and around the area of Ukunda, about ten kilometers south of Mombasa. The attendees (and many of the musicians) at these performances were members of the predominantly Digo (Mijikenda) Muslim community of the area. Taarab has become extremely popular among Digos in both Kenya and Tanzania since the late twentieth century, as is demonstrated by the success in the mid-1990s of the Digo-language taarab song "Kumanya Digo" (To Know the Digo), recorded by Tanzania's Babloom Modern Taarab with anthropologist Kelly Askew on vocals (Askew 2002, 266). This cathection to a marked "Swahili" music is part of a broader trend among Digos and other Muslim Mijikenda in rural areas of alignment with urban Swahili culture and identity (Parkin 1985, 1989). Many rural Digos in Kenya, particularly those with social ties to Mombasa, identify as "Swahili," and so hear taarab as *their* music. Based solely on my firsthand experiences with live taarab in Mombasa in the first decade of the twenty-first century, I would find it difficult to argue with this assessment.

August 14, 2005. We alighted from the *matatu* seemingly in the middle of nowhere, and walked along winding paths through palm trees and vegetation. It was nearly pitch black. The trees were merely shadows against a dark gray sky. There were others with us, also making their way toward the event.

"*Ni haha tu*" (It's just here), assured Badmash. I initially took his use of the Digo "*haha*" in place of the Swahili "*hapa*" as a friendly jibe directed at all the Digos conversing around us. But after he had repeated the phrase a few times, it became clear that he didn't realize he was doing it. A Swahili poet of Arab descent, Badmash was very much an *Mswahili*. But his work and his life were here now, among the Digos.

The *kiwanja*, the "field" for the event, was large and well lit. The band had set up under a canvas canopy that seemed barely adequate to protect them from the immanent rain. Most of the members were busy assisting the guitarist with a repair on his instrument when we arrived. This went on for some time, despite a scolding from the patron.

Attendees arrived by the dozen. Groups of women huddled together in conversation and laughter, the reds, oranges, and yellows of their *kanga* wraps vibrant in the flood lights.

The band finally began to play around 10 p.m., striking up a *chakacha* groove with a simple melodic riff by (synthesized) strings laid over top. Three drummers—one on a drumkit, another on congas, and the third on a set of rototoms—hammered away at the groove, intent on getting the crowd to dance. The electric bassist, meanwhile, supplied a line of staccato notes that danced over the top.

Gyrating young women flooded the area under the canopy, coming within inches of the musicians. There was no need for them to get so close in order to hear the music, which was blasting from a pair of large

PA speakers. This was their way of signaling that they were dancing with and for the *music* rather than the young men in attendance. A few intrepid young men slipped into the throng at the edges.

After fifteen minutes or so, a large man stepped up to the lead microphone and began to sing in a nasal tenor. Three female singers seated alongside the instrumentalists held their mics close to their chests in anticipation of joining in on the refrain. After a few minutes, the refrain finally arrived, and the women's voices stretched out on top of the instrumental sounds.

Each song lasted for around twenty minutes, always culminating in a long, repetitive vamp to allow the dancing to continue.

The crowd got rowdier as the night wore on, much to the chagrin of Badmash, who complained about it after the evening was over. Young men started to dance up against young women suggestively. An adolescent boy got in on the act, his chest pressed against a grown woman's ample behind. Meanwhile, at the edges of the *kiwanja*, alcohol and marijuana were consumed openly, and young men and women paired off and walked together into the darkness.

The party only ended when the first hint of sunlight began peeking over the horizon. In announcing the last song, the lead singer mentioned that people have to go to work in a few hours (it was a Sunday night). The comment was met by jeers from inebriated men, one of whom yelled something in Digo that elicited peals of laughter. Badmash later told me that it was, "We have no jobs! Let the *ngoma* continue!"

HERITAGIZATION

The twenty-first century has seen an effort to revive contemplative taarab in Mombasa, but through a particular process of *heritagization*. In the broadest terms, heritagization is about transforming an object, place, or practice into an iconic representation of a cultural past. As I use the term here, it is a process that is always oriented both inward, toward a community, and outward, toward a wider world. Thus, Zein l'Abdin's Arab taarab, though understood by many during the 1970s as a representation of Swahili culture, only began to be *heritagized* after the turn of the twenty-first century, when Zein became a regular performer at official events and cultural festivals on the Swahili coast.

The twenty-first century has been an era of intensive heritagization on the

Swahili coast. State and community efforts to conserve the architecture of Swahili towns began in the 1980s (Abungu and Abungu 1998; Sheriff 2019), partly catalyzed by a growing interest in developing the tourism industry (Samuelson 2016, 236). But they began to bear fruit at the start of the new millennium: Zanzibar's Stone Town and Lamu Town were placed on UNESCO's list of World Heritage Sites in 2000 and 2001, respectively; and, in 2002, Mombasa Old Town was recognized as a "cultural treasure" by the European Union in order to direct funds for the restoration of streets and buildings.[11] At the same time, public and private efforts to develop the tourism industries in all these cities came to center on the idea of heritage, most directly through a focus on cultural festivals (Bissell 2012; Okech 2011).

Amid this ferment of heritagization, older forms of Swahili taarab have been framed as artifacts of a Swahili cultural past. This process has been most intensive on Zanzibar, where taarab featuring traditional Arab instruments has become a lynchpin of the island's local tourism industry, offered up to foreign tourists at hotels and in cultural festivals as a sonic icon of the island's history (Kirkegaard 2001; Topp Fargion 2014, 175–200; Boswell 2008, 62–68; Vander Biesen and De Beukelaer 2014). Zanzibar even saw the emergence of an educational institution with a mission to "preserve the rich musical heritage of Zanzibar" (DCMA n.d.): the Dhow Countries Music Academy (DCMA), established in 2002 with a sizable grant from the Ford Foundation (Topp Fargion 2014, 184–89).

Mombasan taarab has been heritagized at a slower pace than the taarab of Zanzibar, primarily, it would seem, because the city of Mombasa and its people have been only partially integrated into the local tourism industry. The main tourist hotels in Mombasa are beach resorts located outside of the city. To the extent that they offer a cultural experience, it is usually an Arabian fantasy (Kasfir 2004). Zein l'Abdin often performed at those hotels, but not as a purveyor of Swahili taarab. In what were probably the most surreal moments of my fieldwork, I joined Zein in performing Arab music for European guests at North Coast beach hotels. The songs we played were mostly instrumental preludes by twentieth-century Egyptian composers, which Zein called his "Arabian Nights" repertoire. At one performance, our sets were interspersed with performances by belly dancers and a group of male dancers performing a hybrid of Arabian and Punjabi traditional dance styles.

The fact that Mombasan taarab has been heritagized at all is largely due to the efforts of one man, Werner Graebner, who has worked to market the Mombasan taarab of the 1960s and 1970s to European and American audiences as "world music." In addition to producing a number of albums of Mombasan taarab featuring historical recordings as well as newly recorded music, Graebner has presented Mombasan taarab musicians in Europe and the US. He was especially active in bringing Mombasan taarab musicians abroad around the time of my fieldwork, arranging concerts abroad for Zein l'Abdin (accompanied by two percussionists) and an all-star group of his own conception called Mombasa Party, which had a rotating lineup and specialized in the style of 1960s and 1970s Mombasan taarab.

While Graebner and his collaborators within the Mombasan taarab scene have had some success in putting Mombasan taarab on the world stage, the music has remained in the shadow of Zanzibari taarab, because Zanzibar is much better known to international audiences as a site of a unique cosmopolitan culture. Mbaraka noted that when he performed in Germany with Mombasa Party, the group was introduced as "Zanzibari." While Graebner surely wasn't responsible for misrepresenting the origins of Mombasa Party, he has leaned into the association of taarab with Zanzibar in his marketing of the music abroad. A Swahili coast-oriented series that he curates for the label Buda Musique (consisting of eleven albums and two films as of this writing) is titled *Zanzibara*, in reference to historical uses of the term as a toponym for the entire coast.

The first truly local heritage taarab group in Mombasa was an offshoot of Graebner's Mombasa Party led by Mbaraka and percussionist Omari Swaleh Al-Abdi (see chapter 4). Omari initially founded the group in 2005 after he parted ways with Graebner over artistic and personal differences. But Mbaraka quickly settled into a position as a co-leader, because he held a deep interest in the idea of cultural conservation nurtured in part through interactions with Sheikh Nabhany. For a time, Mbaraka worked closely with Nabhany as a volunteer at the Swahili Cultural Centre, an NGO that was established in 1995 in partnership with the National Museums of Kenya and initially directed by Nabhany. By the time I got to know Mbaraka, he was no longer working with the Swahili Cultural Centre, but he spoke often about what he had learned from Nabhany, whom he referred to as his "teacher" (*mwalimu*).

Mbaraka and Omari first called their heritage taarab group Kite cha Pwani, or "Coastal Affection," but later changed the name to Mombasa Taarab: Sanaa ya Kale (the second part meaning "Art of the Past"). A promotional recording that I recorded for the group featured songs from the 1970s by Shani and Morning Star orchestras as well as a classic from the 1950s by Jauharah. The inclusion of a subtitle in the group's name set off by a colon signaled aspirations for a larger project to go along with the music, whether artistic, academic, or social in nature.

FIGURE 6.1 Lelele Africa, 2015. From left to right: Mwanate Kibwana (voice), Mbaraka Ali Haji (harmonium), Mohamed Adio Shigoo (tashkota), and Mohamed Awadh (violin). Photo by Patrick Ondiek. Copyright © Ketebul Music. Used with permission.

The group articulated these aspirations in the text of their 2006 promotional flyer, which was written by Omari with assistance from a native-English-speaking friend. It describes the group's mission as one of "preserving" and "reviving" the taarab of the 1960s and 1970s in order to bring "spiritual and educational benefits to our Swahili community."

Mombasa Taarab lasted only a few years, but they managed to get high-profile performances during that time at official events in the town. A successor group called Lelele Africa, led by Mbaraka, remains active as of this writing. Lelele Africa perform their own compositions as well as songs from the 1950s through the 1970s, but generally embrace the same "golden-age-of-Mombasa-taarab" style as Mombasa Party. The anchor song of their setlist is the Jauharah classic "Kasha Langu" (see chapter 2). They have been more successful than Mombasa Taarab, thanks to a relationship with the Nairobi-based production house and NGO Ketebul Music, which, among other things, led to the group being included in the performance lineup of the 2014 Smithsonian Folklife Festival in Washington, DC.[12]

Though Mombasa Taarab was a direct offshoot of Mombasa Party, neither Omari nor Mbaraka saw the project as a vehicle for performing in Europe or the US. Both men were experienced enough to know that they would need a well-connected agent like Werner Graebner to make that happen. They were, instead, focused on having a *local* impact. In this regard they were directly inspired by the example of DCMA. Both men spoke frequently about their desire to see an institution like DCMA established in Mombasa. While, to be sure, they held out hope of making money from their efforts, they rarely spoke about this as a possibility, much less a goal. Instead, they spoke passionately about the potential resonances of their ensembles in "our Swahili community." Their mission was, in a word, *revival*. Indeed, the aims they articulated in our discussions were much the same as those of other movements of musical revival around the world: "to serve as cultural opposition and as an alternative to mainstream culture, and . . . to improve existing culture" in a way that accords with local understandings of "historical value and authenticity" (Livingston 1999, 68).

At the heart of Omari and Mbaraka's taarab revivalism lay a belief that contemplative taarab needed to be maintained as a bulwark against modern taarab, which they viewed as a corrupting influence in coastal Swahili society. This came through clearly in a focus-group discussion I held with members of Mombasa Taarab before they formally broke away from Mombasa Party.[13] One of the elder members of the group, violinist and composer Seif Omar, opined that modern taarab lyrics are "shameful" (*aibu*). While the music was amenable to his ears, the lyrics were unacceptable—all just insults and backbiting (*matusi*). In the olden days, he said, there were sometimes fierce competitions between poets that were played out in poetic battles—for example, the famous battle between Bhalo and Maulidi Juma—but those poems still fell within the bounds of propriety. The other group members agreed. Putting a finer point on it, Mbaraka said that modern taarab poetry is devoid of any meaningful "message" (*ujumbe*)—exactly the opposite of traditional taarab poetry, which is *all* message. The other elder of the group, singer and tashkota player Kombo Salim Mataka Msijumu, went on to link the meaninglessness of modern taarab poetry directly to the genre's emphasis on dancing. Nobody really cares about the words, he said, because they are all just listening for a beat they can dance to. Chiming back in, Seif Omar then added that in the olden days a person who was caught dancing at a wedding would be locked up in a room until he or she settled down.

Though centered on the idea of taarab as a contemplative art, Omari and Mbaraka's taarab revivalism left little room for the appropriation-centered musical poetics of identity that I have been exploring in this book. Even the idea of taarab as a space of transoceanic connectivity did not hold much importance in their framing of the project. The idea is mentioned only briefly in the flyer, in reference to the group's "Oriental" instrumentation; and in the focus-group interview, Mbaraka minimized the significance of even this facet of the project, comparing their use of Indian and Arab instruments to the presence of Indian and Arabic loanwords in the Swahili language. In short, he embraced a conception of Swahili music culture more in line with Zuhura Swaleh's emphasis on the essential Africanness of authentic Swahili expressions than Zein l'Abdin's emphasis on the originary syncretism of Swahili culture and identity (see chapter 5).

It isn't difficult to imagine ways in which Mbaraka and Omari might have incorporated a greater emphasis on Indian Ocean connectivity into their musical revivalism. After all, the idea of taarab as an Indian Ocean music has been central to the heritagization of taarab on Zanzibar. But I would suggest that heritagizing the tradition of transoceanic musical appropriation in Mombasa would be extremely difficult, if not impossible. To the extent that this tradition can be said to constitute a form of heritage, it is a truly intangible heritage that is not easily placed within a normative "heritage frame" (Coupland and Garrett 2010). This is not only because it flies in the face of notions of cultural authenticity, but also because of the irreducible dialogism, or "eventness" (Bakhtin 2010), of any performance in this tradition (a theme to which I shall return in the epilogue).

Thinking about transoceanic musical appropriation as inherently resistant to a heritagization helps to make sense of why Ali A. Mazrui was so adamant that the "Orientalization" of Swahili music represented a turn away from "authentic Swahili culture" (1996, 160). A concept of "heritage"—specifically, the idea of Africa's "triple heritage," borrowed from the Liberian pan-Africanist Edward Wilmot Blyden—famously lay at the center of Mazrui's scholarship and work as a public intellectual (see Mazrui and Mutunga 2004). Notably, a year and half after my interview with Mombasa Taarab, Mazrui echoed Mbaraka's exact argument about the status of foreign instruments in Swahili music, in a speech marking the opening of the Swahili Resource Centre at the Fort Jesus Museum in Mombasa (Mazrui 2005).[14]

The larger question that arises from this discussion is whether Mombasa's tradition of transoceanic musical appropriation might have a role to play in projects of collective self-representation among the denizens of Kenya's Swahili coast in the twenty-first century. Is it only fit for the inward-facing practices of self-reflection and cultural intimacy that I have described in relation to Indian taarab and Arab taarab, or might it also be incorporated into projects of collective self-representation within the Kenyan public sphere and/or the international arena? As it happens, this question was put to the test around the same time that Mbaraka and Omari were embarking on their heritagization of Mombasan taarab, by the (re)emergence of transoceanic musical appropriation within the new genre space of Kenyan youth music. I turn to this topic next.

SEVEN

Reorienting Appropriation

Swahili Hip Hop

March 6, 2005. Adio finally arrived to collect us. It was time. I left the remains of my beer as I collected my cameras. Shodemo, Farao, and Stinky D slung their small bags of personal effects over their shoulders. We walked out together onto sand that was still radiating heat from the bygone afternoon sun.

The beach was filling up now. In the fading light, young Kenyan men and women, a few whites and Indians among them, bobbed their heads to preconcert music pumping from the PA system. I recognized a recent hit by Redsan, Nairobi's most popular dancehall artist. Small groups of young women danced under the watchful eyes of seated men, playfully kicking up sand with their sandals. A vigorous hip shake gave one woman's hat to the wind. Another glanced at herself on the live video feed. She was present and accounted for at the latest "Mombasa beach party."

Halfway through our walk, the music suddenly dropped out for an announcement. "Please make sure you don't go swimming beyond life savers in the ocean," a man's voice implored over a smattering of groans and heckles. After a brief pause, the announcement continued, but now in Sheng', Nairobi's Swahili-based youth argot: "There are already people that are stark naked! If you decide to enjoy yourself, carry yours!" (There are already *watu ambayo wako ndethe, wako empty kinyama! Uki* decide *kuji* enjoy, *ubebe yako!*). The words echoed—literally and figuratively—off of dozens of Trust Condoms billboards set up around the beach, all featuring the catchphrase "*Ubebe Yako!*" (Carry Yours!) alongside images of young men and women cozying up to each other.

As soon as we entered the hotel room, Adio implored me to take out my video camera. He was bubbling with nervous energy. This would be his first "beach party" gig, and undoubtedly the largest audience he'd ever performed for. The crowd had not come for him—there were no illusions about that. They were there for the headliners: Nairobian *kapuka* singer Nameless, and Tanzanian *bongo flava* star Mista Blue. But this only raised the stakes for Adio.

I tried my best to capture the sort of greenroom footage Adio wanted, focusing in on moments of playful interaction and introspective preparation. For the most part, everyone in the room played along by pretending to ignore the camera. But when it came time to head out to the door, Farao suddenly turned and spoke directly to the lens, wagging his finger with each word. "We're going to do a gig right now," he said in English, "getting major bucks."

The combination of a newly liberalized broadcast media and the advent of affordable digital technologies of music production during 1990s catalyzed the emergence of new local popular musics in Kenya oriented toward the urban youth and grounded in the aesthetics of hip hop and Jamaican dancehall as well as Congolese *soukous* (Nyairo 2004b; Eisenberg 2022). In the first decade of this "millennium music boom" (Nyairo 2004b), these musics strongly embraced key elements from global hip hop culture, most notably the idea that an artist should "represent the real" by embodying and expressing the authentic subjectivity of an urban space, a "'hood" (Forman 2002; Bennett 2000, 133–65; Maxwell 2003, 135–37). This created the conditions for a revival of transoceanic musical appropriation in Mombasa, in a new, outward-facing form, as aspiring youth music artists within the Swahili-speaking Muslim community turned to sounds and images of the Indian Ocean world as a means of representing their version of the real. This chapter explores the earliest iterations of this new mode of musical cosmopolitanism in Mombasa, and what it reveals not only about the possibilities of transoceanic appropriation as an outward-facing project but also about the broader conditions of "cultural citizenship," in Aihwa Ong's

(1996, 737) sense of "self-making and being made in relation to nation-states and transnational processes," for Swahili-speaking Muslims of the Kenyan coast in the twenty-first century.

HIP HOP AND CITIZENSHIP IN KENYA

Following the liberalization of the Kenyan media in the mid-1990s, stiff competition for the ears of the "youth" led to a near-complete monopoly of US hip hop and R&B on Kenya's radio airwaves.[1] Emerging just as the personal computer-based "bedroom studio" was coming into common use in the Kenyan music industry, this new soundscape was soon met with a dialogical response in the form of locally produced youth-oriented music genres, grounded stylistically in hip hop with inflections of Jamaican dancehall, Caribbean *zouk*, and Congolese *soukous*. The advent of these new youth music genres had an enormous impact on the Kenyan media. By the early 2000s, Kenya had become host to a vibrant, youth-oriented mediascape dominated by the sounds, images, and narratives of a fully "indigenized" (Mitchell 2001), albeit intensively "glocal," hip hop culture (see Eisenberg 2022; Nyairo 2004b). I use the term *mediascape* with Arjun Appadurai's definition in mind—that is, as both a media infrastructure and a set of "characters, plots, and textual forms" that subjects use in imagining "scripts" for their and others' lives (1996, 35). I would only add that mediascapes also provide *soundtracks*—affective grooves, tunes, refrains, anthems, and associated lyrical content—for these scripts (Nyairo 2007).

Hip hop culture—a cluster of African American expressive forms (rap music, breakdancing, and graffiti art) and associated stylistic and ideological commitments that emerged in America's postindustrial urban ghettos during the late 1970s and 1980s—has proven highly flexible and highly mobile, having been adopted and adapted by young people, albeit variously and differentially, in diverse locales around the world (Alim 2009). Its presence in Kenya is not surprising, given the foundation provided by Afrodiasporic cultural matrices that had previously taken hold among the country's urban youth—namely, African American soul and Jamaican reggae (Nyairo 2004a). But its pervasiveness in the Kenyan public sphere is nonetheless remarkable. Propagated through radio, television, print media, the internet, and (not least) the sound systems of public service vehicles, hip hop culture has come to suffuse *public space* in urban Kenya, in both the concrete and abstract senses of term. As such, it has become deeply implicated in the ways in which young, urban Kenyans are objectified and subjectified as members of the large and politically significant class of Kenyan citizens known as "the youth."

In line with the overriding emphasis on oppositionality and resistance in the global hip hop literature (Alim and Pennycook 2009; Mitchell 2001; Osumare 2007), scholarship on Kenyan hip hop culture typically approaches the issue of youth citizenship through discussions of the ways in which Kenyan hip hop adherents construct a "youth nation" as an alternative to the country's "tribe"-oriented national imaginary (Behrend 2002, 53). Rare exceptions to this include Nyairo and Ogude's (2005) discussion of how a Kenyan hip hop track became "official state culture" after its use in the 2002 presidential campaign and Evan Mwangi's (2004) analysis of the ways in which masculinist tropes in East African hip hop texts borrow from the discourses of nation building. Here I follow Nyairo, Ogude, and Mwangi in suggesting that hip hop culture in Kenya serves at times as an instrument of normativity in the process of transforming young Kenyans into Kenyan "youth."[2]

The potential normativity of Kenyan hip hop culture became evident in Mombasa during the first decade of the twenty-first century, in the ways in which some local youth music artists began to construct a regional identity for themselves. The agents of this project were reacting to the industrial and thematic centrality of Kenya's capital city in Kenyan youth music. With the country's music studios, radio stations, and media houses largely clustered in Nairobi, most successful Kenyan youth music artists are based there and "a significant share of [their output] generates various discourses of the capital city" (Nyairo 2006, 71). Hence Nairobi has become synonymous with "real" urban youth experience in Kenya's youth-oriented mediascape, forcing artists not from Nairobi to either refashion themselves as Nairobians or work to construct a convincing regional identity that would enable them to argue that they are also a part of the Kenyan "youth nation."

BEING "IN MOMBASA"

The project of developing a "coastal" youth music identity in Kenya began in the mid-1990s, among the young, male, socially conscious rappers who founded the "underground" rap collective Ukoo Flani (the forerunner to the Nairobi-based Ukoo Flani Mau Mau).[3] For decades, Ukoo Flani members have put forward descriptions of urban life in Mombasa performed in a slang register of Swahili that is slightly different from Nairobian underground rap's primary code—the hybrid argot Sheng', which was originally developed, and is still constantly reshaped, by young people in Nairobi's slums and lower middle-class housing estates.

While Ukoo Flani have long been at the forefront of the development of a coastal identity, for a brief moment in 2004 an upstart Mombasan rapper by the stage name Farao (Eric Omondi) stole the mantle of leadership from them. Constructed upon an Ukoo Flani-style midtempo beat sparsely decorated with minor-key synthesizer riffs, Farao's "Mombasani" served as something of an anthem for struggling youth music artists in Mombasa.[4] The verses, comprised of jokes and "disses" aimed at dressing down some of the most successful Nairobi-based youth music artists, are interspersed with a repeating refrain sung in a conspiratorial whisper: "*Mombasani twaja kali / Roundi hii hatutaki utani*" (In Mombasa we're coming up strongly / This round we're not joking). The track ends with a message in spoken English, aimed at the Nairobi-based media establishment and referencing the slogan for what was then Kenya's most popular radio station, Kiss FM: "And to those presenters who don't play coast music: coast music can be played on 'Nairobi's freshest' because it's not Nairobi's, this is *Africa's* freshest. I thought you knew, damn!"

While "Mombasani" is full of clever wordplay, the real key to its affective power lies in its use of the slang word "*Mombasani*" (a nonstandard Swahili lexeme combining *Mombasa* and the locative suffix *ni*), which references an urban Kenyan experience unique to the coast. Literally translated as "in Mombasa," *Mombasani* has long been used as an in-group identifier among young Mombasans of up-country descent (ethnic Embu, Kamba, Kikuyu, Kisii, Luo, etc.) who have lived most of their lives in Mombasa and speak Standard Swahili (inflected with a bit of Sheng', to be sure) as a primary language. Such people often use "*Mombasani*" to refer to their city (e.g., "I come from *Mombasani*") or themselves (e.g., "I am one of the *Mombasani*" [see Mahoney 2017, 20]), though the locative suffix often serves no grammatical purpose.

The idea of using the *Mombasani* concept to construct an authentic Kenyan youth music persona did not originate with Farao. Around the same time Farao's "Mombasani" was released, the term also popped up in a popular track called "Street Hustlers," by Ukoo Flani-affiliated artists Cannibal and Sharama. In a Sheng'-inflected Swahili verse, Cannibal (Ralph Masai) extols the resourcefulness and determination of "*sisi Mombasani*" ("those of us in Mombasa" or, simply, "we *Mombasani*"):

> *Walai, kama mwanamziki ndani ya pwani sikatai* (I swear, as a coastal musician I can't deny)
> *Kusakanya gizani hauwezani nao* (No one is better at searching in the dark)
> *Master ndio sisi Mombasani* (The masters are *sisi Mombasani*)

Farao's contribution was to distil the idea of being a *Mombasani* artist into a nicely flowing, repeatable slogan. This distillation was so successful that *Mombasani* came to be used in blogs and online comments as a generic term for Kenyan coastal youth music. One *Mombasani* artist, Sokoro, even added "Mombasani MC" as a tag to his stage name upon making his return to the scene after a number of years on hiatus.

The branding of Kenyan coastal youth music as *"Mombasani"* would seem to be useful for coastal artists seeking to carve out a place for themselves within Kenyan youth music writ large. But not every coastal youth—not even every *Mombasan* youth—is a *"Mombasani."* Certainly, the *Mombasani* identity is inclusive: it is embraced by young people of different ethnic and even religious backgrounds (while most are Christian, many, like Farao, are Muslim). But a closer look at the *Mombasani* lexeme reveals a limit to this inclusiveness.

The fact that *Mombasani* bears a locative suffix means that it does not literally translate to "Mombasan" when used as a personal moniker; instead, it translates to something along the lines of "person-in-Mombasa," conveying the idea of being *in*, but not *of* or *from*, the city.[5] This is a significant distinction in Kenya. For most Kenyans being a "person *of*" (in Swahili, "*mtu wa*") a place means being a member of whatever "tribe" claims that place as their "ancestral homeland." For the most part, this rule does not apply to Kenya's urban centers—for instance, the phrase "*chali wa Nairobi*" ("Nairobi boy") in Necessary Noize's "Kenyan Girl, Kenyan Boy" clearly means a boy who is at home in Nairobi, *not* a boy whose "ancestral homeland" is Nairobi—but *coastal* urban centers provide an exception to this exception. Centuries older than any up-country town or city, Mombasa and other coastal towns and cities serve as "ancestral homelands" of a sort for certain peoples—namely, Swahili-speaking coastal Muslims—who have been settled there for generations.

The ostensibly inclusive *Mombasani* identity thus rests upon a conceptual opposition to the Swahili coast and its subjects. Being *"Mombasani"* means being a Mombasan who is *not* a subject of the Swahili coast. Accordingly, I never heard young Swahili-speaking Muslims refer to themselves or their city as *"Mombasani"*

Swahili Hip Hop 157

during the course of my fieldwork between 2004 and 2006. *Mombasani* youth music artists did not emphasize the exclusionary aspect of their identity, but it was nonetheless evident in their works—particularly in their videos, which represented the city of Mombasa in a particular way (or we might say, which represent a *particular Mombasa*).

THE OTHER MOMBASA

The videos put out by *Mombasani* artists in the first decade of the twenty-first century typically avoided signs of Mombasa's ancient, "Swahili" heritage, showing only its modern, Kenyan side. We can see how this works by juxtaposing the videos for two different Mombasan(i) youth music tracks whose only real connection is their prominent uses of the word "*Mombasani*": the aforementioned "Street Hustlers" by Cannibal and Sharama, and "Soldier" by R&B-oriented singer CLD (Lennox Mwale).[6] At first glance, these videos offer starkly different portrayals of Mombasa. In "Street Hustlers," the city appears as a collection of gritty spaces that could just as easily be parts of Nairobi or any other major African metropolis. "Soldier," meanwhile, mixes beach vistas with scenes of strangely abandoned urban spaces, all tied together with the recurring trope of oddly placed television sets replaying scenes from the video. But the portrayals of Mombasa in these two videos share two important features. The first is a lack of visual references to Old Town (as I will explain below, "Soldier" does show a small area of the neighborhood, but one that few would recognize as such); the second is the use of storefront security curtains as backdrops for the performers. Security curtains index consumerism and insecurity, key facets of everyday life in a modern African city that are, stereotypically, not to be found in a "Swahili town." The image thus places the performers squarely in the modern, "Kenyan" Mombasa, rather than the ancient, "Swahili" Mombasa (Figure 7.1). *Apropos*, this image also appears in the 2004 video for Necessary Noize's "Kenyan Girl, Kenyan Boy," which is a paean to Nairobi's public transport workers and their role in promoting an authentic "local" youth culture.

In avoiding visual references to Old Town in their videos, *Mombasani* artists worked to represent the real-life experiences of their peers: most *Mombasani* have no compelling reason to visit the Old Town, and some consciously avoid it out of fear of the genie magic and homosexual practices rumored to be common among coastal Arabs and Swahili (Porter 1995). But this absenting of the Swahili coast was also a central tactic of a broader representational strategy for

FIGURE 7.1 Video stills from CLD's "Soldier" (top), and Cannibal and Sharama's "Street Hustlers" (bottom).

Mombasani artists, a strategy aimed at rendering their city as a kind of Kenyan Los Angeles, an urban space that can be just as cosmopolitan or gritty as Nairobi even though it happens to be situated amid beaches and coconut palms.

As an answer to the dominance of Nairobi, the representational strategy I have been describing cannot really be called a form of "resistance." Whatever Farao's fighting words might suggest, the idea of being "*Mombasani*" posed no real challenge to the dominant hip hop imaginary that had emerged in Kenya. On the contrary, this strategy specifically *avoided* the most radical challenge to Kenya's dominant hip hop imaginary that could potentially come from a "coastal" identity: a critique of the marriage between Kenya's dominant hip hop imaginary and its dominant *national* imaginary. The fact is, the same absenting of the Swahili coast that we find in the *Mombasani* representational strategy has long been a part of official expressions of Kenyan national identity. In the iconography of the national currency, for example, the nation has always appeared as untamed wilderness, plantations, and the modern metropolis of Nairobi. The current version of the Kenyan currency doesn't feature images of any urban

Swahili Hip Hop **159**

areas outside of Nairobi. Until 2019, however, the fifty-shilling note carried an image of the iconic, colonial-era elephant tusk installation in Mombasa's Central Business District. This was juxtaposed with an image of camel riders in Kenya's untamed northeast, presumably because the northeast is the other predominantly Muslim area of the country. The Swahili town, with all its iconic potential, was very conspicuously absent—indeed, *absented*—just as it is absented from "Street Hustlers," "Soldier," and other videos by self-described "*Mombasani*" one can find on YouTube.[7]

The absenting of the Swahili coast in Kenya's dominant national imagery already posed a distinct challenge for Kenyan youth music artists who happened to be Swahili-speaking coastal Muslims: How can one position oneself as an authentic purveyor of urban Kenyan youth culture when one's 'hood sits on the periphery of the Kenyan nation? With the burgeoning of the *Mombasani* representational strategy, this challenge only became more daunting. The remainder of this chapter focuses on two young men who met the challenge head-on.

A MOMBASAN ARABESQUE

When I met rapper Showdemo (Mohamed Essajee), he was in Mombasa for what he described as an extended vacation from his life in Bergen, Norway. The child of a marriage between two Old Town natives from different communities (one a Punjabi of the Bohra Muslim sect, the other a Baloch), he grew up speaking Swahili as a first language and identifying variously as "Swahili" and "Arab." As with many landed elites in Kenya, he has family all over the world. Eventually, he took up a life with relatives in Bergen, where he studied theater and entered into a career as a cook.

In our conversations in Mombasa, Showdemo described himself as an amateur rapper with a minor career in Norway. He hoped to participate in the Kenyan youth music scene while he was in town, but didn't much care whether he made any money in the process. He was not in great need of money while staying in Mombasa. Moreover, he was well aware that making a living as a Kenyan youth music artist would require years of hard work developing fame and parlaying that fame into gigs, sponsorship deals, and other opportunities. His goals, then, were to pass the time, develop his performing skills, and earn a bit of respect from his childhood friends in Mombasa.

Most afternoons, Showdemo could be found hanging out with other young men under a fraying Brazilian football banner on the veranda of a mysteriously

FIGURE 7.2 Mohamed Essajee (back row, second from left) posing with friends in their corner of Kibokoni, Mombasa, 2005. Photo by author.

abandoned stone building located in Old Town's high-rent Fort Jesus district. Dressed as "thugs" and "rastas," the young men who gathered there sat around talking, chewing khat, and listening to hip hop CDs on a boombox (Figure 7.2). As the Fort Jesus district is frequented by tourists, these young men included tour guides, souvenir sellers, and others who were not necessarily from the neighborhood. Their afternoon gatherings thus served as a rare site of connection for young subjects of the Swahili coast and their *Mombasani* counterparts. This was not lost on Showdemo, who had use for this sort of social nexus. He was interested in collaborating with experienced local artists—and this, by definition, meant *Mombasani* artists. Yet, as he expressed to me, he was also interested in representing his 'hood, Mombasa Old Town. He thus used his afternoon hangouts as an opportunity to bring *Mombasani* artists whom he gotten to know into his world. One of these *Mombasani* artists was the aforementioned singer CLD, who ended up featuring the distinctive scene underneath the Brazilian football banner in his "Soldier" video.

Showdemo had arrived from Bergen with a hard drive full of prefabricated accompaniments, or "beats," which he had created with Bergen-based friends who were mostly immigrants from the Middle East and Turkey. One beat that he particularly prized was based on a sample of an up-tempo prelude to an Arabic song, featuring a descending melody on *qānūn* (plucked zither) and *nāy* over Arab percussion pounding out a syncopated Arab *malfūf* rhythm. It was taken from a 1979 recording of "Bahibbak yā Lubnān" (I love you Lebanon), a classic Arab nationalist song by legendary Lebanese singer Fayrūz, but Showdemo did not know this until I found out and emailed him about it some years later. Combined with a half-time drum groove, it creates a perfect template for an arabesque hip hop track of the type associated at the time with US producers Scott Storch and Timbaland. Showdemo approached CLD with the idea of collaborating on a track based on his arabesque beat. CLD agreed to participate, but he wanted to bring others on board. He approached a fellow *Mombasani* artist, a rapper by the stage name Redwax (Alex Njuguna), who was then a budding music producer and had connections at a number of studios around town. Redwax secured time for the project at a small studio in Mombasa's Tudor area.

The collaborators (Showdemo, CLD, Redwax, and another rapper by the stage name GK) wrote the refrain and verses for the track together in the studio. A decision was made (no one remembers by whom) to make it an ode to a fictional Arabian woman named Samiya. CLD then asked Anwar, the Arab owner of the studio, how to say "baby" or "my love" in Arabic. Anwar answered "*yā habibtī*" (apparently unaware that Arabic popular songs typically use the gender-neutral *yā habibī*), prompting the first line of the refrain: "*Samiya ya habibti, nakupenda unavovaa*" (Samiya my love, I love the way you dress). The rest of the track was then filled in with similarly sexually charged lines in Sheng'-inflected Swahili, save for brief linguistic departures from Showdemo, who raps one verse in English and inserts a brief Norwegian phrase (a "shout-out" to his friends in Bergen) into the refrain.[8]

As soon as the rough mix of "Samiya" was completed, Anwar encouraged the collaborators to shoot a video.[9] As luck would have it, Ali "Canada" Mbarak, a friend of Showdemo's family, was also in town at the time on his own extended vacation from his life in Canada. Looking to parlay his film school training and family property in Mombasa Old Town into a media production house, Ali agreed to direct and produce a video *gratis*. (AUDIO EX. 32, with video).

FIGURE 7.3 Video stills from Showdemo's "Samiya."

Ali's "Samiya" video offers an orgy of Orientalia, including belly dancers and just about all the Arabian imagery the Mombasa environs can provide: the sixteenth-century limestone walls of Fort Jesus, a large sculpture of an Arabian coffeepot, faux Arabian architecture from a North Coast resort, a camel (kept by a local hotel for giving rides along the beach), and East Africa's own 'ūd virtuoso Zein l'Abdin. For the *pièce de résistance*, Ali Mbarak drew on his Canadian film school training and high-end software to conjure up a flying carpet.

Unlike the audio track, the "Samiya" video begins with a brief 'ūd introduction—a short improvisation (*taqsīm*) performed by Zein. During this introduction, images of Zein playing his 'ūd are interspersed with other arabesque imagery: a man pouring himself coffee from a brass-colored Arabian coffee pot, a reined camel, and a belly dancer in a green dress. The performers then appear, all of them wearing Islamic-Swahili *kanzu* tunics and Islamic head-coverings (*kofia*, turban, or skull cap). As Zein's introduction ends, another light-skinned Arab man (Ali Canada's collaborator, Salim Nasher) climbs onto the flying carpet. He is wearing an Arabian white robe and head covering; in his hand is a reed flute. As the original "Samiya" track begins, Salim soars above Mombasa Old Town, the tall buildings of Mombasa's Central Business District visible in the background. At the first sharp turn, he grips the sides of the carpet in terror (Figure 7.3).

The "Samiya" video turned out to be unique and interesting enough to capture the attention of the Nairobian television producers on whose desk it landed: it was featured on the music video programs of at least two national television networks. But what did a national audience see in this Orientalist fantasy? There are, of course, many possible "readings" of the work. But in considering its reception among up-country Kenyans, one cannot ignore the fact that its imagery, however ridiculous, would not have been unfamiliar to viewers. The Swahili coast had long served as something of an internal Orient for Kenya, and by the first decade of the twenty-first century this had become even more the case. The Kenyan government began to push domestic tourism in the late 1990s (Mahoney 2017, 198–99), thereby directing narratives and images of the Swahili coast once aimed solely at foreigners (albeit also consumed by Kenyans) at Nairobi's growing middle class, as well. "The coast has its own fascination," one Kenyan tourism guide tells this new dual readership. "Towns such as Mombasa, Malindi and Lamu have a unique and special magic. Their Arabian Nights ambience that forever holds one's imagination is simply unforgettable" (Nation Media Group 2002).

For many, if not most, up-country Kenyan viewers, the "Samiya" video surely seemed like a musical advertisement for coastal tourism, complete with images of beaches and arabesque-themed hotels. Some might have asked themselves whether the video was ironically playing on their preconceptions of coastal culture. But while the work is playful, there is nothing in its words or images to suggest an attempt at deconstructing or undermining the status of the Swahili coast as Kenya's internal Orient. If anything, it seems to *celebrate* this status.

I was never able to elicit an answer from Showdemo as to what he had intended to create with his arabesque beat before he got to work with his collaborators; however, I got a sense from our discussions that he might not have intended the kind of (self-)parody that the "Samiya" track and video both turned out to be. His ideas were clearly transformed in the process of working with others to create something for a *national* audience. Though it hardly seems possible when viewing the "Samiya" video, Showdemo's original intent may well have been simply to "represent the real." As I discovered during my fieldwork, the sounds of hip hop arabesque bore a powerful resonance in Showdemo's 'hood.

"WELCOME TO DUBAI!"

I first got a sense of the resonance of hip hop arabesque in Mombasa Old Town while hanging out at Island Fruits, a juice bar run by an unctuous Hadrami man, Swaleh, who made sure the juices were sugary enough for local taste buds and the atmosphere welcoming enough for locals and foreigners alike. As I approached Island Fruits one afternoon, my ethnomusicologist's ears picked up an Arab groove pulsating within it. Coming closer, I heard synthesized organ and strings sounds, a muted electric guitar, and a youthful woman's voice singing Arabic words to a melody punctuated by responses from a synthesizer. The song, I would later learn, was "Ah W Nuṣ" ("By Half" [I Mean It]) by Nancy Ajram, a young Lebanese pop star whose youthful voice and playfully coy dance moves were by then well known by the many Mombasans with access to Arabic satellite television.

"Welcome to Dubai!" Swaleh shouted, exultant, as he saw me enter. Swaleh had never been to Dubai, but he had certainly heard firsthand accounts from friends and family members who had. It is a shopping destination for wealthy Mombasans as well as a place of opportunity for some of Mombasa's musicians and entertainers. More than anything else, however, Dubai is a sign vehicle for many Mombasans, signifying a fantastical Arab modernity, bubbling over with capitalism, ingenuity, progress, development, and a hint of debauchery. By sonically transforming his juice bar into "Dubai," Swaleh promoted it as a suitably modern place for cosmopolitan Mombasans as well as Western tourists, researchers, and students.

I eventually came to hear Swaleh's Dubai soundtrack as a congruous addition to the soundscape of Old Town. I also heard songs by Nancy Ajram, Amr Diab, and other Arab pop stars reverberating from the private cars of wealthy young residents. In the Kisauni District special parliamentary election of 2004, a Swahili candidate even attempted to capture the Old Town vote with Amr Diab's "Layly Nahāry" (Night and Day), blasting it into the narrow alleyways from car-mounted loudspeakers.

But just as soon as I got used to sipping saccharine juices to Arab pop, Swaleh's soundtrack suddenly changed—to US hip hop. What was Swaleh up to? I wondered. Didn't he realize that these new sounds would dissolve the aura of "Dubai" that he had been so keen to instill? Once again, I was not yet listening with the right ears. Swaleh's first hip hop obsession was rapper 50 Cent's "Candy Shop," which features a synthesized string riff outlining the tones of what Western music theory terms the Phrygian mode. The Phrygian mode has long been a favorite Orientalist device in Western music; it places the listener in an imagined Spain or Middle East, depending on how it is used (Scott 1998, 327). In "Candyshop" the mode is deployed with just the right timbres (synthesized strings) and inflections (e.g., a slide downward from the flatted second to the tonic) to place us in "Arabia." Produced by Scott Storch, who has made a career out of incorporating Arab and Indian sounds into his grooves, the track is prime example of US hip hop arabesque.

The success of hip hop arabesque mavens like Scott Storch and Timbaland speaks to the popularity of this aesthetic among US consumers. There is, however, an interesting study waiting to be done on the reception of hip hop arabesque in the Arab world, and in places like Mombasa Old Town where the religion, language, and musical systems of the Arab world have been instantiated. The apparent affinity for US hip hop Arabesque in Mombasa Old Town can be explained, on one analytical level, by its timbral, melodic, and rhythmical similarity to Arab pop and London *bhangra*, musical forms that find their way to Old Town through flows of people and media. Indeed, 50 Cent's "Candyshop" generally elicited the same response from Swaleh's elite Swahili, Arab, and South Asian friends as did Nancy Ajram of Amr Diab. Driving by slowly in their expensive cars, they would yell, "*Kama laaandan!*" (Just like London!).

This slogan was clearly a reference to the experiences some of these highly mobile young men had traveling in London. But it was also something more. London is both the official capital of the United Kingdom and, for many in the Anglophone postcolonial world, the *de facto* capital of the diaspora of the Global South. I heard the word *Londonistan* deployed with bemusement by some in Old Town during my fieldwork. This sensationalist nickname for London, originally coined by European intelligence agents and conservative cultural critics concerned with the prevalence of Islamic extremism, seemed in the conversations of my interlocutors in Mombasa to refer more generally to the prevalence of Middle Eastern, Asian, and African Muslims in the city. To the extent that the "*Kama Laaandan!*" slogan indexes "Londonistan," it points to the possibility that young people in Old Town's private homes, juice bars, and automobiles might appreciate hip hop arabesque for its potential to validate global *Arabness* over the global *Blackness* that lies at the heart of Kenya's dominant hip hop imaginary.

Pierre Bourdieu (1984) describes taste as a recursive process of subjectification and objectification: as social boundaries of taste begin to take shape they are "misrecognized" as "the practical affirmation of an inevitable difference" (56);

and partly through their misrecognition boundaries of taste continue to take shape. In a similar fashion, arabesque sounds that may be *sensible* at some unarticulated (perhaps "unconscious") level within the space of Old Town also work as a "practical affirmation" of Old Town's indexical connection to Dubai, and "Londonistan" hip hop arabesque brings Old Town, Dubai, and "Londonistan" together under the sign of a parallel modernity discrete from a Nairobi-centric Kenyan modernity.

Armed with this nuanced conception of the politics of taste, we may begin to hear and see the "Samiya" track and video a bit differently. We may begin to appreciate how the track began as a response to the hip hop injunction to "keep it real." And we may begin to hear and see, somewhere buried under the video's many layers of parody, a deconstruction of Kenya's dominant hip hop imaginary. It would be difficult, however, to argue that the "Samiya" project actually achieves any sort of social critique. Even if critique were the aim, the work's critical edge is dulled by the intractability—the "rigor mortis" (Bhabha 1995)—of the stereotypes it employs.

"SOMETHING FROM HOME": PRINCE ADIO'S TAARAB TINGE

Showdemo was not the only subject of the Swahili coast who sought to succeed in Kenyan youth music during my time in Mombasa between 2004 and 2007. The case of Prince Adio (Adio Mohamed), the son of Maulidi Musical Party cofounder Mohamed Adio Shigoo, adds another dimension to the present discussion. Unlike Showdemo, Adio was a career musician, whose intent in becoming a youth music artist was not simply to garner fame but to make a living. Before reinventing himself as a youth music artist in 2003, Adio struggled to carve out a career in modern taarab. This career path took him to Nairobi for six years, where he performed with a group that was popular among transplanted subjects of the Swahili coast. When he moved back to Mombasa, he continued with this genre for a while, though he made more money playing American jazz and pop songs on the keyboard on the Tamarind Dhow floating restaurant.

Adio's move to youth music began with experimentation at Jikoni Records, a bedroom studio set up in the mid-1990s by British expatriate Andrew "Madebe" Burchell (1952–2017).[10] Burchell introduced Adio to a music-sequencing software called Frooty Loops, with which Adio ultimately developed a style he referred to in our interviews as "hip hop taarab." Described by Adio as "something from

FIGURE 7.4 Prince Adio performs at a "Mombasa beach party" concert, 2005. Photo by author.

home" (*kitu ambacho ni cha kinyumbani*), this style brings together modern taarab's poetic sensibilities and vocal performance style (most obvious in Adio's nasal timbre) with aspects of dance club-oriented Kenyan youth music, including synth-heavy, riff-based accompaniments; rapping (always performed by another artist in Adio's tracks); and a heavy use of what had become known in Kenya onomatopoeically as the "*kapuka*" beat, which involves a 3+3+2 rhythmic syncopation against a steady pulse.[11] The kapuka beat—which also characterizes 1990s Jamaican dancehall (see Manuel and Marshall 2006, 456–57) as well as reggaeton, zouk, and a number of other Afrodiasporic popular musics—had recently become ubiquitous in Kenyan youth music thanks to dancehall-inspired hits put out by Nairobi's Ogopa Deejays (Eisenberg 2022, 61–62).

When I first met Adio, in 2004, he was already nationally famous for his hip hop taarab track "*Nikiwa Ndani*" (When I'm Inside) (AUDIO EX. 33), recorded at Tabasam Records (the same production house that recorded Farao's "*Mombasani*"). "*Nikiwa Ndani*" is ostensibly a straightforward song about domestic tensions; however, in the typical manner of Swahili taarab poetry, its lyrics invite alternate readings. The first two lines of the refrain, "*Nikiwa ndani, wapiga kelele / Nikitoka nje, unanununika,*" can mean either, "When I'm home you argue with me / When I leave you sulk," or "When I'm inside you are loud / When I pull out you sulk." Adio maintained that this double entendre was unintended,[12] but it is clearly what made the track successful: attracted by the raunchy wordplay, young men working in Nairobi's *matatu*s (public service vans) made it part of the everyday soundtrack of Nairobian commuters. (As late as 2006, I saw the words "*Nikiwa Ndani*" painted on a *matatu*.) Having garnered *matatu* credibility, "*Nikiwa Ndani*" easily made it onto the playlists of Nairobi-based DJs and the major Kenyan radio stations.[13]

By the time of my fieldwork, Adio had released an entire album's worth of hip hop taarab tracks, most of them stronger in composition, arrangement, and production than "*Nikiwa Ndani.*" And yet, he had not managed to replicate the national success he found with that first release. What he had achieved, however, was the establishment of a new Mombasan youth music style distinct from those of *Mombasani* artists. During and after my fieldwork, other Mombasan artists followed Adio's lead, albeit without embracing Adio's "hip hop taarab" label. The most successful of these has been singer and songwriter Sudi Boy (Sudi Mohammed Sudi), who at one point was signed with Adio's own Jungle Masters Records. Though Sudi characterizes his own style as unique, it clearly shares a great deal with that of his acknowledged mentor and "musical brother" Adio (Madiangi 2010). His debt to Adio even extends to the use of close vocal harmonies recorded all on his own voice, an effect used throughout "*Nikiwa Ndani.*"

The national media in Kenya, centered in Nairobi, have mostly ignored Mombasa's hip hop taarab scene. It is not immediately clear why this should be the case. The idea of "fusing" modern taarab with mainstream Kenyan youth music is something that the Nairobi-based Kenyan media and major stakeholders in the music industry in Nairobi clearly view as aesthetically and commercially viable. Celebrated Mombasan R&B and Afro-fusion singer Nyota Ndogo (Mwanaisha Abdalla), who was "discovered" by Andrew Burchell around 1999, received a great deal of praise in her early years for her supposed taarab influences (which, by her own admission, were actually rather slight);[14] and Ukoo Flani co-founder Alai K's experiments in what he has called "Swahili hip hop Afro-soul" have garnered support from the major Nairobi-based international patrons of Kenyan "Afro-fusion" music (the Goethe Institut-Nairobi and Alliance Francaise de Nairobi). Why, then, has the arguably more organic hip hop-taarab "fusion" of Adio and Sudi been virtually absent from the national airwaves in Kenya?

One Nairobian music producer who began his career in Mombasa argues that hip hop taarab artists have trouble reaching a national audience due to their lack of investment in production quality at a time when artists in Nairobi are increasingly recording with high-end, professional equipment.[15] No doubt there is something to this. But another problem hip hop taarab artists have faced is the similarity of their hybrid style to Tanzanian *bongo flava*, a genre that shares hip hop taarab's flowing Swahili lyrics and modern-taarab influences.[16] While *bongo flava* is quite popular in Kenya, being a *Kenyan* artist whose music sounds like *bongo flava* puts one in a difficult position when trying to construct a compelling persona for national circulation. For years after the success of "Nikiwa Ndani," the dominant media narrative about Adio was the "revelation" that he hails from Kenya rather than Tanzania. Similarly, Sudi was asked in his first major press interview whether he was truly Kenyan, as his "music sounds more like Bongo" (Madiangi 2010). In this (feigned) surprise at the fact that an artist like Adio or Sudi could be from Kenya lies a thinly veiled insinuation that their music must be either be an imitation of a foreign genre or a music of people caught between two national identities. In either case, what follows is that their tracks are merely poor substitutes for the "real" *bongo* tracks that have been vetted by the dynamic industry in Dar es Salaam.

BRIEFLY BHANGRA

A restless entrepreneur, Adio was always trying out different ways of monetizing his talents. In addition to his gig on the Tamarind Dhow, he produced albums of Swahili-language Islamic *kaswida* music for the new Islamic radio stations. Shortly after my fieldwork, he started up his own production house and began acting in Kenyan television programs and films. For a brief moment in 2005, he also tried out a different stylistic direction for his youth music: *bhangra*.

Developed in Britain in the 1980s, *bhangra* is a South Asian diasporic music based on a "syncretic fusion of Punjabi folk elements and disco/rock rhythms and instrumentation" (Manuel 1995, 235). In Adio's hands, however, it was something a bit less defined. Adio's *bhangra* experiment began and ended with a single track, entitled "Sikitiko" (Regret), whose accompaniment features (synthesized) Indian string and percussion sounds (*sitar* and *tabla*) mapped onto a rhythm much closer to *kapuka* than a Punjabi folk beat. I did not recognize "Sikitiko" as *bhangra* until Adio informed me that it was intended as such. But I later came to learn that this *bhangra* experiment, however subtle, was something special for Adio, something he was looking at as a possible way of reframing his artistic persona.

One day in 2005, Adio popped in on me at my apartment in Old Town to invite me to a "beach party" music festival at which he was scheduled to perform. He had two other artists in tow: his collaborator, Stinky D, and Farao. "He is a hip hop artist, like Tupac Shakur," Adio told me by way of introducing Farao. "What about *you*?" I countered to Adio. "Aren't *you* a hip hop artist?" Adio quickly shrugged off the idea and started fumbling around for a more suitable genre title, ultimately landing on *bhangra*.

If considered as a claim of personal connection to the global Indian diaspora, Adio's embrace of a *bhangra* identity seems puzzling at first. After all, his Bajuni ethnicity marks him as "African" with perhaps a bit of "Arab" heritage. But as we saw in chapter 3, being an African who happens to have a deep personal investment in Indian culture does indeed make sense in the context of the Swahili coast. Unlike in other parts of East Africa, where diasporic Indians are quite segregated from their African neighbors, on the Swahili coast South Asians have always maintained intimate social and cultural ties with their "African" and other neighbors. Of course, all this is difficult to bring across to a broad Kenyan audience. Rather than try, Adio ultimately abandoned his *bhangra* identity. I witnessed what may have been an important moment for his decision to do so during the filming of the "Sikitiko" video.[17] The video was directed by Ali Canada, the same man who directed "Samiya," and was shot at an Indian-themed hotel in Mombasa (AUDIO EX. 34, with video). At one point during the shoot, Ali decided to demonstrate how he thought Adio should be dancing. With palms facing upward, he thrust his shoulders up and down in a perfect imitation of a Bollywood *bhangra* dance. Most of us in the room found Ali's performance riotously funny, but Adio was not amused. "I don't want to look like them!" (*Sitaki kufanana nao mimi!*), he said sharply.

Later, Adio told me that his hesitance to dance in true Punjabi style and thereby "look like them" stemmed from a concern that he might be accused of imitating Akhil the Brain, an Indian-Swahili singer from Tanzania who had developed his own style of Swahili-language *bhangra*. Specifically, Adio felt the accusation would come from his fellow "Swahili," who can be "big mouths" (*watu wa mdomo sana*). In other words, Adio doubted that his own personal connection to Indian diasporic culture would be understood or accepted even by his fellow subjects of the Swahili coast, much less by a broader Kenyan audience.

Adio's hesitance to commit to a *bhangra* persona surely also had to do with his knowledge of the images of *bhangra* that were already circulating within Kenyan popular culture. Kenyan audiences in 2005 were familiar not only with Akhil the Brain's campy videos but also with Kenyan group Kleptomaniax's Orientalist track "*Belly Naach Di*," which implores listeners to "wiggily wiggily to the bhang-a-ra beat." In other words, the rigor mortis of the *bhangra* stereotype had already set in in Kenya.

AN UNREALIZED COSMOPOLITICS

The difficulties Adio and Showdemo faced in working to (re)present themselves to a national audience illustrate the difficulties subjects of the Swahili coast face in finding a place for themselves within the imagined community of the Kenyan nation. Their failed/aborted experiments—Showdemo's arabesque style and Adio's "*bhangra*" direction—reveal that even the ostensibly post-tribal "youth nation" that is the great promise of Kenyan hip hop culture holds little room for subjects of the Swahili coast. I suggest that Adio and Showdemo ultimately abandoned or transformed these experiments because they understood that the basic premise on which they rested was one that many up-country Kenyans would not easily understand or accept: namely, that East Africa is part of an oceanic world distinct from yet every bit as culturally rich as the Black Atlantic. Of course, there are up-country Kenyans who not only understand but actually embrace a vision of East Africa interconnected with the Indian Ocean world (as we saw in Ngũgĩ's narrative in the prologue). But since the British colonial era, up-country Kenyans have been broadly subjected to and subjectified by images and narratives of the Indian Ocean world as no more than a source of foreign interlopers who dominated and enslaved Africans for centuries before the Europeans came. For Adio and Showdemo, playing for a national audience meant operating within this powerful "regime of representation" (Hall 1997).

Why, then, did Adio and Showdemo work so hard to reach a national audience in the first place? It doesn't seem as though either of them were compelled to do so on financial grounds, given Adio's demonstrated ability to make a living on the local scene and Showdemo's apparent lack of need to make a living from his Kenyan musical projects. Why didn't they simply accept their subaltern status, or perhaps work to challenge the racial and spatial commitments that serve to alienate them and their fellow subjects of the Swahili coast? Given how subjects of the Swahili coast commonly describe themselves as "dispossessed" (Mazrui and Shariff 1994), marginalized, and oppressed, there would seem to be room for a Swahili-coast youth music oriented toward resisting the hegemony of upcountry Kenya.

Asking why Adio and Showdemo failed to politicize their music may seem a bit unfair. But the fact is, at the level of style, their music is already political: by incorporating Indian Ocean sounds that resonate in "Swahili" places, their tracks "provincialize" Kenyan youth music, revealing its underlying Afrodiasporic cosmopolitanism as just one of the many cosmopolitanisms with which subjects of the Swahili coast engage on a daily basis (Simpson and Kresse 2008). It is fair to ask, then, why Adio and Showdemo did not articulate through words (i.e., lyrics and public statements) the (cosmo)political critique that is immanent in their music. The simplest answer to this question, beyond that they weren't interested in being controversial, is that they lacked the words to do so.

Speaking about the Indian Ocean world does not come easy. Unlike the Afrodiasporic world, it has never had an "intellectual elite [committed to articulating] irredentist sentiments and [placing] them in public discourse" (Alpers 2001, 32). David Samper (2004) offers a striking example of how Nairobian rappers deploy conceptions of the Black Atlantic developed by scholars like Melville Herskovits and Paul Gilroy. "Rap is an African thing; not an American thing," one artist told him. "Those Americans doing it there are still from Africa. The blacks there are still Africans" (42). There are simply no Indian Ocean parallels to these well-worn references to Black Atlantic diasporic connections—or for that matter, to powerful Black Atlantic concepts like *Négritude, pan-Africanism*, and *Black power*; not to mention *soul, reggae*, and *hip hop*. If a politicized Swahili-coast youth music is to emerge, it will rely in part upon the establishment of an intellectual discourse on the Swahili coast as a cultural nexus of Africa and the Indian Ocean world that is attentive to the role of music as a space in which subjects make sense of and potentially transform the world. This book represents a small step in this direction.

EPILOGUE

For a Humanistic Musical Anthropology of the Indian Ocean

In February 2005, two groups of musicians hailing from different locales of the Indian Ocean world met on Zanzibar for a special conclave. It was just after the end of the second annual Sauti za Busara (Sounds of Wisdom) music festival in Zanzibar's Stone Town, and a contingent of Yemeni musicians from Seiyun Popular Arts, a music and dance group specializing in urban popular song and traditional dances of the Hadramawt region, had been among the featured acts from overseas. Determined to make the most of what had become an increasingly rare opportunity for the musicians to travel abroad, the group's tour manager, retired BBC producer Paul Hughes-Smith, collaborated with German ethnomusicologist and music entrepreneur Werner Graebner to arrange for them to meet with Zanzibar's historic Swahili taarab orchestra Culture Musical Club. The event was attended by an array of invited guests, myself among them, as well as media crews from a Greek television news outlet and a German radio station.[1]

Culture and Seiyun are sister organizations of a sort, each founded in the heat of the decolonization era of the 1960s with the support of a new government (a transitional colonial government, in Seiyun's case; a postcolonial revolutionary one, in Culture's case). But the connections between them run deeper than this, into the very foundations of the music cultures they represent. Indeed, the Culture-Seiyun conclave promised to recreate, or at least evoke, the transoceanic encounters that shaped the music cultures of the Swahili coast and Hadramawt. In this way, the event reflected the growing importance of the narrative of taarab as an "Indian Ocean music."

When Swahili taarab began to receive serious attention from scholars in the 1990s, ethnomusicologists—Werner Graebner among them—described the genre as an "Indian Ocean music" whose sounds reflect historical processes of "syncretism" (Topp 1994) catalyzed by the Swahili coast's "geo-historical proximity" to "Indian Ocean cultures" (Graebner 1991b, 196). At the time of the Culture-Seiyun conclave, this narrative was being taken up and amplified by variously positioned agents involved in the heritagization of taarab (see chapter 6). Zanzibari taarab, in particular, was coming to be framed as an iconic representation of the Swahili coast's place within an "ancient 'dhow culture'" of the western Indian Ocean (Topp Fargion 2014, 184; cf. Bissell 2012). The official biography of Culture Musical Club on the World Music Expo (WOMEX) website, penned by Graebner around this time, describes the "leisurely sound of taarab" as "the result of hundreds of years of exchange of musical and poetic ideas across the Indian Ocean" (Jahazi Media n.d.).

In a sense, the Culture-Seiyun conclave represented an early, applied experiment in developing a more intensive scholarly focus on taarab as an "Indian Ocean music." As a graduate student just embarking on a long period of field research on Swahili music, I felt fortunate to be a part of it. What actually unfolded there stuck with me, ultimately shaping my approach in this book. That is perhaps reason enough to return to it in this epilogue. But what draws me back to the events of the Culture-Seiyun conclave, in particular, is how they reflect on the possibilities and pitfalls of the of the "Indian Ocean ethnomusicology" that is now taking shape (Byl and Sykes 2020; Boulos et al. 2021; Ulaby 2012; Rasmussen 2016; Sykes and Byl 2023b).

A PARODY OF CONNECTION

There were plenty of smiles, but few words, as the members of Seiyun lugged their instrument cases and bags to Culture Musical Club's rehearsal stage. The Yemenis arranged themselves in a row on the stage, using chairs and microphones already in place for Culture's regular rehearsal sessions. Half of them wore crisp dress shirts paired with casual wraps, while the other half sported the elaborately patterned, bright green sarongs the group had worn for their festival performance the night before. Lead singer and ʿūd player Salem Mayhour took up a central position between two violinists and three percussionists. As he and the violinists tuned their instruments, an elder member of Culture Musical Club approached them to bid them welcome and exchange pleasantries in formal

Arabic. Graebner and Hughes-Smith stood close on either side of the encounter, nodding and smiling.

After a brief test of the microphones, the musicians were ready to begin. The percussionists started off with a driving, polyrhythmic tapestry of *dum*s, *tak*s, and jingles, to which Mayhour added rolling tremolos on his *'ūd*. After a few moments, Mayhour began to sing, his tone forceful yet resonant. The vocal melody unfolded in short phrases, each punctuated by a response from the *'ūd* and violins.

I wondered what the Zanzibaris thought of the sounds coming from their stage. I wasn't well enough acquainted with any of them to ask. The sounds were not radically different than those of Zanzibar's orchestral Swahili taarab. Most of the instruments that were being played were also part of Culture's orchestration, the major exception being the southern Arabian-style bongos (*bingiz*), which are louder and more resonant than the Latin American-style bongos in Culture's percussion section. Other structural aspects of the music would also have been familiar to the Zanzibaris, including the rhythm, as I will explain in a moment. But much in the performance was quite distant from Swahili taarab, including the energetic, almost frenetic feel of the performance, which is a world apart from the "languid charm" (Tracey 1951) of orchestral taarab.

The Zanzibaris sat quietly through Seiyun's first song, and applauded politely at the end. It seemed that this is how the evening would go—an exchange of musical performances, respectfully offered and received. But something unexpected happened during the next song that Seiyun performed. It started out very much like the one before; even the rhythm and tempo were the same. But when Mayhour began to sing the first refrain, the sound of his ensemble suddenly expanded, as members of Culture's women's chorus added their voices to the performance.

Mayhour seemed pleasantly surprised by this development. But soon a curious look crept over his face. He had heard something in the Zanzibari women's singing that puzzled him. Without missing a beat in his singing and playing, he shifted his head slightly to get a better ear on what he was hearing. From my seat, I could just make out what it was: while the Zanzibari women had managed to blend their voices beautifully into the performance, the words they were singing were not those of the song. They were a different set of lyrics altogether, almost entirely in Swahili.

The song that the Yemeni musicians were playing when this remarkable synergy occurred was "Ghālī Ghālī" (My Dear, My Dear), a late twentieth-century classic of the Hadrami repertoire written by Ahmed bin Ghodel and famously recorded by Saudi-based luminary Abdel Rab Idris. The Yemeni musicians perhaps suspected that their Zanzibari hosts would know this song. If so, they were half right. It was not actually "Ghālī Ghālī" that the women of Culture Musical Club knew, but "Mbali Mbali" (Far Away, Far Away), a Swahili stylization of "Ghālī Ghālī" recorded in Mombasa around 1990, by Somali-born taarab singer Asha Abdo Suleiman "Malika" (AUDIO EX. 5).

The addition of the Zanzibari women's voices momentarily transformed the event into what the late anthropologist Dwight Conquergood (1985, 10) would have recognized as a "dialogical performance," an "orchestration" (literal and figurative, in this case) of different voices and sensibilities. At the same time, by singing a Swahili version of the song, the women engaged in a communicative process *in relation to* rather than *with* their guests. This performance-within-a-performance was also dialogical, but in a different way. Its dialogism was largely "internal," in Bakhtin's sense, residing in the relations among its formal elements. Most audibly, it involved a dialogue of languages. The words that the Zanzibari women added to Seiyun's performance—part of the verbal text of Malika's song, composed by Swahili poet Sheriff Maulana—included the Arabic phrase "*anā baḥibak*" (I love you). This phrase is not taken from "Ghālī Ghālī"; nor is it part of the standard lexicon of Arabic phrases commonly used by coastal Swahili speakers. It is, rather, a playful allusion to the Hadrami linguistic and cultural context.

In addition to the dialogue of languages, there was also a dialogue of styles. The perfection of the women's timing and phrasing was its own dialogic commentary, highlighting why Malika chose to appropriate "Ghālī Ghālī" in the first place: the song's inherent Swahiliness. Malika and her ensemble perform the song as a *chakacha*—and it turns out that the song works *perfectly* in that genre. The *sharh* rhythm of "Ghālī Ghālī" is almost identical to the *chakacha* rhythm (as I have discussed). What is more, the repetitive pentatonic riff of "Ghālī Ghālī" plays with and against the metric structure in the same way as a traditional *chakacha* melody. Indeed, the rhythm of the first phrase of the refrain is nearly identical to that of the first phrase of the refrain of Malika's biggest hit, "Vidonge" (Pills), which uses a traditional *chakacha* melody.

The unexpected breakthrough into dialogical performance at the Culture-Seiyun conclave tells two stories about taarab as an "Indian Ocean music." One is about taarab as an outcome of historical processes of migration and exchange, the other about taarab as a space in which agents work to *make sense of* historical processes of migration and exchange. Each of these stories points in a particular direction for an Indian Ocean ethnomusicology. The former situates the dialogical performance as a single data point in a project of describing a cultural milieu and reconstructing the histories of migration and exchange behind it; the latter situates it at the center of an inquiry into what geographer Julia Verne (2012) calls "living translocality," translocality as "a particular condition, a particular way of being in the world" (19). There is, or should be, room for both directions in an Indian Ocean ethnomusicology. But the Indian Ocean ethnomusicology that is currently taking shape is mostly oriented in the former direction.

HERSKOVITS'S GHOST

When Indian Ocean studies first took shape in the 1980s and early 1990s, it was as an historiographical project, centered on the proposition that the Indian Ocean had been the site of a relatively coherent "economic and social world" (McPherson 1993) until the rise of a "truly global economy" at the dawn of the nineteenth century (Pearson 2003, 12; Chaudhuri 1985; McPherson 1993). In the first decade of the twenty-first century, scholars expanded the field by exploring how the Indian Ocean has remained, in Sugata Bose's (2006, 12) words, a "coherently definable interregional arena" despite (or perhaps because of) contemporary globalization (see also Ewald 2000; Metcalf 2007; Vergès 2003). This new emphasis situated Indian Ocean studies as a new kind of area studies, based not on a colonial or cold-war cartography but on empirical and theoretical questions of human connectivity. In this new area studies, "the exploration of the Indian Ocean as a cultural milieu is quite as important as its role as a trading zone" (Bose 2006, 11), opening a wide space for music studies.

The earliest moves to develop a framework for the study of music in the Indian Ocean centered on the region's African diaspora and took inspiration from research on the African diaspora in the Atlantic (Alpers 1997, 2000, 2002; de Silva Jayasuriya 2006, 2008). This work approaches music as empirical evidence of patterns of migration and social integration, as well as diasporic consciousness and identity. As Shihan de Silva Jayasuriya (2008) and Edward Alpers make explicit, it draws from the idea of cultural "retentions" that lay at the heart of the "ethnohistorical method" developed by Melville Herskovits in the Atlantic, albeit in a way that is sensitive to, in Alpers's (2000) words, "the burden of not imposing paradigms developed from the experience of Africans in the diaspora of the Atlantic world, with its particular forms of Euro-American racism and concomitant black responses" (94). Though concerned specifically with the African diaspora, it lays the groundwork for an Indian Ocean ethnomusicology focused on comparative and multisited studies of the Indian Ocean as an "interregional arena," with the aim of producing new understandings of human geography.

The emphasis on ethnohistory and comparison in the emerging Indian Ocean ethnomusicology harmonizes with how the relationship between taarab and the Indian Ocean has been conceptualized within and beyond the academy in recent decades. In both cases we find an emphasis on the "unconscious" cultural transmission that takes place over the *longue durée*. Herskovits and his musical protege Richard Waterman embraced a particularly strong version of this emphasis in their research on Afrodiasporic musics. Influenced by gestalt psychology, they approached the music of Africans and African diasporants as little more than a set of behaviors that are learned and transmitted "below the level of consciousness" (Herskovits 1966, 59; 1941, 19; Waterman 1952, 218; cf. Garcia 2017, 106–7). While, in good Boasian fashion, they took as axiomatic that people of African descent have the same intellectual and creative capacities as any other members of the human species, they rarely treated Afrodiasporic musical expressions as anything other than evidence of embodied cultural dispositions.[2] As such, their work reveals little about the concerns and perspectives of musicians and audiences—and even less about their creativity.

The Herskovits/Waterman approach to the music of the African diaspora is a good example of the mode of thought that Bakhtin (2010) labelled "theoretism," defined by Gary Saul Morson (1991a) as an approach "that first abstracts from concrete human actions all that is generalizable, then transforms the abstractions into a system governed by a set of rules, next derives norms from those rules, and finally denies that anything of significance has been left out in the process" (205). While contemporary scholarship on the music of the African diaspora in the Indian Ocean generally avoids replicating Herskovits and Waterman's strong emphasis on unconscious transmission, some version of its underlying theoretism is always present, because the project of approaching the Indian Ocean as a cultural milieu is mostly understood as an ethnohistorical one of retracing histories of migration and cultural exchange. The problem with this (crypto-) theoretism is, of course, what it threatens to exclude, to make inaudible, in scholarly representations of the Indian Ocean world and its inhabitants: the human experience.

Drawing together a set of empirically grounded works that approach music as a site of "boundary-formation and boundary-crossing in Indian Ocean contexts" (Sykes and Byl 2023a, 6), Jim Sykes and Julia Byl's recent volume *Sounding the Indian Ocean* (2023b) reveals and enacts the emergence of an Indian Ocean ethnomusicology that avoids the quagmire of theoretism and takes us into the human experience by decentering musical form in explorations of music as a site of human mobility and connectivity. As Sykes and Byl put it, this new Indian Ocean ethnomusicology "[refuses] to cordon off music into a domain marked 'culture'" (2023a, 9). I am sympathetic to this way of imagining what an Indian Ocean ethnomusicology can and should offer. However, it leaves open the questions of whether and in what ways Indian Ocean ethnomusicology, and by extension Indian Ocean studies, should attend to the hybridized sounds of Indian Ocean musics. My proposed answer, briefly rehearsed in my contribution to Sykes and Byl's volume (Eisenberg 2023) and enacted more fully in this book, is an approach that I propose to call a *humanistic musical anthropology*. Rather than a particular methodology, the centerpiece of this approach is an empirical and theoretical focus on *creativity*. This approach stands in direct opposition to theoretism, which "can never think about creativity without thinking it away" (Morson 1991b, 1074). When creativity is kept in view (or audible, as it were), an analysis of musical form as an outcome of historical processes of migration and exchange opens up ways of hearing lived experiences and forms of agency and action.

To be sure, a humanistic musical anthropology of the Indian Ocean finds useful models in scholarship on music in the Atlantic African diaspora. But the most relevant works are a generation or two removed from Herskovits and Waterman's studies, nurtured by critical perspectives from postcolonial theory. One broad inspiration for my approach in this book is Samuel Floyd Jr.'s (1995) exploration of the reflexive and critical aspects of Black musical communication. Drawing perspectives from African American cultural history and literary theory, Floyd develops a hermeneutics of Black music that reveals it as a medium of critical commentary on Blackness as an idea and experience. His aim, in part, is to demonstrate that the transatlantic musical "survivals" that Herskovits and Waterman cast as cultural dispositions transmitted "beneath the level of consciousness" are often artistic practices of "*playing with . . . and playing on* the content of cultural memory" (233, emphasis in original).

Floyd's concerns are, of course, specific to the Atlantic context. But his approach provides a model for a musical anthropology of the Indian Ocean world that is sensitive to creative agency. Working in his footsteps, I have explored how musicians and audiences in twentieth-century Mombasa grappled with existential questions of being and selfhood through musical acts of "*playing with . . . and playing on* the content of cultural memory." Of course, not all musical expressions in the Indian Ocean world are acts of embodied theorizing like those exemplified by the musical critics and philosophers I have engaged with in this book. But any musical expression—indeed, any act of "musicking" (Small 1998)—entails creative acts of *sensemaking* that may serve as openings for a dialogic engagement. What is needed for such an engagement, more than any particular musicological knowledge, is an intellectual openness to dialogue, the basis of which Bakhtin (1984a, 299) encapsulates in a phrase that could well be a mantra for the anthropology of music writ large: a "willingness to listen."

NOTES

PROLOGUE *Hints of Elsewhere*

1. Bakhtin famously distinguished between two modes of hybridization in culture and cultural expression: "organic" and "intentional." The former is a largely "unreflective" process through which all cultures, "despite the illusion of boundedness . . . evolve historically" (Werbner 1997, 4); the latter is an artistic act oriented toward reflecting upon—objectifying, playing with, ironizing—this process. While Bakhtin developed this dichotomy in relation to language and literature, it holds obvious heuristic value for culture more broadly, and has been taken up in discussions of musical style (Haynes 2005; Sanga 2010; Weiss 2008). Both modes of hybridization involve "borrowings, mimetic appropriations, exchanges and inventions," but intentional hybridization unfolds through "artistic interventions" (Werbner 1997, 4–5) that seek to generate a "collision between differing points of views on the world" (Bakhtin 1981, 360).

2. The collection is archived in the NYU Abu Dhabi Library under the title *Andrew Eisenberg Collection of East African Commercial Sound Recordings AD.MC.035* (hereafter "Eisenberg Collection"), located at https://findingaids.library.nyu.edu/nyuad/ad_mc_035/. Much of the collection was compiled in collaboration with Jamal Hafidh Jahadhmy, an avid music collector and nephew of taarab musician Zein l'Abdin. Omari Swaleh al-Abdi also provided assistance in the process, by connecting me to an anonymous private collector from whom I received many of the materials analyzed in this book.

INTRODUCTION *Sound, Sense, and Subjectivity in Mombasa*

1. The late Kenyan Swahili poet and scholar Ahmed Sheikh Nabhany (discussed in chapter 5) often used the word *pumbao* to characterize taarab. I translate this word as "amusement," as it carries the same connotations of "enjoyment," "diversion," and "leisure" (see Sacleux 1939, 763). In a 2003 conference presentation, Nabhany uses the word

twice in the same definition of taarab, once as a noun and once as a verb. Sticking with "amusement" for both uses, the definition reads as follows: "taarab is a form of amusement that sees people gather together after work to amuse themselves with lutes, drums, and singers with beautiful, attractive voices" (*Twarabu ni pumbao watu wana kusanyika pahali pamoja baada ya shughuli na kujipumbaza kwa ala za kinanda na vigoma na wenye kuimba kwa sauti nzuri za kuvutia*) (Nabhany 2003, 1).

2. Many coastal Swahili speakers articulate the latter etymology in everyday talk, by pronouncing taarab as "*ta'arab*," thereby emphasizing the Arabic root *'arab* in the same way that is often done with *ustaarabu* (*usta'arabu*).

3. For overviews of taarab's regional varieties, see Askew 2002, 115; Frankl et al. 1998, 23; Graebner 1991b, 188–89; 2005b; Khamis 2005, 147; Ntarangwi 2001; 2003; 2007, 13.

4. Focusing on appropriation as a poetic act cuts against the grain of contemporary discourses of "cultural appropriation" that focus on harms perpetrated by powerful agents against marginalized social groups (e.g., Ziff and Rao 1997; Arewa 2016; Oluo 2019, 142–52). It departs, as well, from the interest in postcolonial studies and the anthropology of consumption on the counterhegemonic potentials of appropriation (see Ferguson 2002; Miller 1995; Hahn 2011). Decentering the questions of power that animate these other discourses is necessary, however, in order to home in on aspects of appropriation in cultural expression that may not be reducible to domination or resistance (Schneider 2003, 221–22; Krings 2015, 16–20). This is especially important, as Matthias Krings (2015) suggests, when examining contexts of bottom-up or lateral forms of "cultural appropriation"—such as transoceanic appropriation on the Swahili coast—where an overriding focus on domination or resistance may obscure "the manifold forms of re-signification involved" (17).

5. These comments come in the midst of a discussion of what Mazrui calls the "Afro-Oriental phase" of Mombasa's historical development, which he suggests came to an end when the British Empire became the dominant power in the region in the late nineteenth century. It seems clear, however, that this observation, which begins with the phrase "over time," refers to the twentieth century. His complaint that "some so-called Swahili composers simply plagiarized the music of some Indian songs and just substituted Swahili lyrics" is clearly aimed at Indian taarab.

6. With respect to Graebner's specific point about Kenya providing a better environment for the screening of Hindi films in the postcolonial period, Ned Bertz (2015, 184) reports that while the independence governments of Tanzania and Zanzibar did, indeed, take a heavy-handed approach to "nationalizing" cinema, they nonetheless allowed Hindi films relatively free rein.

7. Janet Topp Fargion (2014) suggests that Zanzibari taarab was just as deeply influenced by Hindi film music as Mombasan taarab was; it is only that this influence is "harder to pinpoint" in the former than in the latter (82).

8. It is precisely because I understand this book to be a study of Swahili ethnogenesis that I avoid using *Swahili* as a general label for members of the broader population of Swahili-speaking coastal Muslims. In addition to being polysemous and contested in the present, its meaning has evolved over time, and that evolution is part of the story that I aim to tell in this book.

9. The ethnonym *Mijikenda*, meaning "nine villages," has been used since the 1940s (Willis 1993). The constituent communities are Chonyi, Digo, Duruma, Giriama, Jibana, Kambe, Kauma, Rabai, and Ribe.

10. The subjective dimension of this relationship between political in-betweenness and political dissociation is brought out nicely in M. G. Vassanji's novel *The In-Between World of Vikram Lall* (2004), which explores the experiences of an Indian Kenyan man "who wants to belong in Kenya and to Kenya" but continually finds himself "detached" from the country that is his home (Myambo 2012, 172).

11. The British colonial administration initially planned to relocate the population of Mombasa Old Town, but these plans never came to fruition (Willis 1993, 145–60). Until today, the northern section of the neighborhood is still dominated by the same Swahili clans that are thought to have settled the area as far back as the fourteenth century, while the southern section is home to a mix of coastal communities and Indian Ocean diasporants similar to what one would have found in the area at the beginning of the twentieth century. The population survey carried out by the Mombasa Conservation Project in 1990 demonstrates a remarkable population stability in the neighborhood. More than 60 percent of households in the Fort Jesus area and the southern portion of Old Town (the "conservation area") had lived in their homes for more than five years at the time of the survey. Even more telling, nearly 77 percent of households had lived in Mombasa before they had moved into the home the surveyors found them in, and nearly 54 percent of households had kin nearby (MCP 1990, 43–55). One change not taken into account in this survey is the influx of Somalis into Mombasa following the civil war in Somalia in 1991. The Somalis who settled in Old Town were generally Swahili-speaking Somalis (Barawas), who settled in the sections of Kibokoni where this community was already present.

12. On this "Arab racial myth" and its critics in Swahili studies, see Allen 1982; Amory 1994, 65–71.

13. There is some resonance here, as well, with Dror Wahrman's (2008, xiii) use of "regime of identity" to mean a "set of assumptions that define[s] the meaning, significance, and limits of identity."

14. The extent to which modern African ethnicity should be understood as a Western import imposed by colonial administrations is a matter of debate among Africanist anthropologists and historians (Glassman 2000; 2004; 2011, ix–x; Lentz 1995; Mamdani 1996, 183–87; Ranger 1993; Willis and Gona 2013). For the most part, as Gabrielle Lynch (2017, 96)

writes, it is axiomatic among Africanist scholars today that "pre-colonial African identities were relatively fluid, permeable, overlapping, and complex; and that the more bounded and politically pertinent ethnic identities of today are (at least to a certain extent) the product of a colonial order of delineated control and of dual processes of invention and imagination." But historians have complicated this picture. In particular, Jonathan Glassman's work on racial thought in Zanzibar suggests that modern ethnicity in African societies cannot be reduced to a "false consciousness" (Mafeje 1971, 259) that was foisted upon "inert" African subjects by "a single-minded, all-knowing state or collaborating elite" (Glassman 2000, 398). It had "multiple sources" (Glassman 2004), including "locally generated ideas" that became "inextricably entwined" with imported Western concepts (Glassman 2011, x).

15. Sharifs on the Swahili coast trace their origins to Hadramawt, in present-day Yemen (see chapter 4). For decades, Swahilist scholars have generally assumed the claims of Persian origins among some Swahili patricians to be no more than "myths or foundation charters" (Horton and Middleton 2000, 53). But a recent genetic study has provided "direct evidence for Persian-associated ancestry . . . arriving on the eastern African coast by about AD 1000" (Brielle et al. 2023, 872).

16. There is no general term in Swahili for a patrician "confederation," as this social configuration is unique to Mombasa. The Nine Tribes confederation includes the tribes of Mvita, Jomvu, Kilifi, Mtwapa, Pate, Faza, Shaka, Bajuni, and Katwa. Of these, the first four mentioned are considered to be the oldest in the town. They came together as town owners after the Sultan of Malindi conquered it in 1590 with the help of the Portuguese. The Bajuni are the newest, and they are part of a more expansive group originally from the Kenya-Somali border region. The Three Tribes includes the tribes of Changamwe, Kilindini, and Tangana. They are said to have come from the mainland around the same period and settled originally on the far side of the island from the other confederation. According to Berg (1968), the Omani rulers of the eighteenth and nineteenth centuries helped to merge the two confederations. Before the influence of Standard Swahili began to grow in the late twentieth century, the entire Twelve Tribes spoke Mvita Swahili for the most part. The Jomvu and Changamwe, who each have settlements on the mainland, had their own dialects.

17. The line comes from the poem "Kilio Huliya Mwenye" (Change Begins at Home), composed and recited by Ustadh Mau to inaugurate an international conference that I organized with Athman Lali Omar and Ann Biersteker in Mombasa in 2006. The poem has recently been published with an English translation and explication (Raia and Vierke 2023, 200–206).

18. Coined by Steven Feld (1996), the term *acoustemology* "joins acoustics to epistemology to investigate sounding and listening as a knowing-in-action: a knowing-with and knowing-through the audible" (Feld 2015, 12; see also Eisenberg 2013).

19. Lady Welby was the first to employ *sense* as a technical term, using it to describe how

meaning emerges from "the organic response to environment" (Welby [1911], in Hardwick 1977, 169). In her 1903 book *What is Meaning?* she defines *sense* as an "expression-value" derived from immediate engagement with the world, and argues that human beings create *meaning* proper by adding intention and rational ideation to it (Welby 1903, 27–28). Peirce saw in Welby's schema a connection to his own semiotic theory, and adopted *sense* as a synonym for his *immediate interpretant*, which is the basic "impression" of a sign on an interpreting mind, the feeling of possibility that instigates interpretation (Liszka 1996, 78–82; Peirce, in Hardwick 1977, 110). A couple of decades later, Dewey echoed Welby and Peirce in defining *sense* as "meaning which is itself felt or directly had" (Dewey 1929, 261; see also Dewey 1934, 22). William James, for his part, also viewed "sensible experience" as a necessary foundation for other forms of meaning, up to and including "rational meaning" (James 1879).

20. The definition of *ngoma* in Charles Sacleux's highly reputed Swahili-French dictionary reads as follows: "*Tambour . . . Danse au son du tambour, ou danse en gén., ou même toute espèce de séance musicale avec instruments*" (1939, 680).

21. As Steven Feld (1994a) argues, Meyer goes astray in assuming that the habitual nature of musical style means that "extra-musical and socio-musical markings" somehow lie outside of it (148). In actuality, such markings are part and parcel of the "felt probabilities" of a style.

22. Patricia Waugh (1984) draws a similar connection between stylistic appropriation and the poetic function in her discussion of literary parody, which she argues "inserts a metaphoric version of [a work or genre] into the ongoing (metonymic) literary tradition" (69).

23. In music studies today, a focus on the internal workings of a text is more often described as *analysis* or *theory*. But as the late Adam Krims (2000, 27) argued specifically with respect to *theory*, the (mis)use of these terms in music studies to refer to what is more properly described as *poetics* is counterproductive for fostering dialogue between music studies and related disciplines. In other humanities disciplines as well as anthropology, *analysis* tends to mean a specialized hermeneutic procedure, and *theory* an application of broader frameworks of understanding.

24. I use *Swahili coast* in this book in the restricted sense of the East African littoral from southern Somalia in the north to southern Tanzania in the south. But from the perspective of the *longue durée*, and taking into account linguistic and cultural connections, it stretches into Mozambique in the south and includes the Comoros and northwestern Madagascar (LaViolette and Wynne-Jones 2017).

25. Aristotle took mimesis to be "an anthropological constant distinguishing human beings from other animals" (Gebauer and Wulf 1995, 53). This view has been reaffirmed and further developed since the mid-twentieth century in philosophical investigations of modernity by the Frankfurt School theorists (Benjamin 1978, 1979; Horkheimer and

Adorno 2002), anthropological investigations of magic and ritual (Frazer 1957; Mauss 1972; Taussig 1993), and theoretical accounts of human cognitive and cultural evolution (Donald 1991, 2006; Tomlinson 2015; Tolbert 2001).

26. An earlier version of chapter 3 appeared alongside Vierke 2017 and Ivanov 2017, in *Comparative Studies of South Asia, Africa, and the Middle East* (37.2), as part of a special section on "the Indian Ocean as aesthetic space" (Verne and Verne 2017). An important antecedent for all the work listed here is Terence Ranger's classic *Dance and Society in Eastern Africa 1890–1970* (1975), which documents the history of *beni ngoma*, a genre of competitive group performance involving the imitation of British military music and parades that originated on the Swahili coast before spreading throughout the wider region.

27. Appadurai's conception of genealogy draws from Michel Foucault's (1978) Nietzschean conception of genealogy as a critical or "effective" history that seeks to "undermine the self-evidences of our age in order to open possibilities for the enhancement of life" (Mahon 1992, 8). The genealogy I develop in this book is broadly Foucauldian in its focus on "processes of subject formation or self making" within systems of power (Saar 2008, 307). But whereas Foucauldian genealogy typically "reduces discourse/meaning to its effects and treats meaning in terms of power relations" (Bielskis 2005, 163; see also Habermas 1986), I attend to meaning-making as a domain of social practice that is not reducible to a struggle over power/knowledge.

ONE *A Feeling for the Boundaries: Early Recorded Taarab*

1. Mbaruk Talsam, "Basahera Umuongo," Odeon A 24 21 52 (Eisenberg Collection, Series II, 398/9).

2. The year 1930 was the last in which these three companies operated as separate entities, all of them falling under the umbrella of EMI by the end of 1931. But even as the massive EMI merger was brewing—indeed, even for quite some time after it took place—competition between the different companies was fierce, a situation that helped to foster the scramble for taarab (Vernon 1997).

3. The other key members of the collective were Maalim Shaaban Umbaye (discussed below), Subeit bin Ambar, and Buda bin Mwendo. With the exception of Maalim Shaaban, who was primarily a singer and tar (frame drum) player, all the male members of the binti Saad collective played one or more of the following string instruments: *gambus* (a southern Arabian lute), *kamanjā* (Arab/Persian fiddle), *ʿūd*, and violin.

4. A version of the original poem is included in Abdalla 1974.

5. Initiatives by Odeon and the French record company Pathé to record Mombasa-based musicians in 1930 are described in official EMI documents (Graebner 2004b, 3). HMV's role in recording these musicians seems to be less well documented, but Laura Fair was able to retrieve information from an HMV catalog from 1930–1931 pertaining

to a couple dozen releases under the names of four different Mombasa-based singers. I am grateful to her for providing me with this information.

6. One might argue, with some justification, that this has to do with Tanzanian writer Shaaban Robert's hagiography (*wasifu*) of Siti, *Wasifu wa Siti Binti Saad* (1967), which transformed her into "a symbol of progress, industry, and dignity of the modern African woman" in the early postcolonial era (Topan 1997, 300; see also Sanga 2016). But Robert did not pluck Siti from obscurity when he set pen to paper a few years after her death in 1950. The songs of the binti Saad collective were still enjoyed, remembered, and performed on Zanzibar and the Kenyan coast at the time, while those of other taarab musicians who had been active during the interwar years—including the Kenyan coast's Siti Peponi, who was at one point seen as a strong competitor to Siti (Suleiman 1969, 89; Topp Fargion 2014, 121–22)—had already been forgotten or relegated to minor status. My older interlocutors in Mombasa, those born between the late 1930s and early 1950s, all recalled listening to the music of the binti Saad collective growing up, while few could recall any songs by other taarab musicians from the era.

7. The theoretical terms and concepts that I use in discussing aspects of the *Maqām* system in this book are those of contemporary Arab music theory. While this theory is taught and studied on Zanzibar today, it would not have been familiar to the binti Saad collective—especially not during the interwar years, when it was still being standardized in Cairo (Marcus 1989, 12–41). It would most likely be impossible at this point to reconstruct how the members of the binti Saad collective conceptualized and communicated about *Maqām*. The smattering of notes on the matter in Matola et al. 1966 are suggestive but raise more questions than answers.

8. A *dūlāb* is often used in Arab music to quickly and efficiently establish the feeling of a melodic mode (*maqām*) (Farraj and Shumays 2019, 145–46; Touma 1996, 106). For this reason, it was often used on recordings of Arab music during the shellac era (roughly from the first decade of the twentieth century until the end of World War II), when recorded performances were limited to three-minute increments.

9. A "half-flat" pitch in the context of *Maqām* is a diatonic pitch lowered by approximately one quarter-tone. In most cases, including the one under discussion here, a *maqām* with a half-flat tonic is built on the *Sīkāh* trichord, classically spelled E half-flat, F, G. These include *Maqām Sīkāh*, *Maqām ʿIrāq*, and *Maqām Huzām*, all of which fall in the *Sīkāh* "family." The specific modulation in this part of "Basahera" moves from *Maqām Bayātī* on G, the song's primary mode, to *Maqām ʿIrāq* on A half-flat, by way of tonicizing the second scale-degree of *Maqām Bayātī* on G.

10. The only published compilation of poems by members of the binti Saad collective, *Waimbaji Wa Juzi* (Matola et al. 1966), contains a number of commentaries on the meanings of the poems from the last surviving member at the time, Maalim Shaaban, but almost no information about the musical settings of any of the poems.

11. Werner Graebner (2004a, 173–75), Hildegard Kiel (2012), and I have each held focus group interviews with accomplished Zanzibari musicians (different musicians in each case) aimed at gathering reactions to some of the earliest taarab recordings. (My interview was carried out with members of the Dhow Countries Music Academy taarab orchestra during their visit to NYU Abu Dhabi on September 26, 2019.) Graebner reports that his interviewees were "[astonished] that the music was so kaleidoscopic and that it featured quite a number of elements from local ngoma-dances" (174). Both Kiel and I found our interviewees puzzled by certain aspects of the recorded performances, including the melodic modes that were used, which they could not always identify.

12. For a brief history of DCMA, see Topp Fargion 2014, 184–89.

13. The prime example, perhaps, is her iconic version of Maalim Shaaban's "Muhogo wa Jang'ombe" (ca. 1930, Columbia WE 14), which is now the standard version for Zanzibari taarab musicians and listeners. Bi Kidude transformed what was a slow melody in *Maqām kurd* (similar to the Phrygian mode, in Western music theory) to an infectious, upbeat melody in *Maqām 'ajam* (similar to diatonic major). Kidude's version can be heard on her disc *Zanzibar* (1998, Retroafric 12CD). Maalim Shaaban's version is available on *Poetry and Languid Charm: Swahili Music from Tanzania and Kenya from the 1920s to the 1950s* (compiled by Janet Topp Fargion, 2007, British Library Sound Archive: Topic Records TSCD936).

14. A digitized version of Jamal Hafidh's cassette collection comprises part of the Eisenberg Collection.

15. This song was recorded in 1930 by Columbia Records in either Dar es Salaam or Zanzibar. It is available on the 2007 compilation *Poetry and Languid Charm*.

16. Evidence of songs from Lamu being performed by Zanzibari orchestras in the first decades of the twentieth century comes primarily from an unpublished manuscript penned by Zanzibari musician Shaib Abeid Barajab (1890–1974), one of the founders of the Zanzibari taarab orchestra Nadi Ikhwani Safaa, which celebrated its centenary in 2005 and continues to operate to this day. Janet Topp Fargion and Werner Graebner make extensive use of the work in their narratives of early taarab. Abeid writes, "We started to learn these Arabic and Swahili songs . . . and many Swahili songs in the Lamu style. Because at the time we used these melodies from Lamu very much, and their original poetry, and for a wedding taarab they were absolutely necessary" (quoted and translated in Graebner 2004a, 183).

17. As a native of Mombasa, Mbaruk's first language would have been Kimvita. Presumably, he was also quite proficient in Kiamu, the Lamu dialect of Swahili. He would have had no trouble adjusting to speaking the Unguja dialect of Zanzibar, which he used as the basis for much of his poetry. But it seems likely that his speech still bore markers of Kimvita.

18. On Umm Kulthum and her status in Egyptian society, see Danielson 1997. In a recent publication, Swahili linguist Abdulaziz Yusuf Lodhi, apparently echoing popular

sentiment, calls Siti binti Saad "the 'Umm Kulthum' of East Africa" (Lodhi 2019, 231). A popular story, probably apocryphal, has it that Siti binti Saad met Umm Kulthum in India while they were both there to record (Graebner 2004a, 177). An intricate version of this story appears in Zanzibari journalist Nasra Mohamed Hilal's recent Swahili-language hagiography (Hilal 2007, 41).

19. It is not for nothing that Hilal's book carries the title *Mfinyanzi Aingia Kasri*, "The Potter Enters the Palace" (Hilal 2007).

20. The category of comedic skits (*vichekesho*) overlaps with plays (*michezo ya kuigiza*). It also overlaps with songs, which can be comedic as well. In his contextual notes for the poetry collection *Waimbaji wa Juzi*, Maalim Shaaban reports that a couple of songs by Buda bin Mwendo "were sung as comedic skits in a performance for Sultan Seyyid Khalifa" (*iliimbwa kama vichekesho, mbele ya Sultani Seyyid Khalifa*) (Matola et al. 1966, 121).

21. Maalim Shaaban, "Hadithi ya Bibi na Vijakazi Part 1" and "Hadithi ya Bibi na Vijakazi Part 2," Columbia WE 54 (Eisenberg Collection, Series I, 155/6). Comedy routines and stories like this became common fare in commercial recordings marketed to coastal Swahili audiences after World War II. Shaaban's "hadithi" was recorded around 1930, however, making it certainly one of the first such recorded performances in circulation.

22. Aly Ahmed Jahadhmy writes, "Since childhood, Mbaruk showed an ability to make people laugh with jokes and satire: he had a quick tongue, a mastery of Swahili vocabulary, and an ability to use wordplay to mock people. What is more, he was not easily embarrassed, and was therefore able to undertake any sort of skit or satire that might please or entertain" (Jahadhmy, in Matola et al. 1966, 62, my translation).

23. Mbaruk's paternal uncle was also an important figure in *beni*. The Talsam family were patrons of different forms of ngoma, including beni. Mbaruk's uncle made his reputation as "King Talsam" of the beni group Skochi (Jahadhmy, in Matola et al. 1966, 61).

24. Bakhtin adopted *stylization*—or, more precisely, the Russian equivalent, *stilizatsii*—from the Russian formalists. In the formalists' work, it generally refers to an overt appropriation of a foreign style that is carried out in a manner too playful to be considered simple imitation but not playful enough to be considered parody (Ogden 2005, 528). Bakhtin uses the term in much the same way, except that he adds a sociological dimension by considering it as a mode of "double-voicing."

25. The former extreme in music is sometimes referred to as *pastiche* (though this term is rarely used beyond of Western contexts). The latter is often referred to as *parody*, though Bakhtin's phrase "rhetorical parody" is probably more appropriate.

26. Fair builds on Janet Topp Fargion's (Topp 1994) work on the history of Zanzibari taarab in developing this theoretical perspective, and credits her with the idea that the music was in some sense about "belonging."

27. Mbaruk Talsam, "Ya Dana Dana," Odeon A 24 20 79 (Eisenberg Collection, Series II, 401).

28. Abdilatif Abdalla, personal communication, September 7, 2019.

29. The reference to *boriti*, which I have translated as ceiling beams but specifically refers to mangrove poles, might also be heard as a reference to dock work, which many Hadrami men undertook in that period.

30. Personal communication, July 8, 2019.

31. Bi Kidude's revival of her music in the mid-1980s was, in part, a national project, spurred by then-Zanzibari President (later to become President of Tanzania) Ali Hassan Mwinyi (Graebner 2005a, 13).

32. The centuries-old Basheikh Mosque is one of Mombasa Old Town's most iconic edifices, being one of the neighborhood's two surviving mosques constructed in the ancient Ibadi style, with a single limestone minaret. Controlled by the Basheikh clan since the colonial era, its cemetery is the final resting place of prominent clan members who were also, by definition, respected members of Mombasa's Swahili-speaking Muslim community. The mosque is also known as Mnara or Tangana. The latter name refers to the clan of Swahili patricians who controlled it before the Basheikh took it over (Berg and Walter 1968; Meier 2016, 200).

33. The detail about Mbaruk playing his *'ūd* on the veranda comes from Mombasa-born poet Abdilatif Abdalla, who recalls Mbaruk as a fixture in Old Town during his childhood in the 1950s (personal communication, June 1, 2019).

TWO *The Lullaby of Taarab: Radio and Reflexivity in the 1950s*

1. *Tashkota* comes from the Japanese name for the instrument, *taishōgoto*. I never heard the word *tuntunia* used during my time in Mombasa, but it was apparently common in the mid-twentieth century. John Storm Roberts mentions it in a piece written in the 1970s (Roberts 1973, 22). His primary interlocutor in Mombasa was the instrument's main proponent, Yaseen Mohamed Tofeli.

2. This section draws heavily on the work of historian James R. Brennan (cited throughout). Brennan and I carried out research on Sauti ya Mvita around the same time. We shared materials and even conducted two interviews together. The topic was of relatively minor interest for my own research at the time. Thankfully, Brennan's interest ran deeper, and I now benefit from his empirical work and theoretical perspectives.

3. Letter of D. M. Mati, *Mombasa Times*, April 12, 1957.

4. The relationship between Arab and Swahili agents of Sauti ya Mvita may not have been entirely frictionless. According to Hyder Kindy (1972, 165–66), some within the Arab community initially objected to his appointment as assistant provincial information officer. But according to Kindy, this tension was quickly resolved.

5. Copies of these recordings have been circulating informally in Mombasa for decades. Jamal Hafidh Jahadhmy generously provided me with a cassette copy.

6. Waliaula refers in particular to Chiraghdin's classic article "Kiswahili Na Wenyewe" (1974), whose title literally translates as "The Swahili Language and its Owners."

7. The first decade of the twenty-first century was a moment of rebirth for local radio not only in Mombasa, but throughout Kenya, catalyzed by the liberalization of the airwaves at the end of the 1990s. Two privately run Islamic radio stations emerged in Mombasa during my fieldwork. Radio Rahma was launched in late December 2004, during the early phase of my research, and Radio Salaam was just starting up as I wrapped up in 2006. Both have been extremely successful and continue to operate today.

8. Swahili poetry did come to be integrated into the programming of Radio Rahma and Radio Salaam, albeit to a limited extent. Clarissa Vierke (2011, xvi) mentions that Ahmed Sheikh Nabhany regularly read poems on the stations during her time in Mombasa in 2006.

9. Abdalla Mohamed Mbwana, unrecorded interview, Mombasa, September 28, 2005.

10. *Jauharah* is an Arabicized version of the Swahili *johar*, meaning "jewel." The band's name is also commonly rendered as "Jauhar," "Johar," or "Johari."

11. Mbarak Rashid, recorded interview, Mombasa, October 20, 2005. Mbarak Rashid could even recall the exact date of the performance: April 14. According to notes compiled later by Jamal Hafidh Jahadhmy in conversation with Jauharah founding member Abdalla Jemadari, Sheikh-Sir Mbarak al-Hinawy was one of around ten "patron members" of the orchestra. Most were male business leaders and/or politicians from the broader Arab-Swahili community. But there was also one Briton among them, Colonel M. T. Boscawen, who owned a sisal plantation in Tanga and engaged in philanthropic activities in support of Muslim communities in the region.

12. Zein l'Abdin, unrecorded interview, Mombasa, August 11, 2005.

13. Johar, "Kasha Langu," *Johar Volume 1* (Eisenberg Collection, Series III, 67).

14. Mbarak Rashid, recorded interview, October 20, 2005. This was the first of two videorecorded interviews with four founding members of Jauharah Orchestra: Mbarak Rashid, Abdalla Jemadari, Miraji Juma, and Awadh Omar Ruwaily (Awadh Tunda). The interviews were arranged by Jamal Hafidh Jahadhmy and took place at the home of Salim Nasher. All four subjects have since passed away, Mbarak Rashid only six months after the interview took place.

15. The composer is Medhat Assem. On the adoption of tango style in Egyptian music, see Frishkopf 2003.

16. The particular variant used is known in Egyptian/Levantine *maqām* theory as *Maqām ʿAjam ʿUshayrān*, but I have never encountered this term on the Swahili coast.

17. "Arabian Conga" is featured in the collection *Opika Pende: Africa at 78 RPM* (2011, Dust-to-Digital).

18. Siti Ganduri and Party of Ras Maalim Revue, "Kitabu Nimekifungua," 1952, Jambo EA 190 (Eisenberg Collection, Series II, 488).

19. The original recording of the song by Sauti ya Mvita is lost, but Mkali rerecorded it in the 1980s with Mbwana Radio Service: Ali Mkali, "Bembeya Mtoto," *Ali Mkali Volume 1* (Eisenberg Collection, Series III, 5).

20. It is unclear how much of the musical setting of this song is traditional. The Somali Bajuni musicians who recorded a version of "Bembeya Mtoto" in 1970 without crediting Ali Mkali probably believed both its verbal text and its music to be traditional (Williams et al. 1971). But my interlocutors in Mombasa believed them to be Mkali's.

21. The word is normally spelled *bembea* in Standard Swahili (which is based on Kiunguja). *Bembeya* appears to be the preferred spelling for Kimvita speakers, however.

22. Sacleux (1939) lists *bembea* as a variant of *pembea* in a number of dialects of Swahili, including Mombasan Kimvita. But few Swahili dictionaries published in later decades list the words as synonyms, suggesting that using bembea in place of pembea may have come to be heard as a malapropism as Standard Swahili took hold on the Kenyan coast. One exception is Rechenbach's (1967) Swahili-English dictionary, which lists bembea as a "rare" form of pembea. Even for Swahili speakers who believe it to be ungrammatical, the use of bembea in place of pembea nonetheless has a poetic logic to it, due to its etymological connection to *bembeleza*, meaning "calm" or "lull."

23. An example of the use of the *howa* vocable in a Zulu context is featured in the famous Apartheid-era documentary *Rhythm of Resistance* (Marre 1979). The vocable is sometimes glossed in translations as "hush" or "hushaby" (Senkoro 1995, 131; Knappert 1990, 104). But this is imprecise in a way that arguably matters for approaching the meanings of the songs. Whereas *hush* mimics the sound of wind or fluid, *howa* mimics the mournful cry of a human being. The verbal texts of howa lullaby songs often thematize crying and sadness.

24. I have not been able to determine when Ali Mkali's "Howa Howa" was originally recorded. A (re)recording of it is featured along with "Bembeya Mtoto" on the cassette *Ali Mkali Volume 1*, produced by Mbwana Radio Service in the 1980s (Eisenberg Collection, Series III, 5).

25. Siti binti Saad, "Mbembeleze Mtoto," Columbia WE 39 (Eisenberg Collection, Series II, 457/8, listed as "Howa Bibiye 1" and "Howa Bibiye 2"); Maalim Shaaban, "Howa Howa Mwanangu" (Eisenberg Collection, Series II, 383).

26. Such a gendered structuring of public and private has been described by anthropologists working in various societies. Lévi-Strauss constructed much of his structuralist theoretical apparatus around this near-universal fact of culture (1969). Later, Rosaldo (1980) and Ortner (1996) each revisited this idea in order to question both the universality of male dominance and the epistemological underpinnings of structuralist anthropology (cf. Low and Lawrence-Zúñiga 2003).

27. Yaseen & Party, "Nimepata Mwana," Mzuri HL 7-6. The song appears on the recent Afro-7 compilation *Yaseen & Party* (2019, AFR7-DIGI-05).

28. Juma Bhalo & Party, "Howa Howa," Philips HL 7-136 (Eisenberg Collection, Series II, 359).

THREE *The Mouths of Professors and Clowns: Indian Taarab*

1. *Teesri Manzil* (dir. Vijay Anand, 1966).

2. Following the East African convention, I refer to people and cultural artifacts of South Asian extraction as "Indian." The term *South Asian* is rarely used in East Africa; *Asian* is more common, but like Aiyar I find it unsuitable because it is an "inheritance from colonial racial categories" with no corollary in Swahili (Aiyar 2015, 20).

3. On Stambuli Abdillahi Nasser's role in public life in Mombasa, see Kresse 2018, 147–89.

4. Precedents for this approach can be found in Eidsheim 2009, 2008; Feld et al. 2004 (especially the contributions by Fox and Samuels); Harkness 2013; Meizel 2011, 2020.

5. In addition to Zein l'Abdin, I interviewed three noted Swahili poets: Ahmed Sheikh Nabhany, Ahmad Nassir Juma Bhalo, and Khuleita Muhashamy.

6. Besides my own experiences collecting and listening to old taarab recordings with local consultants, I rely here on Graebner 2004a. Based on focus-group work, Graebner divides the melodic/rhythmic content of his samples into eight stylistic categories: "Swahili ngoma" (music of traditional rites), "*kitaarab*" (the sui generis style of early Swahili taarab), "Arabia/Gulf/Red Sea," "Arabic (general)" (presumably Arab music of luminaries from Cairo), "Indian," "European," "Latin," and "*Kimanyema*" (Congolese). "Indian," Graebner writes, "refers specifically to Indian film music." This cannot be the case for the earliest recordings he deals with, which he dates around 1928–1930, as this was before the advent of sound in Indian cinema. It is more likely that the five early Zanzibari taarab recordings that Graebner's specialists recognized as "Indian" were based stylistically on *qawwali* or *ghazal*.

7. I will explore the relationship between Hadrami *ṭarab* and Swahili taarab on the Kenyan coast in chapter 4.

8. These recordings were produced in Nairobi by the Indian-owned Shankardas Company and distributed on the HMV MA series. Examples from both singers can be heard on the compilation *Bellyachers, Listen — Songs from East Africa, 1938–46* (Honest Jon's Records, 2010). I also managed to find other examples (presumably reissues) in Assanand & Sons' leftover stock (Eisenberg Collection, Series I, 37; 111–13).

9. Andrew Burchell, unrecorded interview, Mombasa, August 24, 2005.

10. Ned Bertz (2011) avers that early Hindi musical films "described a similar colonized experience at the hands of the British," and later ones "dealt with issues of globalization and liberalization, developments which coincided in South Asia and Africa" (69). Laura Fair (2009), meanwhile, maintains that for Swahili youth in the post-World War II era,

the films' narratives of romantic love resonated with the ideas of liberation and self-determination that were in the air.

11. "EAP190: Digitising Archival Material Pertaining to 'Young India' Label Gramophone Records," Suresh Chandvankar, British Library, sounds.bl.uk/World-and-traditional-music/Young-India-record-label-collection (accessed July 7, 2023).

12. A sizable collection of these songs is available in the Eisenberg Collection. Fourteen songs are also available for streaming on the British Library's website: "Young India record label collection," British Library, sounds.bl.uk/World-and-traditional-music/Young-India-record-label-collection (accessed July 7, 2023).

13. Zuhura Swaleh, recorded interview, Mombasa, September 18, 2004; Malika (Asha Abdo Suleiman), unrecorded interview, Michigan, USA, May 8, 2006.

14. Lamu Omari, "Boi," Mzuri AM 430 (Eisenberg Collection, Series I, 129)

15. Eisenberg Collection, Series II, in process.

16. Ahmed Sheikh Nabhany, unrecorded interview, Mombasa, October 10, 2005.

17. Most, if not all, Indian taarab poems fall within the category of Swahili poetry that Nabhany called *sama* (presumably from the Arabic *samāʿ*, meaning "hearing") or *mahadhi* ("musical setting"), in which the prosody is determined by the structure of an existing melody (see Shariff 1988, 59–60).

18. Ahmad Nassir Juma Bhalo's 1971 poetry collection *Umalenga wa Mvita* (Nassir 1971) includes poems composed in Bajuni, Hindi, and Giriama, interspersed among his characteristically difficult poetry in often archaic Kimvita (Mombasan Swahili).

19. Urdu is a central component of Hindustani, the most commonly used dialect in Hindi films.

20. There is a similar link between religious and secular vocal training in the Arab world (See Danielson 1990, 21–27; Shannon 2006, 153–54).

21. These details come from Mombasan interlocutors who are Bhalo's contemporaries. (See also Bhalo n.d.).

22. The only surviving Swaleh al-Abdi recording that I am aware of is a single track on John Storm Roberts's 1983 Original Music compilation *Songs the Swahili Sing*.

23. Ahmad Nassir's full name is Ahmad Nassir Juma Bhalo, and he is sometimes referred to as Ustadh Bhalo. To avoid confusion with his cousin, I refer to him here as Ahmad Nassir. For an overview of Ahmad Nassir's life, work, and thought, see Kresse 2007, 139–75.

24. This information comes from more than one anonymous source familiar with Ahmad Nassir and Juma Bhalo. I conducted one interview with Ahmad Nassir, but he declined to discuss his Indian taarab work. Juma Bhalo declined to be interviewed.

25. In addition to the examples in the Eisenberg Collection, two of Maruf's early recordings may be streamed on the South African Music Archive Project website: "Mo-

hamed," samap.ukzn.ac.za/mohamed-east-african; "Sote tu lo uzuriya," samap.ukzn.ac.za/sote-tu-lo-uzuriya-east-african (both accessed February 5, 2017).

26. Jambo EA 421 (Eisenberg Collection, Series I, 188)

27. Aditi Deo, personal communication, January 3, 2011.

28. The oral history was produced by Stephen Muecke, who interviewed Mzee Mombasa in Mombasa in 2000 with the assistance of a translator (Alpers 2002).

29. Eisenberg Collection, Series II, in process.

30. Miss Kiran Pardeshi, "Sauti Yako Nzuri," Young India, SR-128 (Eisenberg Collection, Series II, 530). The recording is also available for streaming on the British Library website: "Sauti Yako Nzuri," Young India record label collection, sounds.bl.uk/World-and-traditional-music/Young-India-record-label-collection/025M-CEAP190X7X14-005ZV0 (accessed February 5, 2017).

31. Jamal Hafidh Jahadhmy, personal communication, June 4, 2005. Jamal believes the original source may be a *qawwali* melody.

32. The word *Banyani* is derived from *Vaniya*, a centuries-old Gujarati term for a particular class of Jain or Hindu merchant. It evidently came into use in East Africa around the mid-nineteenth century, when Hindu traders began arriving in large numbers with the support of the Sultan of Zanzibar (see Nagar 1996, 64; Rechenbach 1967, 25). On pidginized Swahili among East African Indians, see Whiteley 1974, 73–79.

33. The Segeju are a traditionally pastoral people of eastern Kenya and Tanzania.

34. Without denying its unsavory aspects, it is possible to argue that the sense of intimacy between Swahili and Indians conveyed by any Indian taarab performance (a theme I will return to in the conclusion) mitigates the callousness of "Sisi Isilamu," bringing it into the realm of *utani* (a traditional relationship of joking or teasing that exists between people of neighboring ethnic groups in East Africa).

FOUR *Mombasa, Mother of the World": Hadrami Ṭarab*

1. Hadramis are known in Arabic as *Ḥaḍārima* (singular *Ḥaḍramī*), and in Swahili as *Wahadhrami* or *Mahadhrami* (singular *Hadhrami*).

2. The Swahili *sharifu* is derived from the Arabic singular masculine form (*sharīf*). The Arabic title *sayyid* (pl. *sāda* or *sādāt*), which is commonly used as a synonym for *sharīf* in Hadramawt, is also used on the Swahili coast, but mostly as an honorific title for an individual rather than a descriptor for the broader sharif class.

3. The sharifs, in particular, were strictly "wife takers" and not "wife givers" (Ho 2006, 150; Le Guennec-Coppens 1997, 163).

4. Le Guennec-Coppens mentions the presence of these groups on the Swahili coast (1997, 164). I am not aware of any detailed study of their social positioning.

5. The *Shihiri* ethnonym has also come to be used in Hadramawt to refer to Swahili speakers—and in Aden to refer to the small grocery shops of which Swahili speakers are stereotypical proprietors (Muhammad Jarhoom, personal communication, January 9, 2009).

6. Ḥumaynī is thought to be an important antecedent of Swahili poetry (Minerba 2020; Abdulaziz 1979, 59).

7. Khan's earliest recordings were distributed by Odeon. Lambert and Al-Akouri note that it was actually an English branch of the company, which split from the German branch at the start of World War II and operated independently for a short time thereafter (Lambert and Al-Akouri 2019, 62). These were not the first recordings of Hadrami music produced in Aden. Other Hadrami musicians appear to have been recorded during the 1930s, and around 1938, Odeon recorded the music of Hadramis in Indonesia, some of which circulated via diasporic networks back to southern Yemen (Serjeant 1951, 51).

8. The regional styles of Yemeni popular song were codified by cultural reformers following Yemeni independence in 1967, such that musicians and experts today recognize at least four of them—Sanaani (Ṣanʿāʾnī), Yafiri (Yāfiʿī), Hadrami (Ḥaḍramī), and Lahiji (Laḥijī)—with many recognizing a distinct Adeni (ʿAdanī) style as well (Lambert 1993; Miller 2007, 245; Liebhaber 2011; Wagner 2009, 247–53).

9. From the earliest days of Aden's recording industry, Yemeni musicians often worked in styles of regions other than their own. Some of the earliest recordings in Aden were reinterpretations of the ancient tradition of Sanaani sung poetry by musicians from other regions (Lambert and al-Jumāʾī 2013, 68).

10. All of the recordings listed are archived in the Eisenberg Collection, Series I.

11. The specific Hindi film song that El Antari borrows is "Ye Duniya Hai" from the 1949 film *Shair*. I am grateful to Jamal Hafidh Jahadhmy for recognizing it. This information helps to place the recording date between 1949 and 1956. The specific matrix number of the record suggests a date on the later end of that spectrum.

12. Nizar Ghanem, personal communication, May 23, 2021. Tarek Yamani and Rony Afif (2017) transcribe *sharh* in 6/8, and describe it as an "African 6/8 polyrhythm cycle" (3).

13. Farouk Topan (1995, 106) lists some of the reasons for the demise of *vugo* in Mombasa, including the breakdown of the traditional status system to which it was connected.

14. *Ṭarab* is also used in Yemen as another name for the gambus (monoxyl lute) (see Lambert and Mokrani 2013).

15. Yemenis recognize the power of musico-choreological dicent-indices for projects of identity formation and maintenance in their proverb, "a nation that does not dance will die" (Adra 2007).

16. I was told that the song does not have a known composer or a fixed title. The latter issue, according to Omari, is a function of the fact that titles of *ṭarab* songs are determined by their opening lines and the opening line of this song starts with a declaration of the current year.

17. The original words were definitely written by Baisa. Zein l'Abdin once suggested to me that the melody may have been borrowed from a Saudi song, but I have not been able to confirm this. It sounds stylistically "Hadrami" to Muhammad Jarhoom (personal communication, January 9, 2009).

18. One remarkable example is a recent performance by Muhammad Bā MaṬrif in Saudi Arabia, kindly forwarded to me by Jean Lambert (Muḥammad ʿAlawy Bā al-Faqīh 2017).

19. Personal communication, January 9, 2009.

20. Incidentally, this is also true of Swahili poetry, which is not surprising given the likely historical connections between key Swahili poetry genres and *ḥumaynī*.

21. I completed the transcription and translation in consultation with Iman Meiki and Muhammad Jarhoom. An initial rough translation of the song (into Swahili) was provided to me in the field by Swaleh al-Timami.

FIVE *The Musical Philosopher: Zein l'Abdin's Arab Taarab*

1. *Taarab ya kiarabu* is often translated into English as "Arabic taarab" rather than "Arab taarab" (I have done so myself in the past [Eisenberg 2017]). The word *Arabic* creates a potential for confusion, however, as Arab taarab is sung in Swahili rather than Arabic.

2. On Fadhili William, see Paterson 2001.

3. This quote is presumably translated from Swahili by Graebner.

4. Quotations and paraphrases from Zein l'Abdin in this chapter come from notes and recordings taken during dozens of informal interactions over the course of more than a year and half of fieldwork between August 2004 and August 2006 as well as two formal interviews conducted in Mombasa on October 22, 2004 (recorded) and August 11, 2005 (unrecorded).

5. "Moyo Wakupenda Hauna Subira" is featured on *Zein Concerts 9* (Eisenberg Collection, Series III, in process). The poem is by Khuleita Muhashamy. The melody is taken from Umm Kulthum's "Al-Qalb Yʿashaq Kula Jamīl" (The Heart Loves Every Beautiful Thing).

6. "La Waridi" is featured on Zein's *The Swahili Song Book* (2000) and *Zein Concerts 19*, *Zein Concerts 33*, and *Zein Concerts 34* (Eisenberg Collection, Series III, 298). The poem is Zein's own. The main melody is taken from Mbaruk Talsam's "Tausi Kwa Heri" (Goodbye, Peacock), originally released on the Columbia label (WE 19). I acquired a copy of the recording from Werner Graebner in 2005.

7. There is another version of the *goma* rhythm that is set in duple meter. In my experience, that rhythm is actually more common in traditional goma performance. I have never heard it in a taarab context, however.

8. By "basic drum melody" I mean the high and low tones performed by a drummer on the double dumbek (*maradufu*), a set of bongos, or possibly a single dumbek using a

muffled tone in place of the high tone. A percussionist situates each basic melody within a more complex pattern involving other, more subtle sounds; and varies the melody throughout the song to give shape to the song and add excitement. The second drum parts notated for *chakacha* and *vugo* may not always be present. Sometimes, a skilled *duf* player covers a second drum part, by producing high and low tones on different parts of the drumhead.

9. Eisenberg Collection, Series III, 298.

10. The poem, "Bahari ya Tungu," is in Zein's Swahili Songbook, but I have not heard it performed. It does not appear on any of Zein's recordings.

11. The *shaha* title is specific to Lamu (Shariff 1985, xiii; Vierke 2011, 399). The translation "master poet," which I take from Vierke, fits well, given that on the other parts of the coast *shaha* has historically referred to a position of political authority or a status that accrues to a person of great wealth (Sacleux 1939, 828). The traditional title for a great poet in Mombasa is *malenga*. *Malenga* does not carry the same connotations of authority and power as *shaha*, and so might be better translated as "expert poet."

12. Nabhany provided me with a copy of some of these recordings. J. W. T. Allen had originally deposited a copy at the University of Dar es Salaam, but they have since disappeared from that location (Clarissa Vierke, personal communication, August 19, 2019).

13. Filed in the UCLA Library collection under Nabhany, Ahmed Sheikh. [Kenya, Swahili-speaking peoples, 1965–1995] collected by A. S. Nabhany. Record ID 8526. UCLA Library.

14. The Swahili term *mahadhi* is often used to mean "tune" or "melody" (in which case it is a synonym for *lahani*), but it also carries a more general meaning that is best glossed as "musical style." Graebner (1991b, 196) translates it as "tone color" or "style," and notes that it is often used to describe taarab subgenres (e.g., *mahadhi ya Kiarabu* = Arab taarab). The term seems to have a more specific meaning in the context of poetry recitation. Based on her experience grappling with issues of poetry recitation with Sheikh Nabhany and his teacher, Faraj Bwana Mkuu, Vierke (2011) suggests that mahadhi names an "emic understanding" of melody in the Swahili context, which conceives of melodies that sound different to Western ears as multiple variants of the same "prototypical framework" (44).

15. My understanding of the Kuwaiti *dīwāniya* comes largely through discussions with Ghazi al-Mulaifi and direct experience with the Mayouf Mejally *dīwāniya*, of which Ghazi is a regular attendee as well as a chronicler (Mulaifi 2021). I recall thinking upon my first visit to the Mayouf Mejally *dīwāniya* that Zein would have felt at home in the environment.

16. "Shuwaykh min 'Arḍ Miknās" is notable for being a Khaliji setting of an Andalusian poem. It was composed by Bahraini composer Khaled al-Shaykh and popularized by Bahraini musician Ahmad al-Jumairi. "Kamba Haipigwi Fundo" appears on *Zein Concerts 9* (Eisenberg Collection, Series III, 297). I am grateful to Nizar Ghanem for recognizing the source of this melody (asynchronous online discussion, June 28–September 23, 2019).

17. Zein's Kuwaiti-style "Loho ya Kihindi" is featured on *Zein Volume 11* (Eisenberg Collection, Series III, 317), *Zein Concerts 9* (Eisenberg Collection, Series III, 298), and *Zein Concerts 20* (Eisenberg Collection, Series III, 302). Abdullatif al-Kuwaiti's recording is a two-part song, "Yā Badīʿ Al-Jamāl / Yā Ḥamām," which spans two sides of a 78-speed record recorded in Baghdad in 1928 and released on the Odeon label. Both sides of the recording have been made available on Soundcloud by the Qatar Digital Library (https://soundcloud.com/qatar-digital-library/sets/kuwait-shellac-titles).

18. "Maneno Tisiya" is featured on both of Zein's international releases (*Mtindo wa Mombasa* [1989] and *The Swahili Song Book* [2000]), as well as *Zein Concerts 14* (Eisenberg Collection, Series III, 324).

19. I discuss Zein's interest in the relationship between the Arab *Maqām Sīkāh* and traditional Swahili approaches to melody elsewhere (Eisenberg In prep.).

20. The Juma Khan song in question is "ʿAynī Lighayr Jamālikum" (I Look Upon Your Beauty). "Mnazi Wangu" is featured on *The Swahili Songbook* (2000) and *Zein Concerts 9* (Eisenberg Collection, Series III, 298). The Marzuq melody in question is that of the late twentieth-century *dān ṭarab* song "Hayya Layālī Jamīla" (Oh, Beautiful Nights). A version of "Hayya Layālī Jamīla" performed by a solo singer can be heard on the Auvidis/UNESCO release *Yemen: Songs from Hadramawt* (1998). I am grateful to Nizar Ghanem for noting these similarities (Nizar Ghanem, Jean Lambert, and Gabriel Lavin, asynchronous online discussion, June 28–September 23, 2019).

SIX Sea Change: The Twenty-First Century

1. Mbwana Radio Service finally closed its doors in 2022, following the death of the proprietor, M. A. Shali.

2. Maulidi Juma Iha grew up with the most prolific Giriama singer, Bin Hare. He opened the door to the relationship between the Giriama community and Mbwana, by helping to broker Bin Hare's first recordings (Joseph Mwarandu, recorded interview, Malindi, September 3, 2005).

3. Bakari argues that IPK was more likely banned out of fear that Muslims of the Coast Province and North-Eastern Province would be drawn away from KANU en masse (1995a, 246).

4. Mbaraka Ali Haji, recorded interview, Mombasa, May 30, 2005.

5. There have been many rows in Mombasa over the start date of the Ramadan fast (*saumu*), with some opting to ignore the local "sighting of the moon" in favor of starting on a predetermined date drawn up by reformists in Saudi Arabia (Kresse 2007, 177–78).

6. The administration of Sakina Mosque has changed hands many times over the years. During the late 1990s, it was closely associated with IPK. More recently, the mosque has become something of a "battleground" between "mainstream Kenyan Muslim groups

like the Council of Imams and Preachers in Kenya (CIPK) that acts as a bridge between Muslims and the government" and radical reformists sympathetic to the aims (if not the methods) of Al-Shabab insurgents in Somalia (Patinkin 2014).

7. Athman Lali Omar, personal communication, Mombasa, June 29, 2006.

8. Maulidi Juma Iha, recorded interview, Mombasa, June 4, 2005.

9. The genre first took shape in Dar es Salaam and Zanzibar, and among Zanzibaris in Dubai, as a commercialized form of Zanzibar's traditional, Egyptian-oriented orchestral taarab. It also has roots in the earlier tradition of small-group taarab in Tanga, Tanzania, which featured Western instruments and ngoma rhythms (Askew 2002). And there are Kenyan antecedents, as well. Graebner (2004c) suggests that the "first modern taarab song" was the massively popular *chakacha*-style song "Vidonge" (Pills), which has been recorded by many different groups but is most closely associated with Malika.

10. One such song that I heard them perform at a wedding in 2005 is "Chap Chap Mapenzi" (Quickly My Love), based on a melody from a Hindi film song from the 1960s. The song appears on *Silver Star Modern* taarab *Volume 5* (recorded at Mbwana Radio Service around 2004, and now available for download via Amazon Music).

11. The National Museums of Kenya had also applied to UNESCO for World Heritage status for Mombasa Old Town as well as Fort Jesus, the sixteenth-century Portuguese-built structure at the edge of the neighborhood. The latter was approved in 2011.

12. On the activities and impact of Ketebul Music in Kenya, see Morin 2012 and Eisenberg 2022.

13. Omar Swaleh Al-Abdi, Kombo Salim Mataka Msijumu, Mbaraka Ali Haji, Seif Omar, unrecorded interview, Mombasa, September 16, 2004.

14. A draft script of the speech is archived online: https://github.com/jamalmazrui/AliMazrui/blob/master/Uswahili%20International%20-%20Between%20Language%20and%20Cultural%20Synthesis.pdf (accessed January 12, 2022).

SEVEN *Reorienting Appropriation: Swahili Hip Hop*

1. That Kenya's first private radio stations would focus on "the youth" only made sense from a financial perspective: according to Kenya's Ministry of Youth Affairs, "the youth in Kenya number about 9.1 million, and account for 32 percent of the population. Of these, 51.7 percent are female. The youth form 60 percent of the total labor force but the majority are unemployed due to the country's high unemployment level" (Ministry of Youth Affairs [Kenya] 2006, 1).

2. I am also informed here by works on global hip hop that take a more critical approach to the politics of hip hop expressions and scenes—in particular, Ian Maxwell's book on hip hop in Sydney, Australia, which examines the political conservatism of Australia's "hip hop ideoscape" (2003, 121–24), and Geoffrey Baker's on hip hop in Cuba,

which reveals that "resistance links [Cuban] hip hop to the state as much as it separates the two" (2011, 103).

3. *Ukoo Flani*, which translates to "a certain clan," is said to be an acronym for "*Upendo Kwote Olewenu Ombeni Funzo la Aliyetuumba Njia Iwepo*" (love everywhere all who seek teachings of the Creator; there is a way).

4. Two men who were at the time in constant contact with aspiring Mombasan youth music artists impressed upon me the significance of this track: anthropologist Dillon Mahoney, who was then conducting research among young entrepreneurs in various parts of the city (Mahoney 2017), and the late producer Andrew Burchell of Jikoni Records.

5. According to Swahili morphology, *Mmombasa*, without the locative suffix, would mean Mombasan, but such a word does not exist in practice. The idea "Mombasan" would generally be expressed with "*wa Mombasa*."

6. "Street Hustlers" was recorded at Tabasam Records. "Soldier," released in 2007, was recorded at Nairobi's Ketebul Music and also features Nairobi-based rapper Bobby Mapesa. The videos were each shot in Mombasa by different production companies.

7. One interesting exception is the 2011 video for "*Msoto* Millions" by Ukoo Flani and Nairobian ragga artist Jahcoozi. One would expect something different from this video, however, as the track is part of the Goethe Insitut-funded Berlin-Nairobi (BLNRB) project, which brought together German producers and Kenyan artists. Produced by the high-end outfit, DYMK Films, the video features evocative scenes of Old Town.

8. My information about this process comes from informal conversations with Showdemo as well as recorded interviews with CLD (Lennox Mwale, recorded interview, Mombasa, July 15, 2005) and Redwax (Alex Njuguna, recorded interview, Nairobi, February 1, 2012).

9. Alex Njuguna, recorded interview, Nairobi, February 1, 2012.

10. On Andrew Burchell's life and career in Mombasa, and impact on Kenyan popular music, see Eisenberg and Odidi 2018a, 2018b.

11. Adio Mohamed, recorded interview, Mombasa, September 15, 2004.

12. Adio Mohamed, recorded interview, Mombasa, February 2, 2005.

13. This is a common route for a successful Kenyan youth music track; indeed, many artists take new tracks to *matatu* crews before taking them to radio stations. Adio never approached Nairobian matatu crews with "Nikiwa Ndani," however. The track became standard matatu *mahewa* (musical atmosphere) without any effort on his part.

14. Mwanaisha Abdalla, recorded interview, March 12, 2005. In 2003, Nyota Ndogo won the Kisima Award for Best Taarab Singer. In my conversations with her between 2004 and 2006, she often took pains to clarify that she had never claimed to be a taarab singer, and was surprised, and a bit embarrassed, by the Kisima Award. As she also stated to the Kenyan press, she expressed that the award should have gone to Maulidi Juma or another legendary taarab singer. Years later, however, she would embrace her connec-

tions to taarab, joining heritage taarab group Lelele Africa (see chapter 6) for the 2012 Smithsonian Folklife Festival as well as subsequent concerts and recordings.

15. Amin Virani, unrecorded interview, Nairobi, January 22, 2012.

16. *Bongo flava* has received a great deal of scholarly attention. For an overview of the history and sociology of the genre, see Perullo 2007, 2011; Reuster-Jahn and Hacke 2011. Bongo flava artists often play down their taarab influences. The influences are audible, however, especially in vocal style. Little research has been conducted in this area, but Tanzanian musician Adelgot Haule argues that bongo flava incorporates subtle Arabic vocal decorations borrowed from Swahili taarab (Suleyman 2011).

17. At Adio's request, I helped out with the shoot, working (unpaid) as a second cameraman and an extra.

EPILOGUE *For a Humanistic Musical Anthropology of the Indian Ocean*

1. Hughes-Smith's (2005) report on Seiyun's trip to Zanzibar offers some further details about its genesis of the conclave, including the fact that Graebner had hoped it might lead to a recording project but the logistics ultimately proved too complicated.

2. In addition to obscuring a great deal of data and insights, this had the added deleterious effect of allowing racist questions about the intellectual and creative "capacities" of Africans and their descendants to fester. Waterman's attempt to put these questions to rest in his famous "On Flogging a Dead Horse: Lessons Learned from the Africanisms Controversy" (1963) only illustrates this problem, as he does not—because, indeed, he cannot—cite any of his own scholarship as a means of rebuking racist assumptions about the limited creative capacities of Black people.

BIBLIOGRAPHY

Abdalla, Abdilatif. 1974. "Tanzu Za Ushairi Wa Kiswahili Na Maendeleo Yake: 1" [Genres of Swahili Poetry and Their Development: 1] Working paper. University of Dar es Salaam, Taasisi Ya Uchunguzi Wa Kiswahili [Institute of Kiswahili Research].

Abdulaziz, Mohamed H. 1979. *Muyaka: 19th-Century Swahili Popular Poetry*. Nairobi: Kenya Literature Bureau.

Abou Egl, Mohammad Ibrahim Mohammad. 1983. "The Life and Works of Muhamadi Kijuma." PhD dissertation. University of London.

Abrahams, Roger D. 1982. "The Language of Festivals: Celebrating the Economy." In *Celebration: Studies in Festivity and Ritual*, edited by Victor Turner, 161–77. Washington, DC: Smithsonian Institution Press.

Abu-Lughod, Janet L. 1987. "The Islamic City–Historic Myth, Islamic Essence, and Contemporary Relevance." *International Journal of Middle East Studies* 19 (2): 155–76.

Abungu, George, and Lorna Abungu. 1998. "Saving the Past in Kenya: Urban and Monument Conservation." *The African Archaeological Review* 15 (4): 221–24.

Adra, Najwa. 2007. "The State of Dancing Traditions in the Arabian Peninsula." *Conference on Music in the World of Islam*, August 8–18. Assilah, Morocco.

Agawu, Kofi. 2006. "Structural Analysis or Cultural Analysis? Competing Perspectives on the 'Standard Pattern' of West African Rhythm." *Journal of the American Musicological Society* 59 (1): 1–46.

Aiyar, Sana. 2015. *Indians in Kenya: The Politics of Diaspora*. Cambridge, MA: Harvard University Press.

Al-Saqqaf, Abdullah Hassan. 2006. "The Linguistics of Loanwords in Hadrami Arabic." *International Journal of Bilingual Education and Bilingualism* 9 (1): 75–93.

Alim, H. Samy. 2009. "Translocal Style Communities: Hip Hop Youth as Cultural Theorists of Style, Language, and Globalization." *Pragmatics* 19 (1): 103–27.

———, Awad Ibrahim, and Alistair Pennycook, eds. 2009. *Global Linguistic Flows: Hip Hop Cultures, Youth Identities, and the Politics of Language*. New York: Routledge.

Allen, J. W. T. 1968. "The Collection and Preservation of Manuscripts of the Swahili World." *Swahili* 38 (2): 109–17.

———, ed. 1981. *The Customs of the Swahili People: The Desturi Za Waswahili of Mtoro Bin Mwinyi Bakari and Other Swahili Persons.* Berkeley: University of California Press.

Allen, James de Vere, ed. 1977. *Al-Inkishafi (Catechism of a Soul), By Abdalla Bin Ali Bin Nasir.* Nairobi: East African Literature Bureau.

———. 1979. "The Swahili House: Cultural and Ritual Concepts Underlying Its Plan and Structure." In *Swahili Houses and Tombs of the Coast of Kenya*, edited by James de Vere Allen and Thomas H. Wilson, 1–32. London: Art and Archaeology Research Papers.

———. 1981. "The Swahili World of Mtoro Bin Mwinyi Bakari." In *The Customs of the Swahili People: The Desturi Za Waswahili of Mtoro Bin Mwinyi Bakari and Other Swahili Persons*, edited by J. W. T. Allen, 211–30. Berkeley: University of California Press.

———. 1982. "Traditional History and African Literature: The Swahili Case." *Journal of African History* 23: 227–36.

Alpers, Edward A. 1997. "The African Diaspora in the Northwestern Indian Ocean: Reconsideration of an Old Problem, New Directions for Research." *Comparative Studies of South Asia, Africa and the Middle East* 17 (2): 62–81.

———. 2000. "Recollecting Africa: Diasporic Memory in the Indian Ocean World." *African Studies Review* 43 (1): 83–99.

———. 2001. "The African Diaspora in the Indian Ocean: A Comparative Perspective." In *The African Diaspora in the Indian Ocean*, edited by Shihan de Silva Jayasuriya and Richard Pankhurst, 19–52. Trenton, NJ: Africa World Press.

———. 2002. "Imagining the Indian Ocean World." Opening address to *The International Conference on Cultural Exchange and Transformation in the Indian Ocean World*, April 5, University of California Los Angeles.

Alsalhi, Ahmad Ali. 2016. "Ṣaut in Bahrain and Kuwait: History and Creativity in Concept and Practice." PhD dissertation. Royal Holloway, University of London.

Ammann, Ludwig. 2006. "Private and Public in Muslim Civilization." In *Islam in Public: Turkey, Iran and Europe*, edited by Ludwig Ammann and Nilüfer Göle, 77–123. Istanbul: Istanbul Bilgi University Press.

Amory, Deborah. 1994. "The Politics of Identity on Zanzibar." PhD dissertation. Stanford University.

Amselle, Jean-Loup. 1998. *Mestizo Logics: Anthropology of Identity in Africa and Elsewhere.*

Anonymous. 2000. "Mzee Mombasa's Story." *UTS Review: Cultural Studies and New Writing* 6 (2): 181–85.

Appadurai, Arjun. 1992. "Putting Hierarchy in Its Place." In *Rereading Cultural Anthropology*, edited by George E. Marcus, 34–47. Durham, NC: Duke University Press.

———. 1996. *Modernity At Large: Cultural Dimensions of Globalization.* Minneapolis: University of Minnesota Press.

Arens, William. 1975. "The 'Waswahili': The Social History of an Ethnic Group." *Africa* 45 (4): 426–38.

Arewa, Olufunmilayo. 2016. "Cultural Appropriation: When 'Borrowing' Becomes Exploitation." *The Conversation*, June 20, https://theconversation.com/cultural-appropriation.

Aristotle. 1902. *The Poetics of Aristotle*. London: Macmillan.

Askew, Kelly M. 2000. "Following the Tracks of *Beni*: The Diffusion of the Tanga *Taarab* Tradition." In *Mashindano!: Competitive Music Performance in East Africa*, edited by Frank D. Gunderson and Gregory Barz, 21–38. Dar es Salaam: Mkuki na Nyota Publishers.

———. 2002. *Performing the Nation: Swahili Music and Cultural Politics in Tanzania*. Chicago: University of Chicago Press.

———. 2003. "As Plato Duly Warned: Music, Politics, and Social Change in Coastal East Africa." *Anthropological Quarterly* 76 (4): 609–37.

Bakari, Mohamed. 1995a. "Muslims and the Politics of Change in Kenya." In *Islam in Kenya: Proceedings of the National Seminar on Contemporary Islam in Kenya*, edited by Mohamed Bakari and Saad S. Yahya, 234–51. Mombasa: Mewa Publications.

———. 1995b. "The New 'Ulama' in Kenya." In *Islam in Kenya: Proceedings of the National Seminar on Contemporary Islam in Kenya*, edited by Mohamed Bakari, and Saad S. Yahya, 168–93. Mombasa: Mewa Publications.

Baker, Geoffrey. 2011. *Buena Vista in the Club: Rap, Reggaetón, and Revolution in Havana*. Durham, NC: Duke University Press.

Bakhtin, Mikhail M. 1981. *The Dialogic Imagination*. Austin: University of Texas Press.

———. 1984a. *Problems of Dostoevsky's Poetics*. Minneapolis: University of Minnesota Press.

———. 1984b. *Rabelais and His World*. Bloomington: Indiana University Press.

———. 1986. *Speech Genres and Other Late Essays*. Austin: University of Texas Press.

———. 2010. *Toward a Philosophy of the Act*. Austin: University of Texas Press.

Ballinger, Pamela. 2003. *History in Exile: Memory and Identity at the Borders of the Balkans*. Princeton, NJ: Princeton University Press.

Bang, Anne K. 2019. "Hadramis in Africa." In *Oxford Research Encyclopedia of Asian History*, https://doi.org/10.1093/acrefore/9780190277727.013.324.

Barber, Karin. 1987. "Popular Arts in Africa." *African Studies Review* 30 (3): 1–78.

Barthes, Roland. 1977. "The Grain of the Voice." In *Image - Music - Text*, essays selected and translated by Stephen Heath, 179–89. New York: Hill and Wang.

Bauman, Richard, and Charles L Briggs. 1990. "Poetics and Performance as Critical Perspectives on Language and Social Life." *Annual Review of Anthropology* 19: 59–88.

Beck, Rose Marie. 2000. "Aesthetics of Communication: Texts on Textiles (Leso) from the East African Coast (Swahili)." *Research in African Literatures* 31 (4): 104–24.

Beckerleg, Susan. 2009. "From Ocean to Lakes: Cultural Transformations of Yemenis in Kenya and Uganda." *African and Asian Studies* 8 (3): 288–308.

Behrend, Heike. 2002. "'I Am Like a Movie Star in My Street': Photographic Self-Creation in Postcolonial Kenya." In *Postcolonial Subjectivities in Africa*, edited by Richard Werbner, 44–62. London: Zed Books.

Beidelman, T. O. 1997. *The Cool Knife: Imagery of Gender, Sexuality, and Moral Education in Kaguru Initiation Ritual*. Washington, DC: Smithsonian Institution Press.

Benjamin, Walter. 1978. "On the Mimetic Faculty." In *Reflections*, edited by Peter Demetz, 333–36. New York: Schocken Books.

———. 1979. "Doctrine of the Similar (1933)." *New German Critique* 17: 65–69.

Bennett, Andy. 2000. *Popular Music and Youth Culture: Music, Identity, and Place*. New York: Palgrave.

Berg, F. J. 1968. "The Swahili Community of Mombasa, 1500–1900." *Journal of African History* 9 (1): 35–56.

———, and B. J. Walter. 1968. "Mosques, Population, and Urban Development in Mombasa." In *Hadith I*, edited by Bethwell A. Ogot, 47–99. Nairobi: East African Publishing.

Bergson, Henri. 1911. *Creative Evolution*. London: MacMillan and Co. Ltd.

Bertz, Ned. 2011. "Indian Ocean World Cinema: Viewing the History of Race, Diaspora and Nationalism in Urban Tanzania." *Africa* 81 (1): 68–88.

———. 2015. *Diaspora and Nation in the Indian Ocean: Transnational Histories of Race and Urban Space in Tanzania*. Honolulu: University of Hawai'i Press.

Bhabha, Homi K. 1994. *The Location of Culture*. New York: Routledge.

———. 1995. "'Black Male': The Whitney Museum of American Art." *Artforum* 33 (6): 86–87, 110.

Bhalo, Anwar. n.d. "Something About Juma Bhalo." http://jumabhalo.com/fr_aboutjb.cfm.

Bielskis, A. 2005. *Towards a Postmodern Understanding of the Political*. New York: Palgrave.

Bissell, William Cunningham. 2012. "From Dhow Culture to the Diaspora: Ziff, Film, and the Framing of Transnational Imaginaries in the Western Indian Ocean." *Social Dynamics* 38 (3): 479–98.

Blacking, John. 1983. "The Concept of Identity and Folk Concepts of Self: A Venda Case Study." In *Identity: Personal and Socio-Cultural*, edited by Anita Jacobson-Widding, 47–65. Stockholm: Almqvist & Wiksell.

Boninger, James. 1956. "Sauti Ya Mvita Expansion." *Mombasa Times*, September 3, 2.

Booth, Gregory D. 1993. "Traditional Practice and Mass Mediated Music in India." *International Review of the Aesthetics and Sociology of Music* 24 (2): 159–74.

Bose, Sugata. 2006. *A Hundred Horizons: The Indian Ocean in the Age of Global Empire*. Cambridge, MA: Harvard University Press.

Boswell, Rosabelle. 2008. *Challenges to Identifying and Managing Intangible Cultural Heritage in Mauritius, Zanzibar and Seychelles*. Dakar: CODESRIA.

Boulos, Issa, Virginia Danielson, and Anne K. Rasmussen, eds. 2021. *Music in Arabia: Perspectives on Heritage, Mobility, and Nation*. Bloomington: Indiana University Press.

Bourdieu, Pierre. 1980. *The Logic of Practice*. Stanford, CA: Stanford University Press.

———. 1984. *Distinction: A Social Critique of the Judgment of Taste*. Cambridge, MA: Harvard University Press.

Branch, Daniel. 2011. *Kenya: Between Hope and Despair, 1963-2011*. New Haven, CT: Yale University Press.

Braune, Gabriele. 1997. *Küstenmusik in Südarabien: Die Lieder Und Tänze an Dem Jemenitischen Küsten des Arabischen Meeres*. Frankfurt am Main: Peter Lang.

Brayton, Sean. 2011. "Race Comedy and the 'Misembodied' Voice." *TOPIA: Canadian Journal of Cultural Studies* (22): 97–116.

Brennan, James R. 2008. "Lowering the Sultan's Flag: Sovereignty and Decolonization in Coastal Kenya." *Comparative Studies in Society and History* 50 (4): 831–61.

———. 2015. "A History of Sauti Ya Mvita (Voice of Mombasa): Radio, Public Culture, and Islam in Coastal Kenya, 1947–1966." In *New Media and Religious Transformations in Africa*, edited by Rosalind I. J. Hackett and Benjamin F. Soares, 19–37. Bloomington: Indiana University Press.

Brielle, Esther S., Jeffrey Fleisher, Stephanie Wynne-Jones, Kendra Sirak, Nasreen Broomandkhoshbacht, Kim Callan, Elizabeth Curtis, Lora Iliev, Ann Marie Lawson, and Jonas Oppenheimer. 2023. "Entwined African and Asian Genetic Roots of Medieval Peoples of the Swahili Coast." *Nature* 615 (7954): 866–73.

Brown, Nicolas. 1997. "Umbuji Wa Mnazi and the Poetics of Anthropology." *SAPINA* X (2): 177–229.

Brubaker, Rogers, Mara Loveman, and Peter Stamatov. 2004. "Ethnicity as Cognition." *Theory and Society* 33 (1): 31–64.

Burgess, Thomas. 2002. "Cinema, Bell Bottoms, and Miniskirts: Struggles Over Youth and Citizenship in Revolutionary Zanzibar." *International Journal of African Historical Studies* 35 (2/3): 287–313.

Burnett, Jacquetta Hill. 1969. "Ceremony, Rites, and Economy in the Student System of an American High School." *Human Organization* 28 (1): 1–10.

Butler, Judith. 1999. *Gender Trouble: Feminism and the Subversion of Identity*. New York: Routledge.

Byl, Julia, and Jim Sykes. 2020. "Ethnomusicology and the Indian Ocean: On the Politics of Area Studies." *Ethnomusicology* 64 (3): 394–421.

Campbell, Carol A., and Carol M. Eastman. 1984. "*Ngoma*: Swahili Adult Song Performance in Context." *Ethnomusicology* 28 (3): 467–93.

Capwell, Charles. 1995. "Contemporary Manifestations of Yemeni-Derived Song and Dance in Indonesia." *Yearbook for Traditional Music* 27: 76–89.

Castells, Manuel. 2010. *The Power of Identity*, Second Edition. Hoboken, NJ: Wiley-Blackwell.

Chapple, Eliot Dismore, and Carleton Stevens Coon. 1942. *Principles of Anthropology*. New York: Henry Holt & Company.

Chaudhuri, K. N. 1985. *Trade and Civilisation in the Indian Ocean: An Economic History from the Rise of Islam to 1750*. Cambridge: Cambridge University Press.

Chernoff, John Miller. 1979. *African Rhythm and African Sensibility: Aesthetics and Social Action in African Musical Idioms*. Chicago: University of Chicago Press.

Chiraghdin, Latifa S. 2018. *Shihabuddin Chiraghdin: Life Journey of a Swahili Scholar*. Nairobi: Asian African Heritage Trust.

Chiraghdin, Shihabuddin, ed. 1971. "Utangulizi Wa Mhariri." In Ahmad Nassir, *Malenga wa Mvita: Diwani ya Ustadh Bhalo*, 3–24. Nairobi: Oxford University Press.

———. 1974. "Kiswahili Na Wenyewe." *Kiswahili* 44 (1): 48–53.

Chome, Ngala. 2019. "From Islamic Reform to Muslim Activism: The Evolution of an Islamist Ideology in Kenya." *African Affairs* 118 (472): 531–52.

Clayton, Martin, Rebecca Sager, and Udo Will. 2005. "In Time with the Music: The Concept of Entrainment and Its Significance for Ethnomusicology." *European Meetings in Ethnomusicology* 11: 1–82.

Clifford, James. 1994. "Diasporas." *Cultural Anthropology* 9 (3): 302–38.

Collins, Robert O. 1990. *Eastern African History (African History in Documents, Volume 2)*. New York: M. Wiener.

Connor, Steven. 2000. *Dumbstruck: A Cultural History of Ventriloquism*. Oxford: Oxford University Press.

Conquergood, Dwight. 1985. "Performing as a Moral Act: Ethical Dimensions of the Ethnography of Performance." *Text and Performance Quarterly* 5 (2): 1–13.

Cooper, Frederick. 1977. *Plantation Slavery on the East Coast of Africa*. New Haven, CT: Yale University Press.

———. 1980. *From Slaves to Squatters: Plantation Labor and Agriculture in Zanzibar and Coastal Kenya, 1890–1925*. New Haven, CT: Yale University Press.

Cottrell, Stephen. 2010. "An Interview with Ben Mandelson." *Ethnomusicology Forum* 19 (1): 57–68.

Coupland, Nikolas, and Peter Garrett. 2010. "Linguistic Landscapes, Discursive Frames and Metacultural Performance: The Case of Welsh Patagonia." *International Journal of the Sociology of Language* 205: 7–36.

Cox, Arnie. 2016. *Music and Embodied Cognition: Listening, Moving, Feeling, and Thinking*. Bloomington: Indiana University Press.

Culler, Jonathan. 2020. "Poetics." In *Oxford Research Encyclopedia of Literature*, https://doi.org/10.1093/acrefore/9780190201098.013.1000.

Curtin, Patricia Romero. 1984. "Weddings in Lamu, Kenya: An Example of Social and Economic Change (Mariages à Lamu (Kenya): Un cas de changement économique et social)." *Cahiers d'Études Africaines* 24 (94): 131–55.

Daniels, Douglas Henry. 1996. "Taarab Clubs and Swahili Music Culture." *Social Identities* 2 (3): 413–38.

Danielson, Virginia. 1990. "'Min Al-Mashāyikh': A View of Egyptian Musical Tradition." *Asian Music* 22 (1): 113–27.

———. 1997. *The Voice of Egypt: Umm Kulthūm, Arabic Song, and Egyptian Society in the Twentieth Century*. Chicago: University of Chicago Press.

DCMA. n.d. "Dhow Countries Music Academy." *Virtual WOMEX*, https://www.womex.com/virtual/dhow_countries_music.

de Silva Jayasuriya, Shihan. 2008. "Indian Oceanic Crossings: Music of the Afro-Asian Diaspora." *African Diaspora* 1: 135–54.

———, ed. 2006. *Sounds of Identity: The Music of Afro-Asians (Musiké)* 1(2). The Hague: Semar Publishers.

Deleuze, Gilles. 1988. *Bergsonism*. London: Zone Books.

Denning, Michael. 2015. *Noise Uprising: The Audiopolitics of a World Musical Revolution*. New York: Verso Books.

Dewey, John. 1922. *Human Nature and Conduct: An Introduction to Social Psychology*. New York: Henry Holt and Company.

———. 1929. *Experience and Nature*. New York: W. W. Norton & Co.

———. 1934. *Art as Experience*. New York: Penguin.

Di Bona, Elvira. 2017. "Listening to the Space of Music." *Rivista di Estetica* 66: 93–105.

Dolar, Mladen. 2017. "The Comic Mimesis." *Critical Inquiry* 43 (2): 570–89.

Donald, Merlin. 1991. *Origins of the Modern Mind: Three Stages in the Evolution of Culture and Cognition*. Cambridge, MA: Harvard University Press.

———. 2005. "Imitation and Mimesis." In *Perspectives on Imitation: Volume 2, Imitation, Human Development, and Culture*, edited by Susan Hurley and Nick Chater, 283–300. Boston: MIT Press.

———. 2006. "Art and Cognitive Evolution." In *The Artful Mind: Cognitive Science and the Riddle of Human Creativity*, edited by Mark Turner, 3–20. Oxford: Oxford University Press.

Donley, Linda Wiley. 1982. "House Power: Swahili Space and Symbolic Markers." In *Symbolic and Structural Archaeology*, edited by Ian Hodder, 63–73. Cambridge: Cambridge University Press.

Donley-Reid, Linda W. 1990. "A Structuring Structure: The Swahili House." In *Domestic Architecture and the Use of Space*, edited by Susan Kent, 114–26. Cambridge: Cambridge University Press.

Eastman, Carol M. 1971. "Who Are the Waswahili?" *Africa* 41 (3): 228–36.

———. 1984. "Waungwana Na Wanawake: Muslim Ethnicity and Sexual Segregation in Coastal Kenya." *Journal of Multilingual and Multicultural Development* 5 (2): 97–112.

———. 1994a. "Service, Slavery ('Utumwa') and Swahili Social Reality." *Afrikanistische Arbeitspapiere* 37: 87–107.

———. 1994b. "Swahili Ethnicity: A Myth Becomes a Reality in Kenya." In *Continuity and Autonomy in Swahili Communities: Inland Influences and Strategies of Self-Determination*, edited by David Parkin, 83–97. London: School of Oriental and African Studies.

Eidsheim, Nina. 2009. "Synthesizing Race: Towards an Analysis of the Performativity of Vocal Timbre." *Trans: Transcultural Music Review=Revista Transcultural de Música* 13. https://www.sibetrans.com/trans/articulo/57/synthesizing-race-towards-an-analysis-of-the-performativity-of-vocal-timbre.

———. 2008. "Voice as a Technology of Selfhood: Towards an Analysis of Racialized Timbre and Vocal Performance." PhD dissertation. University of California San Diego.

Eisenberg, Andrew J. 2009. "The Resonance of Place: Vocalizing Swahili Ethnicity in Mombasa, Kenya." PhD dissertation. Columbia University.

———. 2010. "Toward an Acoustemology of Muslim Citizenship in Kenya." *Anthropology News*, December 51 (9): 6.

———. 2013. "Islam, Sound, and Space: Acoustemology and Muslim Citizenship on the Kenyan Coast." In *Music, Sound, and Space: Transformations of Public and Private Experience*, edited by Georgina Born, 186–202. Cambridge: Cambridge University Press.

———. 2017. "Taarab." In *Shades of Benga: The Story of Popular Music in Kenya*, edited by Ketebul Music, 287–307. Nairobi: Ketebul Music.

———. 2019. "Resonant Voices and Spatial Politics: An Acoustemology of Citizenship in a Muslim Neighbourhood of the Kenyan Coast." In *Worship Sound Spaces: Architecture, Acoustics and Anthropology*, edited by Christine Guillebaud and Catherine Lavandier, 140–57. London: Routledge.

———. 2022. "Soundtracks in the Silicon Savannah: Digital Production, Aesthetic Entrepreneurship and the New Recording Industry in Nairobi, Kenya." In *Music and Digital Media: A Planetary Anthropology*, edited by Georgina Born, 46–89. London: UCL Press.

———. 2023. "A Feeling for the Boundaries: Sounding the Indian Ocean on the Swahili Coast." In *Sounding the Indian Ocean: Musical Circulations in the Afro-Asiatic Seascape*, edited by Jim Sykes and Julia Byl, 54–74. Berkeley: University of California Press.

———. In preparation. "On Swahili Melody: Theorizing Musical Transculturation on the Kenyan Coast."

———, and Bill Odidi. 2018a. "The Mombasa Years of Andrew 'Madebe' Burchell," Part 1. *Afropop Worldwide*, October 24, http://afropop.org/articles/the-mombasa.

———, and Bill Odidi. 2018b. "The Mombasa Years of Andrew 'Madebe' Burchell," Part 2. *Afropop Worldwide*, October 24, http://afropop.org/articles/the-mombasa.

Eisenlohr, Patrick. 2004. "Temporalities of Community: Ancestral Language, Pilgrimage, and Diasporic Belonging in Mauritius." *Journal of Linguistic Anthropology* 14 (1): 81–98.

El Guindi, Fadwa. 1999. *Veil: Modesty, Privacy, and Resistance*. New York: Berg.

el-Zein, Abdul Hamid M. 1974. *The Sacred Meadows: A Structural Analysis of Religious Symbolism in an East African Town*. Evanston, IL: Northwestern University Press.

Elsner, Jürgen. 2002. "Wedding Music in the Hadramaut." In *Omani Traditional Music and the Arab Heritage*, edited by Issah El-Mallah, 115–27. Tutzing, DE: Hans Schneider Verlag.

Ewald, Janet J. 2000. "Crossers of the Sea: Slaves, Freedmen, and Other Migrants in the Northwestern Indian Ocean, c. 1750–1914." *American Historical Review* 105 (1): 69–91.

Fabian, Steven. 2019. *Making Identity on the Swahili Coast: Urban Life, Community, and Belonging in Bagamoyo*. Cambridge: Cambridge University Press.

Fair, Laura. 1998. "Music, Memory and Meaning: The Kiswahili Recordings of Siti Binti Saad." *Afrikanistische Arbeitspapiere* 55: 1–16.

———. 2001. *Pastimes and Politics: Culture, Community, and Identity in Post-Abolition Urban Zanzibar, 1890–1945*. Athens: Ohio University Press.

———. 2004. "Hollywood Hegemony? Hardly: Audience Preferences in Zanzibar, 1950s–1970s." *ZIFF Journal* 1: 52–58.

———. 2009. "Making Love in the Indian Ocean: Hindi Films, Zanzibari Audiences, and the Construction of Romance in the 1950s and 1960s." In *Love in Africa*, edited by Jennifer Cole and Lynn Thomas, 58–82. Chicago: University of Chicago Press.

Falassi, Alessandro. 1987. *Time Out of Time: Essays on the Festival*. Albuquerque: University of New Mexico Press.

Fardon, Richard. 1987. "African Ethnogenesis: Limits to the Comparability of Ethnic Phenomena," In *Comparative Anthropology*, edited by Ladislav Holý, 168–88. Oxford: Basil Blackwell.

Farraj, Johnny, and Sami Abu Shumays. 2019. *Inside Arabic Music: Arabic Maqam Performance and Theory in the 20th-Century Middle East*. New York: Oxford University Press.

Feld, Steven. 1994a. "Aesthetics as an Iconicity of Style (Uptown Title); or, (Downtown Title) "lift-Up-over-sounding": Getting into the Kaluli Groove." In *Music Grooves: Essays and Dialogues*, by Charles Keil and Steven Feld, 109–50. Chicago: University of Chicago Press.

———. 1994b. "Communication, Music and Speech About Music." In *Music Grooves: Essays and Dialogues*, by Charles Keil and Steven Feld, 77–95. Chicago: University of Chicago Press.

———. 1996. "Waterfalls of Song: An Acoustemology of Place Resounding in Bosavi, Papua New Guinea." In *Senses of Place*, edited by Keith H. Basso and Steven Feld, 91–135. Santa Fe, NM: School of American Research.

———. 2015. "Acoustemology." In *Keywords in Sound*, edited by David Novak and Matt Sakakeeny, 12–21. Durham, NC: Duke University Press.

———, Aaron A. Fox, Thomas Porcello, and David Samuels. 2004. "Vocal Anthropology: From the Music of Language to the Language of Song." In *A Companion to Linguistic Anthropology*, edited by Alessandro Duranti, 321–45. Malden, MA: Blackwell Publishing.

Ferguson, James. 2002. "Of Mimicry and Membership: Africans and the 'New World Society.'" *Cultural Anthropology* 17 (4): 551–69.

Ferudi, Frank. 1974. "The Development of Anti-Asian Opinion Among Africans in Nakuru District, Kenya." *African Affairs* 73: 347–58.

Fisher, George, and Judy Lochhead. 2002. "Analyzing from the Body." *Theory and Practice* 27 37–67.

Floyd Jr., Samuel A. 1995. *The Power of Black Music: Interpreting Its History from Africa to the United States*. New York: Oxford University Press.

Forman, Murray. 2002. *The 'Hood Comes First: Race, Space, and Place in Rap and Hip-Hop*. Middletown, CT: Wesleyan University Press.

Foucault, Michel. 1978. "Nietzsche, Genealogy, History." *Semiotexte* 3 (1): 78–94.

———. 2000. "Truth and Power." In *Power* (*Essential Works of Foucault 1954-1984, Volume 3*), edited by James D. Faubion, 111–33. New York: New Press.

Fox, Aaron A. 2004. *Real Country: Music and Language in Working-Class Culture*. Durham, NC: Duke University Press.

Franken, Marjorie A. 1994. "Dance and Status in Swahili Society." *Visual Anthropology* 7 (2): 99–113.

Frankl, P. J. L., Yahya Ali Omar, and Janet Topp Fargion. 1998. "Kasha Langu: A Popular Song from Mombasa." *Afrikanistische Arbeitspapiere* 55 (Swahili Forum V): 17–25.

Fraser, Nancy. 1995. "From Redistribution to Recognition? Dilemmas of Justice in a 'Post-Socialist' Age." *New Left Review* 212 (1): 68–93.

Frazer, Sir James George. 1957. *The Golden Bough: A Study in Magic and Religion*, Volume 1. London: Macmillan & Company.

Friedrich, Paul. 1991. "Polytropy." In *Beyond Metaphor: The Theory of Tropes in Anthropology*, edited by James W. Fernandez, 17–55. Palo Alto, CA: Stanford University Press.

Frishkopf, Michael. 2003. "Some Meanings of the Spanish Tinge in Contemporary Egyptian Music." In *Mediterranean Mosaic: Popular Music and Global Sounds*, edited by Goffredo Plastino, 43–78. New York: Routledge.

Fuglesang, Minou. 1994. *Veils and Videos: Female Youth Culture on the Swahili Coast*. Stockholm: Almqvist and Wiksell International.

Gaffney, Patrick D. 1994. *The Prophet's Pulpit: Islamic Preaching in Contemporary Egypt*. Berkeley: University of California Press.

Ganti, Tejaswini. 2004. *Bollywood: A Guidebook to Popular Hindi Cinema*. New York: Routledge.

Garcia, David F. 2017. *Listening for Africa: Freedom, Modernity, and the Logic of Black Music's African Origins*. Durham, NC: Duke University Press.

Gaunt, Kyra D. 2006. *The Games Black Girls Play: Learning the Ropes from Double-Dutch to Hip-Hop*. New York: NYU Press.

Gebauer, Gunter, and Christoph Wulf. 1995. *Mimesis: Culture Art Society*. Berkeley: University of California Press.

Gendlin, Eugene T. 1997. *Experiencing and the Creation of Meaning: A Philosophical and Psychological Approach to the Subjective*. Evanston, IL: Northwestern University Press.

Gesthuizen, Thomas. 2019. *Yaseen & Party*. LP Liner notes. Afro-7: AFR7-DIGI-05.

Ghaidan, Usam. 1975. *Lamu: A Study of the Swahili Town*. Nairobi: Kenya Literature Bureau.

Glassman, Jonathon. 1995. *Feasts and Riot: Revelry, Rebellion, and Popular Consciousness on the Swahili Coast, 1856–1888*. Portsmouth, NH: Heinemann.

———. 2000. "Sorting Out the Tribes: The Creation of Racial Identities in Colonial Zanzibar's Newspaper Wars." *Journal of African History* 41 (3): 395–428.

———. 2004. "Slower Than a Massacre: The Multiple Sources of Racial Thought in Colonial Africa." *American Historical Review* 109 (3): 720–54.

———. 2011. *War of Words, War of Stones: Racial Thought and Violence in Colonial Zanzibar*. Bloomington: Indiana University Press.

Goldsmith, Paul. 2011. "The Mombasa Republican Council Conflict Assessment: Threats and Opportunities for Engagement." Report. Nairobi: Kenya Civil Society Strengthening Programme.

Göle, Nilüfer. 2002. "Islam in Public: New Visibilities and New Imaginaries." *Public Culture* 14 (1): 173–90.

Graebner, Werner. 1989a. In *Mtindo Wa Mombasa/The Style of Mombasa*, Zein l'Abdin Ahmed Alamoody, CD Liner notes. Globestyle: CDORBD 066.

———. 1989b. "The First 35 Years of Commercial Recording in East Africa 1928–1963: Processes of Institutionalization." Seminar paper, Institute of African Studies.

———. 1991a. In *Jino La Pembe: Zuhura Swaleh with Maulidi Musical Party*, CD Liner Notes: Globestyle.

———. 1991b. "Taarab—populäre Musik Am Indischen Ozean." In *Populäre Musik in Afrika*, edited by Veit Erlmann, 181–200. Berlin: Museum für Völkerkunde.

———. 2004a. "Between Mainland and Sea: The *Taarab* Music of Zanzibar." In *Island Musics*, edited by Kevin Dawe, 171–98. Oxford: Berg.

———. 2004b. "The Interaction of Swahili Taarab Music and the Record Industry: A Historical Perspective." In *African Media Cultures: Transdisciplinary Perspectives—Cultures De Médias en Afrique: Perspectives Transdisciplinaires*, edited by Frank Wittmann and Rose Marie Beck, 171–92. Cologne: Rüdiger Köppe Verlag.

———. 2004c. "Wape Vidonge Vyao: Taarab as Vital Language in Urban East Africa."

In *Between Resistance and Expansion: Explorations of Local Vitality in Africa*, edited by Peter Probst and Gerd Spittler, 249–74. Münster: Lit.

———. 2005a. "Bi Kidude: The Diva of Zanzibari Music." In *Zanzibara 4: Bi Kidude: The Diva of Zanzibari Music*, CD Liner Notes. Buda Musique 860141.

———. 2005b. "Le Taarab à Mombasa / Taarab in Mombasa." In *Zanzibara 2: L'Age D'or du Taarab De Mombasa 1965-1975, Golden Years of Mombasa Taarab*, CD Liner Notes. Buda Musique 860119.

———. 2014. "The Qanbus Connection: Pre-Taarab Roots on the Northern Kenya Coast." In *From the Tana River to Lake Chad: Research in African Oratures and Literatures. In Memoriam Thomas Geider*, edited by Hannelore Vögele, Lutz Diegner, Uta Reuster-Jahn, and Raimund Kastenholz, 311–23. Köln: Köppe.

———. 2020. "First Modern: Taarab Vibes from Mombasa and Tanga." In *Zanzibara 10: First Modern: Taarab Vibes from Mombasa and Tanga*, CD Liner Notes. Buda Musique 860354.

Habermas, Jürgen. 1986. "The Genealogical Writing of History: On Some Aporias in Foucault's Theory of Power." *Canadian Journal of Political and Social Theory/Revue canadienne de théorie politique et sociale* 10 (1–2): 1–9.

Hahn, Hans Peter. 2011. "Antinomien Kultureller Aneignung: Einführung." *Zeitschrift für Ethnologie* 136: 11–26.

Hall, Stuart. 1997. "The Spectacle of the 'Other.'" In *Representation: Cultural Representations and Signifying Practices*, edited by Stuart Hall, Jessica Evans, and Sean Nixon, 223–90. Los Angeles: Sage.

———. 2017. *The Fateful Triangle*. Cambridge, MA: Harvard University Press.

Hanks, William F. 1987. "Discourse Genres in a Theory of Practice." *American Ethnologist* 14 (4): 668–92.

Hardwick, Charles S., ed. 1977. *Semiotic and Significs: The Correspondence Between Charles S. Peirce and Victoria Lady Welby*. Bloomington: Indiana University Press.

Harkness, Nicholas. 2013. *Songs of Seoul: An Ethnography of Voice and Voicing in Christian South Korea*. Berkeley: University of California Press.

Harrev, Flemming. 1989. "Jambo Records and the Promotion of Popular Music in East Africa: The Story of Otto Larsen and East African Records Ltd. 1952–1963." *Bayreuth African Studies Series* 9, Perspectives on African Music: 103–37.

Harries, Lyndon, ed. 1966. *Poems From Kenya. Gnomic Verses in Swahili by Ahmad Nassir Bin Juma Bhalo*. Madison: University of Wisconsin Press.

Hassan, Scheherazade Qassim. 1998. "Yemen: Songs from Hadramawt." In *Yemen: Songs from Hadramawt*, CD Liner Notes. AUVIDIS/UNESCO D8273.

Haynes, Jo. 2005. "World Music and the Search for Difference." *Ethnicities* 5 (3): 365–85.

Herskovits, Melville J. 1941. "Patterns of Negro Music." *Transactions, Illinois State Academy of Sciences* 34 (September): 19–23.

———. 1966. *The New World Negro: Selected Papers in Afroamerican Studies*. Bloomington: Indiana University Press.

Herzfeld, Michael. 2016. *Cultural Intimacy: Social Poetics and the Real Life of States, Societies, and Institutions*. 3rd Ed. London: Routledge.

Hilal, Nasra Mohamed. 2007. *Mfinyanzi Aingia Kasri: Siti Binti Saad: Malkia Wa Taarab*. Dar es Salaam: Mkuki wa Nyota Publishers.

Hillewaert, Sarah. 2016. "'Whoever Leaves Their Traditions is a Slave': Contemporary Notions of Servitude in an East African Town." *Africa* 86 (3): 425–46.

Hinawy, Mbarak Ali. 1964. "Notes on Customs in Mombasa." *Swahili* 34 (1): 17–35.

Hirsch, Susan F. 1998. *Pronouncing and Persevering: Gender and the Discourses of Disputing in an African Islamic Court*. Chicago: University of Chicago Press.

Hirschkind, Charles. 2006. *The Ethical Soundscape: Cassette Sermons and Islamic Counterpublics*. New York: Columbia University Press.

Ho, Engseng. 2006. *The Graves of Tarim: Genealogy and Mobility across the Indian Ocean*. Berkeley: University of California Press.

Hoffman, Valerie J. 2012. "The Role of the Masharifu on the Swahili Coast in the Nineteenth and Twentieth Centuries." In *Sayyids and Sharifs in Muslim Societies*, edited by Kazuo Morimoto, 197–209. New York: Routledge.

Hofmeyr, Isabel. 2012. "The Complicating Sea: The Indian Ocean as Method." *Comparative Studies of South Asia* 32 (3): 584–90.

Horkheimer, Max, and Theodor W. Adorno. 2002. *Dialectic of Enlightenment: Philosophical Fragments*. Stanford, CA: Stanford University Press.

Horton, Mark, and John Middleton. 2000. *The Swahili: The Social Landscape of a Mercantile Society*. Oxford: Blackwell Publishers.

Hoyle, Brian. 2001. "Urban Renewal in East African Port Cities: Mombasa's Old Town Waterfront." *GeoJournal* 53 (2): 183–97.

Hughes-Smith, Paul. 2005. "Sounds of Wisdom." *The British-Yemeni Society Journal*, https://al-bab.com/albab-orig/albab/bys/articles/hughes_smith05.htm.

Hutcheon, Linda. 2000. *A Theory of Parody: The Teachings of Twentieth-Century Art Forms*. Urbana: University of Illinois Press.

Iliffe, John. 1979. *A Modern History of Tanganyika*. Cambridge: Cambridge University Press.

Ingold, Tim. 2018. *Anthropology: Why It Matters*. Cambridge: Polity.

Isin, Engin F. 2002. *Being Political: Genealogies of Citizenship*. Minneapolis: University of Minnesota Press.

Ivanov, Paola. 2014. "Cosmopolitanism or Exclusion? Negotiating Identity in the Expressive Culture of Contemporary Zanzibar." In *The Indian Ocean: Oceanic Connections and the Creation of New Societies*, edited by Abdul Sheriff and Engseng Ho, 209–38. London: Hurst.

———. 2017. "The Aesthetic Constitution of Space: Mimetic Appropriation of Foreign 'Styles' and the Creation of Transoceanic Connections on the Swahili Coast." *Comparative Studies of South Asia, Africa and the Middle East* 37 (2): 368–90.

Jahazi Media. n.d. "Culture Musical Club." *Virtual WOMEX*, www.womex.com/virtual/jahazi_media/culture_musical_1.

Jakobson, Roman. 1960. "Concluding Statement: Linguistics and Poetics." In *Style in Language*, edited by Thomas A Sebeok, 350–449. Boston: MIT Press.

———. 1987. "What is Poetry." In *Language in Literature*, edited by Krystyna Pomorska and Stephen Rudy, 368–78. Cambridge, MA: Harvard University Press.

James, William. 1879. "The Sentiment of Rationality." *Mind* 4 (15): 317–46.

Janmohamed, Karin K. 1978. "A History of Mombasa, c. 1895–1939: Some Aspects of Economic and Social Life in an East African Port Town During Colonial Rule." PhD dissertation. Northwestern University.

Johnson, Mark. 1997. "Embodied Musical Meaning." *Theory and Practice* 22: 95–102.

———. 2007. *The Meaning of the Body: Aesthetics of Human Understanding*. Chicago: University of Chicago Press.

———. 2013. "Identity, Bodily Meaning, and Art." In *Art and Identity: Essays on the Aesthetic Creation of Mind*, edited by Tone Roald and Johannes Lang, 15–38. Leiden: Brill.

Kapferer, Bruce. 1984. "The Ritual Process and the Problem of Reflexivity in Sinhalese Demon Exorcisms." In *Rite, Drama, Festival, Spectacle: Rehearsals Toward a Theory of Cultural Performance*, edited by John J. MacAloon, 179–207. Philadelphia: Institute for the Study of Human Issues.

———. 1986. "Performance and the Structuring of Meaning and Experience." In *The Anthropology of Experience*, edited by Victor W. Turner and Edward M. Bruner, 188–203. Urbana: University of Illinois Press.

Kasfir, Sidney L. 2004. "Tourist Aesthetics in the Global Flow: Orientalism and 'Warrior Theatre' on the Swahili Coast." *Visual Anthropology* 17: 319–43.

Keil, Charles, and Steven Feld. 1994. *Music Grooves: Essays and Dialogues*. Chicago: University of Chicago Press.

Kenyatta, Jomo. 1968. *Suffering Without Bitterness: The Founding of the Kenya Nation*. Nairobi: East African Publishing House.

Khamis, Said A. M. 2002. "Wondering about Change: The Taarab Lyric and Global Openness." *Nordic Journal of African Studies* 11 (2): 198–205.

———. 2005. "Clash of Interests and Conceptualisation of Taarab in East Africa." *Swahili Forum* 12: 133–59.

Khatib, Muhammed Seif. 1992. *Taarab Zanzibar*. Dar es Salaam: Tanzania Publishing House.

Kiel, Hildegard. 2012. "Travel on a Song: The Roots of Zanzibari Taarab." *African Music Journal* 9 (2): 77–93.

———. 2016. "Love, Grief and the Sea: Taarab Music from Zanzibar." In *Mambo Moto Moto: Music in Tanzania Today*, edited by Bernhard Hanneken and Tiago de Oliveira Pinto, 97–112. Berlin: VWB.

Killius, Rolf. 2017. "The Cradle of Arabic Sawt Music: The Early Musician Generations in Kuwait." *Qatar Digital Library* (blog), June 15. https://qdl.qa/en/cradle-arabic-sawt-music-early-musician-generations-kuwait.

Kindy, Hyder. 1972. *Life and Politics in Mombasa*. Nairobi: East African Publishing House.

Kirkegaard, Annemette. 2001. "Tourism Industry and Local Music Culture in Contemporary Zanzibar." In *Same and Other: Negotiating African Identity in Cultural Production*, edited by Maria Eriksson and Baaz and Mai Palmberg, 59–76. Stockholm: Nordiska Afrikainstitute.

Knappert, Jan. 1977. "Swahili Tarabu Songs." *Afrika und Übersee* 66 (1/2): 116–55.

———. 1979. *Four Centuries of Swahili Verse: A Literary History and Anthology*. London: Heinemann.

———. 1990. "Swahili Songs for Children." *Annales Aequatoria* 11: 99–114.

Kresse, Kai. 2003. "'Swahili Enlightenment'? East African Reformist Discourse at the Turning Point: The Example of Sheikh Muhammad Kasim Mazrui." *Journal of Religion in Africa* 33 (3): 279–309.

———. 2007. *Philosophising in Mombasa: Knowledge, Islam and Intellectual Practice on the Swahili Coast*. Edinburgh: Edinburgh University Press.

———. 2009. "Muslim Politics in Postcolonial Kenya: Negotiating Knowledge on the Double-Periphery." *Journal of the Royal Anthropological Institute* 15 (Supplement 1): S76–94.

———. 2011. "Enduring Relevance: Samples of Oral Poetry on the Swahili Coast." *Wasafiri* 26 (2): 46–49.

———. 2012a. "Interrogating 'Cosmopolitanism' in an Indian Ocean Setting: Thinking through Mombasa on the Swahili Coast." In *Cosmopolitanisms in Muslim Contexts: Models from the Past, Questions for the Future*, edited by Derryl N. MacLean and Sikeena Karmali Ahmed, 31-50. Edinburgh: Edinburgh University Press.

———. 2012b. "On the Skills to Navigate the World, and Religion, for Coastal Muslims in Kenya." In *Articulating Islam: Anthropological Approaches to Muslim Worlds*, edited by Magnus Marsden and Konstantinos Retsikas, 77–99. Dordrecht, NL: Springer.

———, ed. 2017. *Guidance (Uwongozi) by Sheikh Al-Amin Mazrui: Selections from the First Swahili Islamic Newspaper. A Swahili-English Edition*. Leiden: Brill.

———. 2018. *Swahili Muslim Publics and Postcolonial Experience*. Bloomington: Indiana University Press.

Krims, Adam. 2000. *Rap Music and the Poetics of Identity*. Cambridge: Cambridge University Press.

Krings, Matthias. 2015. *African Appropriations: Cultural Difference, Mimesis, and Media*. Bloomington: Indiana University Press.

Lambert, Jean. 1993. "Musiques Régionales et Identité Nationale." *Revue des mondes musulmans et de la Méditerranée* 67: 171–86.

———. 2002. "Music in the Arabian Peninsula: An Overview." In *The Garland Encyclopedia of World Music. Vol. 6: The Middle East*, edited by Virginia Danielson, Scott Marcus, and Dwight Reynolds, 649–61. New York: Routledge.

———, and Rafik Al-Akouri. 2019. "Patrimonialisation «sauvage» et Archéologie Industrielle de la Musique Yéménite." *Annales Islamologiques* 53: 49–94.

———, and Muḥammad al-Jumā'ī. 2013. "La Vie Musicale à Sanaa Dans la Première Moitiè du XXe Siècle." In *Qanbus, Tarab. Le Luth Monoxyle et la Musique du Yémen*, edited by Jean Lambert and Samir Mokrani, 49–79. Paris: CEFAS/Geuthner.

———, and Samir Mokrani, eds. 2013. *Qanbus, Tarab. Le Luth Monoxyle et la Musique du Yémen*. Paris: CEFAS/Geuthner.

Larkin, Brian. 1997. "Indian Films and Nigerian Lovers: Media and the Creation of Parallel Modernities." *Africa* 67 (3): 406–40.

———. 2004. "Bandiri Music, Globalization, and Urban Experience in Nigeria." *Social Text* 81: 91–112.

Larsen, Kjersti. 2008. *Where Humans and Spirits Meet: The Politics of Rituals and Identified Spirits in Zanzibar*. New York: Berghahn Books.

Lavin, Gabriel W. 2016. "Thinking Historically, Being Present: Kuwait, Summer 2016." *Ethnomusicology Review*, https://www.ethnomusicologyreview.ucla.edu/content/thinking-historically.

———. 2017. "A Musical Case Study in Indian Ocean Globalization: ʿAdanyat in Kuwait." MA Paper. University of California Los Angeles.

LaViolette, Adria, and Stephanie Wynne-Jones, eds. 2017. *The Swahili World*. London: Routledge.

Le Guennec-Coppens, Françoise. 1980. *Wedding Customs in Lamu*. Nairobi: Lamu Society.

———. 1989. "Social and Cultural Integration: A Case Study of the East African Hadramis." *Africa* 59 (2): 185–95.

———. 1997. "Changing Patterns of Hadhrami Migration and Social Integration in East Africa." In *Hadhrami Traders, Scholars, and Statesmen in the Indian Ocean, 1750s–1960s*, edited by Ulrike Freitag and W. G. Clarence-Smith, 157–74. Leiden: Brill.

Lentz, Carola. 1995. "'Tribalism' and Ethnicity in Africa." *Cahiers des sciences humaines* 31 (2): 303–28.

Lévi-Strauss, Claude. 1969. *The Elementary Structures of Kinship*. Boston: Beacon Press.

Lidov, David. 1987. "Mind and Body in Music." *Semiotica* 66 (1–3): 69–97.

Liebhaber, Samuel. 2011. "The Ḥumaynī Pulse Moves East: Yemeni Nationalism Meets Mahri Sung-Poetry." *British Journal of Middle Eastern Studies* 38 (2): 249–65.

Liszka, James Jakób. 1996. *A General Introduction to the Semeiotic of Charles Sanders Peirce*. Bloomington: Indiana University Press.

Livingston, Tamara E. 1999. "Music Revivals: Towards a General Theory." *Ethnomusicology* 43 (1): 66–85.

Lodhi, Abdulaziz Yusuf. 2019. "Linguistic and Cultural Contributions of Gujarat in Eastern Africa." In *Knowledge and the Indian Ocean*, edited by Sarah Keller, 225–43. Cham, CH: Palgrave Macmillan.

Loimeier, Roman. 2007. "Sit Local, Think Global: The Baraza in Zanzibar." *Journal for Islamic Studies* 27 (1): 16–38.

Lonsdale, John. 2004. "Moral and Political Argument in Kenya." In *Ethnicity and Democracy in Africa*, edited by Bruce Berman, Dickson Eyoh, and Will Kymlicka, Oxford and Athens: J. Currey and Ohio University Press.

Low, Setha M., and Denise Lawrence-Zúñiga. 2003. "Locating Culture." In *The Anthropology of Space and Place: Locating Culture* (Blackwell Readers in Anthropology 4), edited by Setha M. Low and Denise Lawrence-Zúñiga, 1–48. Malden, MA: Blackwell.

Lynch, Gabrielle. 2011. *I Say to You: Ethnic Politics and the Kalenjin in Kenya*. Chicago: University of Chicago Press.

———. 2017. "The Politics of Ethnicity." In *Routledge Handbook of African Politics*, edited by Nic Cheeseman, David M. Anderson, and Andrea Scheibler, 95–107. London: Routledge.

MacAloon, John J., ed. 1984. *Rite, Drama, Festival, Spectacle: Rehearsals Toward a Theory of Cultural Performance*. Philadelphia: Institute for the Study of Human Issues.

Madiangi, George. 2010. "Sudi's Soul Music Comes of Age." *Buzz, Sunday Nation*, April 2, www.nation.co.ke/Features/buzz/Sudis+soul+music+comes+of+age/-/441236/891730/.

Mafeje, Archie. 1971. "The Ideology of 'Tribalism.'" *Journal of Modern African Studies* 9 (2): 253–61.

Mahon, Michael. 1992. *Foucault's Nietzschean Genealogy: Truth, Power, and the Subject*. Albany: State University of New York Press.

Mahoney, Dillon. 2017. *The Art of Connection: Risk, Mobility, and the Crafting of Transparency in Coastal Kenya*. Berkeley: University of California Press.

Mamdani, Mahmood. 1996. *Citizen and Subject: Africa and the Legacy of Late Colonialism*. Princeton, NJ: Princeton University Press.

———. 2001. *When Victims Become Killers: Colonialism, Nativism, and the Genocide in Rwanda*. Princeton, NJ: Princeton University Press.

Manger, Leif O. 2010. *The Hadrami Diaspora: Community-Building on the Indian Ocean Rim*. New York: Berghahn Books.

Manuel, Peter. 1993. *Cassette Culture: Popular Music and Technology in North India*. Chicago: University of Chicago Press.

———. 1995. "Music as Symbol, Music as Simulacrum: Postmodern, Pre-Modern, and Modern Aesthetics in Subcultural Popular Musics." *Popular Music* 14 (2): 227–39.

———, and Wayne Marshall. 2006. "The Riddim Method: Aesthetics, Practice, and Ownership in Jamaican Dancehall." *Popular Music* 25 (3): 447–70.

Marcus, Scott Lloyd. 1989. "Arab Music Theory in the Modern Period." PhD dissertation. University of California Los Angeles.

———. 1994. "Parody-Generated Texts: The Process of Composition in 'Biraha.'" *Asian Music* 26 (1): 95–147.

Marre, Jeremy (producer). 1979. *Rhythm of Resistance: The Black Music of South Africa*, Directed by Chris Austin and Jeremy Marre. Videorecording. London: Harcourt Films.

Martin, Bradford G. 1974. "Arab Migrations to East Africa in Medieval Times." *International Journal of African Historical Studies* 7 (3): 367–90.

Martin, Thomas. 2020. "Poiesis." *Oxford Research Encyclopedia of Literature*, https://doi.org/10.1093/acrefore/9780190201098.013.1080.

Mathews, Nathaniel. 2013. "Imagining Arab Communities: Colonialism, Islamic Reform, and Arab Identity in Mombasa, Kenya, 1897–1933." *Islamic Africa* 4 (2): 135–63.

Matola, S., Mwalim Shaaban, Wilfred H. Whiteley, and A. A. Jahadhmy, eds. 1966. *Waimbaji Wa Juzi: Mw. Shaaban, Mbaruk Effandi, Siti B. Saad, Budda Bin Mwendo*. Dar es Salaam: Chuo Cha Uchunguzi wa Lugha ya Kiswahili.

Mauss, Marcel. 1972. *A General Theory of Magic*. London: Routledge and Kegan Paul.

Maxwell, Ian. 2003. *Phat Beats, Dope Rhymes: Hip Hop Down Under Comin' Upper*. Middletown, CT: Wesleyan University Press.

Mazrui, Alamin M. 1997. *Kayas of Deprivation, Kayas of Blood: Violence, Ethnicity and the State in Coastal Kenya*. Nairobi: Kenya Human Rights Commission (KHRC).

———, and Willy Mutunga, eds. 2004. *Race, Gender, and Culture Conflict: Debating the African Condition; Mazrui and His Critics, Volume One*. Trenton, NJ: African World Press.

———, and Ibrahim Noor Shariff. 1994. *The Swahili: Idiom and Identity of an African People*. Trenton, NJ: Africa World Press.

Mazrui, Ali. 2000. "The Kenya Coast: Between Globalization and Marginalization." *Kenya Coast Handbook: Culture, Resources and Development in the East African Littoral*, edited by Jan Hoorweg, Dick Foeken, and Robert A. Obudho, 101–14. Münster: Lit.

Mazrui, Ali A. 1996. "Mombasa: Three Stages Towards Globalization." In *Re-Presenting the City: Ethnicity, Capital and Culture in the 21st-Century Metropolis*, edited by Anthony D. King, 158–76. London: MacMillan.

———. 2005. "Uswahili International: Between Language and Cultural Synthesis." Speech delivered at the official opening of the Swahili Resource Center, Fort Jesus Museum, Mombasa, Kenya, July 19.

Mbaabu, Ireri, and Kibande Nzuga. 2003. *Sheng-English Dictionary: Deciphering East Africa's Underworld Language*. Dar es Salaam: Taasisi ya Uchunguzi wa Kiswahili.

Mberia, Kithaka wa. 2015. "Al-Inkishafi: A Ninteenth-Century Swahili Poem." *International Journal of Liberal Arts and Social Sciences* 3 (3): 91–101.

MCP [Mombasa Conservation Project]. 1990. *A Conservation Plan for the Old Town of Mombasa, Kenya*. Mombasa: National Museums of Kenya, Municipal Council of Mombasa, United Nations Development Programme, and UNESCO.

McPherson, Kenneth. 1993. *The Indian Ocean: A History of People and the Sea*. Delhi: Oxford University Press.

Meier, Prita. 2016. *Swahili Port Cities: The Architecture of Elsewhere*. Bloomington: Indiana University Press.

Meizel, Katherine. 2011. "A Powerful Voice: Investigating Vocality and Identity." *Voice and Speech Review* 7 (1): 267–74.

———. 2020. *Multivocality: Singing on the Borders of Identity*. New York: Oxford University Press.

Merleau-Ponty, Maurice. 1962. *Phenomenology of Perception*. London: Routledge.

Metcalf, Thomas R. 2007. *Imperial Connections*. Berkeley: University of California Press.

Meyer, Birgit. 2009. "Introduction: From Imagined Communities to Aesthetic Formations: Religious Mediations, Sensational Forms, and Styles of Binding." In *Aesthetic Formations*, edited by Birgit Meyer, 1–28. New York: Palgrave Macmillan.

———, and Jojada Verrips. 2008. "Aesthetics." In *Key Words in Religion, Media and Culture*, edited by David Morgan, 20–30. New York: Routledge.

Meyer, Leonard B. 2010. *Music, the Arts, and Ideas: Patterns and Predictions in Twentieth-Century Culture*. Chicago: University of Chicago Press.

Mgana, Issa. 1991. *Jukwaa La Taarab—Zanzibar*. Helsinki: MediAfrica Books.

Middleton, John. 1992. *The World of the Swahili: An African Mercantile Civilization*. New Haven, CT: Yale University Press.

———. 2000. "The Peoples." In *Kenya Coast Handbook: Culture, Resources and Development in the East African Littoral*, edited by Jan Hoorweg, Dick Foeken, and Robert A. Obudho, 101–14. Münster: Lit.

Miller, Daniel. 1995. "Consumption and Commodities." *Annual Review of Anthropology* 24 (1): 141–61.

Miller, Flagg. 2007. *The Moral Resonance of Arab Media: Audiocassette Poetry and Culture in Yemen*. Cambridge, MA: Distributed for the Center for Middle Eastern Studies of Harvard University by Harvard University Press.

Minerba, Emiliano. 2020. "From Andalusia to Yemen: The Origin of the Swahili Stanzaic Metres." *Kervan—International Journal of Afro-Asiatic Studies* 24 (2): 63–88.

Ministry of Youth Affairs [Kenya]. 2006. "Kenya National Youth Policy," www.youthaffairs.go.ke/.

Mirza, Sarah, and Margaret Strobel. 1989. *Three Swahili Women: Life Histories from Mombasa, Kenya*. Bloomington: Indiana University Press.

Mitchell, Tony, ed. 2001. *Global Noise: Rap and Hip-Hop Outside the USA*. Middletown, CT: Wesleyan University Press.

Monson, Ingrid. 1994. "Doubleness and Jazz Improvisation: Irony, Parody, and Ethnomusicology." *Critical Inquiry* 20 (2): 283–313.

Moore, Robin D. 1998. *Nationalizing Blackness: Afrocubanismo and Artistic Revolution in Havana, 1920–1940*. Pittsburgh: University of Pittsburgh Press.

Morin, Matthew McNamara. 2012. "Composing Civil Society: Ethnographic Contingency, Ngo Culture, and Music Production in Nairobi, Kenya." PhD dissertation, Florida State University.

Morris, David. 2002. "Touching Intelligence." *Journal of the Philosophy of Sport* 29 (2): 149–62.

Morson, Gary Saul. 1991a. "Bakhtin and the Present Moment." *American Scholar* 60 (2): 201–22.

———. 1991b. "Bakhtin, Genres, and Temporality." *New Literary History* 22 (4): 1071–92.

———, and Caryl Emerson. 1990. *Mikhail Bakhtin: Creation of a Prosaics*. Stanford, CA: Stanford University Press.

Muḥammad ʿAlawy Bā al-Faqīh. 2017. "Shufat Al-Zayn Yatamasha -Al-Fanān Muḥammad Bā MaṬrif." YouTube video, 8:59, February 4. www.youtube.com/watch?v=eulJ5W3S3bA.

Mulaifi, Ghazi al-. 2021. "Kuwaiti Pearl-Diving Music and the Mayouf Mejally Folkloric Ensemble: Beyond an Authorized Heritage Discourse." In *Music in Arabia: Perspectives on Heritage, Mobility and Nation*, edited by Issa Boulos, Virginia Danielson, and Anne K. Rasmussen, 69–84. Bloomington: Indiana University Press.

Mwakio, Philip. 2014. "Taarab Maestro Bhalo Succumbs to Long Illness." *Standard*, April 7, http://www.standardmedia.co.ke/thecounties/article/2000108780/taarab-maestro.

Mwangi, Evan. 2004. "Masculinity and Nationalism in East African Hip-Hop Music." *Tydskrif Vir Letterkunde* 41 (2): 5–19.

Myambo, Melissa Tandiwe. 2012. "Indian Ocean Cosmopolitanism?: M. G. Vassanji's Hybrid Parables of Kenyan Nationalism." *Diaspora: A Journal of Transnational Studies* 16 (1–2): 159–89.

Nabhany, Ahmed Sheikh. 2003. "Mapisi Ya Twarabu Na Kibangala." *Kungamano la Zingiro la Ulimwengu wa Uswahili Katika Bahari ya Hindi* [Conference on the Spread of the Swahili Ecumene in the Indian Ocean]. Zanzibar, February 20–23, 2003.

Nagar, Richa. 1996. "The South Asian Diaspora in Tanzania: A History Retold." *Comparative Studies of South Asia, Africa and the Middle East* 16 (2): 62–80.

Nakassis, Constantine V. 2013. "Citation and Citationality." *Signs and Society* 1 (1): 51–77.

Nassir, Ahmad. 1971. *Umalenga Wa Mvita: Diwani Ya Ustadh Bhalo*. Nairobi: Oxford University Press.

Nation Media Group. 2002. "Jewel in the Crown of Tourism in Kenya." *The What's On Guide*, https://web.archive.org/web/20061115054213/http://www.nationaudio.com/News/DailyNation/whatson/June2002/jewel.htm.

Ngũgĩ wa Thiong'o. 1993. *Moving the Centre: The Struggle for Cultural Freedoms*. London: James Currey.

Novak, David. 2008. "2.5 X6 Metres of Space: Japanese Music Coffeehouses and Experimental Practices of Listening." *Popular Music* 27 (1): 15–34.

———. 2010. "Cosmopolitanism, Remediation, and the Ghost World of Bollywood." *Cultural Anthropology* 25 (1): 40–72.

Ntarangwi, Mwenda. 2000. "*Malumbano* and *Matukano*: Competition, Confrontation, and (De)construction of Masculinity in the *Taarab* of Maulidi and Bhalo." In *Mashindano!: Competitive Music Performance in East Africa*, edited by Frank D. Gunderson and Gregory Barz, 55–66. Dar es Salaam: Mkuki na Nyota Publishers.

———. 2001. "A Socio-Historical and Contextual Analysis of Popular Musical Performance Among the Swahili of Mombasa, Kenya." *Cultural Analysis* 2: 1–37.

———. 2003. *Gender, Identity, and Performance: Understanding Swahili Cultural Realities Through Song*. Trenton, NJ: Africa World Press.

———. 2007. "Music, Identity and Swahili Networks of Knowledge." In *Cultural Production and Social Change in Kenya: Building Bridges*, edited by Kimani Njogu and G. Oluoch-Olunya, 7–26. Nairobi: Twaweza Communications.

NTV Kenya. 2020. "Msanii Wa Taarab Maulid Juma Ataka 'Azikwe Angali Hai' [Taarab Artist Maulidi Juma Wants 'to be Buried While Still Alive']." YouTube video, 3:03, January 25. www.youtube.com/watch?v=kvh322d0HwA.

Nyairo, Joyce. 2004a. "'Reading the Referents': The Ghost of America in Contemporary Kenyan Popular Music." *Scrutiny2* 9 (1): 39–55.

———. 2004b. "'Reading the Referents': (Inter)textuality in Contemporary Kenyan Popular Music." PhD dissertation, University of Witswatersrand.

———. 2006. "(Re)configuring the City: The Mapping of Places and People in Contemporary Kenyan Popular Song Texts." In *Cities in Contemporary Africa*, edited by Martin Murray, 71–94. Gordonsville, VA: Palgrave Macmillan.

———. 2007. "'Modify': Jua Kali as a Metaphor for Africa's Urban Ethnicities and Cultures." In *Urban Legends, Colonial Myths: Popular Culture and Literature in East Africa*, edited by James Ogude and Joyce Nyairo, 125–51. Trenton, NJ: Africa World Press.

———, and James Ogude. 2005. "Popular Music, Popular Politics: *Unbwogable* and the Idioms of Freedom in Kenyan Popular Music." *African Affairs* 104 (415): 225–49.

Ogden, J. Alexander. 2005. "The Impossible Peasant Voice in Russian Culture: Stylization and Mimicry." *Slavic Review* 64 (3): 517–37.

Ogot, Bethwell A. 1995. "The Decisive Years: 1956–63." In *Decolonization and Independence in Kenya, 1940–93*, edited by Bethwell A. Ogot and William Robert Ochieng, 48–71. London: James Currey.

———. 2012. *Kenyans, Who Are We: Reflections on the Meaning of National Identity and Nationalism*. Kisumu, Kenya: Anyange Press.

Okech, Roselyne N. 2011. "Promoting Sustainable Festival Events Tourism: A Case Study of Lamu Kenya." *Worldwide Hospitality and Tourism Themes* 3 (3): 193–202.

Oluo, Ijeoma. 2019. *So You Want to Talk About Race*. New York: Seal Press.

Ong, Aihwa. 1996. "Cultural Citizenship as Subject-Making: Immigrants Negotiate Racial and Cultural Boundaries in the United States." *Current Anthropology* 37 (5): 737–62.

Ortner, Sherry B. 1996. *Making Gender: The Politics and Erotics of Culture*. Boston: Beacon Press.

———. 2005. "Subjectivity and Cultural Critique." *Anthropological Theory* 5 (1): 31–52.

Ostrow, James M. 1990. *Social Sensitivity: A Study of Habit and Experience*. Albany: State University of New York Press.

Osumare, Halifu. 2007. *The Africanist Aesthetic in Global Hip-Hop: Power Moves*. Palgrave MacMillan.

Otterbeck, Jonas. 2012. "Wahhabi Ideology of Social Control Versus a New Publicness in Saudi Arabia." *Contemporary Islam* 6 (3): 341–53.

Padgaonkar, Dileep. 2002. "Zanzibar's Desis [Interview with Abdul Shariff]." *Times of India*, July 27, http://timesofindia.indiatimes.com/home/opinion/Zanzibars-Desis/articleshow/17197983.cms.

Parkin, David. 1985. "Being and Selfhood Among Intermediary Swahili." In *Swahili Language and Society: Papers for the Workshop Held at the School of Oriental and African Studies in April 1982*, edited by Joan Maw and David Parkin, 247–60. Vienna: Beitrage Zur Afrikanistik.

———. 1989. "Swahili Mijikenda: Facing Both Ways in Kenya." *Africa* 59 (2): 161–75.

———. 1994. "Introduction." In *Continuity and Autonomy in Swahili Communities: Inland Influences and Strategies of Self-Determination*, edited by David Parkin, 1–12. London: School of Oriental and African Studies.

Paterson, Douglas. 2001. "Fadhili William: A Remembrance." *Beat*, republished at www.eastafricanmusic.com/fadhili.htm. Last accessed March 12, 2022.

Patinkin, Jason. 2014. "In Kenya's Muslim Port: A Tale of Two Mosques." *Christian Science Monitor*, February 19, www.csmonitor.com/World/Africa/2014/0219/In-Kenya.

Pearson, Michael Naylor. 2003. *The Indian Ocean*. London: Routledge.

Peña, Manuel H. 1980. "Ritual Structure in a Chicano Dance." *Latin American Music Review/Revista de Música Latinoamericana* 1: 47–73.

Perullo, Alex. 2007. "'Here's a Little Something Local': An Early History of Hip Hop in Dar es Salaam, 1984–1997." In *Dar es Salaam: Histories from an Emerging African Metropolis*, edited by James R. Brennan and Andrew Burton, 250–72. Dar es Salaam/Nairobi: Mkuki na Nyota/British Institute in Eastern Africa.

———. 2011. *Live from Dar es Salaam: Popular Music and Tanzania's Music Economy*. Bloomington: Indiana University Press.

Petrilli, Susan, and Augusto Ponzio. 2005. *Semiotics Unbounded: Interpretive Routes through the Open Network of Signs*. Toronto: University of Toronto Press.

Porter, Mary Ann. 1995. "Talking at the Margins: Kenyan Discourses on Homosexuality." In *Beyond the Lavender Lexicon: Authenticity, Imagination, and Appropriation in Lesbian and Gay Languages*, edited by William Leap, 133–53. New York: Gordon and Breach.

Pouwels, Randall L. 1987. *Horn and Crescent: Cultural Change and Traditional Islam on the East African Coast, 800-1900*. Cambridge: Cambridge University Press.

Prestholdt, Jeremy. 2008. *Domesticating the World: African Consumerism and the Genealogies of Globalization*. Berkeley: University of California Press.

———. 2011. "Kenya, the United States, and Counterterrorism." *Africa Today* 57 (4): 2–27.

———. 2014. "Politics of the Soil: Separatism, Autochthony, and Decolonization at the Kenyan Coast." *Journal of African History* 55 (2): 249–70.

Prins, A. H. J. 1965. *Sailing From Lamu: A Study of Maritime Culture in Islamic East Africa*. Assen: van Gorcum.

———. 1967. *The Swahili-Speaking Peoples of Zanzibar and the East African Coast (Arabs, Shirazi and Swahili)*. London: International African Institute.

———. 1971. *Didemic Lamu: Social Stratification and Spatial Structure in a Muslim Maritime Town*. Groningen: Instituut voor Culturele Antropologie der Rijksuniversiteit.

Racy, Ali Jihad. 1991. "Creativity and Ambiance: An Ecstatic Feedback Model from Arab Music." *World of Music* 33 (3): 7–28.

———. 2003. *Making Music in the Arab World: The Culture and Artistry of Tarab*. Cambridge: Cambridge University Press.

Radano, Ronald. 2003. *Lying Up a Nation: Race and Black Music*. Chicago: University of Chicago Press.

Raia, Annachiara. 2020. "Texts, Voices and Tapes: Mediating Poetry on the Swahili Muslim Coast in the 21st Century." *Matatu* 51 (1): 139–68.

———, and Clarissa Vierke, eds. 2023. *In This Fragile World: Swahili Poetry of Commitment by Ustadh Mahmoud Mau*. Leiden: Brill.

Ranade, Ashok Da. 2006. *Hindi Film Song: Music Beyond Boundaries*. New Delhi: Bibliophile South Asia.

Ranger, T. O. 1975. *Dance and Society in Eastern Africa, 1890-1970: The Beni Ngoma*. Berkeley: University of California Press.

Ranger, Terence. 1993. "The Invention of Tradition Revisited: The Case of Colonial Africa." In *Legitimacy and the State in Twentieth-Century Africa*, edited by Terence Ranger and Olufemi Vaughan, 62–111. London: Palgrave Macmillan.

Rappaport, Roy A. 1999. *Ritual and Religion in the Making of Humanity*. Cambridge: Cambridge University Press.

Rasmussen, Anne K. 2016. "Performing Islam around the Indian Ocean Basin: Musical Ritual and Recreation in Indonesia and the Sultanate of Oman." In *Islam and Popular Culture*, edited by Karin van Nieuwkerk, Mark LeVine, and Martin Stokes, 297–322. Austin: University of Texas Press.

Rechenbach, Charles William. 1967. *Swahili-English Dictionary*. Washington, DC: Catholic University of America Press.

Reinwald, Brigitte. 2006. "'Tonight at the Empire': Cinema and Urbanity in Zanzibar, 1920s to 1960s." *Afrique histoire* 5 (1): 81–109.

Reuster-Jahn, Uta, and Gabriel Hacke. 2011. "The Bongo Flava Industry in Tanzania and Artists' Strategies for Success." Department of Anthropology and African Studies, Johannes Gutenberg Universität, Mainz, Working Paper 127.

Ricoeur, Paul. 2004. *The Rule of Metaphor: The Creation of Meaning in Language*. London: Routledge.

Robert, Shaaban. 1967. *Wasifu Wa Siti Binti Saad: Mwimbaji Wa Unguja*. Nairobi: Evans Brothers.

Roberts, John Storm. 1973. "Songs the Swahili Sing." *Africa Report* 18 (5) (September–October): 18–22.

———. 1998. *Black Music of Two Worlds: African, Caribbean, Latin, and African-American Traditions*. New York: Schirmer Books.

Rosaldo, Michelle Z. 1980. "The Use and Abuse of Anthropology: Reflections on Feminism and Cross-Cultural Understanding." *Signs* 5 (3): 389–417.

Saar, Martin. 2008. "Understanding Genealogy: History, Power, and the Self." *Journal of the Philosophy of History* 2 (3): 295–314.

Sacleux, Charles. 1939. *Dictionnare Swahili-Français*. Paris: Institut D'Ethnologie.

Said, Amira Msellem. 2012. *Waswifu Wa Ahmed Sheikh Nabhany*. London: JC Press.

Saleh, Ali, Fiona McGain, and Kawthar Buwayhid. 2008. *Bi Kidude: Tales of a Living Legend*. Zanzibar: Gallery Publications.

Saleh, Seif Salim. 1988. "Historia Na Muundo Wa Taarab." *Lugha na Utamaduni* 1: 8–11.

Salim, Ahmed I. 1970. "The Movement of 'Mwambao' or Coast Autonomy in Kenya, 1956–1963." *Hadith* 2: 212–28.

———. 1973. *Swahili-Speaking Peoples of Kenya's Coast, 1895–1965*. Nairobi: East African Publishing House.

———. 1976. "'Native or Non-Native?': The Problem of Identity and the Social Stratification of the Arab-Swahili of Kenya." In *Hadith 6: History and Social Change in East Africa*, edited by Bethwell A. Ogot, 65–85. Nairobi: East African Literature Bureau.

———. 1985. "The Elusive 'mswahili': Some Reflections on His Identity and Culture." In *Swahili Language and Society*, edited by Joan Maw and David Parkin, 23. Vienna: Beiträge Zur Afrikanistik.

Salim, Swalha. 1983. "A History of the Yemeni Arabs in Kenya, 1895–1963." PhD dissertation, University of Nairobi.

Salvadori, Cynthia. 1989. *Through Open Doors: A View of Asian Cultures in Kenya*, Revised Edition. Nairobi: Kenway Publications.

Samper, David A. 2004. "'Africa is Still Our Mama': Kenyan Rappers, Youth Identity, and the Revitalization of Traditional Values." *African Identities* 2 (1): 37–51.

Samuels, David W. 2004. *Putting a Song on Top of It: Expression and Identity on the San Carlos Apache Reservation*. Tucson: University of Arizona Press.

Samuelson, Meg. 2016. "Producing a World of Remains in Indian Ocean Africa: Discrepant Time, Melancholy Affect and the Subject of Transport in Capital Art Studio, Stone Town, Zanzibar." *African Studies* 75 (2): 233–56.

Sanga, Imani. 2010. "The Practice and Politics of Hybrid Soundscapes in Muziki Wa Injili in Dar es Salaam, Tanzania." *Journal of African Cultural Studies* 22 (2): 145–56.

———. 2016. "The Archiving of Siti Binti Saad and Her Engagement with the Music Industry in Shaaban Robert's *Wasifu Wa Siti Binti Saad*." *Eastern African Literary and Cultural Studies* 2 (1-2): 34–44.

Schafer, R. Murray. 1994. *The Soundscape: Our Sonic Environment and the Tuning of the World*. Rochester, NY: Destiny Books.

Schneider, Arnd. 2003. "On 'Appropriation'. A Critical Reappraisal of the Concept and Its Application in Global Art Practices." *Social Anthropology* 11 (2): 215–29.

Schutz, Alfred. 1951. "Making Music Together: A Study in Social Relationship." *Social Research* 18 (1/4): 76–97.

Scott, Derek B. 1998. "Orientalism and Musical Style." *Musical Quarterly* 82 (2): 309–35.

Seeger, Charles. 1951. "Systematic Musicology: Viewpoints, Orientations, and Methods." *Journal of the American Musicological Society* 4 (3): 240–48.

Senkoro, F. E. M. K. 1995. "Viewing Gender through Tanzanian Lullabies." In *Other Worlds, Other Lives: Children's Literature Experiences, Proceedings of the International Conference on Children's Literature, 4-6 April 1995*, edited by Myrna Machet, Sandra I. I. Olën, and Thomas van der Walt, 119–36. Pretoria: University of South Africa.

———. 2005. "Understanding Gender through Genre: Oral Literature as a Vehicle for Gender Studies in East Africa." In *Gender, Literature and Religion in Africa*, edited by Elizabeth Le Roux, 5–24. Dakar: Codesria; Codesria Gender Series #4.

Serjeant, Robert Bertram. 1951. *South Arabian Poetry. I: Prose and Poetry from Hadramawt*. London: Taylor's Foreign Press.

Shannon, Jonathan Holt. 2003. "Emotion, Performance, and Temporality in Arab Music: Reflections on Tarab." *Cultural Anthropology* 18 (1): 72–98.

———. 2006. *Among the Jasmine Trees: Music and Modernity in Contemporary Syria*. Middletown, CT: Wesleyan University Press.

Shariff, Ibrahim Noor. 1973. "Waswahili and Their Language: Some Misconceptions." *Kiswahili* 43 (2): 67–75.

———. 1983. "The Function of Dialogue Poetry in Swahili Society." EdD dissertation. Rutgers University.

———. 1988. *Tungo Zetu: Msingi Wa Mashairi Na Tungo Nyinginezo*. Trenton, NJ: Red Sea Press.

———, ed. 1985. *Umbuji Wa Kiwandeo: Tungo Za Ahmed Sheikh Nabhany*. Nairobi: East African Publishing House.

Sheriff, Abdul. 1987. *Slaves, Spices and Ivory in Zanzibar: Integration of an East African Commercial Empire into the World Economy, 1770–1873*. Athens: Ohio University Press.

———. 2019. "Contradictions in the Heritagization of Zanzibar 'Stone Town.'" In *Travelling Pasts: The Politics of Cultural Heritage in the Indian Ocean World*, 221–45. Leiden: Brill.

Silverstein, Michael. 1993. "Metapragmatic Discourse and Metapragmatic Function." In *Reflexive Language: Reported Speech and Metapragmatics*, edited by John Arthur Lucy, 33–58. Cambridge: Cambridge University Press.

Simpson, Edward, and Kai Kresse. 2008. "Cosmopolitanism Contested: Anthropology and History in the Western Indian Ocean." In *Struggling with History: Islam and Cosmopolitanism in the Western Indian Ocean*, edited by Edward Simpson and Kai Kresse, 1–41. New York: Columbia University Press.

Small, Christopher. 1998. *Musicking: The Meanings of Performing and Listening*. Middletown, CT: Wesleyan University Press.

Spear, Thomas. 1984. "The Shirazi in Swahili Traditions, Culture, and History." *History in Africa* 11: 291–305.

St John, Graham, ed. 2008a. *Victor Turner and Contemporary Cultural Performance*. New York: Berghahn Books.

———. 2008b. "Victor Turner and Contemporary Cultural Performance: An Introduction." In *Victor Turner and Contemporary Cultural Performance*, edited by Graham St John, 1–37. New York: Berghahn Books.

Stokes, Martin. 1994. "Introduction: Ethnicity, Identity and Music." In *Ethnicity, Identity, and Music: The Musical Construction of Place*, edited by Martin Stokes, 1–27. Oxford: Berg.

Strobel, Margaret. 1975. "Women's Wedding Celebrations in Mombasa, Kenya." *African Studies Review* 18 (3): 35–45.

———. 1979. *Muslim Women in Mombasa, 1890–1975*. New Haven, CT: Yale University Press.

Suleiman, A. A. 1969. "The Swahili Singing Star Siti Bint Saad and the Tarab Tradition in Zanzibar." *Swahili* 39 (1–2): 87–90.

Suleyman, Miguel. 2011. "How Swahili Poetry Has Shaped Today's Popular Music." *Citizen*

(Tanzania), October 25, http://thecitizen.co.tz/uhuru/16461-how-swahili-poetry-has-shaped-todays-popular-music.html.

Swartz, Marc J. 1979. "Religious Courts, Community, and Ethnicity Among the Swahili of Mombasa: An Historical Study of Social Boundaries." *Africa* 49 (1): 29–41.

———. 1996. "Politics, Ethnicity, and Social Structure: The Decline of an Urban Community During the Twentieth Century." *Ethnology* 35 (4): 233–48.

Sykes, Jim, and Julia Byl. 2023a. "Introduction." In *Sounding the Indian Ocean: Musical Circulations in the Afro-Asiatic Seascape*, edited by Jim Sykes, and Julia Byl, 1–29. Berkeley: University of California Press.

———, eds. 2023b. *Sounding the Indian Ocean: Musical Circulations in the Afro-Asiatic Seascape*. Berkeley: University of California Press.

Tagg, Philip. 2013. *Music's Meanings: A Modern Musicology for Non-Musos*. New York: Mass Media Music Scholar's Press.

Taussig, Michael. 1993. *Mimesis and Alterity: A Particular History of the Senses*. New York: Routledge.

Thompson, Katrina Daly. 2011. "How to be a Good Muslim Wife: Women's Performance of Islamic Authority During Swahili Weddings." *Journal of Religion in Africa* 41 (4): 427–48.

Tolbert, Elizabeth. 2001. "Music and Meaning: An Evolutionary Story." *Psychology of Music* 29 (1): 84–94.

Tomlinson, Gary. 2015. *A Million Years of Music: The Emergence of Human Modernity*. New York: Zone Books.

Topan, Farouk. 1995. "Vugo: A Virginity Celebration Ceremony Among the Swahili of Mombasa." *African Languages and Cultures* 8 (1): 87–107.

———. 1997. "Biography Writing in Swahili." *History in Africa* 24: 299–307.

———. 2006. "From Coastal to Global: The Erosion of the Swahili 'Paradox.'" In *The Global Worlds of the Swahili: Interfaces of Islam, Identity and Space in 19th- and 20th-Century East Africa*, edited by Roman Loimeier and Rüdiger Seesemann, 55–66. Berlin: Lit.

Topp, Janet. 1994. "A History of Taarab Music in Zanzibar: A Process of Africanisation." In *Continuity and Autonomy in Swahili Communities: Inland Influences and Strategies of Self-Determination*, 153–65. London: School of Oriental and African Studies.

Topp Fargion, Janet. 2002. "The Music of Zenj: Arab-African Crossovers in the Music of Zanzibar." *Journal des Africanistes* 72 (2): 203–12.

———. 2007. "Poetry and Languid Charm: Swahili Music from Tanzania and Kenya from the 1920s to the 1950s." CD Liner Notes. British Library Sound Archive: Topic Records TSCD936.

———. 2014. *Taarab Music in Zanzibar in the Twentieth Century: A Story of 'Old is Gold' and Flying Spirits*. Surrey, UK: Ashgate.

Touma, Habib Hassan. 1996. *The Music of the Arabs*. Portland, OR: Amadeus Press.

Tracey, Andrew. 2006. In *Colonial Dance Bands 1950 & 1952*, CD Liner Notes. Utrecht: SWP Records with International Library of African Music.

Tracey, Hugh. 1951. "Recording Tour, May to November 1950 East Africa." *Newsletter. African Music Society* 1 (4): 38–51.

Trimingham, J. Spencer. 1964. *Islam in East Africa*. Oxford: Clarendon Press.

Trondman, Mats, Anna Lund, and Stefan Lund. 2011. "Socio-Symbolic Homologies: Exploring Paul Willis' Theory of Cultural Forms." *European Journal of Cultural Studies* 14 (5): 573–92.

TUKI. 2001. *Kamusi Ya Kiswahili-Kiingereza (Swahili-English Dictionary), Toleo La Kwanza*. Dar es Salaam: TUKI (Taasisi ya Unchunguzi wa Kiswahili), Chuo Kikuu cha Dar es Salaam.

Turino, Thomas. 1999. "Signs of Imagination. Identity, and Experience: A Peircian Semiotic Theory for Music." *Ethnomusicology* 43 (2): 221–55.

Turner, Bryan S. 1987. "A Note on Nostalgia." *Theory, Culture & Society* 4 (1): 147–56.

Turner, Edith. 2012. *Communitas: The Anthropology of Collective Joy*. New York: Palgrave Macmillan.

Turner, Victor. 1967. *The Forest of Symbols: Aspects of Ndembu Ritual*. Ithaca, NY: Cornell University Press.

———. 1969. *The Ritual Process: Structure and Anti-Structure*. Chicago: Aldine Publishing Co.

———. 1974. "Liminal to Liminoid, in Play, Flow, and Ritual: An Essay in Comparative Symbology." *Rice Institute Pamphlet-Rice University Studies* 60 (3): 53–92.

———. 1979. "Frame, Flow and Reflection: Ritual and Drama as Public Liminality." *Japanese Journal of Religious Studies* 6 (4): 465–99.

———. 1982. *From Ritual to Theatre: The Human Seriousness of Play*. New York: Performing Arts Journal Publications.

———. 1984. "Liminality and the Performative Genres." In *Rite, Drama, Festival, Spectacle: Rehearsals Toward a Theory of Cultural Performance*, edited by John J. MacAloon, 19–41. Philadelphia: Institute for the Study of Human Issues.

———. 1986. *The Anthropology of Performance*. New York: PAJ Publications.

———, and Edith Turner. 1982. "Performing Ethnography." *Drama Review: TDR* 26 (2): 33–50.

Ulaby, Laith. 2012. "On the Decks of Dhows: Musical Traditions of Oman and the Indian Ocean World." *World of Music* 1 (2): 43–62.

Urkevich, Lisa. 2014. *Music and Traditions of the Arabian Peninsula: Saudi Arabia, Kuwait, Bahrain, and Qatar*. New York: Routledge.

Van Gennep, Arnold. 1960. *The Rites of Passage*. Chicago: Chicago University Press.

Vander Biesen, Ivan, and Christiaan De Beukelaer. 2014. "Tourism and Imagining Musical Traditions on the East African Coast: Harmony and Disharmony." *World of Music* 3 (1): 133–54.

Vassanji, M. G. 2004. *The In-Between World of Vikram Lall*. New York: Knopf.

Vergès, Françoise. 2003. "Writing on Water: Peripheries, Flows, Capital, and Struggles in the Indian Ocean." *Positions: East Asia Cultures Critique* 11 (1): 241–57.

Verne, Julia. 2012. *Living Translocality: Space, Culture and Economy in Contemporary Swahili Trade*. Stuttgart: Franz Steiner Verlag.

———, and Markus Verne. 2017. "Introduction: The Indian Ocean as Aesthetic Space." *Comparative Studies of South Asia, Africa and the Middle East* 37 (2): 314–20.

Vernon, Paul. 1997. "Odeon Records: Their 'Ethnic' Output." *Musical Traditions*, July 31, https://www.mustrad.org.uk/articles/odeon.htm.

Vierke, Clarissa. 2011. *On the Poetics of the Utendi: A Critical Edition of the Nineteenth-Century Swahili Poem "Utendi Wa Haudaji" Together with a Stylistic Analysis*. Münster: LIT Verlag.

———. 2012. "Mafumbo: Considering the Functions of Metaphorical Speech in Swahili Contexts." In *Selected Proceedings of the 42nd Annual Conference on African Linguistics*, edited by Michael R. Marlo, Nikki B. Adams, Christopher R. Green, Michelle Morrison, and Tristan M. Purvis, 278–90. Somerville, MA: Cascadilla Proceedings Project.

———. 2016. "From across the Ocean: Considering Travelling Literary Figurations as Part of Swahili Intellectual History." *Journal of African Cultural Studies* 28 (2): 225–40.

———. 2017. "Poetic Links across the Ocean: On Poetic Translation as Mimetic Practice at the Swahili Coast." *Comparative Studies of South Asia, Africa and the Middle East* 37 (2): 321–35.

Wagner, Mark S. 2009. *Like Joseph in Beauty: Yemeni Vernacular Poetry and Arab-Jewish Symbiosis*. Leiden: Brill.

Wagner, Roy. 2001. *An Anthropology of the Subject: Holographic Worldview in New Guinea and Its Meaning and Significance for the World of Anthropology*. Berkeley: University of California Press.

Wahrman, Dror. 2008. *The Making of the Modern Self*. New Haven, CT: Yale University Press.

Waliaula, Ken Walibora. 2013. "The State of Swahili Studies: Remembering the Past, Present, and Future." *Studies in Literature and Language* 6 (2): 8–17.

Walibora, Ken. 2021. "Pwani Si Kenya: Coastal Consciousness and Contesting Kenyanness." In *Illusions of Location Theory: Consequences for Blue Economy in Africa*, edited by Douglas Yates and Francis Onditi, 287–302. Wilmington, DE: Vernon Press.

Walker, Iain. 2005. "Mimetic Structuration: Or, Easy Steps to Building an Acceptable Identity." *History and Anthropology* 16 (2): 187–210.

———. 2008. "Hadramis, *Shimali*s and *Muwalladin*: Negotiating Cosmopolitan Identities Between the Swahili Coast and Southern Yemen." *Journal of Eastern African Studies* 2 (1): 44–59.

———. 2010. *Becoming the Other, Being Oneself: Constructing Identities in a Connected World*. Cambridge: Cambridge Scholars Publishing.

Ward, Jonathan. 2011. *Opika Pende*. [Book packaged with audio collection]. Atlanta, GA: Dust-to-Digital.

Warner, Michael. 2002. *Publics and Counterpublics*. New York: Zone Books.

Waterman, Christopher A. 1990. *Juju: A Social History and Ethnography of an African Popular Music*. Chicago: University of Chicago Press.

Waterman, Richard A. 1952. "African Influence on the Music of the Americas." In *Acculturation in the Americas: Proceedings of the XXIXth International Congress of Americanists*, edited by Sol Tax, 207–18. Chicago: University of Chicago Press.

———. 1963. "On Flogging a Dead Horse: Lessons Learned from the Africanisms Controversy." *Ethnomusicology* 7 (2): 83–87.

Waugh, Patricia. 1984. *Metafiction: The Theory and Practice of Self-Conscious Fiction*. London: Routledge.

Wegulo, Francis N., and Cleophas Ondieki. 1987. *Our Nation, Kenya: Pupils' Book for Standard Five*. Nairobi: Longman GHC Series.

Weidman, Amanda. 2015. "Voice." In *Keywords in Sound*, edited by David Novak and Matt Sakakeeny, 232–45. Durham, NC: Duke University Press.

Weiss, Sarah. 2008. "Permeable Boundaries: Hybridity, Music, and the Reception of Robert Wilson's *I La Galigo*." *Ethnomusicology* 52 (2): 203–38.

Welby, Virginia. 1903. *What is Meaning?: Studies in the Development of Significance*. London: Macmillan and Co., Ltd.

Werbner, Pnina. 1997. "Introduction: The Dialectics of Cultural Hybridity." In *Debating Cultural Hybridity: Multi-Cultural Identities and the Politics of Anti-Racism*, edited by Pnina Werbner and Tariq Modood, 1–26. London: Zed Books.

Whiteley, Wilfred Howell, ed. 1974. *Language in Kenya*. Nairobi: Oxford University Press.

Williams, Chet, Hassan Hussein, and Haussein Sheikh. 1971. *Baijun Ballads: Somali Songs in Swahili; Haussein Shiekh and Radio Mogadisco Swahili Singers*. Smithsonian Folkways FW 08504 [original release: Asch AH 8504].

Williams, Raymond. 1977. *Marxism and Literature*. Oxford: Oxford University Press.

———. 2020. *Culture and Materialism*. London: Verso.

Willis, Justin. 1993. *Mombasa, the Swahili, and the Making of the Mijikenda*. Oxford: Clarendon Press.

———, and George Gona. 2013. "Tradition, Tribe, and State in Kenya: The Mijikenda Union, 1945–1980." *Comparative Studies in Society and History* 55 (2): 448–73.

Willis, Paul. 1978. *Profane Culture*. London: Routledge and Kegan Paul.

Wilson, Gordon M. 1958. *Mombasa Social Survey*. Nairobi: Kenya Government, Ministry of African Affairs.

Yahya, Saad S. 1998. "Who Owns the Kenya Coast? The Climaxing of Land Conflicts on the Indian Ocean Seaboard." Unpublished report. Nairobi.

Yamani, Tarek, and Rony Afif. 2017. *The Percussion Ensemble of the Arabian Peninsula*. Abu Dhabi: Tarek Yamani/Abu Dhabi Foundation.

Young, Robert J. C. 2005. *Colonial Desire: Hybridity in Theory, Culture and Race*. London: Routledge.

Ziff, Bruce, and Pratima V. Rao, eds. 1997. *Borrowed Power: Essays on Cultural Appropriation*. New Brunswick, NJ: Rutgers University Press.

Zuckerkandl, Victor. 1956. *Sound and Symbol: Music and the External World*. Princeton, NJ: Princeton University Press.

———. 1973. *Man the Musician: Sound and Symbol*, Volume Two. Princeton, NJ: Princeton University Press.

INDEX

Swahili and Arab Muslim names are alphabetized by first name except for names of published authors, who are cited according to the last-name first convention.

"Aaja Aaja" (Com), 67
Abdalla, Abdilatif, 42
Abdalla Kadara, 123
Abdel Rab Idris, 176–77
Abdel-Rahim Said Mohammed Basalim, 58–59
Abdurahman Ali Ali, 79
Abubakar, Amina, 123
Abu Bakr Salim, 120
acoustemology: defined, 186; of place, 16, 186n18; of urbanity, 55–56
Adio Mohamed (Prince Adio), 167–73
Ahmad Mahfouz Bin Brek, 101, 122
Ahmad Nassir (Ahmad Nassir Juma Bhalo), 52, 65, 75, 78, 79, 83, 123, 127
Ahmed al Jumairi, 130
Ahmed bin Ghodel, 176–77
Ahmed Sheikh Nabhany: *contrafacta* of, 130–31; cultural ambiguity project of, 129–30; musical philosophizing and, 126; musical poetics of Swahili culture and, 129–33; photo of, 124; poetry of, 123–25; program of conservation of, 134; Swahili Cultural Centre and, 147; viewpoint of, 34, 75; Zein l'Abdin and, 22–23, 114, 123, 125, 126, 129
"Ah W Nuṣ" ("By Half" [I Mean It]) (Ajram), 165
Ajram, Nancy, 165, 166

Akhil the Brain, 171
Ali "Canada" Mbarak, 162–63, 171
Ali Mkali, 62–65, 73
Ali Swaleh, 105
Ali wa Lela, 116
Allen, J. W. T., 125
Alpers, Edward, 178
Al-Shihr, 43
Alwi Shatry, 125
ambiguity, of Swahili, 8–10
Amr Diab, 165, 166
Amselle, Jean-Loup, 134
Anasi Shembwana, 122
Appadurai, Arjun, 21, 154
appropriation: cultural, 184n4; defined, 2; genealogy of, 21–23; heritagization and, 149–50; mimetic, 39; in music, 18; of taarab (sung poetry), 3
Arab, Swahili *versus*, 8
arabesque, Mombasan, 160–64
"Arabian Conga" (Siti Ganduri), 61–62
Arabian *contrafacta*, 130–31
Arab music theory, 189n7
Arab-Swahili identity, 51
Arab taarab: class politics and, 122; compounding culture and, 133; conservator in, 122–25; education of musician in, 115–19;

Egyptian songs in, 119, 120; Hadrami *ṭarab* in, 120–22; Kuwaiti songs in, 119; Kuwaiti style of, 131–33; Latin American songs in, 119; musical philosophizing and, 125–29; musical poetics of Swahili culture and, 129–33; origin of, 48–49; overview of, 112–14; repertoire of, 119–20; resounding in, 133–35; Swahili songs in, 119, 120

Aristotle, 187n25

Asha Abdo Suleiman (Malika), 73, 117–18, 119, 177

Askew, Kelly, 143–44

"Aso Subira Hanali" (One Who Lacks Patience Had Nothing) (Zein l'Abdin), 113–14

Assanand & Sons, Ltd., 47–48

"Awaara Hoon" (I Am a Vagabond) (Kapoor), 75

Badbes, Omar, 100, 122

"Bahibbak yā Lubnān" (I love you, Lebanon) (Showdemo), 162

Bakari Aziz Omar, 79

Bakhtin, Mikhail, 18–19, 21, 183n1

"Bā Nuṭlub al-Mūla" (Bin Brek), 101

barazas, 127–28

"Basahera Umuongo" (Talsam), 24–25, 26, 28–29, 32, 36–38, 40

Basheikh Mosque, Mombasa, 192n32

beach party, example of, 152–53

becoming-resonance, 135

"*Belly Naach Di*," 172

"Bembeya Mtoto" (Ali Mkali), 62–63, 64

Berg, F. J., 9

Berlin-Nairobi (BLNRB), 203n7

Bertz, Ned, 71

Bhabha, Homi, 80

Bhalo, Ahmad Nassir Juma, 52, 65, 75, 78, 79, 83, 123, 127

Bhalo, Mohamed Khamis Juma, 65, 67–68, 72, 74, 76–80, 79, 83

bhangra, 170–72

Bhosle, Asha, 73

Bi Kidude, 31, 190n13

Bin Brek, Ahmad Mahfouz, 101, 122

binti Saad, Siti. *See* Siti binti Saad

binti Saad collective: appropriation by, 31–32; artistic integrity of, 32; characteristics of, 31; crosscurrent of reflexivity in, 49; Dhow Countries Music Academy (DCMA) and, 31; elite taarab and, 34–35; foreign styles appropriations of, 39; *howa* lullaby of, 63–64; hybridized soundworlds of, 28–30, 32; Indian style of, 32–33; "Kijiti" of, 38; members of, 188n3; mimetic appropriations of style of, 39–40; physical positioning of, 35–36; style and identity in, 29; stylistic approach of, 29; stylistic hybridization in, 31–32; taarab form of, 33–36; theatrical expression of, 36–38

Bi Salima Zeina, 34

Blacking, John, 104

Blyden, Edward Wilmot, 150

Bollywood *contrafacta*, 67, 72, 73

bongo flava, 170, 204n16

Bose, Sugata, 178

boundaries, objectification of, 39–40

Bourdieu, Pierre, 76, 166–67

Brennan, James R., 51

Britain, in East Africa, 3–4, 30

Buda Swedi, 34

Burchell, Andrew, 71, 167, 169

Butler, Judith, 80

Bwana Zena, 35

Byl, Julia, 180

"Candy Shop" (50 Cent), 165–66

Cannibal (Ralph Masai), 156, 158, 159

Capwell, Charles, 101

chakacha, 118–19, 133, 134

chali wa Nairobi ("Nairobi boy"), 157

"Chap Chap Mapenzi" (Quickly My Love), 202n10

Chera, Jumaa Bakari, 79

Chiraghdin, Shihabuddin, 54

chokra, 89–90

Chuba Shee, 71, 80

citations, function of, 33
citizenship, 14, 15, 154–55
CLD (Lennox Mwale), 158, 161–62
Clifford, James, 111
clowns, of Indian taarab, 69, 80–84, 89
Columbia Records, 25
comedy, 38
commerce, in Mombasa, 13
Congolese *soukous*, 153, 154
Conquergood, Dwight, 177
contrafacta, 130–31
creativity, 180
crosscurrent of reflexivity, 48–49
cultural citizenship, 153–54
cultural intimacy, 107, 108
cultural performances, reflexive frame of, 104–6. *See also* wedding celebration
Culture Music Club, 174–76

"Damu Imenikauka" (Jauharah Orchestra Musical Club), 59
dance, 107–8, 143
decolonization, 50–51
Denning, Michael, 25
Dewey, John, 16, 187n19
Dhow Countries Music Academy (DCMA), 31, 146, 149
Diamond Star, 137
Digos, taarab popularity among, 143–44
disjuncture, Swahili and, 10–11
dissociation, of Swahili, 6–8
Dolar, Mladen, 37
domestic labor, 14
"Door Koi Gaye" (Someone Sings in the Distance), 84–85
drumming: basic drum melody of, 199–200n8; *chakacha* in, 118–19, 133, 134; compounding culture and, 133; in Hadrami *ṭarab*, 91–92; *kapuka* beat of, 168; for "Kuwaiti" (Zein l'Abdin), 130; melodies of, 120, 121; *sharh* in, 101, 134; *twarila ndia* ("drum of the street"), 132–33
Dubai, 165–67

duf, 117
dūlāb, 189n8

East Africa, 3–4, 6–8, 30. *See also specific locations*
East African Sound Studios Ltd. (East African Records, Ltd.), 47
Eastman, Carol, 9
Egyptian songs, in Arab taarab, 119, 120
Eidsheim, Nina, 68
Eisenlohr, Patrick, 107
ethnicity, modern regime of, 10–11
ethnohistorical method, 178–79

Fair, Laura, 26, 27, 33, 38, 40, 71
Farao (Eric Omondi), 156, 157
Farid al-Atrash, 121
Farraj, Johnny, 28–29
Feld, Steven, 16, 69, 104
50 Cent, 165–66
Floyd, Samuel, Jr., 180
Fox, Aaron, 69
Frankl, P. J. L., 59

Ganduri, Siti, 61–62
Gendlin, Eugene, 16
genealogy, of appropriation, 21–23, 188n27
"Ghālī Ghālī" (My Dear, My Dear) (Ghodel), 176–77
Ghanem, Nizar, 44
ghazal (light classical song), 70
Gilroy, Paul, 173
Giriama *ngoma* songs, 137
Glassman, Jonathan, 10, 186n14
Graebner, Werner, 3, 115–16, 132, 146–47, 149, 174, 175, 190n11

Habib Swaleh Ahdaly, 114
Hadrami Arabs, 41–42, 43, 44–45, 93–96
Hadrami sharifs, 13, 94, 95
Hadrami *ṭarab*: in Arab taarab, 120–22; class politics and, 122; drumming in, 91–92; Indian taarab link with, 111; overview

of, 91–93, 96–101; popular songs of, 99;
sharh of, 101; sounding diaspora and,
106–11; Swahili taarab and, 100; wedding
celebrations and, 101–6. *See also specific
musicians*; *specific works*
half-flat pitch, 189n9
Hall, Stuart, 10
harlequin poetics, 84–88
harmonium, 73
Harrier, Lyndon, 52
henna, at wedding celebrations, 102
heritagization, 145–51
Herskovits, Melville, 173, 178, 179
Herzfeld, Michael, 89
high-order meaning, 106
Hindi musical films, 71–72, 74, 75. *See also
specific films*
hip hop: at beach party, 152–53; citizenship
and, 154–55; culture of, 153, 154; Kenyan
side of, 158–60; Mombasan arabesque in,
160–64; *Mombasani* concept in, 156–58;
popularity of, 153; public space of, 154–55;
regional identity in, 155; taarab tinge in,
167–70; unrealized cosmopolitics and,
172–73. *See also specific musicians*; *specific
works*
"Hiya Hiya al-Sanīn" (These are the Years)
(Abu Bakr Salim), 120
"Howa Howa" (Ali Mkali), 63
"Howa Howa Mwanangu" (Maalim Shaaban),
65
howa lullaby, 63–65
Hucheon, Linda, 2
Hughes-Smith, Paul, 174
humanistic musical anthropology, 180
hybridization, 29, 44, 183n1
hybridized soundworlds, of binti Saad
collective, 28–30, 32

identity, 17–19, 69, 172–73
in-betweenness, of Swahili, 6–8
Indian Ocean ethnomusicology, 173, 178–81
Indian taarab: Bollywood *contrafacta* in, 67,
72; characteristics of, 80; clowns of, 69,
80–84, 89; decline of, 69–70; defined, 2;
development of, 73–76; gender disparity
of, 74; Hadrami *ṭarab* link with, 111;
harlequin poetics and, 84–88; harmonium
and, 73; Hindi musical films and, 71;
Hindustani-Swahili poetry in, 75–76;
influences to, 70–71; intimacy of, 89–90;
origin of, 48, 69–73; overview of, 66–67;
poetics of vocality and, 68–69; popularity
of, 72; prosody in, 75; requirements for,
80; resonance of Indianness in, 83–84;
romance and, 74; singing in, 68–69, 73,
74–75, 76; tabla drums and, 73. *See also
taarab (sung poetry)*
Al Inkishafi, 128–29
instrumentation, of taarab orchestras, 48
intentional hybridization, 29, 183n1
intermusicality, 32–33
irony, x, 2, 18, 38, 44
Islamic Party of Kenya (IPK), 138–39
Island Fruits, Mombasa Old Town, 165

Jahadhmy, Aly Ahmed, 191n22
Jakobson, Roman, 18
Jamal Hafidh, 55
Jamal Hafidh Jahadhmy, 31, 70, 98, 126
Jarhoom, Muhammad Ahmed, 98, 109
Jauharah Orchestra Musical Club, 57–59, 116
Jayasuriya, Shihan de Silva, 178
Jemadari, Abdalla, 60
Johnson, Mark, 16
Juma Bhalo, Mohamed Khamis, 65, 67–68, 72,
73, 74, 76–80
Jumbe Ali, 71, 80
Junaidi Al Noor (Mzee Mombasa ("Old Man
Mombasa")), 82–83

"*Kama Laaandan!*" (Just like London!), 166
"Kamba Haipigwi Fundo" (The Rope is Not
Tied) (Sharif Mohamed Saggaf), 130
kangas, 42
Kapferer, Bruce, 105–6

Kapoor, Raj, 75
kapuka beat, 168
"Kasha Langu" (My Strongbox) (Jauharah Orchestra Musical Club), 58–59, 148
Keil, Charles, 104
Kenya: citizenship in, 154–55; currency of, 159–60; as internal Orient, 7; mediascape in, 154; modern regime of ethnicity in, 10; Mwambao ("coastline") movement and, 51; national identity of, 159–60; political challenges in, 138–39; Swahili in, 3–4; tourism and, 7–8, 164. *See also specific locations*
Kenya African National Union (KANU), 138
"Kenyan Girl, Kenyan Boy" (Necessary Noize), 157, 158
Kenyatta, Jomo, 7
Khadija Husein, 124
Khalid Balala, 138–39
Khuleita Said Muhashamy, 123
"Kijiti" (binti Saad collective), 38
Kilindini, 13, 186n16
Kindy, Hyder, 49, 53–54, 55
Kite cha Pwani, 147–48
Kleptomaniax, 172
Kresse, Kai, 5, 20, 125, 126, 127
"Kumanya Digo" (To Know the Digo) (Babloom Modern Taarab), 143–44
Kumar, Kishore, 80
kupamba, 102
"Kuwaiti" (Zein l'Abdin), 130
Kuwaiti songs, 119, 128, 131–33

Lamu, Kenya, 84, 107
Lamu Omari, 74
Lamu taarab, 34–35
language, 18, 39, 51
Larkin, Brian, 71, 80
Latin American songs, in Arab taarab, 119
Lavin, Gabriel, 96–97
"Layly Nahāry" (Night and Day) (Amr Diab), 165
Lelele Africa, 148

listening, 15–17
Lodhi, Abdulaziz Yusuf, 190–91n18
"Loho ya Kihindi" (The Indian Writing Tablet) (Zein l'Abdin), 130, 131
Loimeier, Roman, 128
London, England, 166
Londonistan, 166–67
ludic *ṭarab* song, 108
lullaby, *howa*, 63–65
Lynch, Gabrielle, 185–86n14

Maalim Said, 52–53
"Maashuki" (Jauharah Orchestra Musical Club), 59, 60
mafumbo, 25, 38
mahadhi, 200n14
Mahfood Bawazir, 98
Mahmoud Mau, 15
Malika (Asha Abdo Suleiman), 73, 117–18, 119, 177
Malindi, 84
Mandelson, Ben, 119
"Maneno Tisiya" (Nine Words) (Kijuma), 132–33
Mangeshkar, Lata, 73
Maqām: ʿIrāq, 41, 44, 189n9; Ṣabā, 132; system, 28
maradufu (double dumbek), 117
Masai, Ralph (Cannibal), 156, 158, 159
maskani, 126–28
Maulidi Festival, 107
Maulidi Juma Iha, 71, 77–78, 79, 117, 136, 142
Maulidi Musical Party, 79, 118
Mau Mau uprising, 6, 47
Mazrui, Alamin M., 9–10
Mazrui, Ali A., 2, 150
Mazrui, Amin bin Ali, 13
"Mbali Mbali" (Far Away, Far Away) (Malika), 177
Mbaraka Ali Haji, 136, 139–40, 147–48, 149–50
Mbarak Rashid, 59
Mbaruk Talsam: background of, 35, 46; "Basahera Umuongo" of, 24–25, 26, 28–29,

32, 36–38, 40; as comedian, 37; description of, 191n22; family of, 191n23; influence of, 98; musical style of, 28–29; performance of, 24; photo of, 45; popularity of, 46; stylistic approach of, 35; writings of, 120; "Ya Dana Dana" of, 40–45
"Mbembeleze Mtoto" (Siti binti Saad), 63
mediascape, 154
medium of social reflexivity, 26
metaphor, 18
Meyer, Birgit, 51
Meyer, Leonard B., 17
Middleton, John, 7, 8
Mijikenda, 5
mimesis, 19–21, 76, 187n25
"Mimi" (a name) (Jauharah Orchestra Musical Club), 59
mipasho, 143
Mkali, Ali, 62–65, 73
Mkuu, Faraj Bwana, 123
"Mnazi Wangu Sitwati Kwa Mkoma" (I Won't Trade a Date Palm for a Doum Palm), 133
modern regime of ethnicity, 10–11
Mohamed Adio Shigoo (Mohamed Mbwana), 77, 79, 118, 148, 167
Mohamed Awadh, 148
Mohamed "Bombom" Abdalla, 112
Mohamed Essajee (Showdemo), 160–64, 167, 172–73
Mohamed Khamis Juma Bhalo, 65, 67–68, 72, 74, 76–80, 83, 167–73
Mohamed Kijuma, 34, 35, 132
Mohamed "Tenge" Yusuf, 69, 71
Mohammed (Bonzo) Hassan, 84–88
Moi, Daniel Arap, 138
Mombasa: Afro-Oriental phase of, 184n5; *baraza* culture in, 127; Basheikh Mosque in, 192n32; commerce in, 13; communitarian privacy in, 141; contours of, 6; dissociation in, 6–7; ethnic classifications in, 30; Fort Jesus district in, 161; independence and, 6–7; Indian influences in, 84; Islamic sounds in, 141; new environment in,

136–42; Old Town of, 6, 12, 70, 127, 140–41, 185n11, 192n32; patricians in, 13, 14; photo of, 12, 161; portrayal of, in hip hop music, 158–59; religious opposition to live music in, 70; religious politics in, 137–38; resonances of, 45–46; Sakina Mosque in, 139–41, 201–2n6; slavery in, 13; stability and prosperity in, 47; Swahili in, 3–4; taarab in, 1–4; tourism in, 146; Twelve Tribes communities of, 11–13, 186n16. *See also* Swahili coast
"Mombasani" (Farao), 156
Mombasani concept, 156–59
Mombasan taarab, 47–48, 49
Mombasa Party, 147
Mombasa Taarab: Sanaa ya Kale, 147–50
"Mombasa Umm al-Dunyā" (Mombasa, Mother of the World) (Saleh Said Baisa), 108–11, 120
mood, in music, 18
Morson, Gary Saul, 179
"Moyo Wakupenda Hauna Subira" (The Loving Heart Has No Patience) (Zein l'Abdin), 120
"Mpenzi Wangu Kanitoka" (And Then My Love Left Me) (Musa Maruf), 81–82
"*Msoto* Millions" (Flani and Jahcoozi), 203n7
Mtoro bin Mwinyi Bakari, 8, 39
Muhammad Juma Khan, 96–97, 98, 133
Muhammed Seif Khatib, 2
"Muhogo wa Jang'ombe" (Bi Kidude), 190n13
Musa ("Famous Musa") Maruf, 80–83
music: celebratory space-time and, 103–4; learned habits in, 17–18; mimetic appropriation in, 18; mood in, 18; multivocality in, 19; phonographic, 26; poetics of identity and, 17–19; self-understanding in, 18; sensemaking and, 16–17; sociological stylistics and, 19. *See also specific types*
musicked poetry, 1
Muslims, as second-class citizens, 7
Mvita, Nine Tribes of, 13, 186n16

Mwale, Lennox (CLD), 158, 161–62
Mwambao ("coastline") movement, 51
Mwanaisha Abdalla (Nyota Ndogo), 169, 203–4n14
Mwanasaada Said (Mimi) Kondo, 64–65
Mwanate Kibwana, 148
Mwangi, Evan, 155
"Mwiba wa Kujitoma" (A Thorn in the Flesh) (Muhammad Juma Khan), 133
Mzee Mombasa ("Old Man Mombasa") (Junaidi Al Noor), 82–83
Mzuri label, 47–48

Nabhany, Ahmed Sheikh. *See* Ahmed Sheikh Nabhany
Nairobi, 155, 159–60, 169
Nakassis, Constantine V., 33
Nasher, Salim, 163–64
Nasser, Stambuli Abdillahi, 67
Necessary Noize, 157, 158
Ng'ambo, 36–38
ngoma, 17, 53–54
"*Nikiwa Ndani*" (When I'm Inside) (Prince Adio), 168–69
"Nimepata Mwana" (Yaseen and Mimi), 65
Njuguna, Alex (Redwax), 162
nostalgia, x, 2, 18, 128–29
nostalgic pastiche, 125–26
Ntarangwi, Mwenda, 78, 139, 142
Nyota Ndogo (Mwanaisha Abdalla), 169, 203–4n14

Odeon, 25, 198n7
Ogopa Deejays, 168
Omani Arabs, 13
Omar, Yahya Ali, 59
Omar Awadh Ban, 116
Omar Badbes, 100, 122
Omari Swaleh al-Abdi, 77, 89, 91–92, 101, 105, 117, 147–48, 149–50
Omondi, Eric (Farao), 156, 157
Ong, Aihwa, 153–54
orchestras, taarab, 48, 57–61

organic hybridization, 29, 183n1
Orientalization of Mombasa music, 2, 3, 48–49
Ortner, Sherry, 4
Our Nation, Kenya (Wegulo and Ondieki), 7

parade of paradoxes, 4–15
Parkin, David, 4, 5
parody, 2, 88, 164, 167, 175–78, 187n22, 191n24
patricians, Swahili, 13, 14
Peirce, Charles Sanders, 16
phonographic music, development of, 26
Phrygian mode, 166
poetics: defined, 18; literary, 18; mimesis in, 20; musical, xi, 18; of Swahili culture and identity, 69, 129–33; of vocality, 68–69
poetry: *humanynī*, 96, 109, 198n6; recitation of, 52, 193n8; taarab and, 1, 44, 75, 122–23, 130, 142–43, 149, 196n17
Porcello, Thomas, 69
Pouwels, Randall, 94
Prestholdt, Jeremy, 20
Prince Adio (Adio Mohamed), 167–73
Prins, A. H. J., 9, 20
prosody, in Indian taarab, 75

qawwali (Muslim devotional music), 70

R
Racy, Ali Jihad, 104
radio, 50, 54–55, 193n7, 202n1. *See also* Sauti ya Mvita (Voice of Mombasa)
Radio Rahma, 54–55
Rafi, Mohammed, 80
Raid al-Sunbati, 120
Ramadan, 139–40
Rappaport, Roy, 106
Redsan, 152
Redwax (Alex Njuguna), 162
Reeves, Jim, 73
reflexivity: citationality and, 33, 38; crosscurrent of, 48–49; medium of social, 26; public/collective, 68, 93, 104–7
regime of ethnicity, Swahili, 14–15

religion, 51
revivalism, 149–50
Roberts, John Storm, 2–3, 122
"Rock the Baby" (Ali Mkali), 61–65
romance, in Indian taarab, 74

saa moya ("hour one"), 111
Saidi Mberera, 112
Saigel, K. L., 81
Sakina Mosque, 139–41, 201–2n6
Saleh, Seif Salim, 17
Saleh Abdallah El Antari, 99–100
Saleh Said Baisa, 108–10, 120
Salem Mayhour, 175, 176
Salim, Ahmed Idha, 52
Salim Bagmesh, 98, 105, 109–10
"Samiya" (Showdemo), 162–64, 167
Samper, David, 173
Samuels, David, 69
Sauti ya Mvita (Voice of Mombasa), 48, 49–56
ṣawt form, 130, 131–32
Schutz, Alfred, 104
Scott, Jimmy, 68
Seeger, Charles, 104
Seif Omar, 149
Seiyun Popular Arts ensemble, 122, 174–76
sensemaking, 16–17, 186–87n19
Shaaban, Maalim, 34, 35, 36, 65
Shaib Abeid Barajab, 190n16
Sharama, 158, 159
sharh, 101, 134
Shariff, Ibrahim Noor, 9–10
Sharif Mohamed Saggaf, 130
Sheriff "Badmash" Maulana, 143, 144–45, 177
Shihiri ethnonym, 95–96
Showdemo (Mohamed Essajee), 160–64, 167, 172–73
Shumays, Sami Abu, 29
"Shuwaykh min ʿArḍ Miknās" (A Little Sheikh from the Land of Meknes), 130
"Sikitiko" (Regret) (Prince Adio), 170–71
"Silie Mwanangu" (Zuhura Swaleh), 65
Silverstein, Michael, 107

Simpson, Edward, 20
"Sina Nyumba" (I Have No Home) (Yaseen Mohamed Tofeli), 75
singing voice, 68–69, 73, 74–75, 76
"Sisi Isilamu" (Bonzo), 84–88
Sitara Bute, 73–74, 137, 139–40
Siti binti Saad: background of, 35; characteristics of, 28; description of, 191n18; "Mbembeleze Mtoto" of, 63; musical style of, 27; as national icon, 45; performance of, 24, 25; photo of, 34; popularity of, 26–27; theatrical skills of, 37; "Wewe Paka" (You Cat) of, 32, 33
Siti Ganduri, 61–62
slavery, 13, 14
social belonging, 11
sociological stylistics, 30–33
socio-symbolic homology, 114
"Soldier" (CLD), 158, 159, 161–62
"Something From Home" (Prince Adio), 167–70
sounding, 15–17
sounding culture, 52–55
Spear, Thomas, 13
Storch, Scott, 166
storytelling, 52–53
"Street Hustlers" (Cannibal and Sharama), 156–57, 158, 159
structures of feeling, 4
stylization, 39, 191n24
Subeit bin Ambar, 34
Swahili: ambiguity of, 8–10; Arab *versus*, 8; citizenship challenges of, 14, 15; culture of, 14–15; defined, 4, 8; disjuncture and, 10–11; dissociation of, 6–8; ethnicity space of, 11, 13–15, 51; Hadrami cultures and, 44–45; identity of, 69; in-betweenness of, 6–8; and Indian, 83; migrants as, 30; Mijikenda, 5; mimesis in, 19–21; in Mombasa, 3–4; musical poetics of culture of, 129–33; orchestrating, 57–61; paradox of, 4–15; photo of, 53; regime of ethnicity of, 10, 14–15; structures of feeling and, 4

Swahili coast: absenting of, in hip hop culture, 159–60; adaptability on, 20; changing ideas on, 30; diversity of, 40; Hadrami *ṭarab* in, 96–101; heritagization and, 145–51; identity challenges of, 8, 9, 40, 172–73; in-betweenness of, 6–8; Islamic reform in, 138; lived experience on, 15; location of, 187n24; tourism and, 7, 164. *See also specific locations*

Swahili Cultural Centre, 147

Swahili hip hop Afro-soul, 169

Swahili songs, in Arab taarab, 119, 120

Swahili-space schema, 15, 84, 93–96

Swahili taarab, 49, 100. *See also* taarab (sung poetry)

Swartz, Marc, 53

Sykes, Jim, 180

taarab (sung poetry): appropriation of, 3; characteristics of, 25, 26, 27, 183–84n1; dance-oriented, 143; defined, 1, 17; elite forms of, 33–34; gender dynamics of, 34; heritagization and, 145–51; as Indian Ocean music, 174–75, 177–78; modern, 142–45; as musicked poetry, 1; overview of, 1–4; performance function of, 33–34; political unrest and, 139; responsibility of, 56–57; sensemaking in, 17; song and theatrical expression in, 36; stylistic paths of, 2. *See also specific types; specific works*

tabla drums, 73. *See also* drumming

Tagg, Philip, 33

ṭarab (Hadrami popular song), 71, 104, 107. *See also* Hadrami *ṭarab*

tashkota, 48

taste, boundaries of, 166–67

Taussig, Michael, 20

theatrical expression, in taarab, 36

theoretism, 179

theory, defined, 187n23

Topp Fargion, Janet, 32, 40, 184n7

Tracey, Hugh, 57, 59, 60

Turino, Thomas, 107

Turner, Edith, 103

Turner, Victor, 93, 104–5

twarila ndia ("drum of the street"), 132–33

Ukoo Flani, 155–56

Umm Kulthum, 35, 120, 190n18, 199n5

urbanity, acoustemology of, 55–56

uswahili (Swahili-space, Swahili culture), 14–15

utamaduni (culture, urbanity), 56, 60–62, 133

Verne, Julia, 178

"Vidonge" (Malika), 73

Vierke, Clarissa, 20, 125

vocal anthropology, 69

vocalic space, 56

vocality, poetics of, 68–69

vocal timbre, 19

vugo, 102–3

Wagner, Roy, 17

Waliaula, Ken Walibora, 133–34

Walker, Iain, 20

Waterman, Richard, 179

wedding celebration: characteristics of, 96, 128; cultural intimacy and, 107; description of, 92–93; diasporic calibration and, 107; dicent-indices at, 107–8; disruptions at, 142; emblems of culture in, 106–7; example of, 112–14, 137; Hadrami *ṭarab* and, 101–6; *kupamba* at, 102; musician popularity at, 98; photo of, 79, 105; reflexive frame of, 104–6; space-time at, 103–4; Swahili accent and, 108; taarab music in, 70; *vugo* at, 102–3

Welby, Victoria Lady, 16, 186–87n19

Werber, Pnina, 29

"Wewe Paka" (You Cat) (binti Saad), 32, 33

William, Fadhili, 117

Williams, Raymond, 4

Willis, Paul, 114

"Ya Dana Dana" (Talsam), 40–45

Yakuti, Sururu, 112, 117

Index **245**

Yaseen Mohamed Tofeli, 48, 64–65, 75
Yemen, Hadrami *ṭarab* and, 101
Young India, 72
the youth, hip hop impact on, 154–55

Zanzibar, 27, 45, 146, 174–77
Zanzibari taarab, 147, 175, 184n7
Zein l'Abdin (Zein l'Abdin Ahmed Alamoody): Ahmed Sheikh Nabhany and, 22–23, 114, 123, 125, 126, 129; "Arabian Nights" repertoire of, 146; Arab turn of, 119; "Aso Subira Hanali" (One Who Lacks Patience Had Nothing) of, 113–14; audience of, 128–29; background and education of, 115–19; class politics and, 122; collaboration with, 77, 117; compounding culture and, 133; as conservator, 122–25; *contrafacta* of, 130–31; cultural ambiguity of, 134–35; Hadrami *ṭarab* and, 120–22; home of, 126–27; "Kamba Haipigwi Fundo" (The Rope is Not Tied) and, 130; Kuwaiti style of, 131–33; "Loho ya Kihindi" (The Indian Writing Tablet) of, 130, 131; ludic *ṭarab* song of, 108; "Maneno Tisiya" (Nine Words) (Kijuma) and, 132–33; "Mnazi Wangu Sitwati Kwa Mkoma" (I Won't Trade a Date Palm for a Doum Palm) and, 133; "Moyo Wakupenda Hauna Subira" (The Loving Heart Has No Patience) of, 120; musical philosophizing and, 125–29; musical poetics of Swahili culture and, 129–33; nostalgic pastiche and, 125–26; overview of, 22–23, 101–2; performances of, 57, 108, 109, 112–14, 146; photo of, 129; as poet, 122–23; quote of, 32; recollections of, 54–55; recordings of, 116; repertoire of, 119–20; *ṣawt* form and, 130, 131–32; viewpoint of, 31–32; at wedding celebration, 112–14; *Zein Concerts 9* of, 120; Zein Trio of, 122
Zein Musical Party, 116, 117
Zein Trio, 122
Zuckerkandl, Victor, 104
Zuhura Swaleh, 65, 73, 117, 118
Zuhura Swaleh and Party, 118

MUSIC / CULTURE
A series from Wesleyan University Press
Edited by Deborah Wong, Sherrie Tucker, and Jeremy Wallach
Originating editors: George Lipsitz, Susan McClary, and Robert Walser

The Music/Culture series has consistently reshaped and redirected music scholarship. Founded in 1993 by George Lipsitz, Susan McClary, and Robert Walser, the series features outstanding critical work on music. Unconstrained by disciplinary divides, the series addresses music and power through a range of times, places, and approaches. Music/Culture strives to integrate a variety of approaches to the study of music, linking analysis of musical significance to larger issues of power—what is permitted and forbidden, who is included and excluded, who speaks and who gets silenced. From ethnographic classics to cutting-edge studies, Music/Culture zeroes in on how musicians articulate social needs, conflicts, coalitions, and hope. Books in the series investigate the cultural work of music in urgent and sometimes experimental ways, from the radical fringe to the quotidian. Music/Culture asks deep and broad questions about music through the framework of the most restless and rigorous critical theory.

Marié Abe
Resonances of Chindon-ya: Sounding Space and Sociality in Contemporary Japan

Frances Aparicio
Listening to Salsa: Gender, Latin Popular Music, and Puerto Rican Cultures

Paul Austerlitz
Jazz Consciousness: Music, Race, and Humanity

Shalini R. Ayyagari
Musical Resilience: Performing Patronage in the Indian Thar Desert

Christina Baade and Kristin McGee
Beyoncé in the World: Making Meaning with Queen Bey in Troubled Times

Lisa Barg
Queer Arrangements: Billy Strayhorn and Midcentury Jazz Collaboration

Emma Baulch
Genre Publics: Popular Music, Technologies, and Class in Indonesia

Harris M. Berger
Metal, Rock, and Jazz: Perception and the Phenomenology of Musical Experience

Harris M. Berger
Stance: Ideas about Emotion, Style, and Meaning for the Study of Expressive Culture

Harris M. Berger and Giovanna P. Del Negro
Identity and Everyday Life: Essays in the Study of Folklore, Music, and Popular Culture

Franya J. Berkman
Monument Eternal: The Music of Alice Coltrane

Dick Blau, Angeliki Vellou Keil, and Charles Keil
Bright Balkan Morning: Romani Lives and the Power of Music in Greek Macedonia

Susan Boynton and Roe-Min Kok, editors
Musical Childhoods and the Cultures of Youth

James Buhler, Caryl Flinn, and David Neumeyer, editors
Music and Cinema

Patrick Burkart
Music and Cyberliberties

Thomas Burkhalter, Kay Dickinson, and Benjamin J. Harbert, editors
The Arab Avant-Garde: Music, Politics, Modernity

Julia Byl
Antiphonal Histories: Resonant Pasts in the Toba Batak Musical Present

Corinna Campbell
The Cultural Work: Maroon Performance in Paramaribo, Suriname

Alexander Cannon
Seeding the Tradition: Musical Creativity in Southern Vietnam

Daniel Cavicchi
Listening and Longing: Music Lovers in the Age of Barnum

Susan D. Crafts, Daniel Cavicchi, Charles Keil, and the Music in Daily Life Project
My Music: Explorations of Music in Daily Life

Jim Cullen
Born in the USA: Bruce Springsteen and the American Tradition

Anne Danielsen
Presence and Pleasure: The Funk Grooves of James Brown and Parliament

Peter Doyle
Echo and Reverb: Fabricating Space in Popular Music Recording, 1900–1960

Andrew Eisenberg
Sounds of Other Shores: The Musical Poetics of Identity on Kenya's Swahili Coast

Ron Emoff
Recollecting from the Past: Musical Practice and Spirit Possession on the East Coast of Madagascar

Yayoi Uno Everett and Frederick Lau, editors
Locating East Asia in Western Art Music

Susan Fast and Kip Pegley, editors
Music, Politics, and Violence

Heidi Feldman
Black Rhythms of Peru: Reviving African Musical Heritage in the Black Pacific

Kai Fikentscher
"You Better Work!" Underground Dance Music in New York City

Ruth Finnegan
The Hidden Musicians: Music-Making in an English Town

Daniel Fischlin and Ajay Heble, editors
The Other Side of Nowhere: Jazz, Improvisation, and Communities in Dialogue

Wendy Fonarow
Empire of Dirt: The Aesthetics and Rituals of British "Indie" Music

Murray Forman
The 'Hood Comes First: Race, Space, and Place in Rap and Hip-Hop

Lisa Gilman
My Music, My War: The Listening Habits of U.S. Troops in Iraq and Afghanistan

Paul D. Greene and Thomas Porcello, editors
Wired for Sound: Engineering and Technologies in Sonic Cultures

Tomie Hahn
Sensational Knowledge: Embodying Culture through Japanese Dance

Edward Herbst
Voices in Bali: Energies and Perceptions in Vocal Music and Dance Theater

Deborah Kapchan
Traveling Spirit Masters: Moroccan Gnawa Trance and Music in the Global Marketplace

Deborah Kapchan, editor
Theorizing Sound Writing

Max Katz
Lineage of Loss: Counternarratives of North Indian Music

Raymond Knapp
Symphonic Metamorphoses: Subjectivity and Alienation in Mahler's Re-Cycled Songs

Victoria Lindsay Levine and Dylan Robinson, editors
Music and Modernity among First Peoples of North America

Noel Lobley
Sound Fragments: From Field Recording to African Electronic Stories

Laura Lohman
Umm Kulthūm: Artistic Agency and the Shaping of an Arab Legend, 1967–2007

Preston Love
A Thousand Honey Creeks Later: My Life in Music from Basie to Motown—and Beyond

René T. A. Lysloff and Leslie C. Gay Jr., editors
Music and Technoculture

Ian MacMillen
Playing It Dangerously: Tambura Bands, Race, and Affective Block in Croatia and Its Intimates

Allan Marett
Songs, Dreamings, and Ghosts: The Wangga of North Australia

Ian Maxwell
Phat Beats, Dope Rhymes: Hip Hop Down Under Comin' Upper

Kristin A. McGee
Some Liked It Hot: Jazz Women in Film and Television, 1928–1959

Tracy McMullen
Haunthenticity: Musical Replay and the Fear of the Real

Rebecca S. Miller
Carriacou String Band Serenade: Performing Identity in the Eastern Caribbean

Tony Mitchell, editor
Global Noise: Rap and Hip-Hop Outside the USA

Christopher Moore and Philip Purvis, editors
Music & Camp

Rachel Mundy
Animal Musicalities: Birds, Beasts, and Evolutionary Listening

Keith Negus
Popular Music in Theory: An Introduction

Johnny Otis
Upside Your Head: Rhythm and Blues on Central Avenue

Jeff Packman
Living from Music in Salvador: Professional Musicians and the Capital of Afro-Brazil

Kip Pegley
Coming to You Wherever You Are: MuchMusic, MTV, and Youth Identities

Jonathan Pieslak
Radicalism and Music: An Introduction to the Music Cultures of al-Qa'ida, Racist Skinheads, Christian-Affiliated Radicals, and Eco-Animal Rights Militants

Thomas M. Pooley
The Land Is Sung: Zulu Performances and the Politics of Place

Matthew Rahaim
Musicking Bodies: Gesture and Voice in Hindustani Music

Matthew Rahaim
Ways of Voice: Vocal Striving and Ethical Contestation in North India and Beyond

John Richardson
Singing Archaeology: Philip Glass's Akhnaten

Tricia Rose
Black Noise: Rap Music and Black Culture in Contemporary America

David Rothenberg and Marta Ulvaeus, editors
The Book of Music and Nature: An Anthology of Sounds, Words, Thoughts

Nichole Rustin-Paschal
The Kind of Man I Am: Jazzmasculinity and the World of Charles Mingus Jr.

T. Sankaran, Matthew Harp Allen, and Daniel Neuman, editors
The Life of Music in South India

Marta Elena Savigliano
Angora Matta: Fatal Acts of North-South Translation

Joseph G. Schloss
Making Beats: The Art of Sample-Based Hip-Hop

Barry Shank
Dissonant Identities: The Rock 'n' Roll Scene in Austin, Texas

Jonathan Holt Shannon
Among the Jasmine Trees: Music and Modernity in Contemporary Syria

Daniel B. Sharp
Between Nostalgia and Apocalypse: Popular Music and the Staging of Brazil

Shayna M. Silverstein
Fraught Balance: The Embodied Politics of Dabke Music in Syria

Helena Simonett
Banda: Mexican Musical Life across Borders

Mark Slobin
Subcultural Sounds: Micromusics of the West

Mark Slobin, editor
Global Soundtracks: Worlds of Film Music

Tes Slominski
Trad Nation: Gender, Sexuality, and Race in Irish Traditional Music

Christopher Small
The Christopher Small Reader

Christopher Small
Music of the Common Tongue: Survival and Celebration in African American Music

Christopher Small
Music, Society, Education

Christopher Small
Musicking: The Meanings of Performing and Listening

Andrew Snyder
Critical Brass: Street Carnival and Musical Activism in Olympic Rio de Janeiro

Maria Sonevytsky
Wild Music: Sound and Sovereignty in Ukraine

Tore Størvold
Dissonant Landscapes: Music, Nature, and the Performance of Iceland

Regina M. Sweeney
Singing Our Way to Victory: French Cultural Politics and Music during the Great War

Colin Symes
Setting the Record Straight: A Material History of Classical Recording

Kelley Tatro
Love and Rage: Autonomy in Mexico City's Punk Scene

Steven Taylor
False Prophet: Field Notes from the Punk Underground

Paul Théberge
Any Sound You Can Imagine: Making Music/Consuming Technology

Sarah Thornton
Club Cultures: Music, Media, and Subcultural Capital

Michael E. Veal
Dub: Soundscapes and Shattered Songs in Jamaican Reggae

Michael E. Veal
Living Space: John Coltrane, Miles Davis, and Free Jazz, from Analog to Digital

Michael E. Veal and E. Tammy Kim, editors
Punk Ethnography: Artists and Scholars Listen to Sublime Frequencies

Robert Walser
Running with the Devil: Power, Gender, and Madness in Heavy Metal Music

Dennis Waring
Manufacturing the Muse: Estey Organs and Consumer Culture in Victorian America

Lise A. Waxer
The City of Musical Memory: Salsa, Record Grooves, and Popular Culture in Cali, Colombia

Mina Yang
Planet Beethoven: Classical Music at the Turn of the Millennium

ABOUT THE AUTHOR

Andrew J. Eisenberg is associate professor and program head of Music at NYU Abu Dhabi, and Global Network associate professor of Music at NYU New York. He served as a postdoctoral research associate on the European Research Council-funded "Music, Digitisation, Mediation" project, and currently co-directs NYU Abu Dhabi's Music and Sound Cultures (MaSC) lab. His writings on music and auditory culture in urban East Africa have appeared in a range of journals and edited volumes, including *Keywords in Sound* and *Music* and *Digital Media: A Planetary Anthropology*.